THE MAKING OF MORAL THEOLOGY
A Study of the Roman Catholic Tradition

THE MAKING OF MORAL THEOLOGY

A Study of the
Roman Catholic Tradition

JOHN MAHONEY

The Martin D'Arcy Memorial Lectures 1981–2

CLARENDON PRESS · OXFORD

Oxford University Press, Walton Street, Oxford OX2 6DP

Oxford New York Toronto
Delhi Bombay Calcutta Madras Karachi
Petaling Jaya Singapore Hong Kong Tokyo
Nairobi Dar es Salaam Cape Town
Melbourne Auckland

and associated companies in
Berlin Ibadan

Oxford is a trade mark of Oxford University Press

Published in the United States
by Oxford University Press, New York

First published 1987
First issued as a Clarendon Paperback 1989

British Library Cataloguing in Publication Data

Mahoney, John
The making of moral theology: a study of
the Roman Catholic tradition.—(The
Martin D'Arcy memorial lectures; 1981–2)
1. Christian ethics—Catholic authors
I. Title II. Series
241'.042   BJ1249
ISBN 0–19–826730–4

Library of Congress Cataloging in Publication Data

Mahoney, John 1931–
The making of moral theology.
(The Martin D'Arcy memorial lectures; 1981–2)
Bibliography: p.
Includes index.
1. Christian ethics—History. 2. Catholic Church—
Doctrines—History. I. Title. II. Series.
BJ1249.M1644 1987   241'.042   86–19188
ISBN 0–19–826730–4

Typeset by Cambrian Typesetters, Frimley, Surrey
Printed in Great Britain
at the University Printing House, Oxford
by David Stanford
Printer to the University

CONTENTS

INTRODUCTION

This study was born of a happy conjunction, for the author, of a sabbatical year from Heythrop College, University of London, after serving for a period as Principal, and an invitation to deliver the Martin D'Arcy Memorial Lectures in Campion Hall, University of Oxford, in the Spring of 1982; and the author is grateful to the Governors of Heythrop College and to the then Master of Campion Hall, Father Paul Edwards of the Society of Jesus, for the possibility and the honour of contributing to the memory of a former distinguished Jesuit Master of the Hall.

The theme for the annual D'Arcy Lectures is chosen by the member of the Society of Jesus invited into the lectureship, and the writer welcomed the opportunity to devote them to exploring the history of his subject of moral theology, which has exercised a continuous, formative, and even at times dominant, influence on the development of the Roman Catholic Church's thinking and behaviour through the centuries, and which has been undergoing little short of an upheaval in the aftermath of the Second Vatican Council and the conciliar criticism of the discipline. An initial attractive project to focus attention upon 'makers of moral theology', such as Augustine and Aquinas, was soon abandoned as incurring the dangers of inflating the importance of some lesser, if still significant, personalities, such as Abelard and Pope Pius XII, and, more importantly, of not according sufficient attention to the other major influences—the intellectual movements and currents of thought and practice in the Church, the universities and the papacy, Church Councils, and other events, which have all contributed to and conspired to form what the author finally decided to term 'The Making of Moral Theology'.

Rather than proceed, however, in the manner of a history, on a broad chronological front from New Testament times to the present in describing events in moral theology in an even-handed way without attention to what hindsight had identified as the highways, as distinct from byways, in moral theology, it seemed more fruitful to approach the subject in a more thematic manner and to select for historical description followed by reflection and comment what emerged upon consideration as the eight most significant aspects in the history of moral theology. These formed the topics of the original lecture series and now constitute the eight chapters of the current work. Such a final structure, and the order in which the topics have been arranged and presented, result, it is hoped, in a cumulative treatment of the subject which at the same time conveys its historical progression, development and fortunes.

The interest evoked by the D'Arcy Lectures on the Making of Moral Theology as so presented, and the absence of any sustained study of the subject hitherto, led the author to conclude that publishing the lectures in their original inevitably brief form might prove more tantalizing or cursory than informative to a wider public, and he has given such time as has been available since resuming teaching moral and pastoral theology at Heythrop College to expanding their contents considerably in the hope that their published form will be of interest to a general readership as well as to students of moral, theological, ecclesiastical, ecumenical, and historical matters. To this end also the abundant citation in the notes of primary theological and historical authorities is intended to provide something of a source-book, as well as to substantiate positions and conclusions, sometimes perhaps controversial, adopted by the author.

The technical term *theologia moralis*, referring to a distinctive science systematically separate from other branches of theology, has been in general use only since the end of the sixteenth century and the Thomist renaissance which followed the Council of Trent, but, of course, formal consideration of Christian moral behaviour is as old as the New Testament records of the moral teachings of Jesus and of Paul as they applied to the early Christian community. Nevertheless, the subject of moral theology as the study of Christian moral behaviour received its definitive orientation for centuries to come from the sixth-century popular development of the monastic practice of regular private confession of personal sins. This traditional preoccupation with sin makes it inevitable that our opening chapter should trace and reflect upon the influence upon Catholic life, and upon moral theology and its developing literature, of auricular Confession as it has developed through the Middle Ages and the Reformation to the present day. No less influential in its own way upon the growth of moral reflection in the Western Church has been the legacy bequeathed to it by its greatest early bishop-theologian, Augustine of Hippo, which provides the subject of our second chapter and which, particularly in its consideration of man's moral capabilities and of sexual morality, has perpetuated for centuries a mood of pessimism which moral theology is only beginning to shake off in this latter half of the twentieth century.

It was the Neoplatonist Augustine, also, in his impassioned despair of man's resources and his appeal to divine grace, who pointed the way towards what would become the theology of the supernatural; while it was the Church's greatest theologian, the thirteenth-century friar, Thomas Aquinas, who daringly incorporated into Christian thinking a rediscovered Aristotelianism, thus laying the foundations of a Christian metaphysics of nature and of natural law which would endure to the present. The competing claims for nature and supernature (Chapter Three) were to erupt in the politico-religious controversy we know as Jansenism, which rocked the Church and made a battlefield of moral theology in the seventeenth and eighteenth centuries, and found the beginnings of a resolution only in recent times under the influence of existentialist thought.

The question of authority—and of the function of Christian teaching authority in the field of moral behaviour—which was so central to the Jansenist controversy forms the subject of our fourth chapter, which traces the history of *magisterium* in the Church, both as the exercise of teaching authority on the part of the University *magistri* (or Masters in Theology) and their successors, and as the teaching authority in 'matters of faith and morals' on the part of the Church's hierarchy and the papacy. In the former case, the history of Probabilism as a means of coping with moral dilemmas is considered, along with the hostility which it evoked from the Jansenists (including Pascal) and the condemnations of its wilder excesses of permissiveness which it provoked from the universities and the papacy. In the case of the hierarchical, and especially the papal, *magisterium*, our study of the now hallowed phrase 'faith and morals', as it first appears in a major Church document in the Council of Trent, leads to the conclusion that the term 'morals' (*mores*) referred on that occasion not to matters of ordinary Christian morality but to the traditional religious and devotional practices which were under sustained theological and

historical attack from Martin Luther and his supporters in their bid
to reform the Church. The decline in the authority of post-
Tridentine moral theologians on account of Probabilism and
Jansenism, the Jansenist and Gallican attacks on Roman authority,
and the further encroachment on it by the French Revolution and
its secularization of many universities, all contributed to an
increased centralization in a diminishing Church and to a concentration upon the teaching authority of the papacy which found its
culmination in the declaration of papal infallibility by the Vatican
Council of 1870. And from our study of the Council's proceedings
and its aftermath we advance the conclusion that the definition of
papal infallibility in morals was hurried and ambiguous. That papal
prerogative has never manifestly been exercised, but the subsequent
expansion of 'infallibility by association' in a number of increasingly
detailed papal pronouncements on moral matters has almost totally
eclipsed all other moral thought and initiative in the Church and
gives rise to the reflections on authority in moral matters which
close the fourth chapter.

The question of individual moral responsibility, to which
Probabilism had attempted to do justice with inadequate resources,
is made the more acute as a central teaching authority develops and
expands. Accordingly, our fifth chapter, on 'subjectivity', proceeds
to the topics of conscience and of the traditional distinction
between 'objective' morality and 'subjective' morality. From
Abelard to Aquinas to the fourteenth-century nominalist school of
thought, the varying fortunes of the individual's role and intention
and his relationship to the will of God are considered, along with
the growing significance attached to 'invincible ignorance' as an
excusing factor from the imputing of moral responsibility and
ultimately, in the Christian dispensation, from eternal damnation.
The Church's changing attitude to unbelievers, however, and the
steady dilution of its strong principle of 'no salvation outside the
Church', provide important evidence of a growing awareness of the
inadequacy of benighted ignorance to explain away moral behaviour which is not in accord with the Church's teaching. This more
positive recognition of unique and variable features of objective
reality in individual cases enables us to analyse and assess the
intimidating strictures of Pope Pius XII on 'situation ethics'. And it
finds confirmation in the *volte-face* of the Roman Catholic Church
on ecumenism and in its positive evaluation of other, formerly

'heretical', Churches in only the past thirty or so years—a culmination of its moral as well as its dogmatic teaching which prompts concluding reflections on the interplay between objectivity and subjectivity in the moral life.

A significant factor in the maturing of moral theology through the centuries has been the durability of certain terms and concepts, such as 'nature', '*magisterium*', 'unbeliever', and 'conscience'. And much of the renewal which has recently been taking place in theology, including moral theology, can be viewed as a slow cracking of traditional conceptual moulds and categories. No category, however, has proved so fundamental or so immune to questioning in the making of moral theology as the concepts and terminology of law in which moral obligations have invariably been expressed. And our sixth chapter examines the origins and deployment of the language of law as a striking instance of the power of concepts and ideas in moral theology. What it further discloses is the historical predilection of moral theologians for the Platonist and voluntarist approach to law which underlay and further vitiated the whole fundamentally legal controversy over Probabilism despite the strong espousal by St Thomas of an Aristotelian and rational understanding of the function of law. This went some way to mitigating the weaknesses of such analogical language when applied to God's moral expectations of man, but it was itself severely strained by Aquinas's eventually identifying the central element of the 'New Law' of the Gospel as the presence of God's Spirit in the hearts of individual believers. Basically, however, a predominantly legal approach to morality is seen to proceed from, and to reinforce, an impoverished conception of the Christian God, particularly when its analogical character is systematically ignored, and our final chapter pursues more generally the modern implications for moral theology of this line of reflection.

No historical study of the making of moral theology could ignore, however, the major papal intervention of the present century on a moral issue, and our penultimate chapter concentrates upon the encyclical *Humanae Vitae* of Pope Paul VI. The purpose of the chapter is not to study yet again the vexed question of contraception, but to identify and reflect upon what we have termed 'the impact of *Humanae Vitae*' upon the Church and upon twentieth-century moral theology in the reactions it occasioned as the first major testing of the Church and of moral theology after the Second Vatican Council. Those reactions were to raise for urgent and continuing consideration profound questions about the *locus* of moral teaching authority in the Church and in the 'college of bishops' as well as in the Bishop of Rome at their head. They also probed the functions of reasoning and argumentation in moral theology and their relationship to moral insight; the *sensus fidei* and the exercise of prophecy in the Christian community; the role of conscience and the gift, and gifts, of the Spirit to the whole People of God; and the function and future of moral theology; as well as the Church's perception of its own identity as a reflecting community.

The reverberations of *Humanae Vitae* remain a feature of contemporary moral theology in the Roman Catholic Church, but much else falls to be considered in our final chapter, which takes the form, not of a conclusion to our historical study, but of a perspective on the present scene and of a proposal for the future. No decades in the history of moral theology have been so productive of literature on the subject as the past two, not even the decades of high casuistry. Nor have any decades witnessed to such an extent, in the five centuries since the formal identification of moral theology as a theological science, the lack of an agreed systematization and the exploration, speculation, experimentation, and altercation to be found today in the literature of moral theology, not only relating to the many new and urgent questions facing society and individuals, but equally in the examination of the very foundations and methodology of the subject.

Rather than attempt the questionable, and indeed impossible, task of attempting to describe in short compass all that has been taking place in the discipline, we have devoted our final chapter, 'A pattern in Renewal?', to an examination of the terse call by the Second Vatican Council for particular improvement in the subject of moral theology, and of the difficulties attendant upon that improvement as greater than the Council itself appreciated, before offering an identification of two major features which appear to be emerging as moral theologians tackle the problem of long overdue renewal in their subject. These features we have described as a pervasive drive towards integration and totality at every level of moral analysis, culminating in a divine principle of totality which forms the ultimate context for all moral evaluation; and at the same time a consistent bid to acknowledge diversity and respect it throughout the whole field of moral reflection and behaviour, as an instance in moral theology of the pluralism which is struggling for expression in theology as a whole. To explain and complete these features we suggest a third as called for, which we have described as the recovery of mystery, the serious acknowledgement that moral theology, perhaps unlike Christian ethics, is a branch of theology, or the consideration of the being and activity of God, with the consequences which that entails. As a conclusion, we offer, in the light of these three characteristics of totality, diversity, and mystery, a consideration of the Church as *koinonia*, or fellowship. As such it is called to be a sacrament, a symbolic agency in society, of that *koinonia* which has been impressed upon mankind as a whole as the image of its creator who thus calls all men in the fellowship of the Holy Spirit to an ultimate sharing in the divine nature of the Trinity of persons in the living God. From this theological perspective it emerges that the task for moral theology is that of being a communal activity exercised by the entire *koinonia* of Christ's disciples, enabling his Church to image forth *koinonia* in action as well as in content. Its programme is to aid man as a whole to discover in himself a destiny and a moral vocation to the shared *koinonia* with God which is the Creator's mysterious plan of love for mankind, and of which the Church is both the provisional expression in history and an agent in society. Sharing in this architectonic design of human and divine fellowship, and applying it and disclosing it in the diversity of human situations, appear to offer a future programme for moral theology, as enabling God's sons and daughters who are driven by the Spirit of Christ (Rom. 8: 14) to contribute 'in all wisdom and insight' to the human destiny which the Epistle to the Ephesians describes (1: 9–10) as 'the mystery of his will, according to his purpose which he set forth in Christ as a plan for the fullness of time, to unite all things in him'.

A feature of this study which may surprise readers who are not familiar with Roman Catholicism is the extent to which moral theology, while claiming to be a science and therefore to enjoy at least some measure of autonomy, has been heavily dependent upon the approval, sanction, and direction of ecclesiastical, and notably papal, authority. One reason for this, of course, is to be found in the Roman Catholic belief, as stemming from the community of disciples founded by Christ, in a diversity of functions in that community, and notably belief in the office of *episkope*, or oversight, as established for the maintaining of fidelity to 'the commandments of God and the faith of Jesus' (Rev. 14: 12). To that extent a healthy distribution of function within 'the household of faith' (Gal. 6: 10) can serve to reinforce the respect of the moral theologian towards his material as the patrimony of the Christian community, and his responsibility to, as well as for, his fellow-believer, 'the brother for whom Christ died' (1 Cor. 8: 11). It can also serve to foster the strongly corporate and cohesive family sense which is a valuable feature of Roman Catholicism, even when it derives from social or cultural factors almost as much as from shared religious considerations. At the same time, in the exercise of such 'oversight' within the Roman Catholic community, such non-religious factors can have, and undoubtedly have had, the effect of at times introducing imbalances, with consequent reactions, between various sectors within the Church. And this finds expression in recent years in the considerable attention given to the relationship between the moral theologian and the *Magisterium*, on which this study comments from time to time and to which the author hopes it will as a whole also have made some contribution.

Surprise may also be experienced that in this historical study of the making of moral theology no consideration is given either to the existence and developments of the subject outside the confines of the Roman Catholic Church, or to the attitudes and observations of other Christian writers concerning the subject as developed within Roman Catholicism. Apart from the need to define some boundaries to an already lengthy treatment of the subject, what such considerations serve to highlight is that, until very recently indeed in the making of moral theology, the attitudes and the enterprises of others were of little, if any, concern to Roman Catholic moralists, far less to the leaders in their community, unless to condemn them. It is a most welcome feature of the past fifteen or so years that dialogue has sprung up and begun to flourish, partly at the instigation of the Second Vatican Council, between the various moral traditions of Christianity in a way which has contributed constructively to that cracking of moulds and renewal of the subject which characterize much contemporary Roman Catholic writing. And it is in this context of Christian fellowship that all references in the following work to 'the Church' as implying the Roman Catholic Church are to be read as expressive solely of stylistic brevity, and in no sense to be understood as making exclusive claims either for Roman Catholicism or for its particular science of moral theology. Paradoxically perhaps, the hope of the author is that, in providing a historical critique from within the tradition and concentrating upon the resources of that tradition, he will have made some contribution towards that self-understanding and mutual understanding which are indispensable to ecumenism.

Finally, these chapters do not claim to present a moral history of the Church, or an account of how Christians have actually thought and behaved in their everyday moral lives, for, of course, theory and practice are rarely completely harmonious in any sphere of life, not least in the moral life. And this not just because of what the Christian tradition calls the human propensity to sin, or that 'concupiscence' which the Council of Trent, perhaps wryly, described itself as 'both acknowledging and experiencing' (*DS* 1515); nor just because at times the historical vagaries of moral views within the community of the Church lead one to hope for a not inconsiderable disparity between theory and ordinary Christian practice. More fundamentally, such disparity as has existed may also on occasion be seen as intrinsic to the whole enterprise of moral theology as it attempts to comprehend and articulate in human and refracted terms the mystery of God's continuous call to individuals to share increasingly in his life through his chosen medium of human personal freedom.

In the course of producing this work the author has had cause to be grateful for the interest and encouragement of many friends and colleagues. In particular he wishes to acknowledge his indebtedness to various fellow-Jesuits for comments and suggestions, including Professor Emeritus F. C. Copleston, Dr William Daniel, Fr Vincent Turner, Dr Clarence Gallagher, Dr Norman Tanner and Dr Gerard J. Hughes. In the end, this study of The Making of Moral Theology remains a personal essay for whose faults the author is responsible, but which, for whatever virtue it may contain, he dedicates to his mother as an expression of love and gratitude.

ACKNOWLEDGEMENTS

Biblical quotations are taken from the Revised Standard Version unless otherwise noted. The quotation on p. 257 from *Mending Wall* is taken from *The Poetry of Robert Frost* edited by Edward Connery Lathem; copyright 1930, 1939, © 1969 by Holt, Rinehart and Winston. Copyright © 1958 by Robert Frost. Copyright © by Lesley Frost Ballantine. Reprinted by permission of Henry Holt and Company.

BIBLIOGRAPHY

The bibliography is limited for the most part to recent works and secondary sources which are referred to in the course of this study, and is aimed at providing convenient reference for the reader rather than at furnishing an encyclopaedic bibliography on moral theology. Individual titles and details of patristic, medieval, and scholastic works and of conciliar and papal documents are not listed, except for some recent papal encyclicals and editions of works in English translations when the author has not preferred to offer his own. Otherwise the bibliographical entries under *Sigla* may be consulted as identifying the standard and most accessible collections of many primary sources to which reference is made.

SIGLA

AAS   *Acta Apostolicae Sedis*, vols. 1 (1909) – 76 (1984) (Vatican Press). Superseding the earlier *Acta Sanctae Sedis* (1865–1908), *AAS* is the monthly official publication of the Papacy, containing the authentic promulgation of Church laws, the official texts of papal and conciliar documents, the proceedings of 'Sacred Congregations', or Vatican Departments, and the announcements of ecclesiastical decisions and appointments.)

COD   *Conciliorum Œcumenicorum Decreta*, ed. J. Alberigo, *et al.* (Bologna, 1973³). (A one-volume collection, in the original, of all the decrees of all Ecumenical Councils, first published on the eve of the Second Vatican Council. The third edition includes all the documents of Vatican II. An accompanying English translation of this edition is currently in preparation under the editorship of Dr Norman Tanner.)

CTS   Catholic Truth Society, London. (Publishes in English translation various conciliar, papal and other Vatican documents.)

DS   Denzinger, H. J., and Schönmetzer, A., *Enchiridion Symbolorum et Definitionum* (Barcelona, 1963³²). (First published by Denzinger in 1854, and revised and updated in subsequent editions (including one by Karl Rahner), 'Denzinger' is a one-volume collection, with brief notes in Latin, of chronological excerpts in the original languages of the dogmatic definitions and doctrinal statements of Councils and Popes. Where possible, passages in this study are for convenience referred to by a number in *DS*. Otherwise reference is made to either *COD* or *AAS*. An English equivalent, with Concordance to *DS*, is *The Christian Faith in the Doctrinal Documents of the Catholic Church*, edd. J. Neuner, and J. Dupuis, (London, 1983 (rev.)).

DTC   *Dictionnaire de Théologie Catholique* (Paris, 1899–1953).

NCE   *New Catholic Encyclopaedia* (New York, 1967–79).

PG   *Patrologiae Cursus Completus, Series Graeca*, ed. J. P. Migne. (The Abbé Migne (d. 1875) founded his own publishing house and enlisted the energies of other French priests in his project to produce a universal library of Christian w;itings in the original languages and with introductions, notes and, where necessary, translations in Latin. The 161 volumes of the Greek series cover the years AD 120–1438, to which are occasionally added corrections and supplementary material. In numerous cases, 'Migne' has been superseded by critical editions, but in general his *PG* and *PL* are referred to whenever possible.)

PL   *Patrologiae Cursus Completus, Series Latina*, ed. J. P. Migne. (See above, *PG*. The Latin writers covered in 221 volumes date from the period AD 200–1206.)

STh   Thomas Aquinas, *Summa Theologiae*. (Written explicitly for beginners, the *Summa* of St Thomas is the Christian masterpiece of the Middle Ages. A new translation in 60 volumes has been published by the English Dominicans (Blackfriars–London, 1964–81). The standard way of referring to *STh* is by volume (e.g., 1a 2ae), question, and article, followed at times by reply to an objection (e.g., *STh*, 1ae 2ae, q. 106, a. 3 ad 4).)

Abbott, W. M., *The Documents of Vatican II* (London, 1966).

Abelard, Peter, *Ethics*, ed. D. E. Luscombe (Oxford, 1971).

Acta Concilii Vaticani Secundi, vol. iv (Rome, 1978).

Adomnan's Life of Columba, edd. A. O. and M. O. Anderson (Edinburgh, 1961).

Alfaro, J., 'Nature: The Theological Concept', *Sacramentum Mundi*, edd. K. Rahner *et al.*, vol. iv (London, 1969), pp. 172–5.

Alszeghy, Z., *Nova creatura. La nozione della grazia nei commentari medievali di S. Paolo* (Rome, 1956).

Amann, E., 'Laxisme', *DTC*, vol. ix/1, col. 37–86.

Angelini, G., and Valsecchi, A., *Disegno storico della teologia morale* (Bologna, 1972).

Anglican–Lutheran Diaologue, The Report of the European Commission (London, 1983).

Anglican–Roman Catholic International Commission (ARCIC), *The Final Report* (London, 1982).

Aristotle, *The Nicomachean Ethics*, trans. H. Rackham. (Loeb Classical Library; London, 1947).

Armas, G. (ed.), *La Moral de San Agustin* (Madrid, 1954).

Athenagoras, *see* Justin Martyr.

Aubert, J. -M., *Le Droit romain dans l'œuvre de saint Thomas* (Paris, 1955)

—— 'Hiérarchie de valeurs et histoire', *Revue des Sciences Religieuses* 44 (1970), pp. 5–22.

Aubert, R., *La Théologie catholique au milieu du XXᵉ siècle* (Paris, 1954).

—— 'Pius IX, Pope', *NCE*, vol. xi, pp. 405–8.

—— (ed.), *The Christian Centuries, vol. v: The Church in a Secularised Society* (London, 1978).

Augustine, *The City of God*, trans. H. Bettenson (London, 1972).

Barnard, L. W., *Justin Martyr: His Life and Thought* (Cambridge, 1967).

Bede, *The Ecclesiastical History of the English Nation* (London, 1910).

Bellarmini, Roberti Cardinalis, *Opera Omnia* (Paris, 1870).

Bellinger, G., *Der Catechismus Romanus und die Reformation* (Paderborn, 1970).

Bévenot, M., 'St Thomas and the Erroneous Conscience', in *Thomistica Morum Principia*, vol. ii (Rome, 1961).

—— ' "Faith and morals" in the Council of Trent and Vatican I', *Heythrop Journal* 3 (1962), pp. 15–30.

Bieler, L., *The Irish Penitentials* (Dublin, 1963).

—— 'Penitentials', *NCE*, vol. xi, pp. 86–7.

Blumenkranz, B., 'La survie médiévale de S. Augustin à travers ses apocryphes', *Augustinus Magister: Études augustiniennes*, vol. ii (Paris, 1954).

Bonner, G., *St. Augustine of Hippo* (London, 1963).

Bossy, J., *The English Catholic Community*, 1570–1850 (London, 1975).

Bouscaren, T. L., *Canon Law: A Text and Commentary* (Milwaukee, 1963).

Boyle, J. P., 'The Ordinary Magisterium: Towards a History of the Concept', *Heythrop Journal* 20 (1979), pp. 380–98.

Braeckmans, L., *Confession et Communion au moyen âge et au concile de Trente* (Gembloux, 1971).

Brodrick, J., *The Life and Work of Blessed Robert Bellarmine*, 1542–1621. 2 vols. (London, 1928).

Brown, B. F., 'Natural Law', *NCE*, vol. x, pp. 251–6.

Brown, P., *Augustine of Hippo* (London, 1967).

Burnaby, J., *Amor Dei: A Study of the Religion of St. Augustine* (London, 1960).

Butler, B. C., 'Infallibile: Authenticum: Assensus: Obsequium. Christian

Teaching Authority and the Christian's Response', *Doctrine And Life* 31 (1981), pp. 77–89.

Butler, C. B., *The Vatican Council*. 2 vols. (London, 1930).

Butler's Lives of the Saints, ed. H. Thurston (London, 1937).

Catechismus ex decreto Concilii Tridentini ad parochos . . . editus (Leipzig, 1840).

Chadwick, H., *The Sentences of Sextus: A Contribution to the History of Early Christian Ethics* (London, 1959).

—— *Early Christian Thought and the Classical Tradition* (Oxford, 1966).

Chambers, R. W., *Thomas More* (London, 1938).

Codex Iuris Canonici, (Rome, 1917; revised Rome, 1983).

Cognet, L., 'Jansen, Cornelius Otto', *NCE*, vol. vii, pp. 817–19.

—— 'Jansenism', ibid., pp. 820–4.

Congar, Y., *Tradition and Traditions* (London, 1976).

—— 'Pour une histoire sémantique du terme "magisterium" ', *Revue des sciences philosophiques et théologiques* 60 (1976), pp. 84–97.

—— 'Bref historique des formes du "magistère" et de ses relations avec les docteurs', ibid., pp. 98–112.

Copleston, F. C., *A History of Philosophy* (London, vol. i (rev.), 1947; vol. ii, 1950).

Cragg, G. R., *The Church and the Age of Reason* (London, 1972).

Cross, F. L., *The Early Christian Fathers* (London, 1960).

Curran, C. E. *Contemporary Problems in Moral Theology* (Notre Dame, Indiana, 1970).

Daniel, W., *The Purely Penal Law Theory in the Spanish Theologians from Vitoria to Suarez* (Rome, 1968).

D'Arcy, E., *Human Acts: An Essay in their Moral Evaluation* (Oxford, 1963).

Davis, H., *Moral and Pastoral Theology*. 4 vols. (London, 1935).

Delhaye, Ph., *The Christian Conscience* (New York, 1968).

—— (ed.), *Pour relire Humanae Vitae* (Gembloux, 1970).

Deman, Th., 'Probabilisme', *DTC*, vol. xiii, col. 417–619.

Doyle, E., 'Peaceful Reflections on the Renewal of Moral Theology', *Clergy Review* 62 (1977), pp. 393–401.

Dubois, M. M., *Saint Columbanus: A Pioneer of Western Civilization* (Dublin, 1961).

Dulles, A., *The Resilient Church* (Dublin, 1978).

Dupré, L., 'Situation Ethics and Objective Morality', *Theological Studies* 28 (1967), pp. 245–57.

Farmer, D. H., *The Oxford Dictionary of Saints* (Oxford, 1978).

Ferguson, J., *Pelagius: A Historical and Theological Study* (Cambridge, 1956).

Filson, F. V., *The Gospel According to Matthew* (London, 1960).

Finsterwalder, P. W., *Die Canones Theodori Cantuariensis und ihre Überlieferungsformen* (Weimar, 1929).

Flick, M., and Alszeghy, Z., *Il Vangelo della grazia* (Florence, 1964).

Ford, J. C., and Kelly, G., *Contemporary Moral Theology, vol. ii: Marriage Questions* (Cork, 1963).

Franzelin, J. B., *Theses de Ecclesia Christi Opus Posthumum* (Rome, 1887).

Fritz, G., and Michel, A., 'Scolastique', *DTC*, vol. xiv/2, col. 1691–1728.

Frost, R., *The Poetry of*, ed. E.C. Lathem (London, 1971).

Fuchs, J., *Human Values and Christian Morality* (Dublin 1970).

Gamer, H. M., *see* McNeill.

Ganns, G. E. (ed.), *Constitutions of the Society of Jesus* (St Louis, 1970).

Gilby, T. (ed.), *Summa Theologiae*, vol. xxviii, (London, 1960).

Gilleman, G., *The Primacy of Charity in Moral Theology* (London, 1960).

Gilson, E., *The Christian Philosophy of St Augustine* (London, 1961).

Glorieux, P., 'Sommes théologiques', *DTC*, vol. xiv, col. 2341–64.

Guilley, P., *La culpabilité fondamentale* (Gembloux, 1975).

Guitton, J., *The Modernity of St. Augustine* (London, 1959).

—— 'Parallèle de s. Augustin et de Newman', *Augustinus Magister*, ii (Paris, 1954), pp. 1105–10.

Hamel, E., 'Fontes graeci doctrinae de epikeia', *Periodica* 53 (1964), pp. 169–185.

—— 'L'usage de l'épikie', *Studia Moralia*, vol. iii (Rome, 1965), pp. 48–81.

—— 'Conferentiae episcopales et Encyclica "Humanae Vitae",' *Periodica* 58 (1969), pp. 243–349.

—— 'Vari tipi di legittimazione in teologia morale', in *Ortodossia e Revisionismo* (Rome, 1974).

Häring, B., *The Law of Christ*, vol. i (Cork, 1963).

Harris, P., *et al.*, *On Human Life* (London, 1968).

Hay, M., *The Prejudices of Pascal* (London, 1962).

Heckler, K., 'Jansenism', *Sacramentum Mundi*, ed. K. Rahner *et al.*, vol. iii (London 1969), pp. 171–4.

Hennessy, J. J., *The First Council of the Vatican: The American Experience* (New York, 1963).

Horgan, J., *Humanae Vitae and the Bishops* (Irish University Press, 1972).

Hughes, W. D. (ed.), *Summa Theologiae*, vol. xxiii (London, 1969).

Innocent III, Pope, see Lothario dei Segni.

Jedin, H., 'The Council of Trent and Reunion: Historical Notes', *Heythrop Journal* 3 (1962), pp. 3–14.

—— and Dolan, J., *Handbook of Church History*. 10 vols. (London, 1965–81).

The Jerome Biblical Commentary (London, 1968).

John Paul II, Pope, Encyclical Letter *Redemptor Hominis*, AAS 71 (1979), pp. 257–324; CTS (1979).

—— *Familiaris Consortio*, AAS 74 (1982), pp. 81–191; CTS (1981).

—— *Reconciliatio et Paenitentia*, AAS 77 (1985), pp. 185–275; CTS (1984).

Justin Martyr and Athenagoras, The Writings of, trans. M. Dods, G. Reith, and B. P. Pratten (Edinburgh, 1867).

Kelly, J. N. D., *Jerome: His Life, Writings, and Controversies* (London, 1975).

Kenny, J. P., 'Supernatural', NCE, vol. xiii, pp. 812–6.

Kidd, B. J. (ed.), *Documents illustrative of the Continental Reformation* (Oxford, 1967).

Kilpatrick, G. D., *The Origins of the Gospel According to Saint Matthew* (Oxford, 1946).

Knowles, D., *The Evolution of Medieval Thought* (London, 1962).

Knox, R. A., *The Belief of Catholics* (London, 1927).

Lampe, G. W. H., *A Patristic Greek Lexicon* (Oxford, 1961).

Leff, G., *Medieval Thought* (London, 1962).

Liddell, H. G., and Scott, R., *A Greek– English Lexicon*. 2 vols. (Oxford, 1925).

Lothario dei Segni, *On the Misery of the Human Condition*, ed., D. R. Howard (New York, 1969).

Lottin, O., *Le droit naturel chez s. Thomas et ses prédécesseurs* (Bruges, 1931).

—— *Psychologie et morale aux XIIe et XIIIe siècles*. 4 vols. (Louvain, 1942–9).

—— *Principes de morale*. 2 vols. (Louvain, 1947).

Lubac, H. de, *Surnaturel* (Paris, 1946).

—— *Augustinisme et théologie moderne* (Aubier, 1965).

Luther, Martin, *Werke* (Weimar, 1883–1980).

McCormick, R. A., 'Notes on Moral Theology: January–June 1968: The Encyclical *Humanae Vitae*', *Theological Studies*, 29 (1968), pp. 725–41.

McNamara, M. A., *Friends and Friendship for St. Augustine* (New York, 1958).

McNeill, J. T., *A History of the Care of Souls* (London, 1952).

—— and Gamer, H. M., *Medieval Handbooks of Penance* (New York, 1938).

Mahoney, J., 'Obedience: Consent or Conformity?', *The Way, Supplement* no. 6 (May, 1968), pp. 5–19.

—— 'Understanding the Encyclical: Six Pastoral Questions', *The Month*, n.s. 40 (1968), pp. 233–44.
—— *Seeking the Spirit: Essays in Moral and Pastoral Theology* (London, 1981).
—— 'The Sharing Church', *The Month*, 2nd n.s. 14 (1981), pp. 346–9.
—— *Bioethics and Belief: Religion and Medicine in Dialogue* (London, 1984).
—— 'Moral Reasoning in Medical Ethics,' *The Month*, 2nd n.s. 18 (1985), pp. 293–9.

Mansi, J. D., *Sacrorum Conciliorum nova et amplissima collectio*. 54 vols. (Arnheim, 1901–27).
Maritain, J., *Neuf leçons sur les notions premières de la philosophie morale (Paris, 1949)*.
Markus, R. A., *Saeculum: History and Society in the Theology of St Augustine* (Cambridge, 1970).
Matteucci, B., 'Jansenistic Piety', *NCE*, vol. vii, pp. 824–6.
Meier, A. M., *Das peccatum mortale ex toto genere suo* (Regensburg, 1966).
Michel, A., 'Pénitence, du IVᵉ Concile du Latran à la Réforme,' *DTC*, vol. xii col. 948–1050.
Monden, L., *Sin, Liberty and Law* (London, 1966).
Monumenta Ignatiana, Epist., vol. IX (Madrid, 1909); *Exercitia Spiritualia* (1919).
Moriones, F. (ed.), *Enchiridion theologicum Sancti Augustini* (Madrid, 1961).
Murphy, F. X., 'Moral Theology, History of (to 700)', *NCE*, vol. ix, pp. 1117–19.
Murphy, J. L., *The Notion of Tradition in John Driedo* (Milwaukee, 1959).

Newman, J. H., *Apologia pro vita sua* (London, 1959).
—— *An Essay on the Development of Christian Doctrine*, ed. J. M. Cameron (London, 1974).
Noonan, J. T., *Contraception* (New York, 1967).
Novak, M. (ed.), *The Experience of Marriage* (London, 1965).

Obermann, H. E., *The Harvest of Medieval Theology* (Cambridge, Mass., 1963).
Ó Fiaich, T., *Columbanus in his own Words* (Dublin, 1974).

Palmer, P. F., 'Penance, Sacrament of', *NCE*, vol. xi, pp. 73–8.
Pantin, W. A., *The English Church in the Fourteenth Century* (Cambridge, 1955).
Pascal, B., *Les Provinciales*, ed. L. Cognet (Paris, 1965).

Paul VI, Pope, Encyclical Letter *Humanae Vitae, AAS* 60 (1968), pp. 481–503; *CTS* (1968).

Pius XI, Encyclical Letter *Casti Connubii, AAS* 22 (1930), pp. 539–92; *CTS* (1959).

Pius XII, Pope, Encyclical Letter *Mystici Corporis Christi, AAS* 35 (1943), pp. 193–248; *CTS* (1952).

—— Encyclical Letter *Humani Generis, AAS* 42 (1950), pp. 561–78; *CTS* (1957).

Plato, *Laws*, trans. R. G. Bury (Loeb Classical Library; London, 1926).

—— *Euthyphro*, trans. H. N. Fowler (Loeb Classical Library; London, 1953).

—— *Republic*, trans. P. Shorey (Loeb Classical Library; London, 1946).

—— *The Statesman*, trans. H. N. Fowler (Loeb Classical Library; London, 1952).

Pluralismo, Commissione teologica internazionale (Bologna, 1974).

Portalié, E., 'Augustin (Saint)', *DTC*, vol. i, col. 2268–472; Eng. trans. *A Guide to the Thought of St Augustine* (London, 1960).

Poschman, B., *Penance and the Anointing of the Sick* (London, 1964).

Potts, T. C., *Conscience in medieval philosophy* (Cambridge, 1980).

Price, E., 'Sexual Misunderstanding', *The Clergy Review* 65 (1980), pp. 157–63.

Pyle, L. (ed.), *The Pill and Birth Regulation* (London, 1964).

—— *Pope and Pill* (London, 1968).

Rahner, K., *Theological Investigations*. 20 vols. (London, 1961–84).

—— *Nature and Grace* (London, 1963).

—— 'The Theology of Risk', *The Furrow*, 19 (1968), pp. 266–8.

Rock, J., *The Time Has Come* (London, 1963).

Rohmer, J., *La Finalité morale chez les théologiens de saint Augustin à Duns Scotus* (Paris, 1939).

Roland-Gosselin, B. (ed.), *Œuvres de s. Augustin*, i (Paris, 1949).

Romero, O., 'Political Dimension of Christian Faith from an Option for the Poor', *Convergence* (Pax Romana; Switzerland–Belgium, no. 1–2, 1981).

Scarisbrick, J. J., *Henry VIII* (London, 1968).

Scott, J. B., *Francisco de Vitoria and the Law of Nations* (Oxford, 1934).

Southern, R. W., *The Making of the Middle Ages* (London, 1953).

Spanneut, M., *Le Stoïcisme des pères de l'Église* (Paris, 1957).

Suarez, F., *Opera Omnia* (Paris, 1856).

Sullivan, F. A., *Magisterium: Teaching Authority in the Catholic Church* (Dublin, 1983).

Sweeney, G., 'The Primacy: the small print of Vatican I', in A. Hastings (ed.), *Bishops and Writers* (Wheathampstead, 1977).

Tentler, T. N., *Sin and Confession on the Eve of the Reformation* (Princeton, 1977).

Thils, G., *L'infaillibilité pontificale* (Gembloux, 1969).

Tuchman, B. W., *A Distant Mirror: the calamitous 14th century* (New York, 1978).

Ullman, W. 'Innocent III, Pope', *NCE*, vol. vii, pp. 521–4.

Valsecchi, A., *Controversy: The birth-control debate 1958–1968* (London, 1968).

Vatican Council II, *Decrees*, etc., *AAS* 57 (1965)–58(1966). See also, Abbott.

Vereecke, L., *Storia della teologia morale moderna*. 4 vols. multicopied (Accademia Alfonsiana, Rome, 1979–80).

Vermeersch, A., 'Soixante ans de théologie morale', *Nouvelle Revue Théologique* 56 (1929), pp. 863–84.

Vernet, F., 'Latran, IVᵉ Concile œcuménique du', *DTC*, vol. viii, col. 2652–67.

Vorgrimler, H. (ed.), *Commentary on the Documents of Vatican II*. 5 vols. (London, 1967–9).

Walker, G. S. M., *Sancti Columbani Opera* (Dublin, 1957).

Walsh, M. J., 'Ecumenism in Wartime Britain (1)', *Heythrop Journal* 23 (1982), pp. 243–58.

Williams, C., 'Conscience', *NCE*, vol. iv, pp. 198–202.

Zalba, M., *Theologiae Moralis Compendium*. 3 vols. (Madrid, 1958).

1

THE INFLUENCE OF AURICULAR CONFESSION

To begin a historical study of the making of moral theology with an examination of the influence of auricular confession may appear to some an intriguing, and to others an unattractive prospect; but however one regards it there is no doubt that the single most influential factor in the development of the practice and of the discipline of moral theology is to be found in the growth and spread of 'confession' in the Church. In his examination of the development of confession in the Western Church one authority comments, 'one of the most remarkable transformations in the history of Church discipline is the gradual admission, leading ultimately to the requirement, of the frequent penance which had long been earnestly rejected'.[1] The purpose of this opening chapter, then, is to trace how the Church's development and practice of the confessing of sins has been of profound importance in the making, and the interests, of moral theology, and to offer some reflections on that formative influence.

An added advantage of such a beginning to our study is that, in the process, something of a historical framework of the subject will emerge, within which it will be possible to situate the material of subsequent chapters and topics. And for the purpose of this chapter, and indeed for the development of moral theology itself, it is convenient to identify in that development four stages: the patristic period; the age of the rise and spread of the penitential movement and literature, embracing the sixth to the ninth centuries; the Fourth Council of the Lateran, held in Rome in 1215 under the powerful reforming Pope Innocent III, which saw Scholasticism approaching its most self-confident period and the enactment of the Church's law of annual private confession; and the Council of Trent, convened to stem the Reformation flood in the sixteenth century, which consolidated and reaffirmed the

[1] John T. McNeill, *A History of the Care of Souls* (London, 1952), p. 93.

Church's teaching on confession, as on many other subjects, and whose influence, although waning, is still a most powerful feature in Church thinking and behaving. It should be noted that the concern of this study is not with the specifically sacramental nature of the rite of penance, but with the element of personal acknowledgement of sins, and with how that powerfully influenced the making of moral theology.

The Patristic Period

From the beginning, the Christian community was conscious of sayings of Jesus referring to the forgiveness of sins within the Church, whether in the explicit statement to the Apostles, 'whose sins you shall forgive, they are forgiven them; and whose sins you shall retain, they are retained' (John 20: 22–3), or in his conferring on Peter 'the keys of the kingdom of heaven', and in his promising to Peter (Matt. 16: 19) and to the Twelve (Matt. 18: 18) that whatever they bind on earth shall be bound in heaven; and whatever they loose on earth shall be loosed in heaven. As Palmer comments, 'Christian tradition will interpret the power of binding as the power to excommunicate the sinner, the first step in the discipline of Penance, and the power of loosing as the power of reconciling the sinner to the community, the final step'.[2]

The recognition of this discipline of Penance, however, and its scope, proved extremely contentious in the Church of the early centuries. It was one thing for Church communities or authorities to expel a sinner from their midst, partly to prevent contamination and partly to shock him into repentance, following the precedent of Paul's directive to the Church in Corinth (cf. 1 Cor. 5). It was quite another whether he should then be left to God's mercy or be received back into the communion of the Church if he repented. On what Poschmann describes as the 'most important problem of the relationship of ecclesiastical to divine forgiveness'[3] opinions were to be sharply and acrimoniously divided in the growing Church, particularly with the development of currents of fervent perfectionism and the emerging phenomenon of those who apostatized from the Church in times of State persecution and then had a change of heart.

[2] P. F. Palmer, 'Penance, Sacrament of', *NCE*, vol. xi, p. 74.
[3] B. Poschman, *Penance and Anointing of the Sick* (London, 1964), p. 12.

Controversy centred largely on the puritanical figure of Tertullian (died c.220), the influential African convert who wedded Christian thought with the Latin language and introduced a strong legal bias to that thought. Eventually, however, the Church's practice settled round the teaching of its first great Council, convened at Nicaea in 325 by the Emperor Constantine to affirm the divinity of Christ against Arianism. Among its various disciplinary decrees the Council affirmed a 'humane' policy of readmitting to Communion after appropriate periods of penance excommunicates and any who had fallen away during persecution, or in any other way given up their religion.[4] Granted, however, that readmission to the community was in principle possible, there remained the further question whether such a 'humane' attitude should cover all sins. To Tertullian a century previously, when he had moved into strict Montanism, the news that adultery and fornication as well as idolatry and homicide would be forgiven was evidence not just of a 'most humane' but also of an 'extremely soft' attitude.[5]

This triad of sins comprising idolatry, adultery, and homicide obviously created particular difficulties for many opposed to any relaxation of the Church's penitential discipline; and the thinking behind it appears to rely on an exegetical development which translated into these three sins the findings of the 'Council' of Jerusalem which enjoined all Christians to 'abstain from what has been sacrificed to idols and from blood and from what is strangled and from unchastity' (Acts 15: 29). Since, moreover, the decisions of this Council were arrived at by the Apostles in conjunction with the Holy Spirit (Acts 15: 28), it appeared to some that idolatry, adultery, and homicide must constitute sinning 'against the Holy Spirit', which, according to Jesus, was *the* sin which would never be forgiven (Matt. 12: 31–2).[6] It is not altogether surprising, then, that even thus early a form of moral casuistry is to be glimpsed in considerations of what is to count as, or equivalent to, the prohibitions of Acts. Sacrificing to idols quickly came to include apostasy and heresy;

[4] *COD*, pp. 7, 11.
[5] 'Mollissima et humanissima disciplina', Tertullian, *De pudicitia*, c. 5 (PL 2, 989).
[6] Thus Tertullian as Montanist in *De pudicitia*, c. 12 (PL 2, 1002). Augustine was aware of the triad and also of the view that each element constituted a sin against the Holy Spirit, but he knew of no proof (*Sermo* 352: PL 39, 1558; *Epist* 71, 7, 4; PL 38, 448). And in any case, his own understanding (which prevailed) of the only unforgivable sin was that of hardness of heart which refused forgiveness to the end. *Epist* 187, 3, 7: PL 33, 818.

strangulation and blood applied to any form of homicide; and unchastity obviously covered all serious sexual transgressions. Bishop Cyprian of Carthage (d. 259), for instance, was to judge that a consecrated virgin who had sinned should do 'full penance' as an adulteress, not of her husband but of Christ.[7] And he it was, in the latter half of the third century who was most concerned to adapt the penances decreed in various regional councils to 'the cases, wills, and needs of individuals'.[8]

Two features of this developing penitential discipline which were to have major influence in the centuries to follow were, first, that all authorities were agreed that public exclusion from, and reconciliation with, the Church could be availed of only once in one's lifetime. Even that had been a hard battle to win against the Montanists and Novatianists. And secondly, the penitential practices to be undertaken for various major transgressions before full readmission years later could be extremely demanding, not to mention humiliating, even when all due allowances had been made. Various 'canonical' penances for the several major sins were laid down in the canons of local church councils, decretals, and letters of bishops, including Basil and Gregory of Nyssa in Asia Minor, whose influence extended into the Western Church.[9] And even after the completion of his penance and readmission to the Eucharist, the Christian was still a marked man, disqualified for life from various activities ranging from military service to marital relations.[10] Consequently, if he did not fulfil his penance completely or transgressed any of the later obligations, he was canonically at fault and sins were multiplied. And in its very rigour and complexity the whole elaborate and hard-won penitential system became self-defeating for ordinary Christians. Caesarius, bishop of Arles in the sixth century, was to protest in a sermon on behalf of a typical parishioner, 'I'm in the army. And I'm married. How can I do penance?'[11] The final result seems to have been that great numbers of ordinary Christians must have lived in what could only be called a permanent state of ecclesiastical delinquency. Until they were dying. For, as Poschmann concludes, the one permissible 'ecclesiastical penance gradually ceases to have any part in the ordinary course of life, and becomes merely a means of preparing for

---

[7] *Epist* 4, 4: *PL* 4, 370.   [8] Poschman, op. cit., p. 55.
[9] Cf. ibid., pp. 82–3.   [10] Ibid., pp. 105–6.
[11] Ibid., pp. 107–8.

death'.[12] Moreover, as McNeill points out, with the collapse of the Western Roman Empire 'the conquests of the Visigoths and Franks fundamentally transformed the West.... The new barbarized society could not be subjected to the old discipline which had already proved too severe for the Roman Christians'.[13] And he concludes, 'An effective reform of ecclesiastical penance was only possible if there was a retreat from the rigid principle which forbade its repetition'.[14]

The Celtic Penitential Movement

The major breakthrough was to come from the Western edge of Europe, where under monastic influence the practice of repeated private confession and forgiveness of sins, including not only monks but also local Christian lay people, began to develop. It appears that the monastic tradition of the spiritual direction of individual monks by an older monk or a superior lent itself to the more formal expression of a private penitent–confessor relationship, which was eagerly grasped at and became an important element in the pastoral work of monasteries and of itinerant monks and others.

But the problem of penance still remained, or indeed increased, with the introduction of repeated confession of sins. And as a guide to the growing numbers of individual confessors there developed the fascinating and repelling literature which we know as the Penitential Books, which may have originated in Welsh synods held under the influence of St David in the sixth century, before proliferating in Ireland and spreading thence with the Celtic missionary movement to the Frankish lands, England, Italy, and Spain, stimulating other native products as they went.[15] His edition of the Irish Penitentials,[16] mostly written in Latin but some in Old Irish, illustrates Bieler's judgement that 'the private character of the "Celtic" penance and the absence of diocesan organization and episcopal jurisdiction in [Wales and Ireland] explain why the penitentials were not decreed by synods but were the work of

[12] Ibid., p. 107.
[13] John T. McNeill and Helena M. Gamer, *Medieval Handbooks of Penance* (New York, 1938), p. 22.
[14] Op. cit., p. 123.
[15] McNeill and Gamer, *Handbooks*, pp. 24–6.
[16] Ludwig Bieler, *The Irish Penitentials* (Dublin, 1963).

individuals, often of abbots of great monasteries. These authors fixed penances in accordance with Sacred Scripture, canonical and monastic tradition, and their own spiritual judgment'.[17]

Terse and strikingly elliptical in style as they were, the Penitentials' primary function was to provide priests with a tariff of penances to be enjoined for various sins. But as the genre developed, various Penitentials also included instruction on how confession of sins was to be made, providing meticulous lists of questions which the confessor should put to the penitent man, woman, or child; classifications of deadly sins, and family trees of sins, according to the authoritative lists of Cassian and Pope Gregory the Great; and frequently advice on how to deal with penitents according to their social or ecclesiastical status and the circumstances of their case.

The origin and purpose of the penitential literature is well described in the opening of the Penitential of St Columbanus, which dates from about 600 and is described by McNeill as essentially a Celtic book which includes adaptations to a Frankish environment: 'True penance is not to commit things deserving of penance but to lament such things as have been committed. But since this is undone through the frailty of many, not to say everyone, the measures of penance need to be known. A scheme of these has been handed down by the holy fathers, so that in accordance with the greatness of the offences the length of the penances should be ordained'.[18] The European influence of such a work may be gauged from the career and reputation of its author (not to be confused with Columba of Iona), who founded abbeys in France, Switzerland, and Italy in his reforming zeal, and is considered by Farmer 'the greatest of Ireland's many apostles to the Continent of Europe,' and by Poschman as 'that ardent, eccentric and strongwilled pioneer of the missionary activity' of the Irish and Anglo-Saxon monks who 'made a decisive contribution to the establishment of medieval civilization'.[19]

A later Penitential, possibly dating from the eighth century, and

---

[17] *Idem*, 'Penitentials', *NCE*, vol. xi, p. 86.
[18] Bieler, *The Irish Penitentials*, p. 97. Cf. McNeill and Gamer, op. cit., p. 250.
[19] D. H. Farmer, *The Oxford Dictionary of Saints* (Oxford, 1978), p. 89; Poschman, p. 131. The Penitential of Columban, included in Bieler, op. cit., is edited with other works in G. S.M. Walker, *Sancti Columbani Opera* (Dublin, 1957). Tomás Ó Fiaich, in an English selection of the works, observes that the Penitential of Columban 'was the earliest penitential in the Irish tradition to be employed on the continent' (*Columbanus in his own Words* (Dublin, 1974), p. 73). On the European

falsely ascribed to Bede, informs priests that among their books they should possess a Penitential 'so that thou mayest, first of all examine the distinction of all cases, without which judgment cannot stand . . . . For not all are to be weighed in one and the same balance, although they be associated in one fault, but there shall be discrimination for each of those, that is: . . . [etc]'.[20]

The spirit of the Penitentials is very often described by their compilers as healing, or medicinal, and it exemplifies the principle of curing vices by the application of their contrary virtues, a principle which is seen to go back through the monastic Cassian to pre-Christian thought.[21] And the crisp observation is made that a priest who tells tales outside of confession is more of a detractor than a doctor.[22] But it has to be acknowledged that although there is much positive material to be found in the Penitentials taken as a whole, the overall impression gained from them is coloured more by vice than by virtue. They constitute at best an unsuccessful attempt to apply with some degree of humanity an appallingly rigid systematized approach to sin, and no one ever appears to have asked the serious theological question to what end (other than social order) all this suffering was really being imposed. Instead, there was a concern to catalogue major sins, including homicide, adultery, and magic, sometimes apparently haphazardly, but increasingly with the addition of the various subdivisions of the eight 'principal vices' of Cassian: gluttony (not surprising when sustained fasting was so popular a practice and penance), fornication, avarice, anger, dejection and sloth (typically monastic preoccupations), and boasting and pride. In all this classification the authority of many of the Fathers is drawn upon, as also that of earlier Penitentials; canons of various synods and councils; the New Testament (with a predilection for the Pauline 'works of the flesh' of Galatians chapter five and First Corinthians chapter six); the Old Testament, especially and ominously the Books of Leviticus and Exodus, although, curiously, not the Decalogue as such; and, as Columban modestly adds, 'the personal understanding of the author'.[23]

---

influence of Columban(us), and the extent of subsequent devotion to him, cf. Marguerite Marie Dubois, *Saint Columbanus: A Pioneer of Western Civilization* (Dublin, 1961), pp. 107–10.

[20] McNeill and Gamer, *Handbooks*, p. 223.   [21] Ibid., p. 44.
[22] Ibid., p. 110.   [23] Bieler, op. cit., p. 99.

In assessing liability to penance in individual cases the confessor was enjoined, as we have seen, to take various factors into account, and it is interesting to deduce from the varieties of penance imposed according to circumstances a developing tradition concerning moral responsibility. There is care to distinguish between ignorance, inadvertence, carelessness, and contempt.[24] But there is also a crude magical realism to be noted in the approach to the Eucharistic species, whether in dealing with accidents,[25] or in penalizing any negligence, or even stammering, in pronouncing the words of consecration despite the warning given by their being clearly marked 'danger' in the Missal.[26] There is guilt, though lesser, attached to sinful intention which is not put into effect for lack of opportunity.[27] To induce another to sin incurs the same penalty as the sin itself,[28] and in pursuing enquiries about any sinful behaviour the confessor should be careful to ask 'how it came about'.[29] Spontaneous thoughts and desires are distinguished from those deliberately fostered.[30] And in putting them into action, premeditated murder, for instance, merits exile for ten years, and should be distinguished from impulsive killing which results in exile for only six years.[31] A habit of sin in a particular area may be considered more culpable than a single act, rather than diminishing responsibility; although the greater penance for the former may arise simply from the number of individual acts involved, or indeed from a feeling that a greater penance will be an incentive to break the habit.[32]

External factors have also to be taken into account. A bishop's guilt is greater than a priest's, and a priest's than a layman's.[33] The fifth-century document known as the First Synod of St Patrick, which was really a circular letter to the clergy of Ireland approved by Patrick, expected a more becoming style of dress not only from

---

[24] Cf. McNeill and Gamer, pp. 106, 172.
[25] Cf. McNeill and Gamer, pp. 104–6; Bieler, pp. 132–3.
[26] Bieler, pp. 63 and 133, n. 10.
[27] McNeill and Gamer, pp. 88–9.
[28] Ibid., p. 101.
[29] Ibid., p. 198.
[30] Bieler, p. 75.
[31] McNeill and Gamer, p. 91.
[32] Ibid., p. 92, Bieler, pp. 76, 83, 129.
[33] McNeill and Gamer, p. 88.

priests but also from their wives.[34] Cases of those who were sick, those who had to work, and those unable to make restitution for injustices committed, were considered individually. And one salty piece of advice to confessors is to take particular care over the confessions of sailors, since not only do many have wives in several ports, but some of them even think it is permissible![35]

On marriage, it is interesting to note that the seventh-century Penitential of Theodore, Archbishop of Canterbury, which is addressed to 'all Catholics of the English',[36] repeats much of the standard material on marital abstinence for penitential or ritual reasons, and the decree that a woman having an abortion after the fortieth day from conception should do penance as for the more serious act of murder,[37] but takes a considerably more lenient view than others on questions of remarriage. This Theodore considers permissible in cases of proven impotence, in the case of a married slave being given his or her freedom, and in a number of cases of prolonged separation, even to the extent of including the partner who eventually returns.[38] Why Theodore should differ so from other Penitentials is not clear, but the reason may lie in his personal background, since before being appointed to Canterbury by Pope Vitalian, becoming 'the effective organizer of the Church in England',[39] he had been a Greek monk, originally from Tarsus, and the Eastern Church's view on divorce and remarriage was not so absolute as that of the West.[40]

[34] Bieler, pp. 1–2, 54. ('Quicumque clericus ab hostiario usque ad sacerdotem sine tunica visus fuerit atque turpitudinem ventris et nuditatem non tegat, et si non more Romano capilli eius tonsi sint, et uxor eius si non velato capite ambulaverit, pariter a laicis contempnentur et ab ecclesia separentur'.)

[35] On various mitigating circumstances, cf. McNeill and Gamer, pp. 103, 106, 213. On the interrogating of sailors, cf. the fourteenth century 'belated specimen' of the penitentials noted by W. A. Pantin, *The English Church in the Fourteenth Century* (Cambridge, 1955), p. 206, and quoted, p. 273: '. . . quia in singulis terris et regionibus quas ingrediuntur, vel contrahunt matrimonia de facto cum diversis mulieribus, credendo hoc sibi licere, . . . '). Cf. p. 209.

[36] McNeill and Gamer, p. 182. Cf. P. W. Finsterwalder, *Die Canones Theodori Cantuariensis und ihre Überlieferungsformen* (Weimar, 1929).

[37] McNeill and Gamer, p. 197.

[38] Ibid., pp. 209–12. For the Latin text, cf. *PL* 99, 933–5.

[39] John T. Noonan, *Contraception* (New York, 1967), p. 192. For Noonan's magisterial survey of the penitential literature on sexual morality, cf. pp. 190–210.

[40] For a variety of views on divorce and remarriage during the penitential period, cf. McNeill and Gamer, pp. 95, 273; Bieler, pp. 89, 91, 117, 179 (and n. 6), 195 (and n. 7), 197. Bede, in his *Ecclesiastical History* (bk. 4, chap. 1), refers to a fear of Theodore's sponsor for the archbishopric of Canterbury that he might 'according to

Detailed consideration of the actual forms of penance imposed by the penitential literature is not strictly relevant to the topic of this chapter, which is more concerned with the moral thinking and climate underlying the whole penitential movement, but two features in particular were to have a profound effect not only on the life but also on the fate of Christian Europe. The usual forms of self-mortification enjoined were fasts of varying intensity and duration, deprivation of sleep, multiple genuflections and recitations of psalms, long periods of standing or of silence, different degrees of discomfort at night, beatings and, of course, sexual abstinence. Columbanus decreed that for a particular transgression the penitent should 'abstain for three years from the more tasty foods and from his wife',[41] although he had also insisted that marital abstinence should always accompany whatever other penances were undertaken.[42] Occasionally more philanthropic penances were imposed, such as clerics giving of their superfluity to the poor, almsgiving in general, and the release of slaves.[43] Those who might, for reasons such as sickness, be unable to perform the more demanding penances were permitted to have recourse to redemption; that is, to 'redeem' the penance by philanthropy, buying back prisoners of war, releasing slaves, and, in later centuries, building churches and

the custom of the Greeks, introduce anything contrary to the true faith into the church where he presided'. He also records (chap. 5) that the Synod of Hertford, held in 673 and presided over by Theodore, included in its decrees 'that no man quit his true wife, unless, as the gospel teaches, on account of fornication. And if any man shall put away his own wife, lawfully joined to him in matrimony, that he take no other.' Evidence of differences between Roman and Greek usages is common in Theodore's Penitential, as also of differences between the (Roman) English and the (Celtic) Scots. Cf. chap. IX, 'Qui ordinati sunt Scotorum vel Britonum episcopi qui in Pascha vel tonsura catholicae non sunt adunati Ecclesiae, iterum a catholico episcopo manus impositione confirmentur. Licentiam quoque non habemus eis poscentibus chrisma vel eucharistiam dare, nisi ante confessi fuerint velle nobiscum in unitate Ecclesiae' (*PL* 99, 932). An early editor of the Penitential of Theodosius, the French scholar, Jacques Petit, draws attention to its reference to 'some unusual practices of certain churches, or others which the Fathers wished in their outstanding indulgence to be tolerated on account of the weakness of very many people'. On the disparity of attitudes to divorce and remarriage 'on account of fornication, prolonged absence, captivity, or other matter', Petit recalls the comment of Origen that some Church rulers appeared to have permitted such behaviour in order to avoid worse (*PL* 99, 904).

[41] 'iii annis paeniteat abstinens se a cybis suculentioribus et a propria uxore', Bieler, p. 102.
[42] Ibid., p. 103, 'for penance ought not to be halved'.
[43] Cf. McNeill and Gamer, p. 106; Bieler, p. 81.

monasteries or endowing colleges.[44] And alongside this there developed also the practice of penance by proxy, when the penitent might pay or even support others, eventually including priests, to share his penance or assume it in its entirety.[45] It was this ominous connection, for the best of intentions, between money payments and the remission of punishment which was to contribute eventually to the trafficking in indulgences, and to lead many penitents and pilgrims to Rome—and many protesters to Wittenberg.

The other significant development was the pilgrimage. An interesting form of penance which would repay further study is that of exile, to which reference is occasionally made. It is frequently qualified as 'unarmed' or 'without arms',[46] and this presumably precluded the penitent's taking up easy employment abroad as a mercenary soldier, a somewhat inappropriate career if the original sin was homicide, as seems often to have been the case. One tradition has it, in fact, that the arrival on Iona from Ireland in 563 of the future St Columba was due to his having been exiled as a result of instigating a war between his own family and King Diarmid of Ireland in which three thousand of the king's men were slain.[47] It would be interesting to know how many others of the

[44] Cf. Poschmann, pp. 76–80, 128.

[45] McNeill, *History*, pp. 122–4.

[46] The Irish Penitentials refer to 'dura penitentia in peregrinatione extranea', sometimes equivalent to being 'in aexilio', or 'peregrinatione perenni', or being a 'peregrinus'. Cf. Bieler, pp. 68, 98, 118–20, 182. Crimes incurring such wandering abroad include incest, wilful murder, theft or injury, and breaking into the place of keeping the Gospel book (ibid., pp. 68, 118–20, 182). The Penitential of Columban decreed 'Si quis clericus homicidium fecerit et proximum suum occiderit, X annis exul paeniteat' (p. 98), and 'Quicumque fecerit homicidium, . . . iii annis inermis exsul in pane et aqua paeniteat' (p. 102). The Penitential of Finnian refers to a penitent going 'unarmed except for a staff' (p. 86).

[47] Cf. *Butler's Lives of the Saints*, ed. H. Thurston (London, 1937), vol. vi, p. 115. *Adomnan's Life of Columba* (edd. A. O. and M. O. Anderson (Edinburgh, 1961)) refers to Columba's leaving Ireland at the age of 42 'on pilgrimage for Christ' ('de Scotia ad Brittaniam pro Christo peregrinari volens enavigavit') and to his spending the remainder of his life in continuous fasts and vigils (p. 186). Later in the work Columba refers to having completed thirty years 'meae in Britannia perigrinationis' and to his frequent prayer that he now be allowed to die (p. 514). No reason is given by Adomnan for Columba's leaving Ireland, but in the course of describing a vision of angels experienced by Saint Brendan, he explains that the occasion was Columba's attendance at an assembly as a consequence of his having been excommunicated by 'a certain synod for certain insignificant and quite excusable causes' (p. 468). As a result of Brendan's vision and eulogy of Columba, the others present did not dare to proceed further with excommunicating the saint, but on the contrary venerated and honoured him (p. 470). The editors of Adomnan's

waves of Irish monks who re-Christianized Europe in their wanderings were victims of that early ecclesiastical penal system which condemned delinquents to a period, or even a lifetime, of 'foreignness', or *peregrinatio*, as it was also termed in the Penitentials.[48] Thus was born also the Christian pilgrimage, wandering abroad to good purpose, as a form of *absolvitur ambulando* and a means of expiating one's sins through the intercession of the Blessed Virgin and the saints whose shrines dotted Europe.[49] Not that it was all penance and piety by any means, as the Canterbury pilgrims of Chaucer abundantly testify.

Life consider other sources for the view that Columba's missionary activities stemmed from punishment for past behaviour, but seem indisposed to accept this explanation (pp. 72–4). In the light of the penitential tradition of exile, however, and the fact of Columba's excommunication, which even Adomnan's veneration cannot gloss over, it appears not unlikely that his 'pilgrimage' was at least partly instigated by either the canonical requirement or the personal desire for penance for his past.

[48] Cf. Bieler, p. 228, 'Si quis autem ex meditatione odii et post vota perfectionis [i.e., vows of religion] alium occiderit, cum peregrinatione perenni mundo moriatur.' Adomnan's *Life of Columba*, written almost a century after the saint's death, records several instances of the abbot receiving, or hearing the confession of, men who had come to Iona 'ad delenda in periginratione peccamina'. Columba's practice seems to have been to sentence such 'pilgrim penitents' to several years' monastic labour on the neighbouring Hebridean island of Tyree where he also had a monastery. That this island was something of a monastic penal settlement for *peregrini* appears also from the description of its abbot bringing with him there from Ireland a royal and bloodthirsty prince 'ut in suo apud se monasterio per aliquot peregrinaretur annos'. Cf Anderson, 36a–b, 87a–b, 32a–b.

A Scot cannot refrain from noting among all the edifying and wondrous tales which Adomnan has to record of Columba his encounter with what appears to have been (or become?) the Loch Ness Monster. On his travels over the 'spine' of Britain Columba once had occasion to cross the River Ness (*fluium nesam*), where a 'water beast' (*aquatilis bestia*) had attacked and killed one of the local Picts while swimming. Undeterred, the blessed man bade one of his companions swim across and sail back a boat for the party from the other bank, which the obedient monk immediately began to do. 'But the monster (*bilua*) was lurking in the depth of the river, its appetite for prey whetted rather than satisfied. Feeling the water above it disturbed by the swimmer, it suddenly erupted and rushed with a mighty roaring and open jaws upon the swimmer, who was by then in mid-stream'. The watching 'barbarians' and monks were terrified, but Columba traced a sign of the cross in the air and invoked the name of God, commanding the ferocious beast 'No further! Do not touch him! Get back immediately!'. 'On hearing these words of the saint, the beast fled in fright as if dragged away with ropes, even though it had got only a short pole's distance from the man', a turn in events which led all who had observed the proceedings to magnify the God of the Christians. (Latin text in Anderson, 74b–75b.)

[49] Cf. H. Jedin and J. Dolan (edd.), *Handbook of Church History* (London, 1969), vol. iii, p. 111.

And more ominously, the practice also helped to spawn the horrors of the Christian crusades, now no 'unarmed exile' but a consecrated using of the sword to wipe out one's sins and the enemies of the Church at one blow, as may be seen in the declaration of the Council of Clermont, called by Pope Urban II in 1095, that crusading to Jerusalem 'would count for all penance'.[50]

Many of the developments, for good and ill, of the Celtic penitential movement are to be seen in miniature in the concluding passage of the Penitential of Columban:

Confessions are to be made with some diligence, especially with regard to disturbances of the mind, before going to Mass in case it should happen that one approaches the altar unworthily or not with a clean heart. It is better to wait until the heart is healthy and distanced from scandal and envy than to draw close boldly to the judgement of the tribunal. For the altar is the tribunal of Christ, and his body there with the blood judges those who approach unworthily. And so, just as we must beware of capital and carnal sins before communicating, so also we must abstain and be cleansed from the interior vices and sicknesses of an ailing soul before the union of true peace and the bond of eternal salvation.[51]

In this passage the echoes of the penitential Psalm 51 and the allusions to Pauline discipline on the Corinthian eucharist (1 Cor. 11: 27–8) are clear. So also is the traditional theme of healing, characteristic of much of the penitential literature. The thoroughness and comprehensiveness with which confession is to be made can also be noted, as also the close link between confession and reception of Communion and the implied frequency of confession. What predominates, however, is the forensic imagery and the dread of Christ's judgement. In a sin-haunted medieval Europe, as described in the work of Tentler and Tuchman, the judgement theme was to become all-pervasive, not least in art, and most notably in the last judgement scenes given such colourful prominence in the 'judgement', or 'doom', windows and wall-paintings of so many cathedrals and village churches, climaxing in the condemnatory Christ of Michelangelo in the heart of Rome, the Sistine

---

[50] Cf. *DS* 868, proem: 'qui pro sola devotione, non pro honoris vel pecuniae adeptione, ad liberandum Ecclesiam Dei Ierusalem profectus fuerit, iter illud pro omni paenitentia reputetur'.

[51] Latin text in Bieler, p. 106.

Chapel.[52] And the court-of-law imagery was to be developed further and systematized theologically to become enshrined in due course in the 'sacred tribunal' teaching of the Council of Trent on confession.

There is much to be said for the view that the Catholic Church has never quite shaken off, or recovered from, the penitential movement of the sixth to the sixteenth centuries. In its earliest stages it was an attempt to draw Christians out of folk religion, magic, and pagan customs, and in that lies much of the interest of the penitential books for the social historian. From the theological point of view, it may be said that of all early Christian literature they make the greatest attempt to draw close to the real life of God's often nominal people in their weakness. And if they are selective in their subject-matter, negative in their approach, and shocking in their more lurid passages, they were the best that many an uneducated priest had to hand in his desire to exercise his healing ministry of God's forgiveness. Perhaps McNeill puts it best when he writes of such books that they were 'products, no less than correctors, of a primitive society'.[53]

The reaction of hierarchies to this spread of repeated private confession and to the inconsistent and unauthorized literature which accompanied it to stimulate and guide it, no less than to the flood of enthusiastic Irish missionaries purveying it, was one of extreme disapproval. Not a few local synods denounced the handbooks for their errors, contradictions, and lack of proper authority; and there were calls to burn them and to reaffirm or reinstate the old system of public penance. Charlemagne in 813 called synods of his entire empire in various cities to bring about

---

[52] W. A. Pantin, describing *The English Church in the Fourteenth Century* ((Cambridge, 1955), p. 239), observes that 'from the point of view of religious instruction, the most impressive feature in most churches would be the great painting of the Last Judgement over the chancel arch'. Barbara W. Tuchman, in *A Distant Mirror* (New York, 1978), writes (p. 34): 'No one doubted in the Middle Ages that the vast majority would be eternally damned. *Salvandorum paucitas, damnandorum multitudo* (few saved, many damned) was the stern principle maintained from Augustine to Aquinas.' Thomas N. Tentler, in *Sin and Confession on the Eve of the Reformation* (Princeton, 1977), p. 160, records 'the extraordinary opinion of Duns Scotus' that it is not unbelievable 'that there are many in the Church who live for a year without mortal sins', a view which Tentler considers 'is directly opposed to Gregory the Great's encouragement to find sins everywhere'. It was clearly unbelievable to Pope Innocent III; cf. *infra*, p. 17.

[53] McNeill, *History*, p. 135.

reforms in the Church, including some control over the penitential books.[54] And, as Jungman informs us, when the elimination of the penitentials proved impossible, the Church perforce adapted its thinking to the new movement and to its pastoral success, and the Carolingian reform synods had new, more uniform, and duly approved books composed.[55]

For, from the first, and despite the disapproval of higher ecclesiastics, the parochial clergy no less than the monks welcomed the penitential literature and the growing practice of repeated and private *Confession*, as the whole penitential rite came revealingly to be called from the eighth century.[56] On the whole, the level and standard of education of the clergy was low and they needed all the help they could get from these practical and indispensable ready reckoners, although it may be doubted how much they were capable of also exercising the discretion in application which the authors were often at pains to stress. The existing canonical collections were very bulky, and, with the dissemination of properly authorized summaries, often mingling ancient penitential canons with excerpts from the Celtic-inspired penitentials, priests were increasingly required to possess such a summary in order to standardize the penances to be imposed.[57]

For by now, from the eighth century, regular confession was becoming a general rule. The Dialogue of Egbert, archbishop of York in the middle of that century, tells us:

For, since the times of Pope Vitalian and Theodore, Archbishop of Canterbury, this custom, thank God, has grown up in the Church of the English and has been coming to recognition as lawful, that not only the clerics in the monasteries but also laymen with their wives and families should during these twelve days come to their confessors and with tears and almsgiving cleanse themselves from the fellowship of carnal concup-

---

[54] Poschmann, pp. 134–5; Jedin and Dolan, *Handbook*, vol. iii, p. 98. Among the decrees of the Council of Chalon-sur-Saône (813), it was enacted that 'the measure of penance to those who confess their sins ought to be imposed, as was said above, either by the institution of the ancient canons, or by the authority of the Holy Scriptures, or by ecclesiastical custom, the booklets which they call "penitentials" being repudiated and utterly cast out, of which the errors are obvious, the authors undetermined (*certi errores, incerti auctores*)', McNeill and Gamer, *Handbooks*, pp. 401–2.

[55] In Jedin and Dolan, op. cit., p. 310, n. 2.

[56] Cf. Poschmann, p. 138.

[57] Jedin and Dolan, op. cit., p. 310.

iscence [cf. 1 John 2: 16] that they may be the purer when they partake of the Lord's communion on the Lord's nativity.[58]

Elsewhere in Europe of around the same time, regular confessions were now becoming obligatory, sometimes as often as three times a year, although not always without resistance.[59] And so it continued for the next four centuries, during which the early Scholastic theologians developed, clarified, and systematized not only the Church's law in general, but also its doctrine of the seven Sacraments, and what exactly in theological terms was going on in the encounter between priest and penitent—a speculative debate which was to continue for centuries. We have a glimpse of some current practice in the writings of one of the most exciting and excitable figures of the scholastic age, the logician-theologian Peter Abelard. We shall later be considering in more detail his major contribution to subjectivity in morals, but it is of interest to note here his acerbic comments on the administration of Confession. He was 'no reformer of the penitential system as such',[60] and was, on the contrary, highly indignant that it was not being properly administered. He complains of priests who do not know the canonical rules or how to assign 'satisfactions', with the result that they often promise penitents a vain security and deceive them, a good case of the blind leading the blind, and both falling into a ditch![61] 'So when priests who do not know these canonical rules have been unwise, with the result that they impose less satisfaction than they should, penitents thereby incur a great disadvantage since, having wrongly trusted in them, they are later punished with

---

[58] McNeill and Gamer, *Handbooks*, p. 243, where the view of Watkins is cited (n. 3), that this is probably 'the earliest example of habitual confession generally practised in a Christian community'. The abandonment of public penance in England in the seventh century is acknowledged in the closing passage of the Penitential of Theodore, where, after contrasting the Roman practice of reconciling those who had completed penance with the Greek practice, he adds, 'Reconciliatio in hac provincia non est, quia et publica poenitentia non est' (*PL* 99, 936).

[59] Poschmann, pp. 138–40.

[60] D. E. Luscombe, *Peter Abelard's Ethics* (Oxford, 1971), p. xxxiii.

[61] Ibid., p. 105. For a contemporary's acerbic comment on Abelard, cf. ibid., p. 104, n. 2. The reference to Matt. 15: 14 on the blind leading the blind and their common fate becomes commonplace in treatments of the requirements of confessors, and will recur in the Fourth Lateran Council as well as in the observations of Aquinas. Its connection with penance is apparently first made by Augustine, *De Poenitentia*, 10, 25; *PL* 40, 1122.

heavier penalties for that for which they could have made satisfaction here by means of lighter penalties.'[62]

The Fourth Lateran Council

It was against this historical, theological and pastoral background that in 1215 the reforming Pope Innocent III, described by Ullmann as 'one of the greatest popes in the Middle Ages',[63] convoked a General Council of the Church. Innocent had been trained as a theologian and a canonist at the Universities of Bologna and Paris. His essay *de miseria humane conditionis* proved one of the most gloomy and popular works of the Middle Ages,[64] and he it was 'who brought into clearest possible relief the exclusively legal function of the pope as successor of St Peter'.[65] Three months after annulling the *Magna Charta* which the Barons of England had forced from King John, Innocent presided over a Council of more than twelve-hundred prelates, which affirmed that there was no salvation outside the Church; condemned various heretics; approved the term 'transubstantiation'; founded what was to become the Inquisition; forbade the founding of any further religious orders; appealed for a Crusade against Islam; and, more to our purpose, imposed on the whole Church the obligation of what is popularly known today as 'Easter duties', which still figures with a few modifications in the Church's legislation.[66]

On reaching the age of discernment, everyone of the faithful, of either sex, is faithfully at least once a year to confess all his sins in private to his own priest, and is to take care to fulfil according to his abilities the penance enjoined on him, reverently receiving the sacrament of the Eucharist at least at Easter . . . . Otherwise he is to be barred from entering the church in his lifetime and to be deprived of Christian burial at his death. This saving statute is to be frequently made public in churches, so that nobody may don the veil of excuse through the blindness of ignorance.[67] . . . The priest

---

[62] Luscombe, p. 109. Cf. p. 111 for Abelard's castigation of bishops who are prodigal in relaxing penances in recompense for alms.

[63] W. Ullman, 'Innocent III, Pope', *NCE*, vol. vii, p. 521.

[64] Cf. Pantin, op. cit., p. 198; Lothario dei Segni, *On the Misery of the Human Condition*, ed. D. R. Howard (Bobbs-Merrill, New York, 1969).

[65] Ullmann, loc. cit.

[66] Cf. the *Code of Canon Law* (1917), can. 906; revised edn. (1983), cann. 988–9.

[67] Latin text in *DS* 812.

is to be discerning and careful, so that like a skilful doctor he can apply wine and oil [cf. Luke 10: 34] to the wounds of the injured person, diligently asking for the circumstances of the sinner and of the sin, through which he can prudently understand what advice he ought to give, and what sort of remedy to apply, trying various things to heal the sick person.[68]

The Council went on to impose absolute secrecy on the part of the priest, on pain of himself doing perpetual penance in a strict monastery; but it added that, should he need more prudent advice, he might carefully seek it without revealing the identity of the penitent.[69]   •

In future, the Council also decreed, annual provincial councils were to be held to ensure observance of its decrees.[70] Bishops were also to ensure a supply of suitable priests to administer the sacraments according to the various rites and languages in use,[71] as also of assistants to help the bishops in preaching and hearing confessions.[72] Every cathedral should have a Master of Theology whose duty would be to instruct the clergy in Scripture and especially in what concerns the care of souls.[73] In fact, the Council concluded, quoting Pope Gregory the Great, 'the ruling of souls is the art of arts', and bishops are strictly obliged to educate future priests, since it is better to have a few good ones than a lot of bad ones. 'If a blind man leads a blind man, both will slip into a ditch.'[74]

According to Jedin, the Fourth Council of the Lateran was followed throughout Europe by 'vigorous synodal activity' everywhere;[75] but Iserloh informs us that this could not make much headway against the many pastoral shortcomings, at the root of which lay the inadequate education of the parochial clergy, especially 'the poorly paid vicars, by whom the frequently absentee holders of pastoral benefices had their functions performed'.[76] And Raymond of Peñaforte, who later became Master General of the Dominican Order and whose *Summa of Cases*, written in the years following the Council, was to have widespread influence, distinguished between the knowledge to discern sins and the power to absolve, but concluded sadly that 'many simple priests have the power who have not the knowledge'.[77] Another late thirteenth-

---

[68] DS 813.   [69] DS 814.   [70] COD, pp. 212–13.
[71] COD, p. 215.   [72] Ibid., pp. 215–16.   [73] Ibid., p. 216.
[74] Ibid., p. 224.   [75] Op. cit., vol. iv, p. 172.   [76] Ibid., p. 575.
[77] McNeill, *History*, p. 146.

century writer found it necessary to identify a basic minimum requirement that 'as judge in matters of conscience he must be able to distinguish between what is sin and what is not, and between sin and sin'.[78]

It has been suggested that the Fourth Lateran decree on annual confession was aimed primarily at enabling parish priests, at a time when the Albigensian heresy was spreading alarmingly, to know among their parishioners who were really Catholics;[79] but it is also acknowledged that the decree had important repercussions on the theology, and even more on the practice, of confession. For the requirements of the Council were exacting, the confessor having to be able to help the mostly uninstructed penitent to confess 'all his sins' and to enquire about their and his particular circumstances. It was from this disciplinary decree for the whole Church that there developed the next great body of confessional literature, the *Summas* for confessors, or confessors' compendiums. These works were 'learned theological treatises, very different indeed from the simple and untheological penitentials. They were a natural sequence of the legislation of 1215'.[80]

They were also the inevitable product of a period in the Church obsessed by a desire to classify, digest, summarize and reconcile all possible data on any given subject. The most influential work of classification was in Church Law, in the epoch-making *Decrees* of Gratian (1140), which claimed to be a 'concord of discordant canons' deriving from the whole history and literature of the Church, and also from Roman and Germanic law and the laws of other European nations.[81] There were summas of medicine as well as of law, summas of grammar, logic, rhetoric, and literary style, summas of theology and of the various branches of theology, of sacraments in general and in particular, and especially of marriage

---

[78] Jedin and Dolan, vol. iv, p. 576.

[79] A. Michel, in *DTC*, vol. xii, col. 950. Cf. Aquinas, *infra*, n. 84.

[80] McNeill, *History*, p. 145. On the Summas for confessors, and also the more popular manuals of Confession, cf. Tentler, pp. 31–46. The originator of the *Summa confessorum* was the Dominican canon lawyer, Raymond of Penaforte, writing in the immediate aftermath of the Fourth Lateran Council (ibid., p. 31). Broomfield, however, suggests that the first such *Summa* to appear was that of Thomas of Chobham, which began to circulate about 1216. Cf. L. Braeckmans, *Confession et Communion au moyen âge et au concile de Trente* (Gembloux, 1971), p. 66, n. 2.

[81] The whole vast work of compilation, in the 1833 edition of Richter, comprises vol. 187 of Migne's *PL*.

and of penance.[82] And there were produced, in abundance, summas for confessors, summas of moral cases, summas of moral theology, examples of a literary growth with its roots in the penitential literature, coming to flower in the twelfth to the fifteenth centuries throughout Europe, including England, surviving the gales from Germany in the sixteenth century to take on new growth after the Council of Trent, weathering the icy frost from Jansenist France in the seventeenth century, and still flowering sturdily in the middle of the twentieth century. And all concentrated on the hearing and the making of auricular Confession.[83]

Observance of the legislation of 1215 quickly became itself possible matter for sin and confession, as doubts were raised and entertained about almost every word of the decree, especially, for instance, whether 'sins' meant only mortal sins or also included all those daily lapses which had been recognized as far back as Augustine as both inevitable and innumerable.[84] And so was born

---

[82] Cf. P. Glorieux, art. 'Sommes théologiques', *DTC* xiv, col. 2341–64. On the emergence of summas in the early twelfth century, cf. R. W. Southern, *The Making of the Middle Ages* (London, 1953), pp. 204–5.

[83] On the development of the literature in England, cf. Pantin, op. cit., ch. ix.

[84] Teaching some forty years after the Council, Thomas Aquinas found it necessary to discuss the obligatory nature of its decree of annual confession if one was not conscious of having sinned seriously. He conceded that this was not required by divine ordinance (*ex iure divino*), but was a matter of being bound by a precept of positive law. Even in such cases, there were advantages in the realization that one was a sinner, in approaching the Eucharist with greater reverence, and in helping priests to know their subjects, 'lest a wolf lie hid in the flock'. It was considered by some theologians, however, that the Church's legislation obliged only those who had committed mortal sins. 'All' could not possibly refer to venial sins 'quia nullus omnia confiteri potest'. If this were so, the Church's precept would be fulfilled by presenting one's self to the priest and showing one was without awareness of mortal sin ('et se ostendat absque conscientia mortalis esse'). This would count as confession. (*Summa Theol.*, *Suppl.* q. 6, art. 3 et ad 3). Aquinas's justification for confessing all one's sins, which he qualifies as 'those he remembers', is not juridical but medicinal. A doctor does not treat just one ailment, but the whole state of the patient and its complications. Medicine for one ailment could aggravate others, and so medicine for one sin could be an incentive for another by going to the opposite extreme (ibid., q. 9, art. 2). And the priest should draw upon the canons of penance as a doctor using the science and art of medicine, applying them 'according to a divine prompting', since strong medicine could weaken a patient (ibid., q. 18, art. 3). The penitent should be careful, for his part, not to confess 'aliud quam sua conscientia habeat, sive in bonum sive in malum'. 'The mouth should accuse only what the conscience possesses.' If he is in doubt about whether his sin was mortal or venial, he is bound to confess it as doubtful and await the judgement of the priest. 'Qui aliquid committit vel omittit in quo dubitat esse peccatum mortale, peccat mortaliter, discrimini se committens' (ibid., q. 6, art. 4 et ad 3).

the notorious line of self-questioning and the inevitable literature on whether various types of behaviour or individual actions constituted a mortal sin to be confessed, or were 'only' venial sins. To this was added the striving on the part of the confessor to 'enquire diligently' into all the circumstances of the penitent and his sins, on the clear presumption that the penitent himself was incapable or even untrustworthy.

Precision and development in the Church's teaching on the act and scope of confessing one's sins are to be found a century later in the conditions placed by Pope Clement VI on his coming to the aid of the Armenians against the Sultan, which included accepting the belief that 'it is necessary for salvation to confess all mortal sins perfectly and distinctly to one's own priest or with his permission' to another.[85] In 1415 the Council of Constance, which had been summoned to arbitrate on the merits of three rival claimants to the papacy, also took the opportunity to condemn various views attributed by Oxford scholars to John Wyclif, including the view that 'vocal confession to a priest was introduced by Innocent, and is not as necessary as he lays down. If one has offended a brother only in thought, word, or deed, it is sufficient to repent only in thought, word, or deed.'[86] Later in the same century the Council of Florence, in the course of its abortive attempts to win over the Greeks, summarized the Latin Church's doctrine on the Sacraments, including that of Penance. The 'quasi-material' of this Sacrament are the three acts of the penitent: contrition; oral confession; and satisfaction according to the judgement of the priest. 'The oral confession involves the sinner confessing completely to his priest all the sins he remembers.'[87]

To help the confessor cope with all this he now had at his disposal no lack of literature, but, as Pantin concludes, 'unfortunately, books in themselves were not enough; what was needed was a systematic training and formation of the clergy, . . . and that solution was not to be reached until the Council of Trent in the sixteenth century.'[88] In the meantime, however, an often inadequate and frequently almost illiterate clergy was charged with administering to the laity a procedure which was acknowledged by all to be embarrassing and onerous on them. If, in addition, the confessor

---

[85] *DS* 1085. Cf. *DS* 1050, proem.
[87] *DS* 1323.

[86] *COD*, pp. 397–9.
[88] Op. cit., p. 218.

was zealous, or incompetent, or zealous and incompetent, it is really not surprising if at least such bungling with souls could be described as a torturing of conscience. Accordingly, Martin Luther was to level at the Church's practice 'a double charge of perverse laxity in penance and oppressive rigidity in the hearing of confessions.'[89]

The Council of Trent

But the Catholic Church would have none of that, or indeed of any of the other complaints of Luther and his supporters. After much political and ecclesiastical manœvring throughout Europe, including England, a General Council of the Church was convened at Trent, in the Alps above Lake Garda, with the aim of defining Catholic dogma and reforming the Church. Given the strong Protestant criticisms against current practice and doctrine on Confession, Trent felt it necessary to give thorough treatment to the subject, in 'teaching to be observed by all for ever'.[90] Prescinding from the historical and dogmatic aspects of that teaching, we may note for our purposes the definitive doctrine of Trent on the confessing of one's sins, as a further indication of the way in which moral theology was to develop in subsequent centuries. Expounding on the divine institution of the Sacrament, the Fathers of Trent wrote, 'Christ our Lord wished the baptized who have subsequently

---

[89] McNeill, *History*, pp. 165–6. On the adequacy and competence of confessors in the years following the Fourth Lateran decree, Aquinas has some uncharacteristically trenchant comments. In a rare polemical work, directed against the secular priests at Paris University who were attacking the mendicant orders in general, and Aquinas in particular on his papal appointment as Master of Theology there, Aquinas vigorously defended the academic and apostolic work of the friars, and their marked superiority over the secular clergy in these fields. The Lateran Council's decree that every metropolitan church have a theological teacher was not observed because of the lack of educated men among the secular priests, whereas the religious orders provided even more teachers than the minimum required. A similar situation obtained with regard to popular preachers. And in the hearing of confessions the need was no less, on account of the ignorance of many priests, which is highly dangerous in the hearing of confessions. In his *de Poenitenita*, Augustine had advised seeking out a knowledgeable priest as confessor, lest both fall into a ditch which a fool refused to avoid. Cf. Aquinas, *Contra impugnantes Dei cultum et religionem*, cap. 4–5, in *Opuscula Theologica*, vol. ii (Marietti, 1954). For the background to the work, cf. ibid., Intro., pp. 1–2. On the role of embarrassment, or shame, in the medieval making of confession, cf. Tentler, pp. 128–30. On Luther's view, cf. infra, p. 126, n. 33.

[90] DS 1667.

committed some wrong to stand as guilty men before this tribunal, so that they could be released through the sentence of priests, not once but as often as they penitently took refuge in it from the sins they had committed'.[91] What is at stake is a matter of 'what is demanded by divine justice'.[92]

The confession element of the Sacrament of Penance was instituted by the Lord as a complete confession of sins, and he left priests as his vicars, as presidents and judges, . . . to pronounce sentence of forgiveness or retention on all mortal crimes. Priests could not exercise this judgement without knowing the case, nor observe equity in imposing punishments, if sins were declared only generically and not rather in species and individually.[93] . . . It follows from this that penitents should list in confession all the mortal sins of which they are conscious after diligent reflection . . . . All mortal sins, even of thought, make men 'sons of wrath' (Eph. 2: 3) and enemies of God, and it is necessary to seek forgiveness of God for all with open and ashamed confession. So, when the faithful are careful to confess all the sins which come to mind there is no doubt that they are laying them all before the divine mercy to be forgiven. Those who act otherwise and knowingly hold some sins back are putting forward nothing to be forgiven by the divine goodness through the priest. 'For if a sick man is embarrassed to uncover his wounds to a doctor, medicine does not cure what it does not know about.'[94]

It further follows that in confession those circumstances are also to be explained which change the species of the sin, since without them the sins themselves are not completely exposed or known to the judges, and a correct estimation of the seriousness of the crimes is impossible, as is the appropriate penalty to be imposed on penitents for them.[95] . . . And it is impious to call confession which is commanded to be made in this way impossible or a torturer of consciences. It is certain that the Church requires of penitents only that each examine himself rather diligently and explore all the nooks and shadows of his conscience, and then confess those sins by which he remembers he has mortally offended his Lord and God. Other sins which do not occur to him as he considers diligently are understood as included universally in the same confession.[96]

The Council reaffirmed the teaching of the Fourth Lateran Council on the obligation of confessing at least once annually, and thoroughly approved the practice of confessing during Lent.[97] It considered the absolution conferred by the priest as the dispensing

[91] DS 1671.   [92] DS 1672.   [93] DS 1679.
[94] DS 1680.   [95] DS 1681.   [96] DS 1682.
[97] DS 1683.

of another's kindness, describing it as 'like an act of judgement by which sentence is pronounced by him as by a judge'.[98]

As well as being a conserving and defining Council, Trent was also much concerned with reform within the Church, and it passed many 'Decrees on reformation'. One such, of relevance to this study, was based on the work of the English Cardinal Pole, and concerned the foundation of a diocesan seminary system, decreeing that cathedrals and other major churches institute colleges for young men of the locality who aspired to the priesthood, in such a way that 'this college be a perpetual seedbed (*seminarium*) of God's ministers'. A detailed programme of studies was laid down, in which the seminarians should learn liberal arts, 'Scripture, the ecclesiastical books, homilies of the Saints, and the forms of administering the Sacraments, especially what appears useful for hearing Confessions, as well as of rites and ceremonies'.[99]

One immediate result of the Council was the production in 1566, three years later, of what is popularly known as the Catechism of the Council of Trent. It is more correctly to be considered a Roman Catechism for parish priests as decreed by the Council, and although as such it does not share the status or authority of Trent, it is nevertheless instructive as explaining and applying the conciliar teaching for the benefit of the parish clergy to whom it is addressed. Dealing with confession, the Catechism observes how diligent priests must be in explaining the sacrament, and refers to God as the good pastor binding the wounds of his sheep and healing them with the medicine of penance.[100] Later the priest is portrayed as a presiding judge, to whom the case must be known.[101] It recalls the teaching of the Fourth Lateran, repeated by Trent, on 'the years of discernment' when the Church's ruling on Confession comes into effect, and it interprets this as the ability to discriminate between good and evil exercised at the age when one must deliberate concerning one's eternal salvation.[102] It enjoins that one should make one's confession whenever there is a danger or death, or one

---

[98] 'Ad instar actus iudicialis, quo ab ipso velut a iudice sententia pronuntiatur', *DS* 1685.

[99] *COD*, p. 727.

[100] *Catechismus Concilii Tridentini*, pars. ii, cap. v, q. 1. On this highly influential popularizing work, cf. G. Bellinger, *Der Catechismus Romanus und die Reformation* (Paderborn, 1970).

[101] Ibid., qq. 17, 22.

[102] Ibid., q. 44.

is about to do something which a sinner should not do, such as administering or receiving a Sacrament, or whenever one is afraid of forgetting one's guilt.[103]

On the details of the confession itself, the Catechism continues, 'Since many things are to be observed in confession, some concerning the nature of the Sacrament and others not so necessary, we shall deal with them in detail. Nor is there any lack of booklets and commentaries from which it is easy to obtain an explanation of them all.'[104] 'In confession the utmost care and diligence is to be used, as in all extremely serious matters, and every attention is to be given to healing the wounds of the soul and uprooting sin . . . . One must explain . . . the circumstances which surround each sin and which either increase or lessen its badness. For some circumstances are so serious that they constitute a mortal sin in themselves, and must therefore be confessed.' Instances are given of killing a cleric or a layman, and of how different genera of sins can come about through particular circumstances, such that what may be simple fornication in one case can be adultery, or incest, or sacrilege, in others, 'to use the names given by the doctors in sacred matters in many books'. 'Factors of place and time are sufficiently known from the books of many to be only mentioned here.' And 'whatever does not greatly increase the badness can be omitted without sin.'[105]

These 'books of many' which multiplied after Trent, also now included the works of members of the newly-founded Jesuit order, who added their reflections and solutions of moral cases to those of the Dominicans and the Franciscans who had been active in this field since the thirteenth century. In the actual hearing of confessions also, members of these religious Orders had been, and continued to be, most assiduous, often to the chagrin of the parochial clergy and even of bishops, and occasionally giving rise, or fuel, to disputes within the ranks of the ministers of the Gospel of reconciliation.[106] The founder of the Jesuits, the Basque practical mystic, Ignatius of Loyola, recommended his followers to have a high regard in their ministry for the hearing of confessions and the administration of Holy Communion, and he required all priests of the Society of Jesus to have at least sufficient learning and

---

[103] Ibid., qq. 45, 53. [104] Ibid., q. 46. [105] Ibid., q. 47.
[106] Cf. *supra*, n. 89.

experience of cases of conscience to make them good confessors, seeing in the popular practice of confession not only one of the greatest pastoral aids to the salvation and perfection of souls but also, one may conjecture, one of the most serious pastoral weaknesses of the Church of his day.[107] The modern Redemptorist scholar, Louis Vereecke, describes how Jesuits were trained for the hearing of confessions, especially from case-studies and from manuals, or handbooks, composed by Jesuit moral theologians, which would become the standard textbooks on moral theology used in the Roman College, entrusted to the Jesuits shortly after Trent to become today's Pontifical Gregorian University.[108]

In this and other ways the works, and the influence, of the Jesuit moralists and confessors spread throughout the Church alongside the other great Orders, which included, from the early eighteenth century, the Congregation of the Most Holy Redeemer, or Redemptorists, founded by the most prestigious of all moral theologians, Alfonso of Liguori. His literary output comprised over one hundred books, many of which were no doubt the fruits of his many years of lecturing to his own Redemptorist students before he became a bishop.[109] It is calculated that there exist more than 17,000 editions and translations of his various works.[110] The principal apostolate of the Order which he founded was to give popular missions, in which the hearing of confessions played a major part, and much of his effort went to the preparation of confessors who would be skilled moral theologians and would also have a mastery of casuistry, 'in view of the many modern positive laws, bulls, and decrees that have to be borne in mind'.[111]

In the nineteenth and early twentieth centuries, moral theology continued to focus on the preparation of confessors, and on the

---

[107] Cf. *Constitutions of the Society of Jesus*, ed. G. E. Ganns, (St Louis, 1970), nos. 308, 407.

[108] L. Vereecke, C.SS.R., *Storia della teologia morale moderna*. 4 vols. multicopied (Accademia Alfonsiana, Rome, 1979–80), vol. ii, pp. 110–12. That Ignatius expected an intelligent and flexible application of such studies is evident from his reply to an anxious Jesuit confessor, 'Your reverence should see what the *Summas* say, and then in particular cases act as God inspires you' (V. R. veda quello che scriveno le summe, et puoi nelle particulari faccia come Idio li inspirarà), *Monumenta Ignatiana, Epist. IX* (Madrid, 1909), p. 176.

[109] Vereecke, op. cit., vol. iv, pp. 108–9.

[110] Cf. G. Angelini and A. Valsecchi, *Disegno storico della teologia morale* (Bologna, 1972), p. 121, n.

[111] Quoted McNeill, *History*, p. 292.

discussion of multitudinous moral cases of conscience in the light of the teaching of the Council of Trent on the nature and practice of confession. It concentrated largely on handing on what had been handed down, mostly in Latin textbooks, or occasionally in various European languages, but using a special brand of ecclesiastical vernacular which frequently causes them to read like so many dialects of the Latin. In 1935 one of the most influential of English-speaking moral theologians, the Jesuit Henry Davis, stressed the conservatism and continuity of his subject when he wrote in the Preface to his four-volume *Moral and Pastoral Theology*, 'If . . . references to some of the older authors appear to be infrequent, that will not, it is hoped, be taken to mean that those authors have not been consulted, or that even now they may be disregarded. They have laid the foundations of this science securely and beyond all cavil.'[112] He also acknowledged a special debt to his sources, the great moralists and manualists of the last century and a half, Vermeersch, Prümmer, Merkelbach, Génicot, Salsmans, Lehmkul, and Noldin; and he explained, 'A writer on Moral Theology today must be indebted beyond measure to the labour of past writers, for the matter is one that has been treated with the greatest acumen and scholarship during well nigh three centuries, and there is no room for originality.'[113]

The Preoccupation with Sin

It is clear from this historical review that the growth and massive proliferation of auricular confession in the Church has played an enormous and crucial part in the making of moral theology, and that consideration of the influence of confession makes an appropriate and unavoidable introduction to our study. There is considerably more to be said, of course, on the development of moral theology, as will become evident in the chapters to follow. But the place of confession in that development has historically influenced the subject in three ways which call for comment and reflection: a preoccupation with sin; a concentration on the individual; and an obsession with law.

As a preliminary to considering these features in turn, however,

---

[112] H. Davis, SJ, *Moral and Pastoral Theology*. 4 vols. (London, 1935), vol. i, pp. viii–ix.

[113] Ibid., p. vii.

one point may be made quite simply, and that is that over the centuries the work of confessors and moral theologians has brought God's grace and consolation to countless Christian souls. Bossy writes of John Henry Newman's confessional work in the Oratory of industrial Birmingham in terms which could equally be applied in principle to Philip Neri in the Chiesa Nuova in Rome, and to countless others before and since; 'the chapel where he sat for hours in a bug-ridden confessional seems above all to have represented a source of help, warmth and meaning for factory girls who had lost contact with any other'.[114] Help, warmth, and meaning; the description could scarcely be bettered as a pastoral and theological ideal for the confessor and the moralist. And what the Church's confessional doctrine, and moral theology, have taken to heart above all, it may be suggested, is man in his moral vulnerability; by which is meant not just man in his weakness, but more in his awareness of weakness, his helplessness and *aporia*. It is possible, for instance, with a sympathetic eye, to see even the blunt tariff gradations of the Penitentials and the elaborate casuistical developments which we shall consider later as not just a concern for theoretical and impersonal 'cases', but as a realistic acknowledgement of types of all too human predicaments, and an awareness of the fact that law, even God's, does not automatically answer every human query, but that for many much of life is a series of worried 'but what if's?'

Yet, by the same token, it was the Church's growing tradition of moral theology which was itself heavily responsible for increasing men's weakness and moral apprehension, with the strong sense of sin and guilt which it so thoroughly strove to inculcate or reinforce, and the humiliations and punishments with which it drove its message home. The pessimistic anthropology from which it started, and which served inevitably to confirm and reinforce itself, particularly when the subject was pursued in growing isolation from the rest of theology and developed as a spiritual arm of the Church's legal system, drove moral theology increasingly to concern itself almost exclusively with the darker and insubordinate side of human existence. The miasma of sin which emanates from the penitential literature and from the vast majority of manuals of moral theology is not only distasteful, but profoundly disquieting.

[114] J. Bossy, *The English Catholic Community*, 1570–1850 (London, 1975), p. 320.

It can be argued, of course, that the whole body of literature is professional, intended to help the general practitioner of the Sacrament to diagnose the spiritual ailments of his sick patients, and not intended for morbid reading by the general public. One should not expect more, this defence would claim, from the Summas or the manuals of moral theology in terms of spiritual good health than one does in terms of physical flourishing from textbooks of medical pathology. The analogy, however, although valid in some respects, is also inadequate and misleading in concentrating on, and in the process isolating and exaggerating, one aspect of the moral life, and so militating against any integrated and holistic view of man and his moral vocation. As a consequence of this commitment to spiritual pathology, the discipline of moral theology was to relinquish almost all consideration of the good in man to other branches of theology, notably to what became known as spiritual theology. But inevitably this study of Christian perfection was pursued in a rarified and élitist atmosphere more suited to those few who aspired to the life of the counsels, particularly in the religious orders, than to those laity in the world who would, it was considered, find it sufficiently challenging and formidable to attain even to salvation by observance of the Ten Commandments. Even when the works of moral theology did adopt the scheme, not of sins against the commandments of God and of the Church (as also in the popular catechisms), but of the moral and theological virtues, as in some of the desert and, later, Thomist tradition, it is to be noted that these were still too often seen as remedies for sinful vices, or as alternative moral yardsticks against which to measure the infinite variety of moral delinquency.[115]

The same preoccupation with sin is to be found in the detailed study of moral psychology, and of the varying degrees of moral responsibility which we have noted, in however rudimentary form, in the penitential literature.[116] This was to lead in time to the great scholastic and post-Reformation treatises on the nature of sin, on 'hindrances to voluntariness', on the role of ignorance and the passions in the moral judgement, and on the two major subjective conditions, along with objectively grave 'matter', for mortal sin: 'full knowledge' and 'full consent'. And all this not just as fit subject for academic speculation, but in deadly earnest. For on the

---

[115] Cf. *STh* 2a 2ae.   [116] *Supra*, p. 8.

moralist's and the confessor's conclusions and teaching would depend not only the degree of 'satisfaction', or penitential suffering to be undergone in this life, but also, as Abelard trechantly pointed out, one's fate in the next.[117] It was psychology pursued in a gloomy *gestalt*, and conducted under the sword of Damocles.

What is more, although moral theology made some progress in analysing responsibility for action, it had great difficulty in realizing the need to help the individual to come to terms with his moral responsibility for himself. The penitentials punish even mistakes or accidents, although not quite so severely as deliberate actions.[118] The Fourth Lateran Council enjoins the confessor to enquire diligently about all the circumstances of a sin before deciding on the appropriate penance. The Roman Catechism after Trent stresses the confessor's duty of exhaustive explanation of the circumstances of various sins, and it is difficult to avoid the conclusion that this was aimed at least as much at retrospective disclosure to the penitent of the full iniquity of his past behaviour as at moral guidance for the future.[119] No doubt, much of this reflects a lack of moral information or awareness in many an uneducated or unreflective penitent; but it also reflects a mentality in which objective morality appears to preponderate over subjective guilt, and which all too easily serves to instil, or increase, a pervasive sense of self-mistrust on the penitent's part.

This detail into which the moralist and the confessor were to lead the penitent is interestingly highlighted in the regular recurrence of the term 'diligence' applied throughout the tradition to the examination of conscience, whether by the penitent or by his confessor, which is indicative also in a small way of the Church's predilection for repeating time-hallowed terms and formulae which we shall have occasion to examine later in a much more important context.[120] What we first find in the influential Penitential of Columban in the seventh century as an impersonal observation that confessions should be made 'with some diligence' is interestingly paralleled in Adomnan's life of Columba of Iona, in an episode in which the saint advises a companion to interrogate a particular woman 'rather diligently' about a very serious sin which she is concealing.[121] The need to enquire 'diligently' about the circum-

---

[117] *Supra*, n. 62.   [118] *Supra*, p. 8.   [119] *Supra*, n. 105.
[120] Cf. *infra*, p. 153.   [121] Anderson, op. cit., p. 240.

stances of sins is stressed by the Fourth Lateran Council, but it is
later put squarely on the penitent's shoulders by Trent as a duty of
'diligent reflection', which is also coaxingly described, against
opponents, as the need to examine oneself 'rather diligently'. In its
turn, the Roman Catechism was to urge 'the utmost care and
diligence'; and it is therefore not surprising to find the Church's
1917 Code of Canon Law perpetuating the penitent's obligation of
'diligent self-examination', which the revised Code of 1983 was
content to repeat with regard to the species and number, not now of
'mortal', but of 'serious' sins.[122]

It is this detailed enquiry into what Trent called 'the nooks and
shadows' of conscience which raises one of the major defects which
connection with auricular confession brought about in moral
theology—its preoccupation not just with sin, but with sins. The
requirement of completeness, or 'integrity' in the relating of one's
'mortal', or serious, sins, which called for identifying each and
every one according to circumstances, species and number, and
which underlies present Church resistance to extending the practice
of general absolution,[123] led, as we have seen, to a mentality
disposed to discount sins which were not mortal, but 'only venial',
even if it was concerned with the valid enough question of degress
of seriousness, and therefore of moral responsibility.[124] But
perhaps more significantly, it led also to an approach to the moral
life as discontinuous; 'freezing' the film in a jerky succession of
individual 'stills' to be analysed, and ignoring the plot. Continuity
was discounted, or at most only a 'circumstance', and the 'story' of
the individual's moral vocation and exploration either unsuspected
or disregarded. At times one can observe hints of the opposite, as in
the rules elaborated for dealing with scrupulous penitents or with
those expressing doubt or uncertainty about the subjective sinfulness
of some past piece of behaviour. In such cases it is regarded as
helpful to consider other areas of their behaviour and the overall
direction of their moral life, as a context within which to estimate
the morality of the individual act under examination. But the

---

[122] *Supra*, nn. 51, 68, 94, 96, 105; 'post diligentem sui discussionem', *Code of Canon Law*, 1917, can. 901; 1983, can. 988.

[123] Cf. DS 3832–7; *Code of Canon Law*, 1983, cann. 988, 960, 963; and Pope John Paul II, Exhortation *Reconciliatio et Paenitentia* (CTS, London, 1984), pp. 120–1, 132–4.

[124] Cf. *supra*, n. 84.

prevailing preoccupation is one of pin-pointing sins; and we shall have cause in a later chapter to consider how reaction to this dissection of the moral continuum into disjointed instances has led to a development of a principle of moral totality, where responsibility is considered to arise at least as much from appreciating the sweep and pattern of the whole picture as it is from the individual brush strokes or the coloured dots which go to make it up.

It is considerations such as these which prompt the further reflection that, for all its preoccupation with sin and its busy cataloguing and subdividing of sins, from the family trees of Cassian and Gregory onwards, moral theology has not always appeared to take sin itself seriously enough. It has invested numerous actions with an inherent capacity for moral self-commitment which they could not bear, and has become fascinated by concepts often in a complete divorce from reality. It has, indeed, almost domesticated and trivialized sin, like the scientist or the zoologist handling deadly specimens with careless familiarity. And in its attaching the element of sin so readily in the past to positive Church laws on frequently trivial matters as a sanction to their observance, it has only helped to devalue the currency, and done little to engender and foster a healthy respect for real sin. Such reflections lie behind recent expressions of dissatisfaction with the traditional distinction between mortal and venial sin, as too blunt an instrument for moral analysis and to be explained historically by the Fourth Lateran decree on annual confession;[125] and also behind the powerful development in recent years of the theology of the fundamental moral option, which we shall consider later, and which, it is interesting to note, Maritain considered was latent in Aquinas' explanation of the difference between mortal and venial sin.[126]

Concentration on the Individual

The confessional context which has had such influence in the making of moral theology provides grounds not only for a charge of the latter's preoccupation with sin, but also for the common charge that traditional moral theology has been much too

[125] *Supra*, nn. 67, 84. Cf. Pope John Paul II, ibid., pp. 63–4.
[126] Jacques Maritain, *Neuf leçons sur les notions premières de la philosophie morale* (Paris, 1949), pp. 126–8. Cf. *infra*, pp. 221, 332.

individualistic in its choice of subjects and in its treatment of them, and for the even more common charge that it has devoted more than a little of its attention to sexual morality. The emphasis on sexual sins goes as far back as the preoccupation in patristic times with the *porneia*, or sexual behaviour, listed in Acts 15, and it was luridly present in the penitential literature.[127] It undoubtedly also underlies the Tridentine stress on manifesting even sins of thought,[128] and it was intensified by the seventeenth-century statement of the Holy Office which classified every transgression in matters of sexuality as objectively serious matter constituting mortal sin; a view echoed in the Declaration of 1975 by the Holy Office's successor, the Congregation for the Doctrine of Faith, in its statement that 'according to Christian tradition and the Church's teaching, and as right reason recognises, the moral order of sexuality embraces such important values of human life that every direct violation of that order is objectively serious'.[129] It is evident, in fact, that the Church has always been profoundly ambivalent towards human sexuality; and in our next chapter we shall have occasion to consider some of the historical basis for this attitude.

It should also be stressed, however, in considering its concentration on the individual, that even as far back as the period of the penitential literature moral theology has laid great emphasis on the subject of justice in human relations, and on the need for restitution for harm done to one's neighbour or to society. The sixteenth-century and later work of Spanish moralists particularly, on warfare, human and property rights, and international law, especially as European conquest and colonialism were developing, is of abiding importance.[130] And the impressive tradition of Catholic social teaching developing the series of papal encyclicals inaugurated by Leo XIII's reaction to the miseries perpetrated by the *laissez-faire* spirit of the Industrial Revolution is too easily

---

[127] *Supra*, p. 3–4, and n. 39. Many modern exegetes are inclining to the view that *porneia* in Acts 15, as in Matt. 5 and 19, and 1 Cor. 5, refers to invalid Jewish marriages.

[128] *Supra*, n. 94.

[129] *DS* 2013; 'Atqui, secundum christianam traditionem Ecclesiaeque doctrinam, et sicut recta ratio agnoscit, ordo moralis sexualitatis amplectitur bona vitae humanae adeo praestantia, ut omnis directa violatio eiusdem ordinis obiective sit gravis', *AAS* 68 (1976), p. 89.

[130] On the writings of, e.g., Francisco de Vitoria on colonial expansion, civil and ecclesiastical power, and the morality of war, cf. J. B. Scott, *Francisco de Vitoria and the Law of Nations* (Oxford, 1934).

forgotten when charges of excessive individualism are levelled against the moral teaching of the Church. It is, nevertheless, interesting to note that this social teaching has, until fairly recently, been aimed to quite a large extent at the defence of the individual in society, as in the arguments traditionally marshalled to justify and defend the institution of private property, which only recent teaching has begun seriously to qualify with the corresponding social responsibilities which are entailed. It appears also to be the case that the development and practice of moral theology, as distinct from the Church's official and humanitarian teaching, have concentrated more on the individual's response to the divine command not to steal, and more often in the context of his eternal fate than in the context of the social well-being of others.

This stress on the individual, with a view to his confession, is one reason why the Church's moral tradition has found it difficult to handle the idea of collective responsibility on a large scale. There is no lack of material in the manuals on the morality of petty conspiracies to rob, or to do harm. And one of the most highly developed topics in the tradition is that of 'co-operation', or sharing in the wrongdoing of another. The presumption in all these cases, however, is that the total number of participants is small, and that a large measure of the total responsibility can be assigned to at most a few individuals. It is an approach to 'social justice' in which the influence of confession has led to a concentration on individuals and a reluctance to 'exonerate' them by recognizing a more social meaning to sin and an element of sinfulness in institutions, or, indeed, in social circumstances. And, as moral theology has adopted a wider agenda far beyond, for instance, individual sexual or medical issues, or tax evasion, to address itself to nuclear warfare, environmental and population problems, world poverty, and economic policies at national and international levels, the Church's individualistic moral tradition has experienced considerable difficulty in adapting its thinking to such issues of macro-ethics, as well as to the moral implications of increased democratic participation in public policies and decisions, and to the new social phenomenon of what might be termed responsibility spread thin—except perhaps when it considered the morality of voting for Communist or pro-abortion candidates in local or national elections.

The Obsession with Law

A final reflection on the influence of auricular confession on the making of moral theology concerns the whole legal model of the Sacrament as it developed through the centuries, based as this was on the Church's understanding of the Petrine and apostolic commissions to bind and loose; the Pauline practice of passing judgement; and the general biblical teaching on divine justice, anger, and retribution. The language of the lawcourt is an integral part of the imagery of both Old and New Testaments in describing God's dealings with men; and forensic imagery is widely used of God's judgements. But it must be asked whether the analogy is the most apt to describe what is primarily the Sacrament of God's reconciling forgiveness, rather than a legal apparatus of vindicative justice. We have seen this latter image at work in the early Church's preoccupation with exclusion and readmittance of community sinners, and as a powerful motif, along with the medical image, in the penitential literature.[131] But it reached its most thoroughgoing literal application in the treatment of Trent, and particularly in the conciliar definition that the act of the confessor is a judicial one, on which Monden comments, 'Like many other points of faith, the idea of the *actus judicialis* has been *oversystematized* by a too conceptualist theology'.[132] The consequence has been that the mentality stimulating such over-systematization, and then in turn feeding on it, has impelled moral theology to view sin as above all a transgression of law, and has inculcated concepts of divine justice and retribution, and of God himself, which have bitten deep into the spiritual lives of millions. Moreover, the casting of moral theology for centuries as the handmaid of canon law has only reinforced the predominantly legal approach to morality which has dominated the making of moral theology through its close connection with a primarily penal theology of the Sacrament of penance.

Such has been the theology, pursued in an excessively literal and univocal manner. It has frequently been accompanied by a confessional practice which is mercifully quite different; one exemplifying more, or in some measure, the equally traditional, but

---

[131] Supra, p. 4, 13.
[132] L. Monden, *Sin, Liberty and Law* (London, 1966), p. 45.

theoretically neglected, view of a medical or healing ministry which was systematically overshadowed by the defensive and juridical mentality at Trent, and which shows a more spontaneously human theology. It is as a reaction to this excessively legal tradition that one can best appreciate the relief and eagerness with which many Catholics have embraced various forms of non-directive and client-centred counselling; and as at least an antidote to the forensic extravagances of the past, this is no doubt a healthy and overdue development of the theology of reconciliation. The theologian would have to add, however, that this therapeutic approach also is in its turn only an analogy, or model, of God's relationship with man in his vulnerability. And if the Sacrament of reconciliation is not to be located forever in the Old Bailey, no more is it now to be found exclusively in Harley Street.

In April 1950, Pope Pius XII, who found it congenial to give various professions patron saints, solemnly declared Saint Alphonsus Liguori to be Patron of Confessors *and* of Moral Theologians.[133] The occasion was the two-hundredth anniversary of the first edition of Alphonsus' first major work. In commemorating his career and writings, for which Pope Pius IX had made him in 1871 a Doctor of the Church, Pius XII recalled the testimonies of several other Popes to the quality of his teaching; and he observed that Liguori's moral and pastoral teaching was still thoroughly approved in the whole Catholic world, being frequently and earnestly commended as a safe norm for ministers of the Sacrament of Penance. Perhaps nothing expresses more succinctly than this heavenly patronage and this papal tribute the central influence of confession in the long making of moral theology.

[133] *AAS* 42 (1950), pp. 595–7.

2

THE LEGACY OF AUGUSTINE

The Development of Christian Thought

The earliest Christian writings which we possess after the New
Testament show us the Christian community assimilating the
teaching of Jesus on the great commandment of love, on the Ten
Commandments, and in the Sermon on the Mount, against a
background of the historical continuity of God's action from
creation through Judaism and the Jewish Law to his ever present
Lordship over the world and all human activity. In its early stages
Christian moral teaching was comparatively unreflective and
unsystematic, happy to adopt, and adapt, from popular rules and
codes of conduct whatever seemed congenial to its purpose. The
entry into the Church, however, of educated pagans, and the
growing hostility of outsiders, contributed to developments in
Christian moral thinking and writing arising partly from the
internal dynamism of its message and partly from the need to
commend it and defend it in contemporary society. In this
enterprise the second-century writers whom we know as the
Apologists were not slow, while rebutting popular accusations of
criminal practices and secret vices, to attack the public moral
standards of pagan society and of its gods, while at the same time
seeking common intellectual ground with what they considered
best in pagan thought itself, including pagan ethical thought.[1] In
this continuing dialogue the two main ethical currents of thought
which interacted with developing Christian thought can be identified
generally as Neoplatonism and Stoicism, the former centring on
human aspirations to control passion and to be released from all
material restraints in order to enjoy an intellectual life of
contemplation of the Good, and the latter, at a literally more
mundane level, concentrating on a self-disciplined identification

---

[1] Cf. F. C. Copleston, *A History of Philosophy*, vol. ii (London, 1950), pp. 13–
20; F. L. Cross, *The Early Christian Fathers* (London, 1960), pp. 42–58.

with the *Logos,* or Reason, as the cosmic, almost pantheistic, principle of intelligibility at work in the world.[2]

Alongside such speculative and intellectual developments, of course, and influenced by them, Christian writers and leaders continued to expound and comment on God's Word as it applied to the situations of daily family and social life, not only now in contrast or concord with non-Christian behaviour and thought, but also in often bitter controversy, whether within the Christian community itself or on the fringes of that community. And here the other major ethical current with which the mainstream of a developing theology of Christian moral behaviour had to contend was less a tributary to its thought, as were Neoplatonism and Stoicism in some regards, than a powerful undertow, or cross-current. It can be generally described as a doctrine of ultimate dualism between eternal conflicting powers of light and darkness, good and evil, spirit and matter, which was to be found specifically in its most influential forms in Gnosticism and Manichaeism, combining a strong element of spiritual élitism with a contempt for the bodily which could express itself paradoxically either in the most rigorous and disdainful asceticism or in the most thorough-going self-indulgence.[3]

The Influence of Augustine

It is against this intellectual and social background that we may consider the troubled person of Saint Augustine of Hippo, in

---

[2] Cf. F. C. Copleston, *A History of Philosophy,* vol. i (London, 1947), for the general doctrines. For their influence on Christian thinkers, cf. Cross, *supra,* n. 1; M. Spanneut, *Le Stoïcisme des pères de l'Église* (Paris, 1957); H. Chadwick, *The Sentences of Sextus: A Contribution to the History of Early Christian Ethics* (London, 1959). Not all the Christian Apologists were of such an accommodating temper, however, and the contemptuous polemic of Tertullian ('Quid ergo Athenis et Hierosolymis?') flung down a challenge not only to his heretical adversaries but to all subsequent Christian thinkers. In warning the Colossians against being ensnared by 'philosophy and empty deceit, according to human tradition' (Col. 2: 8), Paul had been drawing upon his own experience of Athens and its corrupting and competing claims to human 'wisdom' (cf. Acts 17: 16–21, 32–3). Jerusalem, the Church, and Christians have nothing in common with Athens, the Academy, and heretics. 'Viderint, qui stoicum et platonicum et dialecticum Christianismum protulerunt. Nobis curiositate opus non est, post Christum Jesum; nec inquisitione, post Evangelium', *Liber de praescriptionibus adversus haereticos,* cap. 7; *PL* 2, 20.

[3] Cf. Peter Brown, *Augustine of Hippo* (London, 1967), pp. 46–60; and G. Bonner, *St Augustine of Hippo* (London, 1963), pp. 157–236, for a fuller treatment.

whom, it has been claimed, 'Western moral thought reached maturity'.[4] Certainly, if one proceeds from the origins of Christian moral thinking to the late fourth and early fifth centuries, when Augustine flourished, one is well justified in judging that in him Christian moral theorizing had come of age. If today one looks back down the arches of some fifteen further centuries of Christian thought and life, on which it is almost impossible to calculate his influence, one would be forgiven for concluding that he has seemed not of an age but for all time.

Born into the lively African Christian Church in what is now Algeria, in 354, of a mixed Christian–pagan marriage, he received his schooling locally and in the nearby city of Carthage, where he became a teacher of rhetoric. His early Christian education seems to have been non-existent, and for nine years or more the growing Augustine found Manichaeism more intellectually satisfying than what he considered the puerilities of the Bible and the conservative Christianity of the local Donatist sect. In pursuit of his career he moved to Rome and then, at the age of thirty, as professor of rhetoric to Milan, which was then the centre of the Western Roman Empire, and where he fell under the spell of Ambrose, the local bishop, as well as of the Neoplatonist writings of Plotinus in Latin. It was here that occurred the famous garden scene of his exhausted moral conversion to Christianity and chastity,[5] followed by his baptism by Ambrose and return to Africa with his illegitimate son and friends to form a Christian commune near his home town. Local pressure, however, led him to be ordained priest and, in 395, bishop in Hippo, where he spent the rest of his life, presiding, arbitrating, conferring, debating, preaching, writing, and above all, attacking the Christian deviations of Donatism, Manichaeism, Arianism and, especially, Pelagianism. He had been bishop for fifteen years when the immortal city of Rome fell to Alaric and his Goths, and for the next twenty years he was to witness the further disintegration of the great Western Roman Empire. As the old man

---

[4] F. X. Murphy, in *NCE* ix, 1118. On Augustine, the standard work in English must be Brown, op. cit. Indispensable for his thought are E. Portalié, *A Guide to the thought of St Augustine* (London, 1960) which is a translation of Portalié's magisterial article in the *DTC*, and E. Gilson, *The Christian Philosophy of St. Augustine* (London, 1961). Cf. also, H. de Lubac, *Augustinisme et théologie moderne* (Aubier, 1965).

[5] Vividly described as God having 'broken the chains that bound me' (Ps. 116: 16) in his *Confessions*, Book 8, culminating in chapter 12.

of seventy-six lay dying in 430, on the eve of the Council of Ephesus, the Vandals were at the very gates of Hippo.

This was the man who, in the words of Newman, 'formed the intellect of Europe'.[6] In his own day he was an intellectual giant, as even the testy Scripture scholar, Jerome, acknowledged in a letter from Jerusalem. 'Well done! You are renowned throughout the world. Catholics venerate you, and look upon you as a second founder of the old faith. And, surely what is a sign of greater glory, all the heretics detest you.'[7] After the disappearance of Western Roman culture into what are popularly known as the Dark Ages, and with the slow re-emergence of some measure of civil order and social stability, it was the writings of Augustine above all, next only to the Scriptures themselves, which helped to bridge the gulf with the Christian and classical past, and to animate the new missionary work of the Church in the European continent. As Portalié writes, echoing the judgment of Harnack and Eucken, 'Augustine collects and condenses in his writings the intellectual treasures of the old world and transmits them to the new.'[8]

In the catechizing of Frankish converts Augustine's little work, *de catechizandis rudibus*, was used as a basic instrument, and found in Europe fields similar to those in North Africa where he had written it 'to immunise catechumens against the seduction of paganism'.[9] In the eleventh century, Anselm of Canterbury, 'like all Western theologians, . . . steeped himself in the writings of Augustine especially',[10] while in the twelfth century, as the Scholastic Age was getting into its stride, Augustine was a notable authority for William of Champeaux and his School of Saint Victor on the left bank of the Seine, as also for its greatest teacher, Hugh of Saint Victor.[11] And his place was now assured for centuries to come by his inclusion as 'the principal witness of theological tradition' in the most enduring theological textbook of the Middle Ages, *The Book of the Sentences* of Peter Lombard. 'Basically conservative, it was a

---

[6] On the role of individuals as initiators in 'the Church of Rome': 'The great luminary of the western world is, as we know, St. Augustine; he, no infallible teacher, has formed the intellect of Europe', *Apologia*, (Fontana, London, 1959), p. 296.

[7] *Epist. 195, inter augustinianas*; PL 33, 891.

[8] Op. cit., p. 84.

[9] Angelini and Valsecchi, p. 77.

[10] Jedin and Dolan, vol. iii, p. 470.

[11] Jedin and Dolan, vol. iv, pp. 45–6.

systematic and clearly and precisely organized summary of all the chief truths of the Christian faith that had been hitherto discussed by theologians. To every question it brought the relevant patristic citations and reliable solutions'.[12] And it remained a universal textbook for theological students until the sixteenth century, when it was replaced by the *Summa* of Theology of Thomas Aquinas, who knew his Lombard thoroughly, having himself, as a junior lecturer at Paris, like many another cut his pedagogical teeth by producing his own *Commentary on the Sentences*.

Aquinas himself, of course, in the thirteenth century, notwithstanding his enthusiastic adoption of Aristotle (whose major works only then became available to medieval scholars in reliable translations), was profoundly influenced by the works and thought of Augustine, whom he cites probably more frequently than any other patristic authority. The influence of Augustine was 'ever present' in the English Church of the fourteenth century, as it continued to be in Paris and in other European universities.[13] And if it could be said of John Henry Newman that he was a hidden *peritus*, after his death, at the Second Vatican Council, the same could be said with even more force of the influence of Augustine at the Council of Trent, all the more so since, in addition to the presence of a strong Augustinian party at Trent, much of the labour of that Council was devoted to examining and attempting to clarify the hallowed teachings of Augustine himself which Luther, the Augustinian monk, had turned against the Roman Church.

Long after Trent the central influence of Augustine was to continue, unwearied although not entirely unquestioned, through the stormy seventeenth and eighteenth centuries of the incredible controversies on grace and the bitterly contested claims of his patronage for French Jansenism. Such was his abiding authority that in 1930 Pope Pius XI addressed the encyclical letter *Ad Salutem* to the whole Catholic Church to commemorate the 1500th anniversary of the death of Augustine. The Pope recalled that the praise for Augustine in the Church, from Popes and others, had been unceasing during and since his lifetime; that the Church's Councils had used Augustine's very words to define Catholic truth; and that the Bishop of Hippo had illuminated not only Christian Africa but the entire Church. This he had achieved not only by his

---

[12] Ibid., p. 89.   [13] Pantin, op. cit., p. 131.

foreful opposition to Donatist attempts to restrict the true Church of Christ to a corner of Africa in his use of the ringing principle 'the judgement of the whole world is reliable' (*securus iudicat orbis terrarum*), which had had such momentous effect in bringing Newman into the Catholic Church;[14] but also in his teaching on God as man's destiny, on the church and the Sacraments and the See of Rome, on the nature of God, the Trinity and Christology. Given the title Doctor of Grace by the Middle Ages, Augustine had forbidden all subsequent theologians to teach, on the one hand, the Reformation and Jansenist view that free will in man is an empty phrase since his lapse from original integrity, and on the other hand the inventions of the Pelagians that God's grace is not freely bestowed on man and does not make all things possible.[15] Although the Pope did not mention it, it is of interest to note also that among other medieval monuments to the prestige of Augustine must be counted 'an incredible number' of apocryphal works attributed to him, and that the political thought of Augustine has also exercised a continual attraction on Western minds.[16]

Augustine's Moral Teaching

Apart from a few monographs on practical ethical subjects, Augustine composed no specific, far less systematic, works on morality, and his moral teaching, often occasional, parenthetical or digressionary, is to be found scattered throughout his enormous literary output of more than 100 books varying from short to very long indeed, over 200 letters and more than 500 sermons. All of this Armas describes as dealing with all, or almost all, the subjects of moral theology, both fundamental and special and constituting

---

[14] *Contra epist. Parmeniani*, 3, 24; *PL* 43, 101. Newman compared 'those great words' of the man who 'was one of the prime oracles of Antiquity' and their effect on him with the 'Tolle, lege' of the child 'which converted Augustine himself', *Apologia*, ch. 3, pp. 184–5.

[15] *AAS* 22 (1930), 201–34. 'Vestigavitque adeo subtiliter feliciterque, ut, Doctor Gratiae nuncupatus deinceps atque habitus, ceteros catholicos posteriorum aetatum scriptores ... prohibuerit, quominus ... docerent aut in homine de pristina integritate deiecto liberum arbitrium esse nomen sine re, ut prioribus novatoribus et iansenistis placuit, aut divinam gratiam nec gratuito nec omnia posse, quemadmodum Pelagiani fabulabantur', ibid., p. 223.

[16] On the Augustinian apocrypha, cf. B. Blumenkranz, 'La survie médiévale de S. Augustin à travers ses apocryphes', *Augustinus Magister; Études augustiniennes* (Paris, 1954), ii, pp. 1003–18. On his political thought, cf. R. A. Markus, *Saeculum: History and Society in the Theology of St. Augustine* (Cambridge, 1970).

'an immense arsenal' for theologians of all subsequent centuries.[17]
In many problem areas the views of Augustine remain highly
influential, whether on the absolute wrongness of suicide, or lying,
or abortion.[18] His teaching on sexual morality has dominated
Catholic thought, as we shall see.[19] And Augustine can reasonably
be regarded as the founder of the Christian doctrine of the just
war.[20] On a more general level one can note his importance, along
with Ambrose and through Gregory and Aquinas, in viewing the
whole moral enterprise in the categories of the four cardinal virtues
united in charity;[21] his influence in establishing the classical
distinction between mortal and venial sins;[22] his laying the founda-
ions of the theology of eternal law;[23] and, of course, his insistence
on the supreme importance of love of God in the Christian life, with
its systematic expression in the famous distinction between
'enjoyment' and 'use'. God alone may be enjoyed (*frui*): creatures
may not constitute the final resting place of our hearts and wills,
but may only be used (*uti*), as instruments and not as ends in
themselves.[24]

'It is for yourself that you have made us, and our heart is restless,
until it repose in you.'[25] For Augustine this most famous and
typical of his aphorisms is not simply a statement of the facts of the
case; it is also the basis of a universal moral injunction. For yourself
(*ad te*), in you (*in te*); Augustine is *par excellence* the theologian of
the preposition. This may be seen most brilliantly in his *de
Trinitate*, in his analysis of the immanent relationships between
Father, Son, and Spirit; but in the *ad* and the *in* of his cry in the
Confessions, it may not be too much to say, we can find summed up
the whole moral thinking of Saint Augustine—the overall orientation,

---

[17] G. Armas (ed.), *La Moral de San Agustin* (Madrid, 1954), p. 39.

[18] On suicide, cf *de civ. dei*, I, 25–27; *PL* 41, 38–40; and *Epist.* 204, 5; *PL* 33,
940–1; on lying, cf. *de mendacio*, 6, 9; *PL* 40, 495; on abortion, *Sermo* 10, 7; *PL*
38, 95.

[19] Cf. *infra*, pp. 60–8.

[20] *Contra Faustum manich.*, 22, 74–5; *PL* 42, 447–8.

[21] Cf. *de mor. Eccl. Cath.*, 1, 15, 25; *PL* 32, 1332.

[22] Cf. *de spir. et lit.*, 28; *PL* 44, 230; *Epist.* 104, 4, 14; *PL* 33, 394.

[23] Cf. *Contra Faustum*, 22, 27; *PL* 42, 418.

[24] 'Frui est enim amore inhaerere alicui rei propter se ipsam, ... sic in huius
mortalitatis vita peregrinantes a Domino, si redire in patriam volumus ubi beati esse
possimus, utendum est hoc mundo, non fruendum', *De Doctrina Christiana*, 1, 4;
PL 34, 20–1.

[25] 'Fecisti nos ad te; et inquietum est cor nostrum, donec requiescat in te', *Conf.*,
1, 1; *PL* 32, 661.

and yet the incompleteness and tension, of man until he find fulfilment, resolution, and rest in God, his supreme Good. Burnaby has suggested that among the three texts of Scripture which sum up Augustine's Christian Platonism is the verse of the Psalm, *mihi autem adhaerere Deo bonum est*: but for me it is good to be near God.[26] The translation is, of course, too weak for Augustine, who saw in the psalmist's words a felicitous correction to the Platonists: for me the supreme Good is cleaving to God. And it can also be suggested that the summation of Augustine's theology of human striving and beatitude, corresponding to the hope and the repose of his statement in the *Confessions*, is to be found above all in the words of his other great love, Paul, that meantime in this life while we are in the body we are distant from the Lord, on a pilgrimage of faith which will culminate in vision: *dum sumus in corpore, peregrinamur a Domino: per fidem enim ambulamus, et non per speciem.*[27] These Augustinian tensions between pilgrimage and homecoming, between using and enjoying, are well expressed together in his statement, 'To enjoy is to cleave to something for its own sake, in love . . . . And thus while we are on pilgrimage from the Lord, in the life of this mortality, if we wish to return home where we can be happy, we must use this world, not enjoy it'.[28]

The Dark Strain in Augustine

It is a striking fact that most studies of, and tributes to, the work of Augustine contain reference to what might be called a dark side to his thought, and to what has been considered a note of pessimism in his character and in his writings. Thus, one writer delicately observes that 'not everything shines with the light of truth' in the theology of Augustine, although such dark spots as are to be found cannot dim the dazzling brightness of his whole work.[29] And Jean Guitton wonders 'to what degree Christianity still suffers from St. Augustine's pessimism,' but concludes that 'when all is said and

---

[26] J. Burnaby, *Amor Dei: A Study of the Religion of St. Augustine* (London, 1960), p. 41, the others, besides this (Ps. 72: 20) being Ps. 15: 2, and Wisd. 7: 27.

[27] 2 Cor. 5: 6–8. Brown, pp. 323–4, brings out well the parallel political and social implications of being a 'resident alien' in ancient Rome.

[28] *Supra*, n. 24.

[29] F. Moriones (ed.), *Enchiridion theologicum Sancti Augustini* (Madrid, 1961), p. xvii.

done it must be admitted that we owe to him far more light than shade'.[30]

Such a conclusion, however, needs qualification. If one considers the whole sweep of Augustine's theological and philosophical output, no one can reasonably doubt both the profundity and the brilliance of his magisterial thought. But if one is concentrating precisely on his moral teaching, it is there that the darkness and the sombre pessimism are most in evidence and, it must be said, at their most dogmatic and devastating. For the Augustinian pessimism to which so many allude is a *moral* pessimism; and what Burnaby refers to as 'Augustine's ethical dualism'[31] must be acknowledged as a major part, if not the preponderant part, of the legacy which was inherited from Augustine by moral theology as the subject developed.

Not by any means that the entire responsibility for this is to be laid at the door of Augustine. As the Aristotelian Aquinas was to stress, whatever is received, is received according to the capacity of the recipient. And the fatal susceptibility of developing moral theology to the pessimistic broodings of Augustine must be attributed, among other factors, to, on the one hand, the growing isolation of Christian moral thinking from other branches of theology, notably from dogmatic and from spiritual theology, and, on the other, to its own preoccupation with confession and sin and its increasing subservience to law in the Church. It is in such factors that we can see a tendency in moral theology to appropriate to itself above all Augustine the anti-Pelagian in order to confirm and reinforce, and to help to explain, the human propensity to death and disaster which seemed so strikingly evident in the chaos of the Dark Ages and subsequent centuries. And unhappily what moral theology was to retain as the major and most influential element of St Augustine's theology of the Christian life was his almost lifelong preoccupation with human sin and frailty. Paul Guilley has observed that the problem of sin and evil 'continually obsessed him', and David Knowles writes in his introduction to *The City of*

---

[30] J. Guitton, *The Modernity of St. Augustine* (London, 1959), pp. 79, 81. P. Guilley, *La Culpabilité fondamentale* (Gembloux, 1975), refers to 'the pessimistic aspect of Augustinian anthropology', and explains its attraction for a West slowly emerging from a new barbarism (pp. 63–4). M. Flick and Z. Alszeghy, *Il Vangelo della grazia* (Florence, 1964), show how the Scholastics felt it necessary to explain away the harshness of some of Augustine's statements (pp. 105–6).

[31] Op. cit., p. 58.

God of 'the problem that was never far from his mind throughout a long life, the problem of sin and evil both in himself and in the whole world of spiritual being'.[32] It is saddening to note how the works of this great and loving man, with their passages of sublime beauty and of moving eloquence, are often flawed by this note of melancholy, of disgust, and even of brutality, towards man in his sinfulness and weakness resulting from his initial fall from God's grace.

For Augustine that original sin of Adam disrupted for all human time the divine order of things, and can be summed up in the cry of Othello the Moor, 'And when I love thee not, chaos is come again'. It began with self-love and pride distorting the order of being between man and God, and resulted immediately in a radical distortion of the order within man himself. *Tu Deo, tibi caro*: you subject to God, and the flesh subject to you, is and should be the natural order of existence; and man's gesture of contempt for God is inevitably echoed in his own being, and reverberates through human history in the ugly discord and disharmony of his own unruly feelings. A just punishment in Adam, is Augustine's verdict, and its repercussions are justly shared by all of Adam's seed, who now experience all too vividly the stirrings of another law in their members.[33] The melancholy consequence of that original sin is that human nature is vitiated, and lust and ignorance are its lot, to such an extent that it lacks even the ability to appreciate the full seriousness of that first wicked act of disobedience which resulted in the whole human race, which had its roots poisoned in Adam, being a 'condemned throng', a *massa damnata*.[34]

---

[32] Guilley, op. cit.; Knowles in Augustine's *The City of God*, trans. H. Bettenson (London, 1972), p. xii.

[33] 'Hoc enim expedit, inferius subjici superiori: ut et ille qui sibi subjici vult quod est inferius se, subjiciatur superiori se. Agnosce ordinem, quaere pacem. Tu Deo, tibi caro. Quid iustius? quid pulchrius? Tu maiori, minor tibi: servi tu ei qui fecit te, ut tibi serviat quod factum est propter te . . . . Si autem contemnis Tu Deo, numquam efficies ut Tibi caro', *Enarrat. in Psalm.* 143, 6; *PL* 37, 1860. 'Haec igitur carnis inobedientia, quae in ipso motu est, etiamsi habere non permittatur effectum, non erat in illis primis hominibus, quando nudi erant, et non confundebantur. Nondum quippe anima rationalis domina carnis inobediens exstiterat Domino suo, ut poena reciproca inobedientem experiretur carnem famulam suam cum sensu quodam confusionis et molestiae suae', *De pecc. mer. et rem.*, 2, 22, 36; *PL* 44, 173.

[34] 'Sed poena aeterna ideo dura et iniusta sensibus videtur humanis, quia in hac infirmitate moribundorum sensuum deest ille sensus altissimae purissimaeque sapientiae, quo sentiri possit quantum nefas in illa prima praevaricatione commissum sit . . . . Hinc est universa generis humani massa damnata', *De civ. Dei*, 21, 12; *PL*

Augustine's vehemence in urging and hammering home what he considered the Pauline and Catholic doctrine of original sin and its consequences ('I didn't *invent* original sin!' he was to protest towards the end of his life[35]) is often explained by two factors in particular—the heat of controversy and his own vivid personal experience. He would have claimed to experience the Pauline 'law of sin which dwells in my members' (Rom. 7: 23) all through his life. As Gilson well expresses it,

the point which dominates the whole history of the controversy is that Pelagianism was a radical negation of Augustine's personal experience . . . . For many long years he had known the law without being able to carry it out . . . he saw it carried out by others, and although he longed with his whole soul to imitate them, he had to admit that he was unable to do so . . . [but] Thanks to Christ's sacrifice, from now on there is a supernatural, divine assistance through which the law becomes something realizable for the human will, and failure to recognize the necessity of this assistance is the very essence of Pelagianism.[36]

The other factor which is frequently advanced in justification, or at least explanation, of Augustine's dark strain is the heat of battle or controversy, particularly in an area in which he had become the acclaimed authority and in which his long, almost obsessive, reflections on the subject had brought him to make some theological sense of his own inner experience. Peter Brown observes of Augustine's role in the anti-Pelagian controversy, 'Not every man lives to see the fundamentals of his life's work challenged in his old age'.[37] In all polemics, however, whether verbal or otherwise, frequently the first casualty is truth. And when the fires of altercation and retaliation have died or faded into history, the dead ashes which remain are cold and often chilling to the touch. What is more, after many a battle or famous victory the field is strewn with

41, 726–7. 'Sed humani generis massam volens ostendere Apostolus de origine venenatam . . . . Quia secundum propaginem carnis in illo eramus omnes, antequam nati essemus, tanquam in parente, tamquam in radice ibi eramus: sic venenata est arbor, ubi eramus', *Serm.* 294, 14, 15; *PL* 38, 1344. 'Iacebat in malis, vel etiam volvebatur, et de malis in mala praecipitabatur totius humani generis massa damnata', *Enchiridion*, 26; *PL* 40, 245.

[35] 'Non ego finxi originale peccatum, quod catholica fides credit antiquitus', *De nupt. et conc.*, 2, 12, 25; *PL* 44, 450.

[36] Op. cit., p. 159.

[37] Op. cit., p. 353.

shrapnel and pieces are picked up to be taken home and polished and become part of life's more ordinary furnishings. Of the two major areas of moral theology in which the legacy of Augustine is most dominant and significant, his teaching on sexual morality will be fully considered later in this chapter. The other, relating to man's freedom and God's grace, can perhaps be best examined for our purposes by considering one piece of shrapnel collected by the Church from Augustine's anti-Pelagian campaign to become a theological maxim enshrined in the Church's moral tradition. It is his statement of the principle that God does not command of man things which are impossible to do.

'Deus impossibilia non iubet'

It may seem contradictory, or at least inconsistent, of Augustine to have maintained that God does not ask the impossible of us in our moral behaviour, in view of his own youthful dissipation and his deeply pessimistic view of universal human experience since the fall of Adam. The main answer is to be found in his theology of God's grace given through Christ to sinners, which in those thus reborn and regenerated makes all things possible in him who strengthens them (cf. Phil. 4:13). Thus it was that Augustine, in his *Confessions* chronicling his early life and conversion, could address God with the words, 'Grant what you command, and command what you wish'.[38] It was to this that Pelagius took exception.[39] The strict Breton, or British, ascetic and reformer who was becoming increasingly influential in Roman Church society aimed to counter mediocre Christianity and to establish a uniform and demanding law of Christian conduct for all before an impartial God. And he would have no divine mollycoddling. Man was not so fallen that he could not brace himself to obey God's commands; the more one stressed his natural handicaps the more one was pandering to him

---

[38] 'Et tota spes mea non nisi in magna misericordia tua. Da quod iubes et iube quod vis . . . . Continentiam iubes: da quod iubes et iube quod vis', *Conf.* 10, 29; *PL* 32, 796. The prayer occurs as a refrain throughout Book 10 of the Confessions, which is devoted to a sustained consideration of temptations to sin. Cf. chapters 31 and 37 (*PL* 32, 798, 804).

[39] As Augustine himself relates in *De dono pers.*, 20, 53 (*PL* 45, 1026), 'Quae mea verba Pelagius Romae, cum a quodam fratre et coepiscopo meo fuissent eo praesente commemorata, ferre non potuit, et contradicens aliquanto commotius, paene cum eo qui illa commemoravit litigavit.'

and in danger of indulging him by relaxing or mitigating what God required of him. And the more one stressed God's initiative and continuing help in grace the more one undermined man's own responsibility for his own actions.[40] Surely a good and just God made man such that his own will-power was sufficient to keep him away from sin?

Not so, replied Augustine, in his work significantly entitled *Nature and Grace*, and developing, as he loved to, the parable of the Good Samaritan (cf. Luke 10: 30–7). Everyone knows that man was created healthy, without fault, and with the power to live rightly. But we are now dealing with a man whom robbers have left on the road only half alive and who has been so grievously beaten up that he cannot get back uphill, to justice. He is still in the inn, recuperating. God, then, does not command things that are impossible. By his command he intimates that you should do what you can, and ask for what you cannot, through the healing medicine of grace.[41]

The Pelagian line of argument was to deny the need for such grace by denying the transmission of Adam's sin to all his descendents and by asserting every man's innate freedom. To meet his threat more than two hundred African bishops assembled in Carthage in 418, in a local Council of which Augustine was 'the soul', and produced a systematic condemnation of the Pelagian doctrines which stressed the centrality of grace not only in enabling us to understand the commandments of God (which Pelagius was disposed to accept) but also in enabling us to love and have the

---

[40] On the Pelagian controversy, cf. Brown, op. cit., pp. 340–407; J. Ferguson, *Pelagius: A Historical and Theological Study* (Cambridge, 1956). Pelagius's fierce reaction to Augustine's prayer of trusting surrender to God arose from his considering it 'as destructive of all moral effort. To Pelagius the vast majority of professing Christians were taking one of two views. Some argued the inevitability of sin, some that only the grace of God could overcome it. Either led to moral sloth', ibid., p. 159.

[41] 'Verum est autem quod ait: "Quod Deus tam bonus quam iustus talem hominem fecerit, qui peccati malo carere sufficeret, sed si voluisset." Quis enim eum nescit sanum et inculpabilem factum, et libero arbitrio atque ad iuste vivendum potestate libera constitutum? Sed nunc de illo agitur, quem semivivum latrones in via reliquerunt, qui gravibus saucius confossusque vulneribus non ita potest ad iustitiae culmen ascendere, sicut potuit inde descendere: qui etiam in stabulo est, adhuc curatur (Lc. 10: 30, 34). Non igitur Deus impossibilia iubet: sed iubendo admonet, et facere quod possis, et petere quod non possis', *De nat. et gratia*, 43, 50; *PL* 44, 271. Cf. *Contra Iul. op. imp.*, 6, 15; *PL* 45, 1534, 'Ideo in hoc agone magis nos Deus voluit orationibus certare, quam viribus.'

power to fulfil them, 'since each is God's gift, to know what we ought to do and to love in order to do it'.[42] The year following Augustine's death saw the General Council of Ephesus condemning Pelagianism in the teaching of his disciple Caelestius.[43] And the Council of Carthage was to be quoted on the subject in the influential *Indiculus* which drew further authority from being wrongly ascribed to Pope Celestine I on account of his warm support for Augustine's memory.[44]

Despite Augustine's sustained and orchestrated opposition, however, Pelagianism became a strong and powerful movement throughout the Church, either in its full-blown version or in what was seen as the insidious and theologically subversive version which maintained that at least in man's initial act of faith in God he did not totally require the help of grace, the view which was later to be described as semi-Pelagianism.[45] Augustine's uncompromising

---

[42] 'Item, quisquis dixerit, eandem gratiam Dei per Iesum Christum Dominum nostrum propter hoc tantum nos adiuvare ad non peccandum, quia per ipsam nobis revelatur et aperitur intelligentia mandatorum, ut sciamus, quid appetere, quid vitare debeamus, non autem per illam nobis praestari, ut quod faciendum cognoverimus, etiam facere diligamus atque valeamus, anathema sit ... cum sit utrumque donum Dei, et scire, quid facere debeamus, et diligere, ut faciamus, ...', *DS* 226. On Augustine's role in the Council, cf. Portalié, op. cit., pp. 31, 190. On the various marches and countermarches of the campaign, cf. Brown, pp. 357–63. It was at this early stage in the controversy that Augustine, in a Sunday sermon, justified his unwearying (for him) preoccupation with those 'men ungrateful for grace who attribute so much to helpless and wounded nature', and adapted Gal. 2: 21 to assert that 'if justification were through *nature*, then Christ died to no purpose'. In exhorting his congregation to expose Pelagian sympathizers, he ended by explaining that through papal intervention the case was now closed. If only this applied also to the error! (*Sermo* 131, chaps. 6, 9, 10; *PL* 38, 732, 734). 'Iam enim de hac causa duo concilia missa sunt ad Sedem Apostolicam: inde etiam rescripta venerunt. Causa finita est: utinam aliquando finiatur error!'
[43] *DS* 267–8. On Caelestius and his dominance in the Pelagian cause, particularly as concerned the controversy over the effects of infant baptism, cf. Ferguson, op. cit., pp. 48–52, 178–9. On his friendship with Nestorius, cf. ibid., p. 115.
[44] *DS* 245; cf. 248. On the *Indiculus*, cf. Portalié, pp. 317–18; on its probable authorship by Prosper of Aquitaine, cf. *DS* 238, proem.; Flick and Alszeghy, op. cit., p. 208. On the esteem which Pope Celestine had for Augustine, cf. *DS* 237.
[45] Cf. Portalié, p. 214. 'Et ipsum igitur initium fidei nostrae, ex quo, nisi ex ipso est? Neque enim hoc excepto ex ipso sunt caetera: sed *ex ipso, et per ipsum, et in ipso sunt omnia*. Quis autem dicat eum qui iam coepit credere, ab illo in quem credidit nihil mereri? Unde fit ut iam merenti caetera dicantur addi retributione divina; ac per hoc gratiam Dei secundum merita nostra dari: quod obiectum sibi Pelagius, ne damnaretur, ipse damnavit', *De praedest. sanct.*, 2, 4; *PL* 44, 962. The term 'semi-Pelagian' was first used by the Reformers in the sixteenth century to characterize Scholastic theologians, becoming frequent in the seventeenth-century controversies on grace. It was first used in official Church teaching in the five

writings on the need for grace dismayed many, including monks in Africa and later in Gaul, on whom the ascetic Cassian was such a potent influence, since all value seemed thereby to be denied to human effort and therefore to their life of monastic striving for perfection. Augustine's attempts to mollify the monks aroused vehement reaction in the monasteries around Marseilles, and the disputes continued to wax after Augustine's death, his views being criticized by Cassian and maintained by the friend who may have been the real author of the *Indiculus*, Prosper of Aquitaine. It was at the instigation of the latter that Pope Celestine, who sent Germanus, bishop of Auxerre, to silence the Pelagians in Britain at St Albans, also wrote to the bishops of Gaul in praise of the memory of Augustine.[46] Eventually, Caesarius, bishop of Arles, in Provence, with the approval of a later Pope, Felix IV, drew up a document of 'moderate Augustinism' which included the affirmation that it is possible for the just to observe God's commands. The document was accepted by a meeting of bishops at Orange in 529, known today as the Second Council of Orange, and the mind of Augustine is to be seen in its profession of faith

that after receiving grace through baptism, all the baptized, with the help and co-operation of Christ, are able and obliged to fulfil what pertains to the soul's salvation, if they are willing to work at it faithfully . . . . [I]n every good work we do not begin it and are then helped by God's mercy, but he first inspires us with faith and love of him, . . . so that we can with his help fulfil those things which are pleasing to him.[47]

The statement of Orange was subsequently approved by Pope Boniface II, and then passed into obscurity for ten centuries until it was finally published only in 1538.[48] The emergence of the

propositions of Jansen (*DS* 2004–5), and later invoked against the Synod of Pistoia (*DS* 2618, 2620). Subsequently the term has become a convenient one to apply to those previously termed Massilians, in southern Gaul, whose opinions were condemned in 529 at Orange. Cf. Flick and Alszeghy, op. cit., pp. 202–3.

[46] Flick and Alszeghy, pp. 203–5. Cf. *supra*, n. 44.

[47] 'post acceptam per baptismum gratiam omnes baptizati, Christo auxiliante et cooperante, quae ad salutem animae pertinent, possint et debeant, si fideliter laborare voluerint, adimplere . . . in omni opere bono non nos incipimus, et postea per Dei misericordiam adiuvamur, sed ipse nobis nullis praecedentibus bonis meritis et fidem et amorem sui prius inspirat, ut . . . cum ipsius adiutorio ea, quae sibi sunt placita, implere possimus', *DS* 397. Cf. 370, *proem.*; Flick and Alszeghy, p. 205.

[48] Flick and Alszeghy, pp. 205, 208–9.

Augustinian teaching of the sixth century into the light of the sixteenth century was quickly seized upon by Catholic theologians, and opportune use made of it against Luther by the Council of Trent in its famous decree on Justification, in a section on 'the possibility of observance of the commandments'. 'No one, however justified, should use that rash formula forbidden by the anathema of the Fathers, that the precepts of God are impossible to observe by a man who has been justified.' For, continued Trent, reverting to the original Augustinian source, 'God does not command things which are impossible, but by his command he intimates that you should do what you can, and ask for what you cannot'. To which it adds, for good measure, 'and he helps you so that you can'.[49]

Having thus entered into the mainstream of the Catholic Church's official teaching, Augustine's axiom that God does not command things which are impossible was put to good use more than once in the years which followed Trent. Thirty years after the Council, the Belgian professor of Louvain University, Michel de Bay, had gone back beyond its teaching and the Scholastic age to study Scripture in the light of Augustine's anti-Pelagian writings, and had fallen foul of the Sorbonne in Paris as well as of other Universities. His extreme Augustinian views on man before and since the Fall were eventually examined and rejected by Rome, and in 1567 Pope Pius V condemned seventy-nine propositions taken from the works of Baius, as he is commonly called, including a statement that the view that God does not command the impossible is to be ascribed not to Augustine but to Pelagius![50]

With this defence of Augustine's and its own title deeds to the principle, the official Church was compelled to defend it again a century later in the first skirmishes of the Jansenist controversy. The bishop of Ypres, Cornelius Jansen, had given a lifetime to a

---

[49] 'Nemo autem, quantumvis iustificatus, liberum se esse ab observatione mandatorum putare debet; nemo temeraria illa et a Patribus sub anathemate prohibita voce uti, Dei praecepta homini iustificato ad observandum esse impossibilia. "Nam Deus impossibilia non iubet, sed iubendo monet, et facere quod possis, et petere quod non possis" [cf. *supra*, n. 41], et adiuvat ut possis', DS 1536. Cf. DS 1568.

[50] 'Definitiva haec sententia, Deum homini nihil impossible praecepisse, falso tribuitur Augustino, cum Pelagii sit', DS 1954. Cf. ibid., n. 1, which explains that Baius had misinterpreted Augustine's *De pecc. mer. et rem.*, 2, 6, 7 (*PL* 44, 155), 'dubitare non possum, nec Deum aliquid impossibile homini praecepisse nec Deo ad opitulandum et adiuvandum, quo fiat iubet, impossibile aliquid esse. Ac per hoc potest homo, si velit, esse sine peccato adiutus a Deo.'

detailed and meticulous study of the works of Augustine, as we shall have cause to consider in more detail in a later chapter, and the pessimistic strain of Augustine was given full rein in Jansen's work published posthumously with the ominous title *Augustinus*. Among the famous Five Propositions which were considered by Rome to sum up the errors of Jansen and his supporters, and which were condemned as such in 1653 by Pope Innocent X, is to be found the statement that 'Some commandments of God are impossible for just men who will and attempt to observe them according to the present strength which they possess; and moreover the grace which would make them possible is lacking to them'.[51]

The bitter theological, religious, and political controversy involved in the Church's long and complicated struggle against Jansenism could only have the effect of it entrenching in its teaching the original polemical statement of Augustine against Pelagianism, and of rendering any qualification or mitigation of its content an apparent accommodation to the view of man and of his access to natural and supernatural resources which was a central feature of Jansenism and which was so repeatedly rejected by the Church. The principle that God asks of no one what is impossible but that his grace is always available thus was confirmed as a central moral and pastoral principle in moral theology in general and in the Church's moral teaching. And eventually in that teaching the wheel came full circle, when what had begun with the Augustine of the *Confessions* as an appeal for the interior grace of chastity and then been expanded by him into a general anti-Pelagian attack, to be espoused in various Church Councils and in papal teaching, was finally applied in 1930 by Pope Pius XI, in his encyclical on marriage, as a theological and pastoral comment on his condemnation of the practice of contraception.

Great care should be taken that regrettable external circumstances do not become the occasion for a more regrettable error. No difficulties can arise which can reduce the obligation of God's commandments forbidding acts which are evil of their inner nature, and in every situation married couples, strengthened by the grace of God, can always be faithful to their duty, and in their marriage preserve chastity from this dreadful stain. For the truth of

---

[51] 'Aliqua Dei praecepta hominibus iustis volentibus et conantibus, secundum praesentes quas habent vires, sunt impossibilia; deest quoque illis gratia, qua possibilia fiant', *DS* 2001. On Jansenism and the Jansenist propositions, cf. *infra*, p. 91.

the Christian faith stands expressed in the teaching of the Council of Trent 'that no one, . . . [etc] . . . should consider the precepts of God impossible . . .'.[52]

The same teaching, the Pope continued, was again solemnly commanded by the Church and confirmed in condemning the Jansenist heresy, which had dared to blaspheme against God's goodness by saying that some commands of God are impossible.[53]

When in 1968 Pope Paul VI repeated unchanged in his encyclical *Humanae Vitae* the teaching of his predecessor on contraception, no explicit reference was made to the general principle of the possibility or otherwise of observing God's commands.[54] It may be possible, however, to discern the Augustinian axiom behind the subsequent teaching on contraception of Pope John Paul II, in his Apostolic Exhortation, *Familiaris Consortio*, issued in 1981, when he writes that the law of God mus• be considered by married couples 'as a command of Christ the Lord to overcome difficulties with constancy . . . . In God's plan, all husbands and wives are called to marriage in holiness, and this lofty vocation is fulfilled to the extent that the human person is able to respond to God's command with serene confidence in God's grace and in his or her own will.'[55]

The loyalty and tenacity with which the Church's moral tradition has preserved the memento of Augustine's anti-Pelagian campaign that God does not command what is impossible suggest three lines

---

[52] 'At cavendum omnino est ne funestae externarum rerum conditiones multo funestiori errori occasionem praebeant. Nullae enim exsurgere possunt difficultates quae mandatorum Dei, actus, ex interiore natura sua malos, vetantium, obligationi derogare queant; in omnibus vero rerum adiunctis semper possunt coniuges, gratia Dei roborati, suo munere fideliter fungi et castitatem a turpi hac macula illibatam in coniugio conservare; nam stat fidei christianae veritas, Synodi Tridentinae magisterio expressa: "Nemo temeraria . . . [*supra*, n. 49]" ', *AAS* 22 (1930), pp. 561–2.

[53] 'Eademque doctrina iterum sollemniterque praecepta est ab Ecclesia et confirmata in damnatione haeresis iansenianae, quae contra Dei bonitatem haec blasphemare erat ausa: "Aliqua . . . [*supra*, n. 51]" ', ibid., p. 562.

[54] 'Ecclesiae doctrina . . . sine dubio multis talis videbitur, ut nonnisi difficulter, immo etiam nullo modo servari possit . . . . Immo eadem servari nequit nisi opitulante Dei gratia, qua bona hominum voluntas fulcitur ac roboratur', *Humanae Vitae*, no. 20; *AAS* 60 (1968) p. 495. It appears hinted at, however, in the passage on marriage as a faithful and exclusive union. 'Quae coniugum fidelitas etsi interdum habeat difficultates, nemini tamen asseverare licet, eam non esse possibilem, cum contra quovis tempore nobilis sit meritisque uber', ibid., no. 9; *AAS*, ibid., p. 486.

[55] 'Huius vocationis praestantia ad effectum deducitur, quatenus persona humana praecepto Dei valet respondere, sereno animo gratiae divinae ac propriae voluntati confisa', *Familiaris Consortio*, no. 34; *AAS* 74 (1982), p. 125.

of reflection. The first is to ask whether the principle, as understood by Augustine, is unduly separatist, both in its consideration of man in himself and in its consideration of man within society. For Augustine, with his Neoplatonist background, man is viewed as 'a rational soul using a mortal earthly body',[56] and although as a Christian Augustine believed in the goodness of the body, and in its eventual resurrection, this seems at times to have been against his earlier Manichaean and later Neoplatonist instincts. For him, grace is almost exclusively isolated in the will of man, in its attempts to exercise a spiritual mastery over the whole self. 'You are to be subject to God, and the flesh to you.'[57] And one consequence of this anti-Pelagian stress on the will's need of grace, and on the sufficiency of God's aid to the will, systematically hammered home by the Council of Trent and subsequent magisterial reactions to Jansenism, has resulted for the Church in an impoverished view of grace which locates it for all practical purposes in the human will, as enabling the individual through sheer supercharged will-power to overcome all other personal and social deficiencies in his attempt to comply with God's commands. Such a separatist view of grace, remote from the totality of the person and abstracting from other resources, or their lack, can easily sound like maintaining that a sufficiently high grade of petrol in a car will substitute for a faulty clutch or even for a lack of viable roads. All that is required is sufficient effort—God-given to be sure, and, if need be, as a return for earnest prayer that God will grant what he commands. But such recourse to earnest prayer can be viewed as simply switching the focus of one's effort and will-power from one sphere of action to a preliminary and prevenient sphere.[58]

Portalié, Brown, and others point out the paradox of Pelagian optimism, that in stressing man's ability it also makes exigent moral demands of him.[59] There is, however, a parallel paradox in the Augustinian view, that with the guarantee of God's grace to the will, absolutely nothing that God commands is impossible of

---

[56] 'Homo igitur, ut homini apparet, anima rationalis est mortali atque terreno utens corpore', De mor. Eccl. cath., I, 27; PL 32, 1332.

[57] Cf. supra, n. 33.

[58] Cf. J. Mahoney, 'Moral Freedom, Grace and Sin', in Seeking the Spirit: Essays in Moral and Pastoral Theology (London, 1981), pp. 34–9. 'Ideo in hoc agone magis nos Deus voluit orationibus certare, quam viribus' (supra, n. 41).

[59] Brown, referring to Portalié, writes of the Pelagians' aiming 'to establish an icy puritanism as the sole law of the Christian community', op. cit., p. 350.

achievement, and thus moral exigence is at least as salient a feature of Augustinism as it is of Pelagianism. Of both, in fact, it can be said that to whom much is given, whether by nature or by grace, of him or his will-power, much is expected. And that, moreover, irrespective of surrounding society. The very intensity of Augustine's intimate personal communion and lifelong dialogue with his God, which is part of his appeal to all individuals, and the interior drama of the will which he so eloquently and often with exquisite sensitivity depicts in the life of the individual, serve to make the rest of mankind spectators rather than participants. Gilson observes that at least in his early years Augustine 'was concerned most of all with the problem of his own destiny. For him, the important thing was to strive for self-knowledge and to learn what must be done in order to be better and, if possible, to be happy'.[60] But grace, like sin, of which it is correlative, must also have a social dimension; and the doctrine of grace needs expanding not only beyond the controversial confines of the will to the other resources of man but also beyond the isolated individual to his surroundings and fellow human beings. With its internally and socially separatist tendencies Augustine's theology of grace is at root unhistorical.

A second reflection on the Augustinian maxim that God does not command the impossible is to do with the theology underlying this principle, and with noting that it is primarily a statement about God, and not about man's moral abilities. To hold another view would be tantamount to admitting that in some circumstances God compels man to sin by demanding of him what he is unable to do, and such action would argue injustice in God himself. It is of interest to note that, in vindicating the teaching of Augustine and its use against Jansenism, Pope Pius XI characterized the Jansenist heresy as daring to blaspheme against the goodness of God by saying that some commands of God are impossible.[61] Divine omnipotence with regard to man is here at the service of divine goodness, and the tenacity with which the Church's moral tradition has clung to the Augustinian defence of God's goodness may go some way towards explaining its continual reluctance to give formal recognition to any ethical theory which entertains the possibility that at times the best a man can do is choose between two evils. Such a forced choice is envisaged as arguing not only a

---

[60] Op. cit., p. 3.   [61] Cf. *supra*, n. 53.

limitation in man in his given circumstances but also a limitation in God's power to transform those circumstances (by injecting grace to the will) and a limitation in his goodness, in requiring, or abandoning, man to do what is evil. We shall have occasion later to explore the implications of this strongly objective view of morality,[62] and for the moment it may suffice to suggest that, to the extent that man's being compelled to make deliberate choice of an evil course of action is seen as somehow a deficiency in God's providence and in divine grace, to that extent it will meet with considerable Augustinian resistance.

The third reflection which the principle that God does not command the impossible evokes is that, from beginning to end of the history of the origin and application of this principle, it appears presumed that we always know exactly what God's commands are. The whole thrust of the tradition is to assert that with grace man cannot be powerless before God's just requirements. The content of God's commands was not an issue between Augustine and Pelagius, Augustine himself acknowledging that Pelagius willingly admitted that God does help us, 'with his law and his teaching'. This Pelagius was prepared to describe as external grace, not strictly necessary, but enabling us to do good more easily than we otherwise would.[63] Nor does the epistemological question figure in subsequent Augustinian controversies, all of which focus attention on fallen and redeemed man's will, and not on his mind. As Gilson comments, in his study of Augustine's thought, 'philosophy is not the knowledge of what we must do but rather the power to do it'.[64] And it may be surmised that one more or less explicit consequence of this in the Church's moral tradition is to regard with suspicion any move which appears to qualify or mitigate God's moral requirements of the individual and at the same time appears by implication to question the efficacy of God's grace whatever the circumstances. Whether or not this be the case, it remains that this Augustinian efficacy only comes into play once one is satisfied that we actually are cognizant of God's precepts.

---

[62] Cf. *infra*, pp. 316–17.

[63] 'Hinc itaque apparet, hanc [Pelagium] gratiam confiteri, qua demonstrat et revelat Deus quid agere debeamus; non qua donat atque adiuvat ut agamus', *De gratia Chr.*, 8, 9; *PL.* 44, 364. It was not Augustine's 'iube quod vis' which Pelagius strenuously rebutted; it was his 'da quod iubes'.

[64] Op. cit., p. 246.

Augustinism and Sexual Morality

We have noted those writers who, while extolling the immense calibre and influence of Augustine's thought, also felt it necessary to acknowledge, and attempt to explain, the dark and pessimistic strain in his works. One important authority who did not consider this necessary was Pope Pius XI. In his encyclical of April 1930, commemorating the 1500th anniversary of Augustine's death, the only note which might be considered negative is his recalling the gentle warning of Pope Leo XIII 'that the authority of Augustine is not to be preferred to the supreme authority of the teaching Church'.[65] Of Augustine's actual teaching, however, there is nothing but praise. It could be argued, of course, that it is not the purpose of a laudatory encyclical to find fault with a saint also considered the greatest Doctor of the Church. But it may be suggested that the reason lies deeper than that, in a genuine affinity which Pope Pius XI himself had with the thinking of St Augustine. He is clear, for instance, that Augustine had much to teach the twentieth century in its educational permissiveness which allowed for co-education and a lack of concern for lust in children and adolescents; in its entertainments which destroy innocence and chastity; and in its immodesty in dress. Augustine, the Pope shows in a lengthy quotation, provides salutary teaching that life is a struggle against evils, calling for the continual need of self-control against sin, even into old age.[66]

The depressed tone of this papal teaching recurred a few months later in the customary Christmas Eve address to the Cardinals and the Roman Curia, when in an extremely gloomy review of the past year and a reference to 'sorrows such as have never before been experienced in history',[67] Pius also referred to an encyclical letter which, despite delays, would shortly be published on the most important subject of Christian marriage.[68] This was the setting in which the famous encyclical *Casti Connubii* was to appear. Its

[65] 'Non ita scilicet—quemadmodum, nonnulli, catholici sensus expertes, censuerunt—ut Augustini loquentis auctoritas supremae ipsi Ecclesiae docentis auctoritati auferatur', *AAS* 22 (1930), p. 204.

[66] Ibid., pp. 223–4.

[67] Ibid., p. 531, referring to the world economic recession, unemployment, anti-religious propaganda, natural disasters especially in Italy, persecution in Mexico, Russia, and China, difficulties for the Church, and the Pope in Italy (pp. 531–3).

[68] Ibid., p. 537.

opening words, 'Of chaste marriage', have a distinctly Augustinian ring, and the theme of chastity is the dominant characteristic of the whole document, which is expressly directed against pernicious errors and depraved practices, some of which had even been conceded by a recent Anglican Lambeth Conference and all of which were gaining acceptance even among Catholics.[69]

A study of the making of moral theology, and here of the legacy of Augustine, can usefully consider the strongly Augustinian approach to human sexuality and marriage which pervades this most important statement on Christian marriage by Pope Pius XI, for it is explicitly based and structured on a systematic analysis of the three values of marriage as propounded by Augustine. In devoting the major section of the encyclical to analysing the three desirable qualities, or *bona*, of marriage, Pius may be seen as following in the line of Western Church teaching as contained in the Bull of union with the Armenians dating from the fifteenth-century Council of Florence, which described the Sacrament of marriage as possessing a 'threefold good' of 'offspring', 'fidelity', and 'indivisibility'.[70] The source for this conciliar teaching is an *opusculum* of Thomas Aquinas, which in turn relies on Augustine's commentary on the Book of Genesis, and it is to that original source that Pope Pius resorts for his theology of marriage. Commenting on the divine institution of marriage, Augustine wrote:

Just because incontinence is evil, it does not follow that marriage, even that in which the incontinent copulate, is not good. This good is not culpable because of that evil, but rather that evil is forgivable because of this good. For the good which marriage possesses and by which marriage itself is good can never be a sin. And this good is threefold: fidelity, offspring, and sacrament. The point of fidelity is that apart from the marriage bond one does not have intercourse with another person. The point of offspring is that it be accepted lovingly, nourished tenderly, and brought up religiously. And the point of sacrament is that the union not be broken and that a man or woman sent away not be married to another even for the sake of offspring. This can be regarded as a pattern for marriage, for it either

---

[69] Ibid., p. 540. No explicit mention is made of Lambeth, but the allusion to it is clear in the encyclical's vehement statement on contraception, ibid., p. 560.

[70] 'Assignatur autem triplex bonum matrimonii. Primum est proles suscipienda et educanda ad cultum Dei. Secundum est fides, quam unus coniugum alteri servare debet. Tertium est indivisibilitas matrimonii, propter hoc quod significat indivisibilem coniunctionem Christi cum Ecclesia', *DS* 1327.

embellishes the fruitfulness of nature or it controls the depravity of incontinence.[71]

In the view of Pope Pius XI these three headings of Augustine are 'rightly considered a most enlightening summary of the whole doctrine of Christian marriage'.[72] The same teaching is to be found more succinctly in Augustine's work on marriage, where he writes, 'All these are the goods on whose account marriage is good; offspring, fidelity, and sacrament'.[73] And it is this order of the Augustinian *bona* of marriage which *Casti Connubii* proceeds to follow, developing each of them in turn, diagnosing the deplorable contemporary abuses of each, and prescribing salutary remedies, all with telling reference as appropriate to the writings of St Augustine.

In so faithfully following Augustine in logic, sentiment, and even tone of language, this twentieth-century Church teaching on Christian marriage may be seen as the outstanding modern instance in recent moral theology of the legacy of Augustine. For him, sexuality was exercised either for children or for lust. St Paul had observed, in advising Christian couples about their mutual sexual rights, that he was writing 'by way of forgiveness, not of command'. But if, Augustine concluded, there was scope for forgiveness, then there must be something culpable connected with even Christian sexual activity.[74] It could not be intercourse as such

---

[71] 'Neque enim quia incontinentia malum est, ideo connubium, vel quo incontinentes copulantur, non est bonum: imo vero non propter illud malum culpabile est hoc bonum, sed propter hoc bonum veniale est illud malum; quoniam id quod bonum habet nuptiae, et quo bona sunt nuptiae peccatum esse nunquam potest. Hoc autem tripartitum est: fides, proles, sacramentum. In fide attenditur ne praeter vinculum coniugale, cum altero vel altera concumbatur: in prole, ut amanter suscipiatur, benigne nutriatur, religiose educetur: in sacramento autem, ut coniugium non separetur, et dimissus aut dimissa nec causa prolis alteri coniungatur. Haec est tanquam regular nuptiarum, qua vel naturae decoratur fecunditas, vel incontinentiae regitur pravitas', *De Gen. ad lit.*, 9, 7, 12; *PL* 34, 397. The mediating text of Aquinas is his *De art. fidei et Eccl. Sacr.*

[72] 'Quae tria capita qua ratione luculentissimam totius de christiano connubio doctrinae summam continere iure dicantur, ipse Sanctus Doctor diserte declaravit, cum ait . . .', *AAS*, ibid., p. 543.

[73] 'Haec omnia bona sunt, propter quae nuptiae bonae sunt: proles, fides, sacramentum', *De bono coniug.*, 24, 32; *PL* 40, 394.

[74] 1 Cor. 7: 6 'by way of concession' (RSV). Augustine's Latin text read 'veniam'. 'Ubi ergo venia danda est, aliquid esse culpae nulla ratione negabitur', *De nupt. et conc.*, 1, 14, 16; *PL* 44, 423. Cf. *supra*, n. 71, 'veniale . . . malum'. It is instructive to note how from his Latin bible Augustine can develop or reinforce entire trains of theological thought. The most notorious instance of this, of course, is his reading of Rom. 5: 12, ἐφ' ᾧ πάντες ἥμαρτον, 'because all men have sinned' (RSV), which Augustine took as 'in quo (i.e., in whom) omnes peccaverunt', and as

between husband and wife, because this had been instituted by God for the growth and continuance of the human race, and it would have occurred between Adam and Eve in Paradise had the Fall not intervened.[75] What would not have occurred before sin entered into human history, however, were the overpowering intensity of sexual pleasure and the rebelliousness of the body, each of which was quite disruptive of human life. Consequently, it was only when sexuality was exercised within marriage with the express purpose of producing offspring, as God had commanded, that the lust and the disorder which now inevitably accompanied even its proper exercise might be considered pardonable. Thus it was that Augustine roundly condemned as a satisfaction of lust the abstaining from intercourse during fertile periods, which the Manichees had advocated as a means of avoiding the production of offspring in which spirit would be imprisoned.[76] Thus also he was able to

apodictic proof of all fallen mankind's primordial identity in Adam. 'Quod autem dicit Apostolus, "in quo omnes peccaverunt": "In quo" non intelligitur nisi in Adam, in quo eos dicit et mori; quia non erat iustum, sine crimine supplicium', *Contra Iulian. op. imp.*, 2, 63; *PL* 45, 1169. Cf. *Contra duas ep. Pel.*, 4, 4, 7; *PL* 44, 614.

[75] 'Quamquam enim iam emissi de paradiso convenisse et genuisse commemorentur; tamen non video quid prohibere potuerit, ut essent eis etiam in paradisco honorabiles nuptiae, et torus immaculatus (Heb. 13: 4): hoc Deo praestante fideliter iusteque viventibus, eique obedienter sancteque servientibus, ut sine ullo inquieto ardore libidinis, sine ullo labore ac dolore pariendi, fetus ex eorum semine gignerentur', *De Gen. ad lit.*, 9, 3, 9; *PL* 34, 395.

[76] 'Nonne vos estis qui nos solebatis monere, ut quantum fieri posset, observaremus tempus, quo ad conceptum mulier post genitalium viscerum purgationem apta esset, eoque tempore a concubitu temperaremus, ne carni anima implicaretur? Ex quo illud sequitur, ut non liberorum procreandorum causa, sed satiandae libidinis habere coniugem censeatis .... Non autem matrimonium est, ubi datur opera ne sit mater: non igitur uxor', *De mor. manich.*, 2, 18, 65; *PL* 32, 1373. It is well known, of course, that Pope Pius XI, heavily dependent although he was on Augustine's views on contraception, departed in this instance from the Bishop of Hippo's teaching in a development which, to the puzzlement of many, has been maintained by his successors. 'Neque contra naturae ordinem agere ii dicendi sunt coniuges, qui iure suo recta et naturali ratione utuntur, etsi ob naturales sive temporis sive quorundam defectuum causas nova inde vita oriri non possit. Habentur enim tam in ipso matrimonio quam in coniugalis iuris usu etiam secundarii fines, ut sunt mutuum adiutorium mutuusque fovendus amor et concupiscentiae sedatio, quos intendere coniuges minime vetantur, dummodo salva semper sit intrinseca illius actus natura ideoque eius ad primarium finem debita ordinatio', *AAS* 22 (1930), p. 561. Although Augustine might have admitted such 'secondary ends' a place in marriage (cf. *infra*, n. 77), he would not have acknowledged them any legitimate weight in the marriage act. In condemning 'any use of marriage in which the act is deliberately deprived of its natural power to procreate life' (ibid., p. 560) as ipso facto an infringement of God's and nature's law,

explain, in ascending order of approval, that a Christian might live at peace with his wife either by fulfilling his carnal need with her, which Paul considered forgivable, or by fulfilling the procreation of children, or by fulfilling a brotherly companionship without physical contact, as Paul commended, having a wife as though he had none (1 Cor. 7: 29), 'which in the marriage of Christians is the most excellent and sublime'.[77] To put the matter more trechantly, 'what father would agree to hand his daughter over to the lust of another man if it were not for children?'[78]

Pius XI was strongly influenced by Augustine's interpretation of the crime and punishment of Onan (cf. Gen. 38: 8–10), which more recent papal teaching has abandoned: 'Illicite namque et turpiter etiam cum legitime uxore concumbitur, ubi prolis conceptio devitatur. Quod faciebat Onan, filius Iudae, et occidit illum propter hoc Deus', *De coniug. adulter.*, 2, 12; *PL* 40, 479; *AAS* ibid., pp. 559–60. The other classic text of Augustine on contraception, which also condemns abortion, is important not only for its historical influence but also for the view of sexuality which it discloses and the contemporary motives and abuses which Augustine was castigating. 'It is one thing to have relations only with a wish to have a child, which is guiltless, and another thing to desire the pleasure of having relations, although only with one's partner, which has pardonable guilt. For even if one has relations not for the sake of producing a child, yet the motive of lust does not oppose the having of a child, either by bad intention or by bad action. Those who do oppose it may be described as married, but they are not; they preserve none of the truth of marriage, but only cover this shameful behaviour with a cloak of respectability. They are betrayed when they go so far as to disown any unwanted children they have. They resent nourishing or keeping those they were afraid to produce. And so, when secret iniquity turns upon the offspring which it has unwillingly produced, it emerges into the light as manifest iniquity, and covert shamefulness is convicted as open cruelty. Sometimes this lustful cruelty, or cruel lustfulness, goes to the length of procuring poisons of sterility. If that does not succeed, it somehow internally extinguishes and eliminates fetuses which have been conceived, wishing its offspring to perish before it lives, or else, if it was already alive in the womb, to be killed before it is born. Surely, if both partners are of such a kind, they are not married; and if they have been so from the start, they have come together more in immorality than in matrimony. If both are not of this kind, then I make so bold as to say that either the woman is some sort of whore of her husband, or he is an adulterer of his wife', *De nupt. et concup.*, 1, 15, 17; *PL* 44, 423.

[77] 'Potest igitur christianus cum coniuge concorditer vivere; sive indigentiam carnalem cum ea supplens, quod secundum veniam, non secundum imperium dicit Apostolus; sive filiorum propagationem, quod iam nonnullo gradu potest esse laudabile; sive fraternam societatem, sine ulla corporum commixtione, habens uxorem tanquam non habens, quod est in coniugio Christianorum excellentissimum atque sublime', *De serm. Dom. in Monte*, 1, 15, 42; *PL* 34, 1250. On the influence on Augustine of the virginal marriage of Mary, cf. *de nupt. et conc.*, 1, 11, 12; *PL* 44, 420.

[78] 'Recitatur liberorum procreandorum causa; ... nisi ad hoc dentur, ad hoc accipiantur uxores, quis sana fronte dat filiam suam libidini alienae? Sed ut non erubescant parentes, cum dant, recitantur tabulae; ut sint soceri, non lenones', *Sermo* 51, 13, 22; *PL* 38, 345.

Behind this teaching of Augustine lay the fact that he had for long years been plagued with his own apparently very strong sexual drives and with the dissipation into which they dragged him. He was not merely humbled by this experience, but rather, as a proud man, he was humiliated by it, and his reason was affronted and philosophically scandalized at the insubordination of his body to the power of his will.[79] It is scarcely surprising that it was in disorderly sexual arousal (and impotence), and in the shame and disgust which accompanied or followed it, that he experienced and witnessed the most blatant instance of that law of sin in his members on which he found St Paul so enlightening, and that he saw in such carnal concupiscence not only the terrible effects of original sin, but also the very channel through which that sin was transmitted from generation to generation. In Paradise there would have been tranquil obedience of the members to intercourse, not this shameful concupiscence of the flesh, which, as Delhaye expresses it, 'soils the soul' of the offspring generated.[80] As it was, in order to procreate, this lust had now to be stimulated and used, so that 'he who legitimately has intercourse by means of shameful lust is putting something evil to good use'.[81]

[79] Cf. *de civ. Dei*, 19, 21; *PL* 41, 649, 'Serviens autem Deo animus, recte imperat corpori, inque ipso animo ratio Domino Deo subdita, recte imperat libidini vitiisque caeteris.'

[80] Rom. 7: 23. 'Ibi homo primitus Dei lege transgressa, aliam legem repugnantem suae menti habere coepit in membris, et inobedientiae suae malum sensit. Quando sibi dignissime retributam inobedientiam suae carnis invenit . . . ubi autem ventum fuerit ut filii seminentur, ad voluntatis nutum membra in hoc opus creata non serviunt, sed exspectatur ut ea velut sui iuris libido commoveat, et aliquando non facit animo volente, cum aliquando faciat et nolente? Hincne non erubesceret humani libertas arbitrii, quod contemnendo imperantem Deum etiam in membra propria proprium perdidisset imperium?' *De nupt. et conc.* 1, 6, 7; *PL* 44, 417–18. 'In paradiso autem si peccatum non praecessisset, non esset quidem sine utriusque sexus commixtione generatio, sed esset sine confusione commixtio. Esset quippe in coeundo tranquilla membrorum obedientia, non pudenda carnis concupiscentia', ibid., 2, 22, 37; *col.* 458. Delhaye, in Guilley, op. cit., p. vi. It was the inherent connection between uncontrolled male carnal 'concupiscence' and the transmission of original sin which enabled Augustine to explain the sinlessness of Jesus born of a virgin, *Contra Iulian. op. imp.*, 6, 22; *PL* 45, 1552. The same line of argument could not, of course, be used of the conception of Mary herself, although Augustine was clearly unwilling to ascribe to the mother of God any stain even of original sin. Cf. *de nat. et grat.*, 36, 42; *PL* 44, 267.

[81] 'Sic insinuantur haec duo, et bonum laudandae coniunctionis, unde filii generentur, et malum pudendae libidinis, unde qui generantur, regenerandi sunt ne damnentur. Proinde pudenda libidine qui licite concumbit, malo bene utitur; qui autem illicite, malo male utitur. Rectius enim accipit nomen mali quam boni, unde erubescunt et mali et boni', *De nupt. et conc.*, 2, 21, 36; *PL* 44, 457.

The modern reader may well react to this Augustinian solution of putting something evil to good use by noting that in so thoroughly pursuing Paul's teaching on the law of sin inherent in his being he had argued himself into a situation against which Paul had earlier warned his readers, that one 'may not do evil that good may come of it' (Rom. 3: 8). Nor did this escape Augustine's most brilliant adversary, the Pelagian Julian, bishop of Eclanum in Southern Italy, who viewed the 'Punic' bishop's views on nature, sin, and sexuality with considerable distaste, and generally charged him with not having shaken off his youthful Manichaeism, with all its tortured hatred of the body.[82] Specifically Julian accused Augustine of teaching in his earlier works that in marriage the wrongfulness of concupiscence is rendered blameless through religion. Augustine's brief rebuttal lacks his usual vituperative confidence.

It cannot be said here, as you think, "Let us do evil that good may come", because marriage is not evil in any respect. The evil in their children which parents have not created, but only found, is not an evil of marriage. In the first married couple, who were not born of parents, it was through sin that there came about the discordant evil of carnal concupiscence, which marriage could put to good use; it was not through marriage, which would then quite rightly be condemned. Why do you enquire, then "whether I apply the term 'purity' or 'impurity' to the pleasure of intercourse between Christian couples"? It is not the pleasure, but the good use of that evil, which is termed "purity"; and because of this good use the evil itself cannot be called "impurity". In fact, impurity is the disgraceful use of that evil, just as virginal purity is its non-use. Thus marital purity is preserved while evil is produced from evil through birth, to be cleansed through rebirth.[83]

---

[82] On Julian, cf. Brown, op. cit., pp. 384–97, 369–71, 46–53.

[83] 'Unde non "crimen eius," sicut calumniando loqueris, "impunitum fit per religionem;" quia nullius est criminis, quando per fidei bonum bene utitur libidinis malo. Neque hic dici potest, ut putas, "Faciamus mala ut veniant bona" (Rom. 3: 8); quia ex nulla sui parte malum sunt nuptiae. Non enim earum malum est, quod in hominibus quos parentes gignunt, non fecerunt, sed invenerunt. In primis autem coniugibus, qui ex nullis parentibus nati sunt, per peccatum accidit carnalis concupiscentiae discordiosum malum, quo nuptiae bene uterentur; non per ipsas nuptias, ut inde merito damnarentur. Quid ergo quaeris, "utrum in coniugibus christianis conventuum voluptatem, pudicitiam, an impudicitiam nominem." Ecce respondeo, Non ipsa nominatur pudicitia, sed eius mali usus bonus; quo usu bono fit ut illud malum nec impudicitia possit. Impudicitia est enim eiusdem mali usus flagitiosus; sicut pudicitia virginalis, nullus. Salva igitur pudicitia coniugali, malum de malo nascendo trahitur, quod renascendo purgetur', *Contra Iulian.*, 4, 8; *PL* 44, 763. On the end not justifying the means, cf. more clearly *Contra mendacium*, 18; *PL* 40, 528.

It looks, at least to a modern theologian, as if Augustine has missed the point of the difficulty into which his jaundiced view of sexual desire had led him, and which his systematic distinction between 'use' and 'enjoyment' was too blunt an instrument to handle with any delicacy. He held, in fact, that all the pleasures of the senses are evil as providing a series of titillating distractions from the main purpose of life—a well-ordered love of God. For him even the pleasure involved in eating and drinking is 'an evil which we put to good use when through it we do no more than is conducive to good health'. Such pleasures of the table are tolerable if closely monitored, because they can always be accompanied by the mental pleasure of good conversation on matters of wisdom. But sexual pleasure, even when approached with the good intention of having offspring, is so engulfing that one cannot think then of anything else at all, far less of wisdom. 'What lover of spiritual good, even if married just for the sake of progeny, would not prefer to procreate children without such pleasure if he could, or at least without such intensity of pleasure?'[84]

The attempt at a controlled, or canalized, 'use' of such intense pleasure in order to fulfil God's command of procreation is not, Augustine seems to argue, creating something evil in order to produce a good effect, but turning to good use an evil which is now, all too regrettably, part of human nature.[85] And perhaps it could be argued that if this 'evil' pleasure is not intended but only incurred as a concomitant of the activity of procreating a child, then the agent

[84] 'Et haec quidem vescendi atque potandi tolerabilis est voluptas, quanta possumus intentione vigilantibus nobis, ut facilius non impleat, quam modum aliquando victus sufficientis excedat: contra cuius concupiscentiam et ieiunando et parcius alimenta sumendo pugnamus; eoque malo bene tunc utimur, quando per illam nonnisi quod saluti conducibile est agimus. Ideo autem hanc voluptatem dixi tolerabilem, quia vis eius tanta non est, ut nos a cogitationibus ad sapientiam pertinentibus, si in eas sumus mentis delectatione suspensi, abrumpat et deiiciat . . . . Illa vero pro qua mecum tantis contentionibus litigas, etiam quando ad eam bona intentione, hoc est, causa propagandae prolis acceditur; tamen in ipso opere suo, quem permittit aliquid, non dico sapientiae, sed cuiuslibet rei aliud cogitare? Nonne illi totus animus et corpus impenditur, et ipsius mentis quadam submersione illud extremum eius impletur? . . . Quis ergo amator spiritualis boni, etiam sola causa sobolis coniugatus, non mallet vel sine ista si posset, vel sine tam magna vi eius filios procreare?' ibid., 4, 13; *PL* 44, 773–4. On the absorption of reason by sexual excitement, which the scholastics also were to consider completely unworthy of man made rational in God's image, cf. *de civ. Dei*, 14, 16; *PL* 41, 424–5.

[85] 'Aliud quippe est malo bene uti, quod iam inerat; et aliud est malum perpetrare, quod non erat, *Contra Iulian.*, 4, 7; *PL* 44, 758.

is 'using' is rather than indulging in it, or 'enjoying' it. But the difficulty for Augustine lies not simply in his experience of being engulfed by such pleasure. Perhaps even more crucial to his position is the unruly character of sexual arousal to which, in the candid climate of the time, he frequently draws attention as an indication of the power of sin and the powerless of the will. The paradox of procreation for sinful man is that such physical and significantly embarrassing disorder needs to be deliberately resorted to, with more or less success, if man is to fulfil his religious duty of procreation. And this aspect of the charge of teaching that the end justifies the means is one to which Augustine does not appear to have given much consideration.

Lacking, of course, from Augustine's introspective make-up was any positive appreciation of women, and he seems to have considered them as little more than sex objects. He could not for the life of him think of any reason why woman should have been given to man other than for the procreation of children, 'as the soil is a help to the seed'. She was physically weaker and her friendship could not compare with that of another man.[86] Love he appears to have evoked from his concubine, whom he had picked out casually and who, on being dismissed so that he could make a respectable marriage, vowed that she would never know another man. And fond of her he may have been, although with a disordered love and 'largely imprisoned by the powerful habit of sating an insatiable concupiscence'. He was not long in procuring another mistress to fill in the two years before his intended marriage, needing a focus for his sexual restlesness and being, as he explained, 'not a lover of marriage, but a slave of lust'.[87] In the event, after his conversion he

---

[86] 'Si autem quaeritur, ad quam rem fieri oportuerit hoc adiutorium, nihil aliud probabiliter occurrit, quam propter filios procreandos, sicut adiutorium semini terra est, ut virgultum ex utroque nascatur', *De Gen ad lit.*, 9, 3, 5; PL 34; 395. Cf. ibid., 9, 11, 19; *col.* 400. On the enormous importance for Augustine of male friends and their companionship, cf. M. A. McNamara, *Friends and Friendship for St. Augustine* (New York, 1958). Interestingly different is the case of Jerome. 'Strongly sexed but also, because of his convictions, strongly repressed as well, his nature craved for female society, and found deep satisfaction in it when it could be had without doing violence to his principles', J. N. D. Kelly, *Jerome: His Life, Writings, and Controversies* (London, 1975), p. 91.

[87] 'In illis annis unam habebam, non eo quod legitimum vocatur, coniugio cognitam, sed quam indagaverat vagus ardor, inops prudentiae', *Conf.*, 4, 2; PL 32, 693–4. 'Interea peccata mea multiplicabantur, et avulsa a latere meo tamquam impedimentum coniugii, cum qua cubare solitus eram, cor ubi adhaerebat, concisum

decided not to marry, feeling that 'there is nothing which overthrows a man's mind so much as female caresses and that physical contact without which one cannot possess a wife . . . . And so, I think quite rightly, and helpfully for my freedom of soul, I have commanded myself not to desire, or seek, or marry a wife'.[88]

It could be urged in defence of later theologians who consciously drew upon Augustine's writings, whether in context or through medieval anthologies such as Lombard or the *Glosses* on Scripture, as it could equally be claimed of the systematic recourse to Augustine in expounding in *Casti Connubii* the Church's teaching on Christian marriage, that to draw upon Augustine is not necessarily to be uncritical nor, in particular, to be wedded to his entire theology of human sexuality and marriage. Gilson remarks that some people 'seem to be born Augustinians; but it would probably be truer to say that each of us has his Augustinian moments, his Augustinian moods'.[89] It also seems necessary to observe, however, that all Augustinian intellectual positions interlock and reinforce each other, so fundamental and all-pervasive are his basic doctrines on both God and man, and so dominant in his thinking is the classical concept of *ordo*, or the divine order of all things.[90] This being so, to quarry texts from Augustine out of the overall landscape of his life and mind-set is to incur the danger of ignoring that they were fashioned within that context and are dug from a particular vein of thought which may contain not only

---

et vulneratum mihi erat, et trahebat sanguinem. Et illa in Africam redierat, vovens tibi alium se virum nescituram. At ego infelix nec feminae imitator, dilationis impatiens, tanquam post biennium accepturus eam quam petebam, quia non amator coniugii sed libidinis servus eram; procuravi aliam, non utique coniugem', ibid., 6, 15; col. 731–2. 'Magna autem ex parte atque vehementer consuetudo satiandae insatiabilis concupiscentiae me captum excruciabat', ibid., 6, 12; col. 730.

[88] 'Nihil esse sentio quod magis ex arce deiiciat animum virilem, quam blandimenta feminea, corporumque ille contactus, sine quo uxor haberi non potest . . . . Quamobrem, satis, credo, iuste atque utiliter pro libertate animae meae mihi imperavi non cupere, non quaerere, non ducere uxorem', *Sol.* 1, 10, *PL* 32, 878. In the *Confessions* he was to recall that God had not only forbidden concubinage but also advised a better state than the 'concession' of marriage, which by God's 'gift' Augustine had accepted. 'Iussisti a concubitu; et de ipso coniugio melius aliquid quam concessisti monuisti. Et quoniam dedisti, factum est et antequam dispensator sacramenti tui fierem', *Conf.*, 10, 30; *Pl.* 32, 796. While Augustine was now enabled to control his sexual stirrings in his waking moments, he continued to be plagued in sleep by the memories and habits of the past; ibid.

[89] Gilson, op. cit., p. ix.

[90] Cf. *infra*, pp. 74–7.

precious elements to be treasured but also impurities to be refined.[91]

With such a strong repugnance for human sexuality as it is experienced, and such a lifelong preoccupation with its disorder as the effect and at the same time the medium of original sin, it is no wonder that for Augustine 'our righteousness in this life consists in the forgiveness of sins rather than in the perfection of virtues'.[92] It was this pervasive sinfulness, in human sexuality and in life in general, which was to preoccupy moral theology in the aftermath of Augustine and in the light of what Guilley terms 'the pessimistic aspect of Augustinian anthropology'.[93] 'The fact that theological speculation in the West was concentrated in the first place on the weakness of fallen man could not but have a decisive influence on its further development.'[94]

The Mind of Augustine

With the separation of the East and the eclipse of Greek culture, Latin theology, derived from St Augustine, dominated the Middle Ages, and inspired the Reformers. So from St Thomas to Malebranche, from St Bernard to Jansenius, the history of theology and philosophy was bound up with the fortunes of Augustinism, just as if this were a second tradition mingled with the first, as if it had given, on the threshold of the new age, a new version of the Christian message.[95]

If the theology is the man, that is eminently so in the case of Augustine in reflecting his subtle and tempestuous mind and the dramatic alternations of his life and thought. Newman, for instance, Jean Guitton suggests, would have found the anti-Donatist bishop hard, violent, and bitter, more African than Latin.[96] And certainly, for all his tenderness and mystic yearning, there is also to be found a violence, not only of language, but also in Augustine's very way of thinking.

In his Introduction to the Bettenson translation of *The City of*

---

[91] To adapt a metaphor applied by Augustine to pagan wisdom, *de doc. chris.*, 2, 40; *PL* 34, 63.

[92] *de civ. dei*, 19, 27 (Bettenson, p. 882); *PL* 41, 657.

[93] Op. cit., p. 63.

[94] Flick and Alszeghy, op. cit., p. 49.

[95] Guitton, op. cit., p. 80, echoing Newman, supra, nn. 6, 14.

[96] 'Parallèle de s. Augustin et de Newman', *Augustinus Magister*, ii (Paris, 1954, p. 1105.

God, David Knowles recognizes Augustine's 'marvellous powers of physchological analysis' which helped to make him 'one of the supreme thinkers and theologians of the Christian centuries'.[97] Yet he also notes that much in Augustine's works presents 'dissatisfaction for those who wish for clear-cut edges'.[98] And he calls attention to that 'characteristic Augustine avoidance of clear distinctions that runs through so much of his thought'.[99] It may be suggested, in fact, that for much of the time Augustine does not make distinctions, he offers dramatic alternatives, highly charged opposing poles. He is not a logician or a Schoolman, but a most skilful rhetorician who is disposed more to set up extremes than to explore the middle ground between them. It is this quality of his mind which often contributes to the appeal of many of those terse phrases and brilliant tensions which have so charmed and delighted his readers, as well as making him the most quotable, and quoted, of theologians. So often with Augustine it appears to be all or nothing, black or white, which he has to offer, as may perhaps be grasped at its most cosmic in his depicting of the two cities and the two loves from which they have sprung. 'We see then that the two cities were created by two kinds of love: the earthly city was created by self-love reaching the point of contempt for God, the Heavenly City by the love of God carried as far as contempt of self'.[100] Underlying the thought of Augustine, it is suggested, there is to be found at work not a philosophical dualism or simply an ethical or moral dualism, but a mental dualism, a dyadic approach to reality. And while such a chiaroscuro of the mind may make for good rhetoric, and certainly for rousing polemics, or for swaying a congregation or a jury, rhetoric and polemic do not always make for good theology. They can lead to violent or extreme language and entrenched positions, in which words become weapons with which to crush an adversary rather than the inadequate counters of that humble exploration of divine reality which should be characteristic of theological discourse.

If this attempt to understand the workings of the mind of Augustine in terms of mental extremism has any validity, then

[97] Trans. Bettenson, p. xi.

[98] Ibid., p. xxii.

[99] Ibid., p. xxi.

[100] *De civ. dei*, 14, 28 (trans. Bettenson, p. 593); *PL* 41, 436. 'Augustine's thought was always in a state of tension', Brown, op. cit., p. 327.

increased significance must be given to the question of Guitton about Augustine's profound influence on all subsequent Christian thought. 'We may ask if the recapitulation of tradition round a *single* survivor does not mean an alteration of it, since it is then depicted in the exclusive colours of an individual mind and career. The qualities, then, of an individual destiny are liable to be taken by many generations as rules of thinking'.[101] As far as moral theology is concerned, one may conclude, that disquiet expressed by Guitton in general is copiously borne out in the legacy of Augustine to this particular subject. Today, however, it is in process of re-assessment, through Augustinian studies; the recovered interest in the Latin West of pre-Augustinian writers and of the great Christian theologians of the East; the long-delayed Catholic renaissance in biblical studies; the positive orientation given to moral theology by the Second Vatican Council; and the reintegration of moral theology with a renewed dogmatic and spiritual theology. In this process the strengths and insights of Augustine will be brought into truer relief and his contributions to the understanding of man's return to God be the more appreciated for being one, but only one, great theologian's dramatic projection of reality, to be balanced by those of others more optimistic and more temperate. In introducing his magnificent series of mature homilies on the Gospel of John, Augustine explained that 'perhaps not even John said what actually is, but even he only as he was able'.[102] At least in his more eirenic moments, Augustine would surely not have wished more to be said of himself.

The legacy of Augustine in Christian thought remains incalculable, ranging from his plumbing what he considered the worst of human misery to soaring passages of great beauty and Latin eloquence. The restlessness of his mind and his heart throughout his long life came to find final resolution only in death and in his indissoluble cleaving to God—his only real good—as fulfilling at last that longing which he described, in concluding his great history of the world, for 'the eternal rest not only of the spirit but of the body also. There we shall be still and see; we shall see and we shall love; we shall love and we shall praise. Behold what will be, in the end,

---

[101] *The Modernity*, p. 78.

[102] 'Forsitan nec ipse Joannes dixit ut est, sed et ipse ut potuit', *In Joan.*, 1, 1; *PL* 35, 1379.

without end! For what is our end but to reach that kingdom which has no end?'[103]

As for Augustine's legacy to moral theology, as the one single individual in Christian history who has had most influence on the making of moral theology, one may recall Gilson's remark that some people seem to have been born Augustinians but that everyone has his Augustinian moods and moments.[104] But the Church was not born Augustinian. And although for 1500 years it has experienced something more than an Augustinian moment in its moral thinking, it now appears to be in the difficult process of shaking off its long Augustinian mood.

[103] *de civ. dei*, 22, 30, 5 (trans. Bettenson, p. 1091); *PL* 41, 804. The monosyllabic English does no justice to the rhythmic beauty and sonority of Augustine's final *rallentando:* 'Ibi vacabimus, et videbimus; videbimus, et amabimus; amabimus, et laudabimus. Ecce quod erit in fine sine fine. Nam quis alius noster est finis, nisi pervenire ad regnum, cuius nullus est finis?'

[104] *Supra*, n. 89.

3

NATURE AND SUPERNATURE

The first two chapters of this study on the making of moral theology have drawn attention to the influence of the major Church institution of confession and to the legacy of the most dominating of Church thinkers in the development of the subject through the centuries. Another major source of development in any subject is the power of ideas—the control exercised on men's minds by major concepts. Of the ideas which have powerfully shaped moral theology in its long making none have achieved more prominence, or perhaps notoriety, than those of 'nature' and of 'the supernatural'. The idea that human nature is to be considered a source of moral knowledge and a basis of moral obligation has been increasingly contested within recent years. And perhaps no other aspect of moral theology is today more elusive, and to many more puzzling, than the whole subject of revelation and grace and the sphere of what is termed the supernatural. The purpose of this chapter is to trace the developments of thought resulting in these two central and contrasting elements, nature and supernature, and to offer some reflections on that development. Since supernatural has the literal meaning of 'above the natural', we may best begin by considering how the ideas of nature, and natural law, have come to occupy so central a place in moral theology.

We have already seen how the early Christian writers and thinkers were prepared to adopt and adapt from the Graeco-Roman culture of their day elements of ethical thought and conventions which appeared to them consonant with living and commending the teaching of Jesus. Of these elements none was more appealing to early Christianity than the glimpses caught by pagan thinkers of an inherently rational structure to reality, as best exemplified in the Stoic teaching on universal order and reason.

Nature, Reason, and Morality

In accepting, and indeed appropriating, Stoic teaching on the moral life as an exercise of man's reason in subordination to a higher

principle of reason which pervades all of reality, early Christian
thinkers were to adopt a principle of divine cosmic and human
order, or *ordo*, which, with contributions from the Book of
Wisdom, has been a major intellectual feature of the history of
Christian moral thinking.[1] The Athenian convert, Athenagoras,
was to explain in his *Apology*, written about 177, that 'man
himself, so far as he that made him is concerned, is well ordered,
both by his original nature, which has one common characteristic
for all, and by the constitution of his body, which does not
transgress the law imposed upon it'.[2] 'We are in all things always
alike and the same, submitting ourselves to reason, and not ruling
over it'.[3] In the contemporary treatise *On the Resurrection of the
Dead* we are informed that, since everything in nature has an end
peculiar to itself, as we know from common sense and observation,
there must likewise be a peculiar end for men 'whose actions are
regulated by the innate law and reason, and who live an intelligent
life and observe justice'.[4]

The final cause of an intelligent life and rational judgment is to be
occupied uninterruptedly with those objects to which the natural reason is
chiefly and primarily adapted, and to delight unceasingly in the contemplation of Him Who Is, and of His decrees, notwithstanding that the
majority of men, because they are affected too passionately and too
violently by things below, pass through life without attaining this object.[5]

The Palestinian theologian, Justin, who was martyred about the
year 165, explains of the Christian God that 'in the beginning he
made the human race with the power of thought and of choosing
the truth and of doing right, so that all men are without excuse
before God [cf. Rom. 1: 20]; for they have been born rational and
contemplative'.[6] God, he explains in his celebrated *Dialogue with
Trypho the Jew*,

---

[1] Cf. Wis. 8: 1, 'She reaches mightily from one end of the earth to the other, and
she orders all things well.'
[2] *A Plea for the Christians*, ch. 25 (trans. Pratten), in *The Writings of Justin
Martyr and Athenagoras* (Edinburgh, 1867), p. 408; Migne, *PG* 6, 949.
[3] Ibid., ch. 35 (p. 419); *PG* 6, 969.
[4] *On the Resurrection of the Dead*, ch. 24 (ibid., p. 455); *PG* 6, 1021.
[5] Ibid., ch. 25 (p. 456); *PG* 6, 1021-4.
[6] *First Apology*, ch. 28 (trans. Dods), in *The Writings of Justin Martyr and
Athenagoras*, p. 31); *PG* 6, 372. It is to Justin that Christian theology is primarily
indebted for the Stoic idea of natural law (φύσεως νόμος) (Spanneut, op. cit., p.
253). For him, in fact, 'the Stoics are first-rate on ethics', H. Chadwick, *Early*

sets before every race of mankind that which is always and universally just, as well as all righteousness; and every race knows that adultery, and fornication, and homicide, and such like, are sinful; and though they all commit such practices, yet they do not escape from the knowledge that they act unrighteously when they do so, with the exception of those who are possessed with an unclean spirit, and who have been debased by education, by wicked customs, and by sinful institutions, and who have lost, or rather quenched and put under, their natural ideas.[7]

One can see in the writings of Tertullian a similar acceptance of the Stoic ethical resources of nature and reason. Romans should not believe the calumnies directed against Christians unless they would behave in a similar manner themselves, for they are fellow human beings.[8] It is to Tertullian, of course, that we owe the historic exclamation which concludes his questionable argument from pagans' spontaneous and everyday invocation of one 'god' that in everyone the soul is 'Christian in its very nature'.[9] It is by this one great God that 'we find this whole fabric of the universe to be once for all disposed, equipped, ordered as it stands, and supplied with the complete guidance of reason'.[10]

Augustine too could find much in common with non-Christian ethical teaching. In what was to become a key-passage for the Middle Ages he explains how Christians can and should use what is true and useful in the profane sciences. As the Hebrews were commanded by God to despoil the Egyptians of their gold and silver, so 'certain most useful moral precepts' are to be found among the Gentiles as minerals of divine providence to be found everywhere which the Christians should take from them for the just purpose of preaching the Gospel.[11] The Stoic influence, however, is most clear in Augustine in his systematic exploitation of the concept of order in the whole of God's creation. Underlying everything is an eternal law of God, 'the divine reason or the will of God commanding the natural order to be respected and forbidding

Christian Thought and the Classical Tradition (Oxford, 1966), p. 11. On the Stoic theme of λόγος (trans. 'reason') and of λόγος σπερματικός in Justin, cf. L. W. Barnard, *Justin Martyr: His Life and Thought* (Cambridge, 1967), pp. 96–9; Chadwick, op. cit., p. 16; *infra*, pp. 102, 344.

[7] *Dialogue*, ch. 93 (*The Writings*, p. 217); PG 6, 697.
[8] 'Homo est enim et christianus, et quod et tu', *Apol.* 8; PL 1, 313.
[9] 'O testimonium animae naturaliter christianae', *Apol.* 17; PL 1, 377.
[10] *Apol.* 11; PL 1, 333–4.
[11] *de doc. chr.*, 2, 40, 60; PL 34, 63. Cf. Gilson, op. cit., pp. 125–6.

its disruption'.[12] 'The idea of the eternal law, which is impressed on us, is the idea by which it is just that everything be perfectly ordered';[13] order, for Augustine, being defined as the disposing of equal and unequal things each in its right place. Hence it follows, according to his famous definition, that 'peace' is that 'tranquility which is to be found in the right ordering of everything'.[14]

All the things which God has created are good, and so the rational soul acts well with reference to them if it maintains order, and if by distinguishing, choosing, and assessing, it subordinates the lesser things to the greater, the bodily to the spiritual, the lower to the higher, and the temporal to the eternal.[15] Within man also 'when reason controls the movements of the soul, man is said to be ordered. For it is not a right order, or even to be called order at all, when the better is subject to the worse'.[16] A popular version of Augustine's ethics, then, might well be a place for everything and everything in its place, a view which he finds aptly illustrated in the physical universe and in the natural properties of bodies. For him 'in every soul, as in every body, there is a weight drawing it constantly, moving it always to find its natural place of rest; and this weight we call love'.[17] This observation by Gilson on what is perhaps Augustine's most famous metaphor of love in terms of gravity is well borne out in *The City of God*:

[12] 'Ergo peccatum est, factum vel dictum vel concupitum aliquid contra aeternam legem. Lex vero aeterna est, ratio divina vel voluntas Dei, ordinem naturalem conservari iubens, perturbari vetans. Quisnam igitur sit in homine naturalis ordo, quaerendum est . . . . Proinde, sicut anima corpori, ita ipsius animae ratio caeteris eius partibus, quas habent et bestiae, naturae lege praeponitur: inque ipsa ratione, quae partim contemplativa est, partim activa, procul dubio contemplatio praecellit', *Contra Faustum*, 22, 27; *PL* 42, 418.

[13] 'Ut igitur breviter aeternae legis notionem, quae impressa nobis est, quantum valeo verbis explicem, ea est qua iustum est ut omnia sint ordinatissima', *De lib. arb.*, 1, 6; *PL* 32, 1229.

[14] 'Pax omnium rerum tranquillitas ordinis. Ordo est parium dispariumque rerum sua cuique loca tribuens dispositio', *De civ. Dei*, XIX, 13, 1; *PL* 41, 640.

[15] 'Sicut enim bona sunt omnia quae creavit Deus, ab ipsa rationali creatura usque ad infimum corpus: ita bene agit in his anima rationalis, si ordinem servet, et distinguendo, eligendo, pendendo subdat minora maioribus, corporalia spiritualibus, inferiora superioribus, temporalia sempiternis; ne superiorum neglectu et appetitu inferiorum (quoniam hinc et ipsa fit deterior) et se et corpus suum mittat in peius, sed potius ordinata caritate se et corpus suum convertat in melius', *Epist.* CXL, 2, 4; *PL* 33, 540.

[16] 'Hisce igitur motibus animae cum ratio dominatur, ordinatus homo dicendus est. Non enim ordo rectus, aut ordo appellandus est omnino, ubi deterioribus meliora subiiciuntur', *De lib. arb.*, 1, 8, 18; *PL* 32, 1231.

[17] Gilson, op. cit., p. 134.

If we were stones, waves, wind or flame, or anything of that kind, lacking sense and life, we would still show something like a desire for our own place and order. For the specific gravity of a body is, in a manner, its love, whether a body tends downwards by reason of its heaviness or strives upwards because of its lightness. A material body is borne along by its weight in a particular direction, as a soul is by its love.[18]

The ordering brought about by love is, for Augustine, spelt out in the two commands of love of God and love of neighbour.[19] And the internal order required of the good loving man can be well expressed in the four controlling virtues of prudence, justice, temperance, and fortitude, which Ambrose and Augustine adopted from Stoicism. Temperance 'bridles the lusts of the flesh to prevent their gaining the consent of the mind'. Prudence helps us avoid mistakes in our choices between good and evil. 'The function of justice is to assign to each his due; and hence there is established in man himself a certain just order of nature, by which the soul is subordinated to God, and the body to the soul, and thus both body and soul are subordinated to God'. Fortitude bears all ills with patient endurance.[20] In a splendid and almost mystical meditation on the divine ordering of all things Augustine observes that God 'created all things in supreme wisdom and ordered them in perfect justice'.[21] And so pervasive is this concept of *ordo* in the thought of Augustine that Roland-Gosselin could conclude, 'the idea of order, law, truth, justice, which is nothing but the idea of reason, is very dear to Saint Augustine. It means that any disorder, whether physical, rational, or moral, is and can only be a partial disorder which is always compensated in such a way that the universal order is never compromised or even disturbed . . . . It is a Stoic concept, but purified of all pantheism and fatalism'.[22] Thus, for man, the

[18] *The City of God*, 11, 28 (trans. Bettenson, pp. 462–3); *PL* 41, 341–2. Cf. *Conf.*, XIII, 9, 10 (*PL* 32, 849): 'pondus meum amor meus; eo feror quocumque feror.'

[19] *De civ. dei*, XIX, 14; *PL* 41, 642–3.

[20] Ibid.; *PL* 41, 628–9.

[21] 'Deus ergo naturarum omnium sapientissimus conditor et iustissimus ordinator', ibid., cap. 13; *PL* 41, 641. Thus Gilson can explain that, for Augustine in considering evil actions, 'the malice of the act is never due to the goodness of its object but to the perversion of our love for this good. In such cases, our error is not in loving what is good, but in violating order by not preferring what is better', op. cit., p. 136.

[22] B. Roland-Gosselin (ed.)., *Œuvres de s. Augustin*, i (Paris, 1949), p. 524. Cf. pp. 525–6.

moral challenge is to locate one's self and all one's actions reasonably, harmoniously, and justly in one's proper place in the divine scheme of things.

To this Christian reflection on the best of pagan ethics, notably in Stoicism, was added its later absorption of key ideas from Roman law, and particularly of the *ius naturale*, or 'the just by nature' of the Roman jurists, which as the expression of universal reason was considered to be the basis of the *ius gentium*, the law of peoples, constructed by Rome as an instrument of its colonial and imperial government.[23] Thus, the seventh-century archbishop of Seville, the learned Isidore, whose famous and fanciful work on *Etymology* had an intriguing effect on the Scholastic age, explained that, unlike human positive legislation, the *ius naturale* is the law observed everywhere by the prompting of nature, such as that ordaining the marriage of man and woman, the procreation and rearing of children, common ownership and freedom, self-defence, and the like.[24] The Church's canonists developed and perpetuated the idea of natural law as of divine origin and as the basis for all justice, described by Rufinus as 'the divine power which nature implants in man, impelling him to do good and avoid evil'.[25]

Aquinas and 'the Law of Nature'

It was in the Dominican friar, the Italian Thomas of Aquino, that in the thirteenth century moral theology was to find its first fully and systematically articulated expression of natural law theory. It is this which has remained the classical exposition embraced by moral

---

[23] Cf. B. F. Brown, 'Natural Law', *NCE*, x, 252. On the Latin development of *ius naturale*, *ius gentium*, and *lex naturalis*, cf. J.-M. Aubert *Le Droit romain dans l'œuvre de saint Thomas* (Paris, 1955), pp. 91–105; O. Lottin, *Principes de morale*, t. ii (Louvain, 1947), pp. 33–6. (For a fuller treatment by Lottin, cf. his *Le Droit naturel chez s. Thomas et ses prédécesseurs* (Bruges, 1931).) Aquinas views *ius naturale* as underlying *ius gentium*, in contrast with *ius civile*, *STh* 1a 2ae, q. 95, a. 4 et ad 1.

[24] 'Jus, aut naturale est, aut civile, aut gentium. Jus naturale est commune omnium nationum, et quod ubique instinctu naturae, non constitutione aliqua habeatur, ut: viri et feminae coniunctio, liberorum susceptio et educatio, communis omnium possessio, et omnium una libertas, acquisitio eorum quae caelo, terra marique capiuntur. Item deposita rei vel commodatae restitutio, violentiae per vim repulsio. Nam hoc, aut si quid simile est, nunquam iniustum, sed naturale, aequumque habeatur', *Etymologiae*, Lib. 5, cap. 4 (*PL* 82, 199).

[25] Quoted *NCE*, ibid. Rufinus was the first systematic commentator on the *Decree* of Gratian.

theology and the Church since his day, and which has also had the deleterious effect of portraying Aquinas as pre-eminently, even exclusively, a moral philosopher to the loss of his far more important contributions as a moral theologian.[26] In the *Summa* of theology, that great Gothic cathedral of human thought which Aquinas explained in his introduction was intended for beginners in theology, he shows how in man's return to the God who is his origin and his destiny he is aided by God's instructing him by law and helping him by grace.[27] The essence of law is to be a rational rule and measure of actions, directing them in an orderly manner to their purpose or end; and this enables Aquinas to offer his famous definition of any law as an order, or arrangement, of reason for the common good.[28] Within this generic concept and definition of law Aquinas's great philosophical advance was to distinguish the eternal law clearly from what Augustine had called its 'impression' on us, and to explore that impression as the raw material in man's constitution for the moral 'law of nature'. All creatures have 'impressed' in their very being inherent tendencies which reflect the ordering and orientation which God their creator wishes for them. Man as a rational being sharing in God's providential activity is aware of what God has impressed in his nature and he is capable of freely accepting and embracing the order of his being and his place in the divine scheme of things. This knowing and free acceptance of his nature as created and destined by God is man's observance of the law of his nature, or of the 'natural law'.[29]

---

[26] Cf. Mahoney, *Seeking the Spirit* (London, 1981), pp. 114–15. On the central role in Aquinas' moral theology of the Spirit and of the wisdom (not prudence) which the Spirit imparts, cf. ibid. On Aquinas's teaching on natural law it is useful to bear in mind the observation of Thomas Gilby, OP, in Aquinas' *Summa Theologiae*, vol. xxviii (London, 1966), p. 170, that 'the terms "*jus*" and "*lex*" are more or less interchangeable in the *Summa*'.

[27] *STh* 1a 2ae, q. 90, proem.

[28] 'Et sic ex quatuor praedictis potest colligi definitio legis, quae nihil est aliud quam quaedam rationis ordinatio ad bonum commune, ab eo qui curam communitatis habet, promulgata', ibid., q. 90, art. 4.

[29] 'Unde cum omnia quae divinae providentiae subduntur a lege aeterna regulentur et mensurentur, ut ex dictis patet, manifestum est quod omnia participant aliqualiter legem aeternam, inquantum scilicet ex impressione eius habent inclinationes in proprios actus et fines. Inter caetera autem rationalis creatura excellentiori quodam modo divinae providentiae subjacet, inquantum et ipsa fit providentiae particeps, sibi ipsi et aliis providens. Unde et in ipsa participatur ratio aeterna per quam habet naturalem inclinationem ad debitum actum et finem, et talis participatio legis aeternae in rationali creatura "lex naturalis" dicitur', ibid., q. 91,

In a major passage Aquinas explores and applies the implications for man of the nature God has given him. The first thing which strikes us about anything is that it is a thing, a being. And the first thing which occurs to our minds as obvious is the principle that we cannot assert that something is a being and at the same time deny it. There is a similar first principle in the area of action, based now not on being and not-being but on good and not-good. Since there is always a purpose to what we do, the first thing we always look for is whether an action we contemplate fits in with our basic human desires, that is, whether or not it is good. In other words, the first thing which occurs to our minds as obvious is the principle that what is good should be brought about and what is evil, or not-good, should be avoided.

We naturally see as good whatever we are naturally inclined to, and the precepts of natural law express in terms of our various inclinations this first moral principle to pursue good and avoid evil.

There is therefore an order of precepts of natural law corresponding to the order of natural inclinations. First, there is an inclination in man towards the good corresponding to what he has in common with all individual beings, the desire to continue in existence in accordance with their nature. In accordance with this inclination those matters which conserve man's life or are contrary to it are governed by natural law. Secondly, there is in man an inclination to some more specific objects in accordance with the nature which he has in common with the other animals. According to this, those matters are said to be of natural law 'which nature has taught all animals', such as the union of male and female, the bringing up of children, and the like. Thirdly, there is in man an inclination to good according to the nature of reason which is peculiar to him. He has a natural inclination to know the truth about God, and to live in society. Accordingly those matters which concern this inclination are matter for natural law, such as that a man avoid ignorance, that he not offend others with whom he should have converse, and other matters relating to this.[30]

---

art. 2. That Aquinas was aware of Augustine's view that the eternal law is 'impressed' on us is evident from ibid., q. 93, art. 2, *sed contra*, 'Augustinus dicit quod aeternae legis notio nobis impressa est'. For the controlling text of Augustine, cf. *supra*, n. 13. The influence of Augustine's insistence on *ordo* is also pervasive in Aquinas's entire treatment of law, with notable support from Aristotle. 'Rationis enim est ordinare ad finem, qui est primum principium in agendis secundum Philosophum', ibid., q. 90, art. 1.

[30] Ibid., q. 94, art. 2, discussing whether natural law contains only one precept or a multiplicity.

Aquinas, then, takes it as axiomatic that we should do what is good and not do what is bad, and he defines good in terms of those fundamental satisfactions to which every human being is essentially and naturally orientated. The general conclusions which he derives from his way of thinking in the light of each fundamental tendency, whether it be towards individual survival, or survival of the species, or in pursuit of truth and of social harmony, then have to be applied in increasing detail, and so he can build up a whole logical scheme of moral reasoning as these tendencies are considered and their realization explored in more and more specific instances. In this way, he points out, one can in theory descend by a series of logical steps from the most general precepts of the law of man's nature to the most particular applications, and the more circumstantial one's conclusions become, the less certain and predictable they are.

In speculative matters [for example, geometry] there is for everyone the same truth in principles as there is in conclusions, although the truth is not known by everyone in the conclusions but only in the principles which are called [by Boethius] 'the general concepts'. In matters of action, however, there is not the same truth or practical rightness for everyone with regard to particulars as there is with regard to what is general . . . .[31]

On the whole it has been the fate of Aquinas's natural law teaching in moral theology that the logical appeal and coherence of his system has been stressed, while the provisionality and contingency of conclusions as they come closer to individual situations, features which he himself carefully built into his theory, have been either neglected or ignored.

In the centuries following Aquinas his teaching on natural law was to become an authoritative and central feature of moral theology and the outstanding example of its respect for, and expectations from, the power of human reasoning in the moral sphere. One line of divergence in the period immediately after him, through nominalism and Occamism and their stress on the absolute power and freedom of God, as we shall have occasion to consider later, was to introduce a note of provisionality to the point of scepticism and moral agnosticism into the whole system.[32] Another line of development, with which we are not concerned in this study,

---

[31] Ibid., q. 94, art. 4.   [32] Cf. *infra*, p. 183.

was pursued through the works of Grotius and Pufendorf, and arose from exploring the implications for natural law not so much of God's absolute power but of the speculative possibility of there not being a God. It was this line of thought which was to result in what Oskar Köhler describes as 'the detheologization of natural law' to become 'at once the foundation of the tolerant state as well as its becoming an absolute concept as the *primum principium* of political and social life'.[33] The mainstream of Thomistic natural law theory, however, is to be found proceeding powerfully through the great Spanish Dominican and Jesuit scholars of the fifteenth and sixteenth centuries—Vitoria, Suarez, and Vasquez—as well as through the Italian Bellarmine, particularly with the universal adoption in the Universities of the *Summa Theologiae* of Aquinas as a universal textbook and a text to be explained, expanded, and applied by the leading theologians of the Church to contemporary issues.

Thus developed, the doctrine of natural law became an increasingly useful resource in official Church teaching on moral matters. The 1864 *Syllabus* in which Pope Pius IX collected and classified eighty of the errors which he had so far had occasion to condemn (and in which he was aided by the future Pope Leo XIII) asserted the need for civil law to conform to the law of nature, and vindicated the indissolubility of marriage as based on natural law.[34] He had also, as early as the first encyclical letter of his pontificate in 1846, made the first papal reference to Communism in describing it as 'a doctrine particularly at variance with natural law',[35] a view on which Pius XI was to elaborate in 1937.[36] But it was with the pontificate of Pope Leo XIII that the doctrine of natural law was to flourish, partly as the result of another Scholastic and Thomistic revival which he strongly and authoritatively encouraged, and partly in its being considered a particularly apt instrument in the development of the Church's social and political teaching in a world which might listen to reason even if it would not heed the revealed word of God. So, against full-blooded socialism, the right of property and ownership was based on human nature and on 'the most holy law of nature'.[37] Duelling was strictly forbidden by

---

[33] In Jedin and Dolan, op. cit., vol. vi, p. 346.
[34] DS 2956; 2967. On the role of the future Leo XIII, cf. DS 2901, proem.
[35] DS 2786.
[36] DS 3772.
[37] DS 3266.

natural law, and the secrecy and disruptive potential of freemasonry were things which nature would not permit.[38] Nature was the basis of the social needs of man,[39] as also of clarifying the relationships between Church and State.[40] The superiority of divine and natural law was asserted over the claims of human legislation, 'for it is just as wrong to command as it is to do whatever violates the law of nature or the will of God'.[41] And the Pope who in 1879 was putting forward the 'golden wisdom' of Thomas Aquinas as the basis of neo-scholasticism was nine years later to deliver a teaching on the eternal law and on natural law which was clearly based on the doctrine of Aquinas:

To see why man needs a law we should consider his power of choice and the need for our wills not to be at odds with right reasoning. The natural law is written and engraved in the minds of individuals because it is human reasoning itself ordering us to act rightly and forbidding us to sin. But that prescription of human reason can have the force of law only if it is the voice and interpreter of a higher reason to which our mind and freedom should be subject. So the law of nature is the eternal law, to be found in rational beings and inclining them to their due act and end, and that in turn is the eternal reason of God the creator who governs the whole universe.[42]

The application of natural law thinking by Leo XIII in his teaching on working class conditions and the rights of workers was to be echoed in later social encyclicals of further Popes;[43] and at the outbreak of the Second World War Pope Pius XII devoted the first encyclical of his pontificate to the subject of natural law, expressing the conviction that the ills of modern society arose from the rejection, in private and public life, and in international relations, of a universal norm of morality, the natural law itself.[44]

This natural law has for its foundation God the all-powerful creator and father of all, the supreme and most perfect lawmaker, and the most wise and just judge of human behaviour. When the eternal Deity is rejected, then the principle of all morality collapses, and silence or feebleness fall upon the voice of nature which teaches the unlearned and even the primitive what is right and wrong, permitted or not permitted, and warns them that some day they will give account before the Supreme Judge of what they have done well and done badly.[45]

[38] *DS* 3272; 3156.   [39] *DS* 3165.   [40] *DS* 3172.
[41] *DS* 3152. Cf. 3132.   [42] *DS* 3247–51. On Aquinas, *DS* 3140.
[43] Cf. *DS* 3267–71, 3956, 3970.   [44] *DS* 3780.   [45] *DS* 3781.

Pope Pius XII and his successors were to continue to see 'right reason' and the moral precepts generated by human nature as a major resource for all men in every area of behaviour, including, of course, the ethics of human reproduction. Pius XII had condemned contraception as contrary to natural law, a teaching repeated by Paul VI in *Humanae Vitae* and renewed by Pope John Paul II in 1981, particularly in the latter's reference to the moral order as revealing and setting forth the plan of God the Creator as a response to 'the deepest demands of the human being created by God'.[46] Pius XII in particular deployed natural law argumentation also to condemn sterilization, as Pius XI had done,[47] and artificial insemination, as Leo XIII had done as early as 1897,[48] as well as the further medical advances of *in vitro* fertilization.[49]

The whole development of Catholic natural law theory has not gone unchallenged, especially in recent years, and this particular application of the persistent confidence of the Church's moral tradition in the power of human reasoning to identify moral claims through a consideration of man's nature raises a host of questions relating not just to the application of this law of nature in particular areas of human behaviour, but also to the more fundamental issues of the presuppositions and methodology of natural law theory in general. Some of these issues will fall to be considered later in this work, but for the present we may turn to some connected questions which have been of equally fundamental importance in the making of moral theology, and in particular to the subject of the supernatural.

The Storm over the Supernatural: Jansenism

Granted that through the use of 'right reason' and recourse to the moral law of man's nature one can come to a correct appreciation of the morality or immorality of different human actions, does it follow that one who thus acts in accordance with reason and natural law will thereby be pleasing to God? The answer to this apparently simple question was for centuries to exercise and often to perplex theologians, and to engage moral theology, and the

---

[46] DS 2715, 2758, 2795, 2791. Pope Paul VI, *Humanae Vitae*, no. 11. Pope John Paul II, *Familiaris Consortio*, no. 34 (cf. nos. 29, 33).
[47] DS 3763.
[48] DS 3323.
[49] DS 3323, proem.

Church, in probably the greatest running battle in the history of theology—the long crisis of Jansenism.

What had enabled Aquinas to exploit the statement of Augustine that God's eternal law is 'impressed' on his creatures, and to explore the constitution and the moral implications of that impression on man, was his full-blooded acceptance of Aristotelian metaphysics. Profoundly imbued and stimulated by the thirteenth century's discovery of the full works of Aristotle, Thomas brought to his examination of human nature a speculative, metaphysical, and not quite unhistorical method of analysis, quite diverse from the Neoplatonist and intensely experiential approach of Augustine. As Gilson explains of Augustine,

> His doctrine is the metaphysics of his own conversion and remains pre-eminently the metaphysics of conversion . . . . He had had actual experience of the radical insufficiency of nature and this is the reason for his constant concern to keep within their actual limits the capacity of essences and the efficacy of their operations . . . [P]articularly attentive to the actual insufficiency of nature to satisfy the desire for things divine which God has placed within it, . . . he underscores its congenital and acquired deficiencies.[50]

Thus it is that 'whereas the nature probed by St Thomas Aquinas is a metaphysically indestructible essence whose intrinsic necessity resists even the corruption of original sin and surrenders to it only the graces removed by it and the powers weakened or vitiated by it, Augustine uses the word "nature" to describe the actual state caused by sin and what there is left in that state to justify man's hope of finding a way out of it.'[51]

Even Augustine, however, could not find himself totally negative in his estimation of man's nature as it existed after Adam's sin of pride and the fall of humankind. He acknowledges that although man's condition was now justifiably wretched, yet God in his goodness 'has filled even this misery with innumerable blessings', including the fact that 'there is still the spark, as it were, of that reason in virtue of which he was made in the image of God: that spark has not been utterly put out'.[52] And in his great survey of

---

[50] Gilson, op. cit., p. 240.

[51] Ibid., p. 239.

[52] 'non in eo tamen penitus exstincta est quaedam velut scintilla rationis, in qua factus est ad imaginem Dei', *De civ. Dei*, XXII, 24 (trans. Bettenson, p. 1071); *PL* 41, 789. Cf., ibid., XIX, 12 (*PL* 41, 639): 'Nullum quippe vitium ita contra naturam est, ut naturae deleat etiam extrema vestiga.'

human history he was to concede that one reason for the past endurance and extent of the Roman Empire was the presence and influence of men of good moral character.[53] Individuals such as Cato were 'good men in their way', and if not saints they were at least 'less depraved' then others.[54] Nevertheless, he points out, 'when such men do anything good, their sole motive is the hope of receiving glory from their fellow men. . . . By such immaculate conduct they laboured towards honours, power and glory, by what they took to be the true way'. And—like the Pharisees—they received their reward in full, from men.[55] 'These were the two motives which took the Romans to their wonderful achievements: liberty, and the passion for the praise of men'.[56] The Stoics had been correct in showing how the Epicureans had vitiated all seemingly moral behaviour by making the pursuit of pleasure the dominant motive and reward; and the same, although perhaps to a lesser degree, must apply to the motive and reward of human glory, 'which may not be a female voluptuary, but is puffed up with empty conceit'.[57]

On one occasion Augustine seems to entertain a less disparaging judgement on the glory that was Rome when he observes that, although he has sufficiently explained why God should have assisted the Romans 'who are good according to the standards of the earthly city' to attain the glory of their Empire, 'it may be that there is another more hidden cause on account of the diverse merits of mankind, which are better known to God than to us'.[58] But his almost invariable way of accounting for the Roman virtues is to

[53] In the preface to Book five of the *City of God* Augustine posed the question 'videamus qua causa Deus, qui potest et illa bona dare, quae habere possunt etiam non boni, ac per hoc etiam non felices, Romanum imperium tam magnum tamque diuturnum esse voluerit', *PL* 41, 141. This will remain his position, that the Romans were 'non boni'.

[54] Bettenson, pp. 201–2; 'per quosdam paucos, qui pro suo modo boni erant', 'non quidem iam sancti, sed minus turpes sunt', *PL* 41, 152–3.

[55] Chap. 15; Bettenson, pp. 204–5; *PL* 41, 160, 'De talibus enim, qui propter hoc boni aliquid facere videntur, ut glorificentur ab hominibus, etiam Dominus ait, *Amen dico vobis, perceperunt mercedem suam* (Matt. 6; 2).'

[56] Chap. 18; Bettenson, p. 208; *PL* 41, 162, 'Haec sunt duo illa, libertas et cupiditas laudis, quae ad facta compulere miranda Romanos.'

[57] Chap. 20; Bettenson, pp. 214–15; *PL* 41, 167, 'Licet enim ista gloria delicata mulier non sit, inflata tamen est, et multum inanitatis habet.'

[58] Chap. 19; Bettenson, p. 213; *PL* 41, 'Romanos secundum quamdam formam terrenae civitatis bonos . . .; potest tamen et alia causa esse latentior, propter diversa merita generis humani, Deo magis nota quam nobis.'

distinguish sharply between true or genuine virtue and its counter-feits. 'It is the conviction of all those who are truly religious, that no one can have true virtue without true piety, that is, without the true worship of the true God; and that the virtue which is employed in the service of human glory is not true virtue.'[59] His standard of true virtue is exacting. 'Virtue is truly virtue when it refers all the good things of which it makes good use, all its achievements in making good use of good things and evil things, and when it refers itself also, to that end where our peace shall be so perfect and so great as to admit of neither improvement nor increase.'[60] Without such overall 'ordering' of one's activities explicitly towards the Christian God all human enterprises lose the name of virtue. 'In serving God the soul rightly commands the body, and in the soul itself the reason which is subject to its Lord God rightly commands the lusts and the other perverted elements. That being so, when a man does not serve God, what amount of justice are we suppose to exist in his being?'[61]

Appearances, then, can be deceptive. 'Not infrequently, to be sure, the obvious vices are overcome by vices so masked that they are reputed virtues; and the king of these is pride, an exalted self-satisfaction which brings a disastrous fall.'[62] This mask of human pride and self-satisfaction also conceals an interior emptiness in such men, an absence of God at work.

Thus the virtues which the mind imagines it possesses, by means of which it rules the body and the vicious elements, are themselves vices rather than virtues, if the mind does not bring them into relation with God in order to achieve anything whatsoever and to maintain that achievement. For although the virtues are reckoned by some people to be genuine and

---

[59] Ibid: 'dum illud constet inter omnes veraciter pios, neminem sine vera pietate, id est, veri Dei vero cultu, veram posse habere virtutem.'

[60] Book XIX, chap. 10; Bettenson, p. 865; *PL* 41, 636, 'Sed tunc est vera virtus, quando et omnia bona quibus bene utitur, et quidquid in bono usu bonorum et malorum facit, et se ipsam ad eum finem refert, ubi nobis talis et tanta pax erit, qua melior et major esse non possit.'

[61] Ibid., chap. 21; Bettenson, p. 883; *PL* 41, 649, 'Serviens autem Deo animus, recte imperat corpori, inque ipso animo ratio Domino Deo subdita, recte imperat libidini vitiisque caeteris. Quapropter ubi homo Deo non servit, quid in eo putandum est esse justitiae; quandoquidem Deo non serviens, nullo modo potest juste animus corpori, aut humana ratio vitiis imperare?'

[62] Book XXI, chap. 16 (Bettenson, p. 994); *PL* 41, 730, 'Nonnumquam sane apertissima vitia aliis vitiis vincuntur occultis, quae putantur esse virtutes, in quibus regnat superbia et quaedam sibi placendi altitudo ruinosa.'

honourable when they are related only to themselves and are sought for no other end, even then they are puffed up and proud, and so to be accounted vices rather than virtues. For just as it is not something derived from the physical body itself that gives life to that body, but something above it, so it is not something that comes from man, but something above man, that makes his life blessed.[63]

On these and similar passages in Augustine two observations may be made. The first is that he ascribes a worthlessness to what is considered human virtue either because it is a sham, bleeding internally from self-satisfaction, or more systematically because he has so defined virtue as to exclude what other men would call virtue. The virtues of the philosophers, 'the morality of the earth-born society', he would call good, but 'a good of little importance', precisely and simply because 'a brief and true definition of virtue is "rightly ordered love" '. Herein lies the significance of the request in the *Canticle* of the Bride of Christ, the City of God, to 'set love in order in me'. And this is for Augustine the key to all true and genuine morality. 'This is true of everything created; though it is good, it can be loved in the right way or the wrong way—in the right way, that is, when the proper order is kept, in the wrong way when that order is upset.'[64] If, then, due and proper love of God does not permeate the whole of man's behaviour and the moral virtues, as it should, why bother to consider them important, or call them virtues?

If it were simply a matter of choosing how virtue is to be defined,

---

[63] Book XIX, chap. 26 (Bettenson, p. 891); *PL* 41, 656, 'Nam qualis corporis atque vitiorum potest esse mens domina, veri Dei nescia, nec eius imperio subiugata, sed vitiosissimis daemonibus corrumpentibus prostituta? Proinde virtutes, quas sibi habere videtur, per quas imperat corpori et vitiis ad quodlibet adipiscendum vel tenendum, nisi ad Deum retulerit, etiam ipsae vitia sunt potius quam virtutes. Nam licet a quibusdam tunc verae et honestae putentur esse virtutes, cum ad se ipsas referuntur, nec propter aliud expetuntur; etiam tunc inflatae ac superbae sunt: et ideo non virtutes, sed vitia iudicanda sunt. Sicut enim non est a carne, sed super carnem, quod carnem facit vivere: sic non est ab homine, sed super hominem, quod hominem facit beate vivere.'

[64] Book XV, chap. 22 (Bettenson, p. 636); *PL* 41, 467, acknowledges that female beauty is a good which is a gift of God, 'sed propterea id largitur etiam malis, ne magnum bonum videatur bonis'. In succumbing to it (Gen. 6: 2), the sons of God chose an 'infimum bonum'; 'Ita se habet omnis creatura. Cum enim bona sit, et bene potest amari, et male: bene, scilicet ordine custodito; male, ordine perturbato . . . . Unde mihi videtur, quod definitio brevis et vera virtutis, Ordo est amoris; propter quod in sancto Cantico canticorum cantat sponsa Christi, civitas Dei, *Ordinate in me charitatem (Cantic.* II, 4).'

little would appear to follow from Augustine's refusal to ascribe the term to non-Christian conduct. But there is a more important observation to be made of his theological attitude and his unwillingness to concede any ultimately real importance to human achievement. 'Those who are endowed with true piety and who lead a good life . . . attribute to the grace of God whatever virtues they may be able to display in this present life, because God has given those virtues to them in response to their wish, their faith, and their petition.'[65] *Da quod iubes, et iube quod vis*! What makes all the difference for Augustine between virtue and vice, as we have seen above, is that 'just as it is not something derived from the physical body itself that gives life to that body, but something above it, so it is not something that comes from man, but *something above man*, that makes his life blessed'.[66] In this appeal to 'something above man' we can discern an intimation of the whole developing theology not of nature but of supernature, which was to result, in the Scholastic age and beyond, in a vast superstructure of 'created grace' apparently overlaid on the natural network of human living and human relationships. It was not enough to love God and one's neighbour; it had to be done with 'supernatural' love. Since the Fall of man and the ruination of his nature, 'none of the perfections God maintains therein has now the slightest value as regards salvation. The rare and precarious virtues which remain can regain their initial supernatural value only if God grants it to them by means of a special assistance adapted to the needs of fallen nature, namely by grace.'[67]

This Augustinian appeal to the need for a supernatural resource in order to engage in truly virtuous behaviour was later to be found in Aquinas transposed into an Aristotelian key, in his teaching on charity as the 'form' of the moral virtues.[68] J. P. Kenny observes of the term 'supernatural' that in its Neoplatonist origin and its introduction into Western thought in the ninth century through

---

[65] Book V, chap. 19 (Bettenson, pp. 213–4); *PL* 41, 166, 'Illi autem qui vera pietate praediti bene vivunt, . . . virtutes suas, quantascumque in hac vita possunt habere, non tribuunt nisi gratiae Dei, quod eas volentibus, credentibus, petentibus dederit.'

[66] *Supra*, n. 63.

[67] Gilson, p. 152.

[68] Cf. the influential study which helped to rehabilitate the moral *theology* of Aquinas; G. Gilleman, *The Primacy of Charity in Moral Theology* (London, 1960). On 'caritas forma virtutum', cf *STh* 2a 2ae, q. 23, a. 8.

translations of the Pseudo-Dionysius it was used to refer to a superior being, and that its full possibilities for theology were to be developed only in the thirteenth century by Aquinas, in his applying the term not just to superior beings but to effects brought about in natural beings which were well beyond their ordinary and native capacities. And this Aquinas was the more able to do by his developing from Aristotle, and for the first time in theology, a firm, stable understanding of what is to be understood by natures and their essential properties.[69] Once that basic substratum was clearly identified, the universe of the supernatural could be confidently explored. And one consequence of this for moral theology was to lay all the stress on supernatural moral activity as alone sufficient for salvation, to the detriment of merely human, natural, and terrestrial moral behaviour. Morality became a two-tier activity in requiring supernatural motivation and even 'infused' moral virtues which alone could count with God.[70] The Christian sat upstairs on the Clapham omnibus.

The Scholastic elaboration of the supernatural in the light of man's natural resources, particularly when contrasted with the Augustinian view of the ruinous state of human nature after the Fall, led to the greatest storm ever to rock moral theology, that to which the name Jansenism is globally applied. At its centre was the posthumous work of Jansen to which we have already referred, the massive intellectual construction of a lifetime which has been given the tragic epitaph by de Lubac of being based on a fatal misunderstanding of one distinction in Augustine's teaching on grace.[71] The storm clouds had been gathering, however, long

---

[69] J. P. Kenny, 'Supernatural' *NCE* 13, p. 812. Cf. H. de Lubac, *Surnaturel* (Paris, 1946), p. 327.

[70] Cf. Aquinas, *STh* 1a 2ae, q. 63, a. 3 on infused moral virtues; a. 4, on how they differ from acquired moral virtues. 'Patet igitur ex dictis quod solae virtutes infusae sunt perfectae, et simpliciter dicendae virtutes, quia bene ordinant hominem ad finem ultimum simpliciter. Aliae virtutes, scilicet acquisitae, sunt secundum quid virtutes, non autem simpliciter. Ordinant hominem bene respectu finis ultimi in aliquo genere, non autem respectu finis ultimi simpliciter. Unde, super illud, *Omne quod non est ex fide, peccatum est* [Rom. 14: 23], dicit Glossa Augustini, *Ubi deest agnitio veritatis, falsa est virtus etiam in optimis moribus*', ibid., q. 65, art. 2. The thought is clearly Augustinian, although the quotation is not, in fact, from Augustine but from his friend and defender, Prosper of Aquitaine, *Sent.* 106; *PL* 51, 441. (Cf. *Summa Theologiae*, vol. xxiii, ed. W. D. Hughes, OP (London, 1969), p. 186.)

[71] H. de Lubac, *Augustinisme et théologie moderne* (Aubier, 1965), p. 59. Cf. *supra*, pp. 52–3.

before the death of Jansen in 1638, in the sixteenth and seventeenth-century controversies over the relationship between man's free act of his will and God's action on him through grace—the famous *De Auxiliis* controversy between Dominican and Jesuit theologians on the Augustinian 'helps' given by God to man to enable him to act well. The Spanish Dominican theologian, Dominic Bañez, propounded the theory which he claimed to be that of Aquinas, that God moves, or almost prods, man into successful action by his grace—the theory of 'physical pre-motion'. But the Spanish Jesuit, Francis Molina, judging such a theory as destructive of human freedom in its attempt to secure divine initiative, depicted God rather as foreseeing the action which man would freely choose to do and in the light of that knowledge giving man the grace to do it. Thus was born the theory of 'middle knowledge', or God's *scientia media*, by which he knows not only what actually is the case and what will be the case, but also what would be the case; that is, not only actuals and futures but also 'futuribles'. This difference in ways of analysing the mechanics of God's actions aroused a quite astonishing controversy and enduring animosity, or *odium theologicum*, between the sons of St Dominic and the sons of St Ignatius and their students and sympathizers, and led to the dispute eventually being called to Rome for papal arbitration, the only official outcome being that neither side was condemned but that in 1611 silence was authoritatively imposed on all the protagonists.[72]

Such silence was too much to hope for, of course, and the faculty of the University of Louvain, strongly Augustinian and anti-Jesuit, continued to combat Molinism, the aim which motivated the young Cornelius Jansen to begin his monumental study of Augustine. Jansen's predecessor as professor of theology at Louvain, Baius, whom we have already met contending that God does sometimes ask the impossible of man, had already run into trouble with other European universities for his views on grace and on human nature, and Rome was eventually drawn to condemn a series of propositions alleged to be found in his various works, including a statement that 'all the deeds of unbelievers are sins, and the virtues of the

---

[72] For a typically irrepressible and enjoyable account of the controversy, cf. James Brodrick, SJ, *The Life and Work of Blessed Robert Bellarmine*, 1542–1621 (London, 1928), vol. i, pp. 1–67. Cf. also *DS* 1997, proem.

philosophers are vices'.[73] Behind this and other assertions of du Bay one can discern a view on the 'basic depravity of man's fallen nature and his impotence of himself to will anything but sin'.[74] And it was this theological anthropology which Jansen was to buttress and build into a complete system through his quarryings in Augustine. The disedifying spectacle of the Louvain theologians condemning the Jesuits as Pelagians for vaunting man's moral freedom, and being in turn condemned of Calvinism, with attempts to prevent Jansen's work being published, culminated in 1653 in papal condemnation of five propositions ascribed to Jansen—an action which only exacerbated the hostilities by adding to controversy over what Augustine had meant further dispute over what Jansen himself had meant.[75]

[73] 'Omnia opera infidelium sunt peccata, et philosophorum virtutes sunt vitia', *DS* 1925. On Baius, cf. *supra*, p. 52.

[74] Palmer, op. cit., p. 262.

[75] The famous 'Five Propositions', *DS* 2001–5, concluding with the comprehensive statement (*DS* 2007) 'by this declaration and definition on the five aforesaid propositions we do not intend in any way to approve other opinions contained in the work referred to of Cornelius Jansen'. Jansenist reception of this papal bull was devious, Antoine Arnaud introducing his celebrated distinction between the question of law (*de jure* the propositions were heretical) and the question of fact (*de facto* they were not what Jansen meant). The Sorbonne expelled Arnaud for propounding this subtlety, which may be thought typical of the worst type of 'Jesuitical' casuistry which Arnaud found so repulsive, and at the request of the French bishops Pope Alexander VII issued in 1656 another bull which aimed to remove any further doubt. 'We declare and define that those five propositions were excerpted from the book *Augustinus* of Cornelius Jansen, bishop of Ypres, and were condemned in the sense intended by Cornelius Jansen, and we again condemn them as such . . .'. (*DS* 2012. For the historical details, cf. *DS* 2001, proem; 2010, proem.) Ten years later, Louis XIV obtained from the Pope a formula of submission to be accepted within three months by all, accepting the papal condemnations and rejecting and condemning 'sincero animo' 'the five propositions excerpted from the book *Augustinus* of Cornelius Jansen and in the sense intended by the author'. (*DS* 2020. Cf. proem.) Jansenist opposition survived, however, and public debate on a 'case of conscience' on whether absolution could be given to anyone professing only external submission and not internal assent to the formula of submission (*DS* 2390) led to yet a further authoritative clarification from Rome in the bull of 1705 entitled 'The Vineyard of the Lord of Hosts'. 'To prevent any occasion of error in future, and so that all the sons of the Catholic Church may learn to listen to the Church, not simply in silence (for the wicked also are silent in darkness, 1 Kgs. 2: 9 [Vulg.]), but also submitting interiorly (*interius obsequendo*), as is the true obedience of an orthodox person; We decree, declare, lay down and ordain by Apostolic authority in this Constitution which will be forever in force that: the obedience owed to the previous Apostolic Constitutions is in no way satisfied by that submissive silence (*obsequioso illo silentio*); but that all the faithful ought to reject and condemn as heretical, not only with their lips but also in their hearts, the meaning condemned in

Jansenism, however, was much more than an academic theo-logical quarrel. As de Lubac observes, it refers also to 'the vast religious and moral movement to which his name is attached'.[76] For the quality of religion in early seventeenth-century France was profoundly depressing. Jedin paints a sombre picture of a clergy almost totally uneducated, both in general and professionally, and of decadence in religious orders, which all gave sad proof that the Church reforms envisaged and demanded by the Council of Trent were largely dead letters.[77] It was from such a background that there arose various reform figures and movements: Bérulle and the founding of the French Oratory; Jean-Jacques Olier and his Compagnie de Saint-Sulpice; Monsieur Vincent de Paul; and the Basque Jean Duvergier de Hauranne, Abbé de Saint-Cyran, to whom, according to de Lubac, Jansenism owed its success and its greatness, and without whom it would have been merely another academic aberration.[78] Saint-Cyran was a convinced Augustinian, and with Bérulle he 'sought to derive from Augustine a method that would make souls realize their total dependence on God and their personal wretchedness'.[79] Among the means chosen to instil this realization, in a throwback to the penitential practice of the early Church, Saint-Cyran introduced the practice of deferring absolution from sins and reception of Holy Communion for several weeks, so that true repentence could be proved by good behaviour, a devout

the five propositions of Jansen's book which the words express, as it is expressed; and that the formula may not be subscribed to in any other intention, mind or acceptance; so that whoever thinks, holds, preaches, teaches, or asserts in word or writing, otherwise or to the contrary with regard to each and every one of these points falls completely under each and every censure . . .' (*DS* 2390). Not even this attempt to block all loopholes was successful, however. Cf. *DS* 2400, proem. Apart, of course, from the immediate interest of Roman reactions to Jansenism, two important questions of principle for moral theology which emerge from the controversy are the possibility of even interior dissent from Roman teaching and whether papal infallibility can extend to what, in the light of the five Jansenist propositions, came to be termed 'dogmatic facts'. On these cf. *infra*, p. 148.

[76] De Lubac, p. 51. A clear guide to the whole tangled tale is readily available in G. R. Cragg, *The Church and the Age of Reason* (London, 1972), ch. 2 and 13. It may not be over-simplifying the intellectual movements which mingled with religious and moral movements, and with political ambitions, to identify them as summed up in a confrontation between Jansenism, with its fierce loyalty to Augustine and its roots in Platonism, and the Society of Jesus, attracted to the cool and rational, even humanist, optimism of Aquinas rooted in Aristotelianism.

[77] Jedin and Dolan, op. cit., vol. vi, pp. 5–10.

[78] Ibid., pp. 21–2; de Lubac, op. cit. p. 53.

[79] Louis Cognet, in Jedin and Dolan, vi, p. 28.

practice adopted with enthusiasm by Mère Angélique Arnaud and her Paris community of Cistertian nuns at Port-Royal.[80]

The Jansenist movement, then, in the words of Cragg, aimed at a purification of the French Church.[81] As such it inevitably fell foul of the political aims of the all-powerful Cardinal Richelieu and the French Court of Louis XIV. Disapproval from Rome, and resistance to such disapproval, also inevitably revived the tension between the claims of the Gallican Church to independence in matters of jurisdiction and discipline from the centralizing bids of Rome beyond the Alps. And the anti-papal and reforming spirit of Augustinian Jansenism also picked out as one of its most dangerous and most insidious foes what it viewed as among the major causes of the decline of true religion, the laxity of morals, and the overweening claims of the papacy: the powerful and papalist Society of Jesus, which had from the first attacked the teaching on grace from Louvain and which had unsuccessfully intrigued to prevent publication of Jansen's *Augustinus*. It was a disciple of Saint-Cyran—the brother of Mère Angélique of Port-Royal and the author of a popular work entitled *On Frequent Communion* (which advocated infrequent reception)—the Sorbonne professor Antoine Arnaud, who led the major spirited attack in his *The Moral Theology of the Jesuits*. And this detailed and painstakingly documented disclosure of the laxism of Jesuit theories of morality was to be put to more eloquent and biting use two years later by another friend of the community of Port-Royal, the young convert mathematician, Blaise Pascal, in his imaginary and anonymous newsletters to a friend in the country. Later in this study we shall have occasion to discuss the moral reasoning castigated in the *Provincial Letters*, our concern for the present being to consider the mentality, and the anthropology, underlying them and the whole Jansenist movement, of which Voltaire wrote, 'I know of no sect more barbarous and more dangerous than the Jansenists. They are worse than the Scottish Presbyterians'.[82]

[80] Ibid., pp. 29–30. Among 101 (!) propositions excerpted from the writings of Quesnel—who succeeded Arnaud as leader of the Jansenists—and condemned by Rome, is the statement that 'it is a wise, enlightening and loving way of acting to provide souls with time to bear with humility and to experience the state of sin, to seek a spirit of repentance and contrition, and at least to begin to satisfy God's justice before they are reconciled' (*DS* 2487).

[81] Op. cit., p. 25.

[82] Quoted in M. Hay's spirited attack, *The Prejudices of Pascal* (London, 1962), p. 20, n. 1. For the events, cf. Jedin and Dolan, vi, p. 37.

Not, of course, that the free-thinking Voltaire was any friend of his former schoolmasters, the Jesuits, whom he regarded as 'enemies of the human race, driven out of three countries, and regarded with horror by the whole earth'.[83] But his comparison of Jansenism with Scottish Presbyterianism may be seen as an indication of the profound affinities with Calvinism of which the Jansenists were continually accused by Jesuits and others in their extreme Augustinian pessimism about the state of fallen man and the selective and impenetrable workings of God's grace.[84] In strict Jansenism, fallen man is completely at the mercy of his desires, whether for evil or for good. Of himself he can delight only in evil, in love of himself and of creatures, and his will is invincibly drawn in that direction. Should God decide to number him, however, among the few He will save, then grace will so flood his will as to conquer and overcome all other delights and draw him irresistibly in love to God and to his will.[85] The effect of such beliefs was, as Mère Angélique was to write, to annihilate man before God,[86] and, as Matteucci observes in describing the rigorist and repressive nature of Jansenist piety, to present Jesus as a severe and inscrutable redeemer and themselves as an élite ranged against the humanistic spirit of the times which seemed to glorify man at God's expense.[87] Among the many and increasingly exasperated Church condemnations of Jansenism we may note its rejection of the extreme views that Christ had not died for all men but only for those who are finally saved and that, as we have already seen, even to the just some of God's commands are impossible since grace is not granted to make them possible.[88] In a later attempt to quell the

---

[83] Quoted in Hay, ibid.　　　　[84] Jedin and Dolan, vi, p. 31.

[85] Cf. Cognet, 'Jansenism', *NCE*, 7, p. 820; K. Heckler, art. 'Jansenism', in *Sacramentum Mundi* (London, 1969), vol. iii, pp. 171–2.

[86] Matteucci, 'Jansenistic Piety', in *NCE* 7, p. 825; de Lubac, p. 51.

[87] Matteucci, ibid. For some indication of Jansenist influence in England, cf. Bossy, op. cit., p. 290. Pope Pius X was not exaggerating when, in 1910, his Decree lowering the age for reception of Communion and encouraging even daily Communion pointed out how Jansenism especially had brought it about that very few were considered worthy to receive Communion daily and were content to receive less frequently, even annually. 'In fact, severity reached such lengths that whole classes were excluded from frequenting the heavenly table, such as merchants or married people' (*DS* 3376).

[88] The fifth of Jansen's condemned propositions was 'it is semi-Pelagian to say that Christ died or shed his blood for absolutely all men' (*DS* 2005). On the restriction of grace to obey God's commands, cf. *DS* 2001 (the first Jansenist proposition) and *supra*, p. 53.

persistent movement Rome's Holy Office issued in 1690 a condemnation of thirty-one 'errors of the Jansenists' which included their views that 'even if there were invincible ignorance of the natural law anyone acting against it in the state of fallen nature would still be guilty of formal sin'; that 'every deliberate human action is either love of God, and therefore charity of the Father, or love of the world, and therefore concupiscence of the flesh, and as such evil'; that 'an unbeliever necessarily sins in everything he does'; that 'whatever is not of Christian supernatural faith operative through love is a sin'; and, for good measure, that 'where anyone finds a teaching clearly based in Augustine he can absolutely hold and teach it, all papal Bulls to the contrary notwithstanding'![89]

In thus responding to what it judged the excessive supernaturalism of Jansenism, the Church's moral tradition was at pains not to exceed the balance which it considered had been achieved by the Council of Trent, drawing upon the fifth century Council of Arles, that although the fall of Adam had weakened and distorted man's freedom of choice it had not extinguished it.[90] It was true that Trent had taught that unbelievers were excluded from the kingdom of God.[91] Nevertheless, it also anathematized anyone who would say 'that all the works done by anyone before justification, and whatever their reason, are sins and deserve God's hatred'.[92] This balance the Church was to continue to aim at in the eighteenth century in condemning views of Pasquase Quesnel, who succeeded Arnaud as leader of the Jansenists, and in condemning similar views

---

[89] 'Tametsi daretur ignorantia invincibilis iuris naturae, haec in statu naturae lapsae operantem ex ipsa non excusat a peccato formali', *DS* 2302. 'Omnis humana actio deliberata est Dei dilectio vel mundi: si Dei, caritas Patris est; si mundi, concupiscentia carnis, hoc est, mala est', *DS* 2307. 'Necesse est, infidelem in omni opere peccare', *DS* 2308. 'Omne, quod non est ex fide christiana supernaturali, quae per dilectionem operatur, peccatum est', *DS* 2311. 'Ubi quis invenerit doctrinam in Augustino clare fundatam, illam absolute potest tenere et docere, non respiciendo ad ullam Pontificis Bullam', *DS* 2330.

[90] 'tametsi in eis liberum arbitrium minime extinctum esset, viribus licet attenuatum et inclinatum', *DS* 1522 (Trent), echoing Arles, 'libertatem voluntatis humanae non existinctam, sed adtenuatam et infirmatam' (*DS* 339). Cf. *DS* 336.

[91] 'divinae legis doctrinam defendendo, quae a regno Dei non solum infideles excludit, ...' *DS* 1544.

[92] 'Si quis dixerit, opera omnia, quae ante iustificationem fiunt, quacumque ratione facta sint, vere esse peccata vel odium Dei mereri, ...: anathema sit', *DS* 1557.

enunciated in 1794 at the Jansenist-inspired Synod of Pistoia.[93] Not, of course, that the Church was entirely optimistic about the natural resources of fallen human nature. It was persuaded that fallen man's ability to do good naturally, or at least not to sin in every one of his actions, was a very precarious one, almost more theoretical than actual, and one which he could not maintain for any extended period of his life. And in this it based itself not only on the experience even of the justified but also on the Pauline interpretation of world history without Christ, in God's solemn triple abandonment of disbelievers to their own unnatural devices (cf. Rom. 1: 24–31).[94]

Good Pagans or Anonymous Christians?

In the storm over the supernatural two of the questions at issue were whether, once man knew what he ought to do he was naturally capable of actually doing it without supernatural aid from God, and whether he was able to do it in the manner in which God wished it done. Generally speaking, it may be said that medieval theology, based on Augustine, was to develop in answer to the former question a theory of 'healing' grace which would restore the full 'natural' resources of man who had on the road to Jericho been not only robbed of his riches but also physically harmed. But in order for man further to act in the way in which God wished, out of a 'supernatural' love, it would be necessary for God graciously to replace the riches with which he had originally freely endowed the victim of sin, by the gift of 'elevating' grace enabling him to raise his sights to God and to rise above his nature and so act well for love of Him. In this way Christ, the Good Samaritan, came to the aid of man who had been, as the axiom expressed it, both 'despoiled of his riches and injured in his nature'.[95] Post-Tridentine theology was to explore both the wounds of fallen nature and the gratuitous quality of the supernatural gifts of God by speculating on the possibility of a human nature which was neither elevated in Adam, nor fallen through sin, nor redeemed in Christ, a state of 'pure nature' and of

---

[93] Cf. *DS* 2401–5, 2438–49; 2619, 2623–4.

[94] Cf. M. Flick and Z. Alszeghy, *Il Vangelo della grazia* (Florence, 1964). pp. 40–67.

[95] 'spoliatus a gratuitis et vulneratus in naturalibus', ibid., p. 183, n. 48. On Augustine, cf. *supra*, p. 49.

its potentialities and its conjectured natural destiny. It was from this concept of pure nature that there was to arise controversy over whether man so constituted would have a 'natural' desire for the Beatific Vision, ultimately sharing fully in the divine life in a way which was somehow 'owed' to him by God who had created in him this natural desire.[96]

In all these speculations and complicated constructs, theology, and the Church in its teaching on nature and supernature, were aiming above all to preserve intact what they considered two fundamental truths: that God's grace is freely given and can in no sense be considered something which he owes to man, or to which man has a right based on any incompleteness or exigency arising from the nature which God created;[97] and that man himself, even after sin, is somehow capable of actively co-operating and responding to God's overtures of grace.[98] More recently, however, such scholastic and neo-scholastic analyses of various types of grace and of the intricate mechanics of grace have come to appear remote, if not obsolete, particularly in their application to the possibility of fallen man's ability to behave in a way which is 'naturally' good without being 'supernaturally' good. Juan Alfaro observes that 'the "super-naturality" of grace does not express what grace is in itself, . . . but it does signify the absolute freedom of God and of his giving of himself to man'.[99] As for 'nature', that, as Alfaro also points out, is 'a theological concept' in relation to grace, but as Karl Rahner has argued, it is a 'vestigial concept', or a remainder 'arrived at by abstraction from divinizing grace in man'.[100] This idea of 'nature' as an abstraction, or as what remains when one considers it in isolation from God's grace, indicates that such an idea or concept has never in fact actually been realized in human history.

Rahner, who has been the principal and most influential exponent of such developments from post-Tridentine and neo-scholastic theology, writes of the traditional theological distinction

---

[96] Cf. Karl Rahner, 'Concerning the relationship between nature and grace', *Theological Investigations*, vol. i (London, 1961).

[97] Cf. the encyclical of Pope Pius XII, *Humani generis*, 'Alii veram "gratuitatem" ordinis supernaturalis corrumpunt, cum autument Deum entia intellectu praedita condere non posse, quin eadem ad beatificam visionem ordinet et vocet' (*DS* 3891).

[98] Cf. Flick and Alszeghy, op. cit., pp. 180–2, 190–1.

[99] J. Alfaro, art. 'Nature', *Sacramentum Mundi*, vol. iv, p. 174.

[100] Ibid., p. 173. As a translation of *Restbegriff* here, 'remainder' appears better than 'vestigial', the latter implying 'traces' of the supernatural in 'nature'.

between nature and grace, 'in this most widespread view of it, grace is a superstructure above man's conscious spiritual and moral life, although it is, of course, also an acknowledged object of his faith and recognized as the highest, the divine, life in him which alone has power to bring him salvation'.[101] 'In short, the relationship between nature and grace is thought of as two layers laid very carefully one on top of the other so that they interpenetrate as little as possible.'[102] But, he maintains, 'it is perfectly acceptable to hold that man's whole spiritual life is permanently penetrated by grace. Just because grace is *free and unmerited* this does not mean that it is rare (theology has been led astray for too long already by the tacit assumption that grace would no longer be grace if God became too free with it). Our whole spiritual life takes place within God's will for our salvation.'[103] He writes of 'grace which enfolds man, the sinner and the unbeliever too, as his very sphere of existence which he can never escape from', and concludes that 'actual human nature is *never* "pure" nature, but nature in a supernatural order'.[104]

Within this scheme of what Rahner calls the 'supernatural existential', what then becomes of 'nature'? Not only is it a *Restbegriff*, or what is left when one withdraws from consideration all reference to grace and the supernatural, but it is well nigh impossible in practice to filter out in one's consideration of human experience the supernatural ingredients in order to collect a 'pure' deposit of the natural.

Certainly the philosopher has his own well-grounded concept of the nature of man: the irreducible substance of human being, established by recourse to human experience independently of verbal revelation. This concept may largely coincide with the theological concept of man's nature, in so far as without Revelation the greater part of what goes beyond this 'theological' nature is not experienced, and at any rate is not recognized *as* supernatural without the help of Revelation to interpret it. But in principle the content of this philosophical concept of man need not simply coincide with the content of the theological concept of man's "pure" nature. It can in concrete fact contain more (i.e., something already supernatural, though not as such). When therefore one undertakes to state with precision what exact content is intended by such a concept of a pure nature, in particular as regards God and his moral law, the difficulties, indeed the impossibility,

[101] *Nature and Grace* (London, 1963), p. 5. [102] Ibid., p. 7.
[103] Ibid., p. 31 (italics in original). [104] Ibid., pp. 32, 35.

of a neat horizontal once again become apparent for us, as the history of theology shows only too clearly.[105]

To the phenomenon of 'good' pagans Augustine had responded, as we have seen, mainly by impugning their motives for acting, so that their virtues were at best only counterfeits of the true virtue which must be motivated and 'ordered' by explicit love for the true Christian God. And this could only be done with help 'from above' on pain of their 'virtuous' conduct being virtuous at best only within the mundane terms of the earthy city or, as later theology was to re-express it, being virtuous only in 'natural' terms. The line which more recent speculation has followed is to decline to take such a systematically derogatory attitude towards ordinary human behaviour, and to argue a case for its being fully acceptable to God as at least 'implicitly' motivated and directed by genuine love which cannot be dissected with such ease as previous theologians have considered. In other words, if it is true that only with the help of God's grace can individuals consistently observe the moral law then two possible conclusions follow. The first, which appealed to Augustine and has been the tendency in the Church's moral teaching for centuries, is that, despite any appearances of isolated virtues to the contrary, the behaviour of unbelievers is frequently sinful. The other is, by contrast, a more generous willingness to accept the genuine worth of the behaviour of unbelievers and to conclude that they are regularly the co-operative recipients of God's grace.

This theological *volte-face* cannot, of course, be an isolated move and it inevitably raises the question of consequent fundamental shifts in other areas of theology, notably those of the function for moral behaviour of what Rahner calls 'verbal Revelation' and of the role of the Church as the, or an, instrument of salvation, as we shall consider in more detail later. Within the doctrine of grace, however, the fundamental issue which a rehabilitation in Christian eyes of the moral behaviour of 'good pagans' raises is how it can come about that they are the willing recipients of the grace of Christ whom they either do not know or have, for one reason or another, rejected but in whose name alone man can be saved. Somehow or other, by a mysterious and hidden dispensation of God, the grace of

---

[105] Rahner, 'Concerning the relationship . . .', *Theological Investigations*, vol. i, pp. 314–15.

Christ is available outside the category of faith and visible adherence to his Church. And so the problem of the good pagan became the hypothesis of the 'anonymous Christian', whose practical conclusions at any rate, whatever may be thought of the sometimes intricate theology underlying it, were adopted by the Second Vatican Council.[106]

The idea of anonymous Christianity is today invariably linked with the name of Karl Rahner as its chief exponent, and it is a logical development of his thinking on the supernatural existential.

No matter what a man states in his conceptual, theoretical, and religious reflection, anyone who does not say in his *heart*, 'there is no God' (like the 'fool' in the psalm) but testifies to him by the radical acceptance of his [own] being, is a believer. But if in this way he believes in deed and in truth in the holy mystery of God, if he does not suppress this truth but leaves it free play, then the grace of this truth by which he allows himself to be led is always already the grace of the Father in his Son. And anyone who has let himself be taken hold of by this grace can be called with every right an 'anonymous Christian'.[107]

[T]his self-communication by God offered to all and fulfilled in the highest way in Christ ... constitutes the goal of all creation and—since God's word and will *effect* what they say—... stamps and determines man's nature and lends it a character which we may call a 'supernatural existential' .... [T]his means that the express revelation of the word in Christ is not something which comes to us from without as entirely strange, but only the explicitation of what we already are by grace and what we experience at least incoherently in the limitlessness of our transcendence.[108]

From such reflections Rahner is able to conclude,

if one believes seriously in the universal salvific purpose of God towards all men in Christ, it need not and cannot really be doubted that gratuitous influences of properly Christian supernatural grace are conceivable in the life of all men (provided they are first of all regarded as individuals) and that these influences can be presumed to be accepted in spite of the sinful state of men and in spite of their apparent estrangement from God.[109]

For the Augustinian explanation that in the good behaviour of

---

[106] Cf. Vatican II, *Lumen Gentium*, no. 16, *Gaudium et Spes*, no. 22, *Ad Gentes*, no. 7. Cf. also, *infra*, p. 202.

[107] K. Rahner, 'Anonymous Christians', in *Theological Investigations*, vol. vi (London, 1969), p. 395.

[108] Ibid., pp. 393–4.

[109] *Idem*, 'Christianity and the non-Christian Religions', in *Theological Investigations*, vol. v (London, 1966), p. 125.

the unbeliever his virtuous conduct is only apparent and superficial, Rahner would substitute the explanation that it is his unbelief which is only apparent, and that the efficacy in history of God's will that all men should be saved can be presumed to prevail over the belief that all men have sinned. What this comes to mean in practice, with regard to the expressly Christian revelation, is that man 'already accepts this revelation whenever he really accepts *himself completely*, for it already speaks *in* him. Prior to the explicitness of official ecclesiastical faith this acceptance can be present in an implicit form whereby a person undertakes and lives the duty of each day in the quiet sincerity of patience, in devotion to his material duties and the demands made upon him by the persons under his care.'[110]

The possibility of a Christianity which is 'anonymous', particularly as elaborated in Heideggerian terms by Rahner, is one which arouses a variety of reactions. Some would view in it a patronizing attitude towards the 'best' of non-Christian moral thinking, past and present. Others might incline to see in it, with its foundation in the refusal to distinguish clearly in human experience between the natural and the supernatural, a threat to the autonomy of moral philosophy. Others might again see it as a covert recruitment drive for Christians from among those who had been previously viewed as rather puzzling good pagans. And yet, modern theologians have by no means been the first to adumbrate a theology of the influence of Christ, and not just of a unitarian God, at work in the thinking and lives of unbelievers. As early as the second century the attitude of some Christians to what they considered the best of pagan thought, including moral thinking, was not just hospitable, as we have seen. It also took on a proprietorial dimension by Christians laying claim to what was good in such thought. Sometimes this is naïvely expressed in terms of laying a prior claim to such thinking as originating with Moses and the Prophets, from whom Plato and other philosophers among the pagans historically derived their doctrines.[111] At other times the acceptability of some pagan ethics

---

[110] 'Anonymous Christians', ibid., p. 394. On Rahner's response to the difficulties raised against his thesis, cf. *idem*, 'Observations on the problem of the "anonymous Christian"', in *Theological Investigations*, vol. xiv (London, 1976), pp. 280–94.

[111] Justin, *First Apology*, ch. 44 (trans. Dods, p. 45), 'For Moses is more ancient than all the Greek writers. And whatever both philosophers and poets have said

would find a more theological explanation in the idea of the Stoic *logos*, or reason permeating all reality, being identified as the creative Joannine *Logos*, or Word of God, whose seed was scattered and sown throughout creation in the minds of men. This doctrine of the *Logos spermatikos* we find developed strikingly in Justin, who refers to 'seeds of truth among all men', and who explains how Christ is 'the Word of whom every race of men were partakers; and those who lived according to reason, [or the Word,] are Christians, even though they have been thought atheists; as, among the Greeks, Socrates and Heraclitus, and men like them; and among the barbarians, Abraham, and Ananias, and Azarias, and Misael, and Elias, and many others ....'[112] The seed was not always permitted to grow undisturbed, and the devils are always at pains to distort the truth, to blind men and to persecute all who thus 'live a reasonable and earnest life'. Their hostile activity is even more strongly directed against those 'who live not according to a part only of the word diffused [among men], but by the knowledge and contemplation of the whole Word, which is Christ'.[113] No doubt, those who have known only a part of the word have often contradicted themselves, but 'whatever things were rightly said among all men, are the property of us Christians'.[114] Nor is it just a matter of the apprehension of truth, in a speculative manner. 'Those who did that which is universally, naturally, and eternally good are pleasing to God.'[115]

concerning the immortality of the soul, ... or doctrines of the like kind, they have received such suggestions from the prophets as to enable them to understand and interpret these things. And hence there seem to be seeds of truth among all men.' *PG* 6, 396. Cf. Tertullian, *Apol.*, chap. 19 (*PL* 1, 440–1). Augustine, *civ. dei*, viii, 11 (*PL* 41, 235) mentions entertaining the suggestion, but he later rejected it (trans. Bettenson), p. 314, n. 23.

[112] Justin, ibid., ch. 46 (Dods, p. 46); *PL* 6, 397. On the espousal of this view by Pope John Paul II, cf. *Redemptor Hominis*, n. 11; *AAS* 71 (1979), p. 276. Cf. also the striking missionary passage in Vatican II, *Ad gentes*, 9; *AAS* 58 (1966), p. 958.

[113] Justin, *Second Apology*, chap. 8 (Dods, p. 78); *PG* 6, 457. He ascribes the admirable moral teaching of the Stoics to 'the seed of reason (τὸ σπέρμα τοῦ λόγου) implanted in every race of men', ibid.

[114] Ibid., ch. 10 (Dods, p. 79); *PG* 6, 460. 'Christ ... was partially known even by Socrates (for he was and is the Word (λόγος) who is in every man)', ibid., p. 80; *PG* 6, 461. ὅσα οὖν παρὰ πᾶσι καλῶς εἴρηται, ἡμῶν τῶν χριστιανῶν ἐστι, ibid., ch. 13 (Dods, p. 83); *PG* 6, 465.

[115] Justin, *Dialogue with Trypho*, chap. 45 (Trans. G. Reith), ibid., p. 144; *PG* 6, 572 (Ἐπεὶ οἱ τὰ καθόλου καὶ φύσει καὶ αἰώνια καλὰ ἐποίουν, εὐάρεστοί εἰσι τῷ θεῷ).

Reason and Revelation

Another fundamental question which can be asked in the light of moral theology's espousal of natural law theory and the Church's persistent confidence in the power of man's rationality to apprehend what he ought to do and ought not to do is, what then is the point or the purpose for morality of Revelation or, for that matter, of religion? Ronald Knox, in his summary of *The Belief of Catholics*, was quite forthright in his reply. 'Neither Catholicism nor any other form of Christianity pretends to have a special morality of its own; religion is meant to enforce, not to supersede, the natural code of morals.'[116] Today the idea of religion 'enforcing' anything has an unpleasant ring of compulsion and sanction, but if Knox is to be understood as meaning that religion *reinforces* knowledge of the natural code of morals then he is closer to the Church's tradition. And yet there has also persisted a view that the matter is not so easily settled, that just as in the area of moral performance there are twin sources of action, the natural and the supernatural, so in the sphere of moral knowledge man has two resources of information, his natural reason and supernatural Revelation.

Pelagius and his followers were prepared to concede the benefit to man of a grace which would illuminate his mind, and in this at least they seem to have been at one with Augustine. The latter's theology of original sin had included in its dire effects not only disorder in the will but also a darkening of the mind, resulting in 'that terrifying abyss of ignorance, as it may be called, which is the source of all error, in whose gloomy depths all the sons of Adam are engulfed, so that man cannot be rescued from it without toil, sorrow and fear'.[117] We have seen, however, that Augustine was to number among the blessings which he could still count after the Fall a spark, or glimmer, of reason which had not been totally extinguished by sin.[118] Scholastic theology was to maintain this tradition of a darkening, although not a complete extinction, of man's capacity for moral knowledge, and found in this the rationale for a divine verbal revelation of such knowledge. As Aquinas explained, after the Fall, 'as time went on, sin too began to take more hold on man, to such an extent that, with his reason

---

[116] Ronald Knox, *The Belief of Catholics* (London, 1927), p. 34.
[117] Augustine, *de civ. dei*, xxii, 22; *PL* 41, 784 (Bettenson, p. 1065).
[118] Cf. *supra*, n. 52.

darkened by sin, the precepts of the law of nature were not enough
for living rightly, and they had to be determined in the written
law'.[119] Over and above natural law and human law, however,
Aquinas also saw a need for a 'divine law', that is, the moral
contents of the Old and New Testaments, as arising from four
considerations. Two of these concern the inadequacy or incompleteness of human law, either to forbid all evil behaviour, which might
have undesirable social consequences, or to cope with interior
acts.[120] The other two considerations relate to man's supernatural
end and to the uncertainty of human judgement. Law directs man
to actions corresponding to his final end, and since man is ordered
towards the end of eternal beatitude, which exceeds the proportion
of his natural human ability, he needs a comparable law from God
directing him to this end. Moreover, because of the uncertainty of
human judgement, especially concerning contingent and particular
matters, a variety of judgements is to be found about human
actions which also gives rise to different and conflicting human
laws. And so that man can know without any doubt what he should
do and not do, he needed to be directed in his own acts by a divine
law which cannot be mistaken.[121]

We have already seen Aquinas express confidence in man's
reason being able to come to some knowledge of God's eternal law
based on the identification of, and respect for, fundamental
tendencies which exist in human nature as created by God. We have
also seen him identify the good which man is morally obliged to
pursue defined in terms of the fulfilment of those tendencies.[122] In
this way he was able to formulate a series of moral precepts of
natural law: some very general in content, which he calls 'primary
precepts'; and others increasingly specific in their content and
conclusion, which he calls 'secondary precepts'. Students of St
Thomas seem agreed that there is a vagueness in his works about
which precepts of natural law were considered primary by him, and

---

[119] *STh* 3a, q. 61, art. 3 ad 2.

[120] *STh* 1a 2ae, q. 91, art. 4.

[121] 'Quia homo ordinatur ad finem beatitudinis aeternae, quae excedit pro-
portionem naturalis facultatis humanae (cf. 1a 2ae, q. 5, a. 5], ideo necessarium fuit
ut supra legem naturalem et humanam dirigeretur etiam ad suum finem lege
divinitus data', ibid. 'Ut ergo homo absque omni dubitatione scire possit quid ei sit
agendum et quid vitandum, necessarium fuit ut in actibus propriis dirigetur per
legem divinitus datam, de qua constat quod non potest errare', ibid.

[122] Cf. *supra*, p. 79.

which secondary,[123] and it is arguable that for him the primary precepts are very general and non-specific, lying within the area between the first axiomatic principle that good is to be done and evil avoided and such precepts as those of the Decalogue. As he explains, 'some matters are derived from the general principles of the law of nature by way of conclusions, as the injunction "not to kill" can be derived as a sort of conclusion from "Do evil to no one".'[124] And he was of the view that the primary principles of the law of man's nature are known to all men, whereas when one begins to become more specific in drawing conclusions from such first principles difficulty can arise from two complicating factors. One of these is the complexity of moral situations, so that as a matter of fact general natural law conclusions do not cover every eventuality.[125] The other is more to do with man's capacity for moral argumentation as it becomes more specific and complicated. In some instances incapacity in individuals is simply a matter of limited natural endowments, but in many other instances the incapacity arises from a variety of moral factors.

There are some very common, or general, precepts of natural law which are known to all, and other secondary and more particular precepts derived from them. The former general precepts can never as such be entirely expelled from men's hearts, but their application to a particular situation can be, if reason is prevented by desire or some other emotion from making the application. Secondary precepts can be driven from men's hearts, either through wrong convictions (as can happen even in speculative matters), or through bad customs or habits, as some thought robbery not a sin, or even vices against nature, as Paul states (Rom. 1: 24–7).[126]

The participation by man in God's eternal law through knowledge, then, can be corrupted and depraved in such a way that the natural knowledge of good is darkened by passions and the habits of sin.[127] For Aquinas, then, not all the conclusions of natural law are

[123] Cf. O. Lottin, *Principes de morale*, t. ii (Louvain, 1947), pp. 37–54, especially p. 49, n. 1.

[124] 'Derivantur ergo quaedam a principiis communibus legis naturae per modum conclusionum: sicut hoc quod est "non esse occidendum", ut conclusio quaedam derivari potest ab eo quod est "nulli esse faciendum malum" ', *STh* 1a 2ae, q. 95, art. 2.

[125] 'Principia communia legis naturae non eodem modo applicari possunt omnibus propter multam varietatem rerum humanarum', ibid., ad 3.

[126] *STh* 1a 2ae, q. 94, a. 6.

[127] 'Ipsa naturalis cognitio boni in [malis] obtenebratur per passiones et habitus peccatorum', ibid., q. 93, a. 6. Cf. *STh* 3a, q. 61, a. 3 ad 2.

universally known, and the more one descends from the general to
the particular, the more possible it is for reason to be unduly
influenced by the emotions, or by customs, or by fallen nature.
'Caesar tells us that the Germans once thought there was nothing
wrong with robbery, even although it is expressly against the law of
nature.'[128]

Aquinas remained, however, convinced that morality is essentially
rational conduct, and as such it must be accessible, at least in
principle, to human reason and wisdom. In his systematic discussion
of the Old Testament as part of divine law he explains that, since all
morality must be consonant with reason, then 'all moral precepts
belong to the law of nature',[129] and the Ten Commandments are
conclusions which 'a little thought' can derive from 'the two first
general precepts of the law of nature', love of God and love of
neighbour.[130] But the Commandments in their turn can be viewed
also as principles which by dint of more subtle and wise
consideration yield further reasonable conclusions.[131] Moreover,

---

[128] *STh* 1a 2ae, q. 94, a. 4, which may be seen as summing up Aquinas' view on
the applicability and the 'knowability' of natural law. 'Sic igitur dicendum est quod
lex naturae, quantum ad prima principia communia, est eadem apud omnes et
secundum rectitudinem et secundum notitiam. Sed quantum ad quaedam propria,
quae sunt quasi conclusiones principiorum communium, est eadem apud omnes ut
in pluribus et secundum rectitudinem et secundum notitiam: sed ut in paucioribus
potest deficere et quantum ad rectitudinem, propter aliqua particularia impedimenta—sicut etiam naturae generabiles et corruptibiles deficiunt ut in paucioribus
propter impedimenta—et etiam quantum ad notitiam; et hoc propter hoc quod
aliqui habent depravatam rationem ex passione, seu ex mala consuetudine, seu ex
mala habitudine naturae; sicut apud Germanos olim latrocinium non reputabatur
iniquum, cum tamen sit expresse contra legem naturae, ut refert Julius Caesar in lib.
de bello Gallico [vi, 23].'

[129] 'Cum moralia praecepta sint de his quae pertinent ad bonos mores, haec
autem sunt quae rationi congruunt, omne autem rationis humanae judicium
aliqualiter a naturali ratione derivatur, necesse est quod omnia praecepta moralia
pertineant ad legem naturae', *STh* 1a 2ae, q. 100, a. 1.

[130] 'Illa duo praecepta sunt prima et communia praecepta legis naturae, quae sunt
per se nota rationi humanae, vel per naturam vel per fidem. Et ideo omnia pracepta
decalogi ad illa duo referuntur sicut conclusiones ad principia communia', ibid., a. 4
ad 3. 'Illa ergo praecepta ad decalogum pertinent quorum notitiam homo habet per
seipsum a Deo. Huiusmodi vero sunt illa quae statim ex principiis communibus
primis cognosci possunt modica consideratione: et iterum illa quae statim ex fide
divinitus infusa innotescunt', ibid., art. 3. The precepts which, for Aquinas, result
immediately from divinely infused faith are those which refer to one's conduct
towards God himself.

[131] 'Illa [praecepta] quae sunt prima et communia, continentur in eis sicut
principia in conclusionibus proximis: illa vero quae per sapientes cognoscuntur,
continentur in eis, e converso, sicut conclusiones in principiis', ibid.

the precepts of the New Law are substantially the same as those of the Old,[132] and in fact the New Law added very little to the precepts of the law of nature.[133] For even the counsels commended by Jesus (the 'evangelical' counsels of poverty, chastity, obedience) can be seen to be reasonable means for some people to achieve their end better and more readily by liberating themselves from the good things of this world, whether it be wealth, or the pleasures of the body, or independence.[134]

In the teaching of Aquinas, then, the purpose of Revelation, so far as morality is concerned, appears to be essentially remedial, not absolutely necessary for man but in practice almost indispensable. In the opening sentence of his *Summa* of Theology, discussing the purpose of God's revelation, he explains that in general man's need for a Revelation about God in order to attain salvation covers not only matters which exceed his natural comprehension but also those which can be investigated by human reason, since this can be carried out 'only by a few people, requires a lot of time and is subject to many errors'.[135] This being so, the Christian revelation contains in its moral teaching no substantial element over and above what is accessible to human reason without such revelation.

Such was to continue to be the Church's doctrine on man's natural knowledge of the requirements of morality, and the tradition was firmly stated in the nineteenth century particularly in papal and conciliar teaching which, in the views of Flick and Alszeghy, 'completed the teaching already formed on fallen man's freedom of will with similar teaching on the powers and weaknesses

---

[132] 'Praecepta novae legis dicuntur esse majora quam praecepta veteris legis, quantum ad explicitam manifestationem; sed quantum ad ipsam substantiam praeceptorum Novi Testamenti omnia continentur in Veteri Testamento', q. 107, art. 3 ad 2. Cf. q. 108, art. 2 ad 1.

[133] 'lex nova, quae praeter praecepta legis naturae paucissima superaddit in doctrina Christi et Apostolorum', q. 107, art. 4.

[134] 'Consilia vero oportet esse de illis per quae melius et expeditius potest homo consequi finem praedictum', q. 108, art. 4, which proceeds to show how reasonable are the counsels given by Jesus, always depending on the aptitude of individuals (*idoneitate hominum*), ibid., ad 1.

[135] 'Ad ea etiam quae de Deo ratione humana investigari possunt necessarium fuit hominem instrui revelatione divina. Quia veritas de Deo per rationem a paucis, et per longum tempus, et cum admixtione multorum errorum homini proveniret . . . . Ut igitur salus hominum communius et securius [*al.* convenientius et certius] proveniat necessarium fuit quod de divinis per divinam revelationem instruantur', *STh* 1a, q. 1, a. 1.

of the intellect in the present state of man'.[136] The occasion for such statements was the movements of rationalism and fideism which largely occupied the Church in that century. Pope Pius IX, the Pope of the First Vatican Council, had some years previously taken exception to the writings of the Munich Professor Frohschammer on the capacity of philosophy and human reason to dispense with Revelation,[137] and the Council was to echo the papal (and Thomist) teaching by asserting that, on the one hand, Revelation was an absolute necessity in disclosing to man the supernatural end destined for him by God, and on the other hand that although not absolutely necessary on other matters it enabled 'those matters relating to God which are not in themselves inaccessible to human reason, to be known by all, even in the present condition of the human race, readily, with firm certitude and without any admixture of error'.[138] Following Vatican I, Pope Pius XI was to allow that in the area of morality 'there are many matters which are not in themselves inaccessible to human reason', but he also warned that the attractions of pleasure and the difficulties of married life can easily deceive people left to themselves and lead to rationalization.[139] The age of Leo XIII, as we have earlier shown, saw a systematic and neo-scholastic expansion in the application of natural law theory,[140] but the cautionary note was once again stressed in 1950 by Pope Pius XII, despite his own confident appeals to human reason and natural law. In his encyclical, *Humani Generis*, which was aimed to quell the post-war 'new theology' apparently undermining the

---

[136] Op. cit., p. 172.

[137] DS 2850–2. Pius IX was clear enough on the value of a 'true and healthy philosophy' in diligently seeking truth and in cultivating human reason, 'which has been darkened but in no way extinguished' by original sin (DS 2853). Trent had applied this description to man's free will, as had the Council of Arles. Cf. *supra*, n. 90.

[138] 'Huic divinae revelationi tribuendum quidem est, ut ea, quae in rebus divinis humanae rationi per se impervia non sunt, in praesenti quoque generis humani condicione ab omnibus expedite, firma certitudine et nullo admixto errore cognosci possint. Non hac tamen de causa revelatio absolute necessaria dicenda est, sed quia Deus ex infinita bonitate sua ordinavit hominem ad finem supernaturalem, ad participando scilicet bona divina, quae humanae mentis intelligentiam omnino superant', DS 3005.

[139] 'Ecclesiam enim constituit ipse Christus Dominus magistram veritatis, in his etiam quae ad mores pertinent regendos ordinandosque, etsi in his multa humanae rationi impervia non sunt', AAS XXII (1930), 580. 'At nemo non videt, quot fallaciis aditus aperiretur et quanti errores admiscerentur veritati, si res singulis relinqueretur solo rationis lumine exploranda, . . .', ibid., p. 579.

[140] *Supra*, pp. 81–2.

whole tradition of the supernatural, but which events may have shown to be more of a panegyric preached over the grave of neo-scholasticism, he admitted that human reason really can by its own natural powers and light come to a true and certain knowledge of God 'and of the natural law imprinted in our minds by the Creator'. But he went on to stress that there are many obstacles to prevent this from happening, since such knowledge carries implications for a personal commitment and for self-denial. The intellect is hampered by emotions and imaginings as well as by the lower desires resulting from original sin.

The result is that in such matters men willingly persuade themselves that what they do not want to be true is really false or at least doubtful. For this reason divine "revelation" must be said to be morally necessary, so that those matters of religion and morality which are not in themselves inaccessible to reason can be known by all, even in the present condition of the human race, readily, with firm certitude and without any admixture of error.[141]

The Scope of Revelation

In so stressing the 'moral', or practical, need for Revelation only as a remedy to overcome the human failings which can impede the natural exercise of ordinary human reason, Pope Pius XII was only continuing the steady moral tradition going back through his predecessors to Aquinas, and indeed to Augustine. Revelation as such has nothing in matters of moral behaviour to add to the best of human thinking, but such human moral thinking is by no means always or invariably at its best. It is interesting to note, however, the reluctance with which many Catholics greet this conclusion and the ways in which they struggle against it, unwilling to accept that, so far as content is concerned, there is nothing specifically distinctive about Christian ethics as compared, for instance, with the best of humanist ethics. At times there appears a persistent

---

[141] 'Licet humana ratio, simpliciter loquendo, veram et certam cognitionem . . . naturalis legis a Creatore nostris animis inditae, suis naturalibus viribus ac lumine assequi revera possit, . . . Humanus autem intellectus in talibus veritatibus acquirendis difficultate laborat . . . . Quapropter divina "revelatio" moraliter necessaria dicenda est, ut ea, quae in rebus religionis et morum rationi per se impervia non sunt, in praesenti quoque humani generis condicione, ab omnibus expedite, firma certitudine et nullo admixto errore cognosci possint', *DS* 3875–6, the final words being from Vatican I, *supra*, n. 138.

seeking for a Christian 'plus factor', a miracle ingredient which will make the significant difference between the two, and there is almost a sense of being cheated or defrauded when this is not forthcoming or is denied.

It may be that such reaction arises from a confusion between religion and morality, akin to some public support for religious schools or education which will teach children how to behave properly, a function for religion which is also mirrored in the minds of some school, and post school, children by their resistance and resentment towards a religion portrayed almost entirely in terms of moral duties and Church regulations. Such an approach to religion is, of course, profoundly unchristian, ignoring the fact that, for the Christian, morality is above all a free response in love to the invitation of a loving and liberating God, and that what is primary in religion is God's actions, not ours, and, basic to Christianity, God's actions in spite of ours.

It may also be, however, that the sense of something missing if Christian and 'human' morality are simply equated is pointing towards the need for an enriched view of morality rather than towards an impoverished view of religion. It might be expressive of a fundamental dissatisfaction with the traditional distinction between nature and supernature as this has been elaborated in the Church's moral teaching, and as it is reflected in moral matters in the distinction between reason and Revelation. To act according to reason and to act according to nature are frequently regarded as synonymous, although it is sometimes suggested that in the thought of Aquinas they betoken two differing and unreconciled approaches to human morality. Latent in this suggestion is the idea that acting reasonably may give more room for moral maneouvre in such disputed areas as contraception than acting according to the profound built-in inclinations of human nature.[142] Such a line of argument, however, does not take sufficiently into account that for man to act according to reason is acting according to his nature as a rational being, and that to act unreasonably would for him be to act

---

[142] 'The Thomistic natural law concept vacillates at times between the order of nature and the order of reason', C. E. Curran, *Contemporary Problems in Moral Theology* (Notre Dame, Indiana, 1970), p. 106. On the following reflections, cf., however, Aquinas, *de Malo*, q. 2, a. 4 (*Quaestiones disputatae* (Rome (Marietti), 1965), vol. ii, p. 474), 'bonum et malum in actibus humanis consideratur secundum quod actus concordat rationi informatae lege divine, vel naturaliter, vel per doctrinam, ver per infusionem'.

unnaturally. Nor does it make clear what constitutes reasonable action, which has to do with the manner in which man reaches his moral conclusions but of itself says nothing concerning the subject-matter about which he should act reasonably. In other words, man's nature includes reason but is more than reason. It has other elements of givenness about which man is to act reasonably but which are not identical with reason, such elements as the volitional, emotional, corporeal, and social aspects of his humanity.

Traditionally, then, to act according to nature has been considered as delivering the content of moral behaviour, and when Revelation has been more than simply remedial in supplying for the actual deficiencies in man's reasonable activity it has been regarded as indicating a supernatural quality conferred by God on that activity rather than as adding anything to the content or the conclusions of morality. The supernatural element has not effected any change in the programme of natural behaviour, but has transformed its quality through making it the carrier of charity, almost as if the Christian were living and acting simultaneously at two different levels. In this scheme of things and way of viewing morality the 'nature' according to which all men must act has continued to be the metaphysical essence as analysed speculatively by Aquinas. It is true that he distinguished different states of human nature before and after sin, but nature itself he considered to remain essentially the same and unchanged.[143] If, however, as Rahner contends, man is living in a supernatural existential, and 'nature' as such is a

---

[143] Cf. *STh* 3a, q. 61, a. 2 ad 2: 'Eadem est natura hominis ante peccatum et post peccatum, non tamen est idem naturae status.' Sin does not affect the constitutive principles of nature or its powers, but it does affect its predisposition to virtuous action (*STh* 1a 2ae. q. 85, a. 1). And it is well known that he viewed the institution of private property as necessary for man only after the Fall, due, no doubt, to sin's affecting man's natural predisposition to live in social harmony (1a, q. 98, a. 1; cf. 2a 2ae, q. 66, a. 2). It may also be noted that he considered man's original justice before the fall as accidental to his nature (1a, q. 100, a. 1), such that changes in the state of human nature are all equally accidental. Moreover, Aquinas distinguishes between nature in general (*natura universalis*) and nature in particular individuals (*natura particularis*) (1a, q. 99, a. 2 ad 1), and it appears that it is in this sense that he can refer to nature being changeable in individuals on account of particular circumstances. 'Natura autem hominis est mutabilis, ideo id quod naturale est homini potest aliquando deficere', as in the case of a madman or a public enemy demanding the return of his sword (2a 2ae, q. 57, a 2 ad 1). Cf. *de Malo* (Marietti, op. cit., p. 477) q. 2, a. 5 ad 13, 'mutabilitatem naturae humanae et diversas conditiones hominum et rerum, secundum diversitatem locorum et temporum.' On the immutability of natural law, as a consequence of the immutability of nature, cf. Lottin, *Principes*, vol. ii, pp. 40–2.

Restbegriff, an incomplete or remainder concept with something missing, then as such a concept it is scarcely an adequate basis for producing the programme of human morality to which all men are, as a matter of fact, invited by God. There cannot be any question of regarding natural law, or what Aquinas preferred to call the law of nature, as a covert or implicit extension of the purely abstract possibility of 'pure' nature. In other words, there is a mysterious or 'supernatural' element to nature itself as it historically exists, to which moral theology with its long indebtedness to Stoic and Aristotelian ways of thinking has not given its attention. One charge made today against the application of natural law theory, in some of its details at least, is that it works with a concept of nature which has been philosophically defective in being too unhistorical, as we shall see later, and in being considered in isolation from the social and technological developments which have come into prominence over the years.[144] To this, it appears, should be added the further possibility that the concept of nature, and the conclusions derived from it, have been theologically defective in not taking sufficiently into account the continuity and the actual—as opposed to the conceptual—indivisibility of God's onward purpose for man in Christ.

The Second Council of Arles, in 473, referred to the 'law of nature' as 'the first grace of God',[145] with an apparent sense of such continuity and cumulative divine purpose. And it may be significant for moral theology that Pope Paul VI made reference to 'principles of a moral teaching on marriage which relies on natural law illuminated and *enriched by divine revelation*'.[146] Enrichment is surely more than correction or than mere remedial potential. But Pope Paul's point is not that what the moral tradition, following Aquinas, held about the equivalence of biblical moral teaching and the natural law is inadequate. It is that a 'natural' view of man as a source for moral reasoning is inadequate and does not correspond to the reality that 'man is made a new creature who can respond in

---

[144] Cf. *infra*, p. 206.

[145] Condemning the view that 'ab Adam usque ad Christum nullos ex gentibus per primam Dei gratiam, id est per legem naturae, in adventum Christi esse salvatos eo quod liberum arbitrium ex omnibus [= *ex toto*] in primo parente perdiderunt' (*DS* 336).

[146] 'principia moralis doctrinae de matrimonio, quae in lege naturali, divina Revelatione illustrata ditataque, nititur', *Humanae Vitae*, n. 4 (*AAS* 60 (1968), p. 483).

love and genuine freedom to the plan of his Creator and Saviour'.[147] The continuity and the interpretation in history of God's work as both Creator and Saviour have the effect, if not of blurring, at least of rendering academic the conceptual distinction between nature and supernature. As Pope Paul concluded, the Church 'can only teach the law which is appropriate to a human life which has been restored to its genuine truth and is led by God's Spirit'.[148]

It may also be a growing dissatisfaction with the traditional concept of 'nature' which has contributed in recent years to the focus of moral attention moving from 'human nature' to 'human person' or 'human dignity'. Thus, the Second Vatican Council was certainly not unaware of the whole moral tradition centred on the law of nature when it nevertheless considered basing objective moral standards on 'the dignity of the human person', and finally decided to propose the need for such standards as based on 'the nature of the [human] person and his acts'.[149] It is also worthy of note that the Council's Decree on Religious Freedom, which Pope Paul VI described as 'one of the major texts of the Council',[150] opened with the statement, 'A sense of the dignity of the human person has been impressing itself more and more deeply on the consciousness of contemporary man'.[151] John Courtnay Murray, the American Jesuit whose labours and writings had done much to forward in the Church the subject of religious freedom, considered this decree 'the most controversial document of the whole Council' and pardonably described the debate on the subject as 'the greatest argument on religious freedom in all history'. The hidden agenda, he explained, was not the issue of religious freedom, but that of the development of doctrine in the Church leading to the conciliar

---

[147] 'Unde homo nova efficitur creatura, quae in caritate germanaque libertate superno sui Creatoris et Salvatoris consilio respondeat . . .', ibid., n. 25 (*AAS*, pp. 498–9).

[148] 'facere autem non potest, quin legem doceat, quae reapse propria est vitae humanae ad eius germanam veritatem restitutae, atque a Spiritu Dei actae', ibid., n. 19; *AAS* 60 (1968), p. 495.

[149] 'obiectivis criteriis, ex personae eiusdemque actuum natura desumptis', *Gaudium et Spes*, n. 51; *AAS* 58 (1966), p. 1072. An earlier draft ran 'obiectivis criteriis, in eadem personae humanae dignitate fundatis', *Acta Concilii Vaticani Secundi*, vol. iv, 6 (Rome, 1978), p. 478.

[150] W. M. Abbott, *The Documents of Vatican II* (London, 1966), p. 674.

[151] 'Dignitatis humanae personae homines hac nostra aetate magis in dies conscii fiunt', *Declaration on Religious Freedom*, n. 1; *AAS* 58 (1966), p. 929.

teaching. 'The course of the development between the *Syllabus of Errors* (1864) and . . . [this decree] . . . still remains to be explained by theologians. But the Council formally sanctioned the validity of the development itself; and this was a doctrinal event of high importance for theological thought in many other areas.'[152]

One such area, as we shall consider later, has to do with the role of the Church in the salvation of individuals.[153] But the founding of the right to religious freedom on the dignity of the individual human person can be seen as further indication of the move from human nature to the human person and his dignity as a basis for moral reasoning. In the circumstances it is significant that the criterion of person rather than nature can be seen flourishing in the thought of Pope John Paul II, notably in the first encyclical of his pontificate, and in his Apostolic Exhortation on the Christian Family, in which, with reference to the subject of contraception, he invites theologians to shed more light on 'the biblical foundations, the ethical grounds and the personalistic reasons behind this doctrine'.[154] It is equally significant that in his encyclical *Redemptor Hominis* the Pope stresses that the object of divine Revelation includes man himself, not now just one 'supernatural' dimension of human nature, but the unitary object of God's love and God's single design and destiny.[155]

The implications of this shift in focus and terminology for moral theology are still unfolding. It may be suggested that what it betokens is the establishment of a single perspective of God's creative and salvific enterprise concerning humankind, and a concentration on individuality and personal destiny, rather than, as formerly, a stress on nature as such and on a uniformly and systematically applied distinction between nature and supernature. If God is historically calling all men and women to ultimate life with him, the invitation has been delivered, and ultimately only God can really say which men have definitely refused the invitation, which have not yet opened it, and which are at present reading it.

[152] Abbott, op. cit. pp. 673, 672.
[153] Cf. *infra*, pp. 194–202.
[154] *Familianis Consortio*, n. 31, AAS 74 (1982), p. 117.
[155] 'Human dignity is the dignity of the grace of divine adoption and at the same time the dignity of the truth within the human race', *Redemptor hominis*, n. 11, AAS 71 (1979), p. 277. Cf. ibid., n. 12 (p. 280): 'the dignity of the human person' is part of the Gospel, and freedom is the condition and foundation of the true dignity of the human person.

As even Augustine acknowledged, 'it may be that there is another more hidden cause on account of the diverse merits of mankind, which are better known to God than to us'.[156] It may also be that the shift of attention which sees divine Revelation as including the mystery of man himself in God's designs of love puts in question the enterprise to identify what is the specific factor in 'Christian ethics', or at least replaces the supposition that there is a 'plus factor' in Christian ethics with the realization that there is a factor missing in any attempt to identify purely natural ethics. As Rahner expresses it, 'Who is to say that the voice heard in earthly philosophy, even non-Christian and pre-Christian philosophy, is the voice of nature alone (and perhaps of nature's guilt) and not also the groaning of the creature, who is already moved in secret by the Holy Spirit of grace, and longs without realizing it for the glory of the children of God?'[157] It may turn out, in other words, that philosophical ethics are really anonymous Christian ethics.

Finally, it may also be that such a unitary approach to the moral enterprise and programme for man will give rather more weight to the Church's claim to competence over the whole field of morality. If, in the past, the basic argument for this universal competence has been that both divine and natural law issue from one and the same God, for the future, even if these can or should be conceived distinctly, they must be seen as God's and the Church's attention focusing on what Pope John Paul II has expressed as man, not in the abstract but in his historical entirety.[158]

---

[156] *Supra*, n. 58.

[157] *Nature and Grace*, p. 42.

[158] 'De homine ideo hic agitur, in tota eius veritate, in universa eius amplitudine. Non agitur de homine *abstracto*, sed vero, ut est, de homine *concreto*, historico, ut aiunt. De quolibet homine agitur, cum quivis comprehenditur mysterio Redemptionis et huius mysterii gratia in omne tempus cum eo Christus se coniunxerit', *Redemptor hominis*, n. 13 (*AAS*, p. 283).

4

'TEACHING WITH AUTHORITY'

Among the various influential factors which have entered into the making of moral theology one of the most dominant has been that of authority; and the aim of this chapter is to explore and to reflect upon how authority in moral matters has developed and been exercised within the Church. If in the previous chapter we considered one instance of the powerful influence of ideas in the development of our subject, in this chapter we turn to consider the strengths and weaknesses of institutions and their technical terminology in relation to the delicate texture of moral behaviour. This is best illustrated by considering the subject of magisterial authority in morals.

Magisterium *in the Church*

As a technical term in the Church's moral tradition, the Latin word *magisterium* has not by any means always possessed the precise significance of 'teaching authority' with which it is invariably used today, nor even when it has had this sense in the past has the exercise of such authority been restricted to the teaching activity of the Church's hierarchy. The development of its use as a synonym for the body of bishops as such and of its application with a capital letter to the Pope in his teaching capacity is of relatively recent origin, as has been amply demonstrated by the outstanding scholar on the Church, the French Dominican Yves Congar.[1] The term *magisterium*, rare in Classical Latin but used with increasing frequency in Christian writings, had the general sense of being a *magister*, or a greater person in charge of anything, as contrasted with a *minister*, or lesser person. This could apply to different areas of responsibility and competence, including that of teaching, and for centuries in the Church the general connotation of responsibility,

---

[1] Y. Congar, 'Pour une histoire sémantique du terme "magisterium" ', *Revue des sciences philosophiques et théologiques*, 60 (1976), pp. 84–97; 'Bref historique des formes du "magistère" et de ses relations avec les docteurs', ibid., pp. 98–112.

or oversight, and its particular application to teaching continued in use side by side. In a famous phrase of Pope Gregory the Great the 'pastoral *magisterium*' is synonymous with the responsibility for souls; and the phrase *mater et magistra* used of the Roman Church in the twelfth century did not have the meaning given it today of 'mother and teacher' but more that of 'mother and governess'.[2]

The specifically teaching aspect of the term is to be found used in the eleventh century in a reference to the *magisterium* of the Church Fathers, and from the next century and the development of theological Schools, as the title of Master, or *Magister*, was being accorded to those who gave public teaching, so the teaching activity or function of such men was referred to as their *magisterium*. It was with the rise, however, of the Universities—which Pantin describes as 'a new organ in the Church'[3]—to become literally international bodies in their staffing, students, interests, and prestige, that the great medieval theologians, Albert, Thomas, Bonaventure, Scotus, and many others, were able to influence their contemporaries not only on account of the inherent brilliance of their teaching but also because of their status in the Church as *Magister* and because of the coveted University chairs in theology which they occupied. Aquinas it was who distinguished between the pastoral *magisterium* of prelates and the academic *magisterium* of the 'masters of theology' as two ways of expounding the contents of Sacred Scripture.[4] Moreover, the Universities themselves and the Faculties of Theology came to exercise, as colleges of theologians, a considerable authority in the Church in their own right, most frequently by commending or censuring the teachings of individual theologians, whether of their own or another University. One of the most striking instances of such activity was the condemnation in 1277 by the University of Paris of teachings of its most illustrious Master, and of the novel Aristotelianism of which in his lifetime Thomas had been a most influential exponent.[5] And the history of European theology is to a very large extent a history of theology as explored, expounded, and disputed in its great University centres.

Over and above their function of scientific teaching, doctors and Universities acquired a position and a role of authority of decisions or of

[2] Ibid., pp. 88–9.
[3] Op. cit., p. 105.
[4] Congar, p. 92; *In 4 Sent.*, d. 19, q. 2, a. 2, qa 2, ad 4.
[5] Cf. Jedin and Dolan, op. cit., vol. iv, p. 256.

calling for submission. The Studium [house of studies] is a third authority alongside the Sacerdotium [priestly estate] and the Regnum [ruling estate]. The Popes themselves use the Universities to publish collections of decretals . . . . There is more than a sounding of opinion. The Faculties judge doctrinal theses.[6]

It was this public recognition accorded to Doctors, Faculties, and Universities in the Church which gave such weight and authority to their general teaching on various matters and their pronouncements on specific subjects or public controversies, as well as underlying their sense of responsibility in theological and Church matters and their sensitivity to criticism and attack. As Karl August Fink concludes, 'since the High Middle Ages the universities, Paris at their head, had assumed the tasks of the *magisterium ordinarium*', the day to day teaching in the Church.[7]

It was not, of course, to be expected that in discharging such a function the Universities or their professors were always at one with the Church of Rome. Early in the thirteenth century Pope Gregory IX had occasion to complain to the Paris theologians of those who put the tail before the head and forced the queen of theology to serve the handmaid of philosophy.[8] And in the centuries to come relationships between the Papacy and the scientific exponents of theology were frequently strained, sometimes amicable and co-operative, and occasionally such that Popes felt obliged to intervene as arbiters of bitter controversy. At times, also, it appeared that the theologians were needed to come to the help and service of the Papacy, either in helping to adjudicate on their colleagues or in providing their expertise on various commissions, or, most strikingly, in the workings of various of the Councils of the Church. This last contribution was perhaps most in evidence at the Council of Constance, to which in 1414 large numbers of theologians and others turned up as the 'greatest congress of the Middle Ages'[9], whose major achievement, apart from voicing a universal yearning for reform of the Church and a control of papal

---

[6] Congar, p. 104.

[7] In Jedin and Dolan iv, p. 451. It is in the context of this magisterial role of the Universities that one can appreciate Henry VIII's seizing with alacrity on the suggestion of Thomas Cranmer that the question of the king's divorce be proposed for judgement to 'those most solemn authorities', J. J. Scarisbrick, *Henry VIII* (London, 1968), pp. 255–8.

[8] 'redigunt caput in caudam et ancillae cogunt famulari reginam', DS 824.

[9] Fink, in Jedin and Dolan, iv, pp. 451–2.

absolutism, was to adjudicate among the rival merits of three claimants to the papacy by persuading one to resign and deposing the other two. Neither Martin V, who was then elected Pope, nor his successors, ever welcomed the claims of Constance, or of the movement of conciliarism to which it gave birth (and to which Luther and others were later to appeal) that a general Council of the Church was superior to the Pope or could be appealed to against the Pope.[10] The Papacy did, however, welcome the verdict of Constance on the Oxford teacher, John Wyclif, in condemning forty-five propositions ascribed to him, including the proposition that 'Universities, study houses, colleges, graduations, and master-ships (*magisteria*) in them were introduced as pagan vanities, and are as much use to the Church as the devil is'![11]

The *magisterium*, or teaching activity, was also to be found, of course, in bishops and in the Pope; and this became increasingly the case with the growth of papal authority during the Middle Ages and as a consequence of the reaction to Reformation doctrines of the common priesthood of the faithful and of the principle of private judgement, the crisis of Jansenism and reaction to the Enlightenment, and most especially of the further loss to Catholicism of many of the European Universities in the aftermath of the French Revolution and the rule of Napoleon. A momentous factor in this concentration of teaching authority as one aspect of the growing centralization of international Church activity on Rome was the sharp distinction, introduced from the middle of the eighteenth century and strongly developed by German canonists and popular catechisms, between the 'teaching Church', the *Ecclesia docens*, and the 'learning Church', the *Ecclesia discens*. The role of the latter was to hear and to obey, particularly as the *Ecclesia docens* became more and more identified with the Church's *magisterium*, as localized and personified in the Church's hierarchy, and especially in the Pope, as ministers (*ministri*) of the *magisterium* of Christ and his Spirit.[12] One consequence of this development, as part of the analysis of the Church's authority into magisterial, ministerial, and jurisdictional (teaching, sanctifying, and ruling),

[10] Cf. *DS*, p. 315; nos. 1375, 1445.
[11] Cf. *DS*, p. 310. 'Universitates, studia, collegia, graduationes, et magisteria in iisdem sunt vana gentilitate introducta; tantum prosunt Ecclesiae, sicut diabolus', *DS* 1179.
[12] Congar, p. 94.

was the almost inevitable identification of the hierarchy as *the* Church and of others of the faithful as members of the Church in only a modified sense, which reached its climax in the appeal of Pope Pius XII to the laity to realize that they too are the Church.[13] Ironically, however, it was also in Pius XII that the claims of *magisterium* in the Church to be the complete prerogative of the hierarchy and the papacy were most strongly expressed, with his references to 'the living *Magisterium*' and 'this sacred *Magisterium*' in a significant personification and use of the capital letter, and with his warning to theologians that they were not to consider themselves teachers, or *magistri*, of the *Magisterium*.[14]

The Meaning of 'Morals' at Trent

The aspect of magisterial activity with which we are here concerned is that which directs itself to moral behaviour, of which the outstanding instance is the traditional couplet of 'faith and morals', used to describe the content of divine Revelation entrusted by Christ to his Church, and to be encountered for the first time in a major Church statement in one of the early decrees of the Council of Trent. Mounting concern over the laxity of morals, particularly of the clergy, was a particular feature of the sixteenth century in Europe, notwithstanding various Church attempts at reform. As early as 1523 the papal legate in Germany, Cardinal Campeggio, had objected that a local Diet at Nuremberg would contribute nothing to peace and harmony in Germany, 'and if, putting aside what concerns faith and religion, some maintain it should be held to restrain and restore the fallen morals and licentiousness of the clergy, I would reply that such corruptions have been sufficiently foreseen and provided for, and many laws have been passed on this matter' which only needed enforcing.[15] Fifteen years later a papal commission which included the English Cardinal Pole reported to

---

[13] Encyclical letter *Mystici Corporis*, DS 3801: 'Minime autem reputandum est, hanc ordine digestam seu "organicam", ut aiunt, Ecclesiae corporis structuram solis hierarchiae gradibus absolvi ac definiri.'

[14] 'ea quae a vivo Magisterio docentur', DS 3886; 'institutionibus et decretis sacri Magisterii', *AAS* 50 (1958), p. 151; 'hoc sacrum Magisterium', DS 3884; 'altrimente sarebbe un fare i Teologi quasi "*magistri Magisterii*"; il che è un evidente errore', *AAS* 48 (1956), p. 709.

[15] B. J. Kidd (ed.), *Documents Illustrative of the Continental Reformation* (Oxford, 1967), pp. 138–9. Cf. *infra*, n. 47.

Pope Paul III that the main source of the abuses and sickness in the Church lay in the manifold unsuitability of the clergy, including those of 'bad morals', and in the system of benefices, including bishoprics.[16]

As was to be expected, then, the Council of Trent devoted much attention not only to theological matters but also to disciplinary decrees and regulations which attempted to control the behaviour of the clergy of all ranks and which stressed the moral standards to be required of them.[17] Of actual moral teaching directed at the laity the Council contained very little, although it did, for instance, commend the cult of saints as encouraging an imitation of them in one's life and morals, and it also forbade the reading of obscene books, 'since regard must be had not only for faith but also for morals, which are often easily corrupted by reading such books'.[18] That the Council was deeply concerned about moral matters appears evident from the agenda which it set itself as it considered 'the magnitude of the subjects to be covered, especially under the two headings of rooting out heresies and reforming morals, which are the main reasons for its assembling'.[19] And the same can be gathered from the papal Bull confirming the completed work of the Council which described that work as 'dealing with, defining, and deciding on the Sacraments and other necessary matters, in order to confute heresies, remove abuses and correct morals'.[20]

This picture of the moral preoccupations of Trent is not, however, a perfectly clear one because of the peculiarity of the Latin word *mores*, a plural noun usually translated as 'morals', but which in its singular form *mos* has the sense of any established practice, or custom, or usage, without any particular moral connotation. In its singular form the word is quite commonly used by Trent to describe a specifically religious or devotional Christian practice, such as traditional devotion to the Blessed Sacrament,

---

[16] Ibid., pp. 308 ff. Cf. *infra*, n. 50.

[17] Cf. the disciplinary decrees elaborated alongside the better-known doctrinal decrees, COD, pp. 643–6, 657–9, etc.

[18] DS 1824, 1857.

[19] 'Haec ... Synodus, ... magnitudinem rerum tractandarum considerans, praesertim earum, quae duobus illis capitibus de exstirpandis haeresibus et moribus reformandis continentur, quorum causa praecipue est congregata ...', DS 1500.

[20] 'quae de sacramentis et aliis rebus, quae quidem necessariae visae sunt, tractanda, diffinienda et statuenda restabant ad confutandas haereses, ad tollendos abusus et emendandos mores, ...', DS 1847.

reservation of the Eucharist, and processions on the Feast of Corpus Christi, various prayers connected with the Sacrament of Penance, and 'that salutary practice' (*mos*) of annual Lenten Confession.[21] This being so, the question arises whether the occurrence in the documents of Trent of the plural form *mores* is to be invariably understood as referring in general to behaviour which has a moral connotation, that is, to 'morals', or whether it is to be seen as occasionally referring to various ecclesiastical, religious, or devotional 'practices', with the result that the traditional phrase 'faith and morals' might in some contexts of Trent be better rendered as 'faith and religious practices'.

The major early decree of Trent in which this phrase is used aimed at identifying and establishing the primary sources of Scripture and Traditions on which the Council would base its whole enterprise of 'removing errors and preserving the purity of the Gospel in the Church', and for more than twenty years scholars have been investigating what precisely the Fathers at Trent understood by the term *mores* in this foundation statement.[22] The most thorough study has been that of John L. Murphy in his examination of *The Notion of Tradition in John Driedo*, the sixteenth-century professor of theology at Louvain whose work very probably influenced the deliberations of Trent.[23] From his study of the writings of Driedo, the background documents of Trent, and the foundation decree of the Council, Murphy concludes that by 'traditions' are meant 'the practices, beliefs, or rites which were given to the Church by Christ or the Apostles . . . separate entities which could be named, some doctrinal in nature, others more disciplinary or liturgical.' He then proceeds to examine further the subdivision by Trent of these traditions into those pertaining to faith and those pertaining to *mores*, concluding that the latter are *apostolic traditions* 'of a ceremonial, liturgical, or disciplinary nature'.[24] His final conclusion on the sense of *mores*,

---

[21] 'pro more in catholica Ecclesia semper recepto', *DS* 1643; 'vetustissimo Catholicae Ecclesiae more', *DS* 1645; 'pie et religiose admodum . . . inductum fuisse hunc morem', *DS* 1644; 'de Ecclesiae sanctae more', *DS* 1673; 'mos ille salutaris confitendi sacro illo et maxime acceptabili tempore Quadragesimae', *DS* 1683.

[22] Cf. M. Bévenot, 'Faith and Morals', *Heythrop Journal*, 3 (1962), pp. 15–30; G. Thils, *L'infaillibilité pontificale* (Gembloux, 1969), pp. 207–09.

[23] J. L. Murphy, *The Notion of Tradition in John Driedo* (Milwaukee, 1959). Murphy's study was a doctoral dissertation for the Gregorian University, Rome.

[24] Ibid., pp. 291–5.

which Congar found attractive, is that 'there surely is no hint in the *Acta* of the Council that the Fathers in speaking of the "mores" were referring to moral principles of any sort, as we would understand the term today. "Mores" at Trent would seem to indicate the practices and customs of the Apostolic Church, some of which touch upon doctrinal matter, others having to do with disciplinary or ceremonial practices.'[25]

If this last sentence is to be understood as implying that the Council never used the term *mores* in a formally moral sense, then it manifestly claims too much.[26] And if it implies that *mores* in the non-moral sense is used by Trent to refer not only to practices but also to formulated doctrines, then it not only blurs the Tridentine distinction between faith and *mores*, but it also confuses the distinction of traditions which Murphy establishes between those of a doctrinal nature and those of a practical nature. Nevertheless, confirmation of his basic conclusion that in its Fourth Session the Council's *Decree on Accepting the Sacred Books and the Traditions*, which we have termed its foundation decree, used the noun *mores* not of moral matters but of religious practices appears forthcoming from a consideration of the religious and theological controversies which preceded and occasioned the Council, and also from examination of the internal argument of the Decree itself.

The two meanings of *mores* which, for convenience, we may term the moral and the religious, are to be found in theological literature for centuries before Trent, and we find Aquinas possibly sensing a need for precision in referring to 'good *mores*' and 'matters involving faith and good *mores*', as contrasted with the religious sense which, not long before his birth, the Fourth Lateran Council had implied in referring to 'the *mores* and rites' of Greek Christians.[27] In the fifteenth century the Council of Florence was to describe the decree of the Council of Jerusalem as appropriate to

---

[25] Ibid., p. 300. Congar found Murphy's conclusion 'entirely convincing', but he also noted that earlier usage, from the twelfth and thirteenth centuries, gave the general meaning of 'faith and morals', *Tradition and Traditions* (London, 1976), p. 158, n. 3.

[26] Cf. Session XXI, Decree on reformation, canon 2, 'ne quis deinceps clericus saecularis, quamvis alias sit idoneus moribus, scientia et aetate . . .', *COD*, 705, 3–4.

[27] Aquinas, *STh* 1a 2ae, q. 100, a. 1; *Quodlib.* III, 4, 2. IV Lateran, 'Licet Graecos . . . honorare velimus, mores ac ritus eorum, in quantum cum Domino possumus, sustinendo, . . .' (*DS* 810). With this sense, cf. Aquinas, *STh* 3a, q. 28, a. 4: 'secundum quod mores illius temporis exigebant.'

the period when one Church would emerge from Jews and Gentiles 'who previously lived according to different ceremonies and *mores*' relating to clean and unclean foods.[28] But earlier in the century we find both senses of the word in connection with the teachings and condemnation of John Huss, the Bohemian reformer who was influenced by Wyclif. On the one hand he is quoted as questioning the legitimacy of any Pope who does not live according to the *mores* of Christ and St Peter, in an obvious moral sense which does not require qualification, but on the other hand he is also quoted as castigating evil-living priests for being unfaithful in their attitude to 'the seven Sacraments of the Church, the keys, Offices, censures, *mores*, ceremonies and sacred things of the Church, the veneration of relics, indulgences and Orders', a catalogue which indicates religious practices rather than the moral sense of the term.[29] On the day Huss's errors were condemned at the Council of Constance he was burned to death, and three years later a papal decree listing the questions to be put to followers of Wyclif and Huss by inquisitors included the interrogation whether they agreed with what the Council of Constance condemned as 'contrary to faith or good *mores*'.[30]

In the sixteenth century, as the Church of Rome gathered its forces against Luther, the Bull *Exsurge, Domine* of 1520 (which Luther publicly burned) listed a series of forty-one errors attributed

---

[28] '[Romana Ecclesia] dicit illi tempori congruisse, quo ex Judaeis atque gentilibus, qui antea diversis ceremoniis moribusque vivebant, una surgebat Ecclesia', *DS* 1350. The meaning of 'mores' is clear from the Council's contrast between that diversity and the later period when all would unit 'in eosdem ritus Evangelii ceremoniasque', ibid.

[29] 'Nemo gerit vicem Christi vel Petri, nisi sequatur eum in moribus: ... quia ad illud officium vicariatus requiritur et morum conformitas et instituentis auctoritas', *DS* 1212. Taken in itself, this statement could refer to 'mores' in the ceremonial sense, but it is perhaps more likely to be the moral sense in view of the charge, 'Papa non est verus et manifestus successor Apostolorum principis Petri, si vivit moribus contrariis Petro .... Et pari evidentia Cardinales ..., nisi vixerint more Apostolorum, servantes mandata et consilia Domini nostri Iesu Christi', *DS* 1213. However, it is difficult to exclude the religious sense of *mores* in the passage where it is listed with various Church practices: 'Sacerdotes quomodolibet criminose viventes, sacerdotii polluunt potestatem, et sicut filii infideles sentiunt infideliter de septem sacramentis Ecclesiae, de clavibus, officiis, censuris, moribus, caeremoniis, et sacris rebus Ecclesiae, veneratione reliquiarum, indulgentiis et ordinibus', *DS* 1208.

[30] 'Item, utrum credat, quod illud, quod sacrum Concilium Constantiense, universalem Ecclesiam repraesentans, ... condemnavit et condemnat esse fidei vel bonis moribus contrarium, hoc ab iisdem esse tenendum pro condemnato, credendum et asserendum', *DS* 1248.

to him, including the statement that 'It is certainly not in the power of the Church or the Pope to lay down articles of faith, or even laws of *mores*, that is, of good works'.[31] At first sight it might appear that by explaining *mores* in terms of laws laying down good works both Luther and his adversaries had in mind explicitly moral teaching on which, together with faith, he denied competence to ecclesiastical authority. Perusal, however, of Luther's original statement in its context indicates rather that he had a quite different sense in mind. Enlarging on the disputation in which he had engaged at Leipzig in 1519 with the papal spokesman, John Eck, who later drew up this papal list of Lutheran errors, and in the context of the dispute over indulgences, on which Pope Leo X had recently pronounced, Luther affirmed, 'It is certainly not in the power of the Church or the Pope to lay down articles of faith, or even laws of *mores*, that is, of good works, on the grounds that all these are handed down in Sacred Scripture. All it has power to do is to declare articles, and secondly, for the external beauty of the Church of God, to regulate ceremonies, which it also discontinues if piety so requires.'[32] It seems clear from this fuller statement of Luther that he was arguing that the Church had competence to declare or identify those articles of faith which were contained in Scripture, but not to invent new ones, such as its doctrine of indulgences; and that it could certainly make regulations from time to time affecting religious ceremonies as appropriate, but it could not pass laws binding universally for all time relating to those 'good works' which attracted and merited the conferring and the gaining of indulgences. That *mores*, then, does not refer in the papal Bull to moral teaching which Luther claimed was not handed down in Scripture, but to religious and devotional practices, is confirmed by his explanation in 1518 to Pope Leo, at the early stage of his

---

[31] 'Certum est, in manu Ecclesiae aut Papae prorsus non esse statuere articulos fidei, immo nec leges morum seu bonorum operum', *DS* 1447.

[32] 'Primo quicquid sit de extravagante illa et declaratoria, certum est, in manu Ecclesiae aut Papae prorsus non esse articulos fidei statuere, immo nec leges morum seu bonorum operum, quod haec omnia in sacris literis sint tradita. Ideo, reliquum est, ut articulorum declarandorum tantummodo potestatem habeat, deinde cerimonias ordinare ad externam speciem Ecclesiae dei, quas rursum destituat, si pietatis ratio postulet', *Resolutiones Lutherianae super propositionibus suis Lipsiae disputatis, 1519*, Conclusio X; *D. Martin Luthers Werke* (Weimar, 1884), vol. ii, p. 427, 8–13. From the opening phrase of Luther it is clear that he is rejecting the Bull of 9th November 1518 sent by Pope Leo X to Cardinal Cajetan justifying the Roman doctrine of indulgences against Luther's earlier attacks. Cf. *DS* 1447 et proem.

conflict with the Church, that 'I was disputing not about faith, not about *mores*, not about the precepts of God or the Church, but, as I have said, about indulgences'.[33] The behaviour which he describes as *mores*, and later as 'good works', cannot be connected with divine or ecclesiastical moral teaching.[34]

What rapidly became a central issue between Luther and the Church of Rome, as one can appreciate from these and other texts, was not primarily criticism of moral standards of behaviour, even that of the clergy and religious orders, but rather a pervasive and popular theology of 'good works' which the Augustinian monk considered to be totally at odds with the sufficiency of faith alone for justification before God. Innumerable religious and devotional practices, devotions to saints, repetitions and applications of private Masses, penitential practices, celibacy, and many other instances of ecclesiastically encouraged or commanded works, were viewed by him and other reformers as so many blasphemous human attempts to 'merit' grace for one's self and others, and so win one's own way to heaven. In other words, it was more the theological thinking underlying many Church practices than any moral aspect which offended the Reformers and which helped explain the evangelical zeal motivating their attack on such practices and on the warrant and authority of the Church in

---

[33] 'Et licet ego non de fide, non de moribus, non de praeceptis dei aut ecclesiae, sed de indulgentiis (ut dixi) disputarem, quae nec praeceptae nec consultae nec meritoriae sunt, . . .', *Appellatio a Caietano ad Papam, 1518*, Werke, ibid., p. 29, 31–3. The distinction is clear between *mores* and the moral law, whether of God or the Church. On the onerous practices (*moribus*) imposed by confessors on their penitents, cf. *Confitendi ratio* (152), Werke, vol. vi, p. 169, 6–12, 'Sed quis omnes tyrannides recenseat, quibus confitentium et poenitentium miserae conscientiae Christianorum mortiferis constitionibus et moribus quottidie exagitantur per ineptos homunculos, qui alligare tantum noverunt onera gravia et importabilia et imponere humeris hominum, quae ipsi nec digito volunt movere? Et factum est hoc saluberrimum poenitentiae sacramentum aliud nihil quam mera tyrannis magnatum.'

[34] For further illumination on Luther's understanding of *mores*, cf. the interesting series of parallels (here italicized) in *Resolutio Lutheriana super propositione XIII. de potestate papae* (1519), Werke, vol. ii, pp. 199, 41–200, 6, 'Vere nimis nihil times, mi Leo, pronunciare, audens *humana statuta evangeliis* aequare, et audacter satis affirmas, iis non servatis nec fidem catholicam servari. Si de contemptoribus et iis qui sub te sunt diceres, recte diceres: nunc contra, quando *mores et fidem, traditiones cum evangelio, verbum hominum cum verbo dei* confundis, nonne homo es? Quis ferat, ut evangelium et fidem non servare putetur, qui sub statutis illis non fuerit? Tu cum tuis serva statuta et canones: illis, qui sunt in oriente, alia sunt *statuta*, sed idem *evangelium*.' It seems clear that Luther is contrasting, on the one hand, human decrees, mores, traditions, and the word of men, with, on the other hand, the gospels, faith, the gospel, and the word of God.

promoting them. Against claims of authority and tradition about various such religious practices Protestants were not slow to put historical objections, and the Confession of Augsburg described to the Emperor, Charles V, how in some States of the Empire the chalice was now given to the laity, 'since this practice (*mos*) has the mandate of the Lord', how the 'practice of the Church' in requiring celibacy of priests was contrary to God's mandate of marriage, and how the dropping of private Masses in favour of public Masses was not 'a new practice in the Church'.[35] As for specific and detailed penitential exercises—'works to merit grace and make satisfaction for sins'—[36]

we retain most traditions which are conducive to orderly behaviour in the Church . . . . But meantime men are advised that such cult does not justify one before God, and that such things are not matter for sin if they are omitted without scandal. This freedom in human rites was not unknown to the Fathers. In the East they observed Easter at a different time from Rome, and when the Romans accused the East of schism because of this dissimilarity, they were informed by others that such practices (*mores*) did not have to be everywhere the same. As Irenaeus said, disharmony over fasting does not destroy the harmony of faith.[37]

The Diet of Augsburg, however, did not succeed in its primary aim of 'bringing pious resolution to dissensions in holy faith and Christian religion',[38] and the Emperor ordered a peace until a

---

[35] 'Laicis datur utraque species sacramenti in Coena Domini, quia hic mos habet mandatum Domini Matt. xxvi [, 27]', Kidd, op. cit., p. 271. 'Quum autem exstet mandatum Dei, quum mos ecclesiae notus sit, quum impurus caelibatus plurima pariat scandala, . . .', ibid., p. 272. 'servatur apud nos una communis missa singulis feriis . . . ubi porrigitur sacramentum his qui petunt. Neque hic mos in ecclesia novus est. Nam veteres ante Gregorium non faciunt mentionem privatae missae: de communi missa plurimum loquuntur', ibid., p. 275.

[36] 'non ut per illa exercitia mereamur gratiam, aut satisfaciamus pro peccatis', ibid., p. 278.

[37] 'Servantur tamen apud nos pleraeque traditiones, quae conducunt ad hoc ut res ordine geratur in ecclesia; ut ordo lectionum in missa et praecipuae feriae. Sed interim homines admonentur, quod talis cultus non iustificet coram Deo, et quod non sit ponendum peccatum in talibus rebus, si omittantur sine scandalo. Haec libertas in ritibus humanis non fuit ignota Patribus. Nam in Oriente alio tempore servaverunt Pascha quam Romae: et quum Romani propter hanc dissimilitudinem accusarent Orientem schismatis, admoniti sunt ab aliis, tales mores non oportere ubique similes esse. Et Irenaeus inquit, "Dissonantia ieiunii fidei consonantiam non solvit" ', Kidd, p. 279.

[38] 'et imprimis de dissensionibus in sancta fide et religione Christiana pie componendis', Kidd, p. 298.

Council of the Church could be convened.[39] Eventually, after many
delays, the Council of Trent was to begin in 1545 to take up what
had been agitating Europe for a generation, the Emperor decreeing
in 1548 an interim religious compromise in his territories by which
many instances of a practice (*mos*) of 'the old Church' and many
'old ceremonies' were to remain in force, including those of
Baptism, the Mass and other Sacraments, services for the dead,
Rogation Days and other processions, and 'the practice (*mos*) and
institution' of regular days of fasting and abstinence.[40]

The counter-attack of Trent was to take due note of the two-
pronged Protestant attack on the various religious and devotional
practices of 'the old Church': the historical attack on their
authenticity as expressive of the Gospel; and, more importantly, the
theological attack on the doctrine of 'good works' which inspired
them. The carefully argued teaching of the Council of Trent on
man's justification by God is the finest achievement of what was by
many standards a great Council, and within that *Decree on
Justification*, comprising sixteen headings and thirty-three concluding canons, serious and detailed consideration was given to the
worth and quality of man's actions after justification, particularly
in the sixteenth chapter, 'The fruit of justification: the merit of
good works and the notion of merit'.[41] The various Scriptural
passages referring to the need for good works and the theme of
reward for perseverance were sifted and balanced, and an elegantly
poised doctrine expressed of which the following is typical.

What is called our justice, since we are justified by it inhering in us, is the
justice of God, since it is poured into us by God through the merit of
Christ. And it should not be forgotten that, although Scripture pays tribute
to good works to the extent that Christ promises reward even to anyone
giving a drink of water to his little ones, and Paul testifies that our present
slight momentary affliction is working in us an eternal weight of glory,

---

[39] 'Imperatoria Maiestas etiam vult atque serio praecipit ut interea pacem per
Imperium colant omnes, ne Saxo sociique novi quid de religione . . . patiantur, . . .
ne veterem religionem sequentes . . . prohibeant, nec denique monasticis utriusque
generis personis, quominus et sacra peragant et delictorum audiant confessionem, et
Coenam Domini suo more administrent, ullum facessant negotium', Kidd, pp. 299–
300.

[40] 'Vigiliae item et exsequiae mortuorum de more veteris Ecclesiae celebrentur
. . . et per annum aliae consuetae processiones pro veteri more observentur . . . mos
et institutum veteris Ecclesiae diebus ieiuniorum . . . retineatur', Kidd, pp. 360–1.

[41] De fructu iustificationis, hoc est, de merito bonorum operum, deque ipsius
meriti ratione, DS 1545.

nevertheless no Christian may either trust or glory in himself rather than in the Lord whose goodness towards all men is so great that he wishes what are his gifts to be their merits.[42]

With such a theology to rebut what it considered the extremism of the Reformers and their Augustinian failure to do justice to the mystery of how God works in man his creature's own works, the Council considered it also necessary to establish the Apostolic authenticity of religious and devotional practices by appeal to the earliest traditions of the Christian community. This it set out to do from the start in what we have called its foundation decree, in which it laid out the method it proposed to adopt throughout the labours of the Council:

Our Lord Jesus Christ, the Son of God, first promulgated the Gospel personally, and then ordered it to be preached through his Apostles to every creature as the source of all saving truth and of all regulation of *mores*. The truth and regulation are contained in the written books and the unwritten traditions received by the Apostles from Christ or coming down to us from the Apostles as dictated by the Holy Spirit. In view of this, the . . . Synod follows the examples of orthodox Fathers in receiving and respecting with equal affection and reverence all the books of the Old as well as the New Testament (the one God being author of both), and also those traditions relating both to faith and to *mores* as either verbally from Christ or dictated by the Holy Spirit, and preserved in continuous succession in the Catholic Church.

After then listing the books of the Bible which it received, the Council concluded, 'Let everyone therefore understand how the Synod is going to proceed after laying the foundation of its confession of faith, and what principal witnesses and resources it is

---

[42] 'Ita neque propria nostra iustitia tamquam ex nobis propria statuitur, neque ignoratur aut repudiatur iustitia Dei; quae enim iustitia nostra dicitur, quia per eam nobis inhaerentem iustificamur, illa eadem Dei est, quia a Deo nobis infunditur per Christi meritum. Neque vero illud omittendum est, quod, licet bonis operibus in sacris Litteris usque adeo tribuatur, ut etiam qui uni ex minimis suis potum aquae frigidae dederit, promittat Christus, eum non esse sua mercede cariturum, et Apostolus testetur, id quod in praesenti est momentaneum et leve tribulationis nostrae, supra modum in sublimitate aeternum gloriae pondus operari in nobis: absit tamen, ut christianus homo in se ipso vel confidat vel glorietur et non in Domino, cuius tanta est erga omnes homines bonitas, ut eorum velit esse merita, quae sunt ipsius dona', *DS* 1547–8. The final balance between merits and gifts here is repeated from the fifth century *Indiculus*, on which cf. *supra*, p. 50. (*DS* 248), and finds an echo in the 1971 *Missale Romanum*, in the first Preface for feasts of saints, 'et eorum coronando merita tua dona coronas'. The idea originates in Augustine; *PL* 33, 880.

going to use in strengthening dogmas and in restoring *mores* in the Church.'[43] In a subsidiary decree the Council went on to defend the Latin Vulgate version of Scripture, and charged 'in order to control impudent spirits, that no one should rely on his own prudence to twist Sacred Scripture to his own meanings in matters of faith and *mores* pertaining to the building up of Christian doctrine, against that meaning which holy Mother Church has held and holds . . . .'[44]

If *mores* in this decree is to be taken in the moral sense it is strange that Trent appeared to find their regulation only in traditions and not apparently in Scripture, for the distinction between saving truth and regulation of *mores* appears to correspond to the distinction between Scripture and traditions.[45] Moreover, the *mores* in question are seen as pertaining to the edification of Christian teaching, a function which might more appropriately be performed by religious and devotional practices. And the fundamental theological controversy over justification and good works which was the basic issue of the Reformers had, as we have seen, led to the desire or the fact of many current changes in the practice of religion which the Council was determined to resist by, as it said, strengthening dogmas and restoring *mores* in the Church. If one accepts that, as Jedin writes, the Council of Trent was 'the official

---

[43] 'Sacrosancta . . . Synodus, . . . hoc sibi perpetuo ante oculos proponens, ut sublatis erroribus puritas ipsa Evangelii in Ecclesia conservetur, quod promissum ante per Prophetas in Scripturis sanctis Dominus noster Iesus Christus Dei Filius proprio ore primum promulgavit, deinde per suos Apostolos tamquam fontem omnis et *salutaris veritatis* et *morum disciplinae* "omni creaturae praedicari" iussit; perspiciensque, hanc *veritatem* et *disciplinam* contineri in *libris* scriptis et sine scripto *traditionibus*, quae ab ipsius Christi ore ab Apostolis acceptae, aut ab ipsis Apostolis Spiritu Sancto dictante quasi per manus traditae ad nos usque pervenerunt, orthodoxorum Patrum exempla secuta, *omnes libros* tam Veteris quam Novi Testamenti, cum utriusque unus Deus sit auctor, nec non *traditiones* ipsas, tum ad *fidem*, tum ad *mores* pertinentes, tamquam vel oretenus a Christo, vel a Spiritu Sancto dictatas et continua successione in Ecclesia catholica conservatas, pari pietatis affectu ac reverentia suscipit et veneratur . . . . Omnes itaque intelligant, quo ordine et via ipsa Synodus post iactum fidei confessionis fundamentum sit progressura, et quibus potissimum testimoniis ac praesidiis in *confirmandis dogmatibus* et *instaurandis in Ecclesia moribus* sit usura', *Decretum de libris sacris et de traditionibus recipiendis*, DS 1501, 1505. Italics added.

[44] 'Praeterea ad coercenda petulantia ingenia decernit, ut nemo, suae prudentiae innixus, in *rebus fidei* et *morum*, ad aedificationem doctrinae christianae pertinentium, sacram Scripturam ad suos sensus contorquens, contra eum sensum, quem tenuit et tenet sancta mater Ecclesia, cuius est iudicare de vero sensu et interpretatione Scripturarum sanctarum . . . interpretari audeat . . .', DS 1507.

[45] Cf. Luther's own contrast between: human statutes and the gospel; mores and faith; traditions and the gospel; the word of men and the word of God; *supra*, 34.

Catholic answer to Protestantism', then an understanding of the teaching of Trent must depend on identifying the Protestant charges which it considered it was answering.[46] Morality as such did not appear to be a major difference between the parties, but religious practices did, and in all the circumstances it might be nearer the truth of Trent to identify its agenda not as 'faith and morals' but, in the phrase used by both Cardinal Campeggio and the Diet of Augsburg, as 'faith and religion'.[47]

Many of the texts of Trent are capable of this interpretation and some appear to require it, while yet other documents both before and after the Council yield more sense when so understood. Thus, in an early attempt to deal with Luther's attack on indulgences, the Dominican papal theologian, Silvester Prierias, had countered that

the Roman Church can decree something about faith and *mores* both in word and by action. There is no difference between the two, except that words are more obvious than actions, but the reason why custom acquires the force of law is because the will of the superior is permissively or effectively expressed in actions. Consequently, just as anyone who thinks badly of the truth of Scripture is a heretic, so also is anyone who thinks badly of the teaching and actions of the Church in matters relating to faith and *mores*.[48]

[46] Jedin, 'The Council of Trent and Reunion: Historical Notes', *Heythrop Journal* 3 (1962), p. 3. 'Since the Bull *Exsurge Domine* of 1520 the highest authority of the Church had been silent. Now, in the dogmatic decrees of the Council of Trent, it authoritatively separated Catholic doctrine from Protestantism.'

[47] 'Itaque neque ad pacem neque ad quietem neque ad concordiam Germaniae congregationem hanc profuturam iudico. Quod si, omissi quae ad fidem et religionem spectant, dixerint aliqui praedictam congregationem suscipiendam esse in hanc rationem ut lapsi mores et cleri licentia coerceatur et restituatur, illud respondere libere possum huiusmodi corruptelae iam satis cautum et provisum et leges in hac re multa latas esse; quae si observari mandentur et ad id me, sufficienti facultate munitum vocaverint, statim omnia fuerint restituta', Kidd, p. 138–9. For Augsburg, cf. *supra*, n. 38. It will be noted that Campeggio refers here also to 'mores', probably in the moral sense, which he is enabled to do without ambiguity by referring to the main bones of German contention as 'faith and religion'. To suggest that these be disregarded and that he simply be given sufficient authority to enforce Rome's legislation indicates in the papel legate a less than adequate appreciation of the total situation in 1524, despite the scene which met him on his entry into Nürnberg. Cf. Kidd, pp. 134–5.

[48] 'Ecclesia Romana sicut verbo ita et facto potest circa fidem et mores aliquid decernere. Nec in hoc differentia ulla est, praeter id quod verba sunt accommodatiora quam facta. Unde hac ratione consuetudo vim legis obtinet, quia voluntas principis factis permissive aut effective exprimitur. Et consequenter, quemadmodum haereticus est male sentiens circa Scripturarum veritatem, ita et male sentiens circa doctrinam et facta ecclesiae, in spectantibus ad fidem et mores, haereticus est', Kidd, p. 32.

And after Trent the Roman Catechism of 1566 does not refer to the Church's competence as that of teaching 'morals', its only use of the phrase 'faith and *mores*' apparently occurring in a polemical reference to self-styled Churches and their practices: 'Just as this one Church cannot err in handing on the regulation of faith and *mores* since it is governed by the Holy Spirit, so all others claiming the name of Church, being led by the spirit of the devil, must incur the most pernicious errors of doctrine and *mores*.'[49]

It remains, however, that before, during and after Trent, the term *mores* was also used in its sense of 'morals' alongside that of devotional or religious practices, and this even when coupled with 'faith'; and this must often result in uncertainty about the precise significance of the word and confusion about its practical bearing.[50] As we shall see later in this chapter such confusion was not absent from the First Vatican Council when it came to define papal infallibility in 'matters of faith and morals'. Nor does it follow, of course, from our conclusion that Trent's foundation decree was directed in the mind of those who composed it to problems of 'faith

---

[49] 'Sed quemadmodum haec una ecclesia errare non potest in fidei ac morum disciplina tradenda, quum a Spiritu sancto gubernetur; ita ceteras omnes, quae sibi ecclesiae nomen arrogant, ut quae diaboli spiritu ducantur, in doctrinae et morum perniciosissimis erroribus versari necesse est', *Roman Catechism*, I, 10, xvi. In part III, in which the Catechism treats of morals in terms of the Decalogue, no reference is made to the Church's competence in *mores*, although the popular sense is apparent in its reference to 'pravis moribus et diuturna perversitate', III, 1, iii.

[50] In 1538, a committee of Cardinals appointed secretly by Pope Paul III reported on ways of 'improving the Church' by diagnosing 'those abuses, most serious diseases, from which the church of God has long been suffering, and especially this Roman curia'. The root cause had lain in some of Paul's predecessors, who had surrounded themselves with advisers to justify their every action, including the disposition of all benefices in the Church. This was the Trojan horse from which all the abuses and sickness of the Church burst forth and evoked the derision of unbelievers. As Aristotle [!] had observed, laws simply had to be obeyed; and dispensations of any kind weakened observance, even by the Pope. Since the Pope cared for the Church through ministers who were all clerics, everything depended on the choice and appointment of such men, and on eliminating all abuses connected therewith. The first such abuse lay in ordaining men with no concern for their quality or qualification, with the result that 'passim quicunque sint imperitissimi, sint vilissimo genere orti, sint malis moribus ornati, sint adolescentes, admitantur ad ordines sacros et maxime ad presbyteratum'. The need was to have such ordinations supervised in every diocese and to have a master to instruct the minor clerics 'et litteris et moribus'. There followed a close analysis of the various abuses of benefices and absenteeism among the higher clergy, not by any means excluding cardinals. Since the Roman church was the *mater et magistra* of other churches, it should be outstanding in 'divinus cultus et morum honestas', Kidd, pp. 307–18.

and religion', that the Church's warrant to teach with authority in matters of morality was in any sense diminished. The most one can conclude is that this issue was not at the forefront of the Reformation battle. In the aftermath of Trent, however, and in the deployment of all the forces of the Counter-Reformation, the authority and prerogatives of the Papacy were strongly propounded, not least by the Jesuit Cardinal Robert Bellarmine, Professor of Controversial Theology at the Roman College, whose adversaries included King James I of England and who was caricatured for this *lèse-majesté* on innumerable Bellarmine jugs. The Italian theologian was not a moralist, of course, but a positive and dogmatic theologian who did much to elucidate Rome's doctrine on the Church and the Papacy, and whose authority and arguments were to play a major part in the debates of Vatican I.[51] In his Third General Controversy, on the subject of the Supreme Pontiff, he first showed with a great wealth of detail 'that the Roman Pontiff and Antichrist have nothing in common', and then proceeded to a close analysis of the Pope's 'spiritual power', including the questions whether the Pope has power to judge controversies of faith and morals, and whether such judgements are infallible.[52]

Bellarmine found common ground with 'heretics' in agreeing that the Pope, even with his advisers, and even with a General Council, can be mistaken in particular controversies of fact, which rely especially on information and human testimony; and that the Pope as a private teacher in faith and morals can make mistakes out of ignorance, like any other teacher. But all Catholics are agreed, he continued, with a welcome precision of language, that the Pope with a General Council cannot make a mistake in laying down decrees of faith or 'general precepts of morals'.[53] 'The Supreme Pontiff cannot be mistaken, not only in decrees of faith but in precepts of morals which are prescribed for the whole Church and

---

[51] It was no coincidence that Bellarmine's *Opera Omnia* appeared in the Vivès edition in 1870.

[52] Ibid., vol. ii, pp. 77–88.

[53] 'His notatis, conveniunt omnes Catholici et haeretici in duobus. Primo, posse Pontificem, etiam ut Pontificem, et cum suo coetu consiliariorum, vel cum generali Concilio, errare in controversiis facti particularibus, quae ex informatione, testimoniisque hominum praecipue pendent .... Deinde Catholici omnes in aliis duobus conveniunt .... Primo, Pontificem cum generali Concilio non posse errare in condendis Fidei decretis, vel generalibus praeceptis morum', ibid., p. 79.

have to do with matters necessary for salvation or with matters which are good or bad in themselves.'[54] He could not make the mistake of commanding the whole Church to practice what is in fact a vice, such as usury, or not to practice what is in fact a virtue, such as restitution for harm, these being good things or bad things in themselves. Nor could he command what is contrary to salvation, such as circumcision or observance of the Sabbath, nor forbid what is necessary to salvation, such as baptism or the Eucharist. To believe otherwise would be to call in question the holiness of the Church professed in the Creed. The Church believes that every virtue is good and every vice bad, and 'the Church would be obliged to believe that vices are good and virtues bad, unless it was willing to sin against conscience. For in doubtful matters the Church is obliged to agree with the judgement of the Supreme Pontiff and to do what he commands and not to do what he prohibits; and lest it should act against conscience, it is obliged to believe that good which he orders, and that bad which he prohibits.'[55]

Thus writes Bellarmine the Counter-Reformation controversialist and the loyal follower of Ignatius Loyola, founder of the Jesuits, and of his rules for thinking with the hierarchical Church.[56] But in raising the whole question of doubtful moral matters he is also touching the apparently simple moral question which was to agitate and dominate moral theology for at least the next century and a half, and to leave its mark on the science even into the twentieth century—the question 'what am I to do when I am not sure what to do?' Bellarmine had asserted that all Catholics were agreed that when the Pope, acting alone or with his advisers, decides something

[54] 'Caput V. De decretis morum. Tertia propositio haec esse potest: "Non solum in decretis Fidei errare non potest summus Pontifex, sed neque in praeceptis morum, quae toti Ecclesiae praescribuntur, et quae in rebus necessariis ad salutem, vel in iis quae per se bona, vel mala sunt, versantur" ', ibid., p. 87.

[55] 'Tenetur enim in rebus dubiis Ecclesia acquiescere iudicio summi Pontificis, et facere quod ille praecipit, non facere quod ille prohibet: ac ne forte contra conscientiam agat, tenetur credere bonum esse quod ille praecipit: malum quod ille prohibet', ibid., pp. 87–8.

[56] Ignatius and his first nine companions were established as the Company of Jesus in 1540 by Pope Paul III in the Bull *Regimini militantis Ecclesiae*, and became 'in time the first, as in operation the most effective, instrument of the Counter-Reformation', Kidd, op. cit., p. 335. In his famous little book, *The Spiritual Exercises*, Ignatius closed with a collection of eighteen rules describing the correct attitude one should have towards the Church. Cf. *Monumenta Ignatiana, Exercitia Spiritualia* (Madrid, 1919), pp. 548–63.

in a matter which is doubtful, then, whether he can be mistaken or not, he is to be listened to obediently by all the faithful.[57] Short of such papal intervention, or perhaps even notwithstanding such intervention, what other criteria were available for resolving moral doubts and what weight in such questions was to be accorded the views, and the teaching authority, of the moral theologian?

When in Doubt: Probabilism

The question was not unreasonable. A Church which of its nature is a conserving body is ever ill-equipped to cope with change, and such was the Church which asserted itself in and after Trent, when a revived Scholasticism based on the works of Aquinas attempted to grapple with the profound changes which had come upon medieval Europe. The task, even when approached positively, was a formidable one, compounded of social changes and divisions, religious antagonisms interacting with nationalism, movements towards individualism and political absolutism, European expansion in America and Asia, the move from urban to national economies, and the increasing diffusion of humanism and human values, with the philosophical and theological optimism thus engendered. Within a severely contracted Roman Catholic Church and with what Universities still remained to the Church and such as were newly founded, moral theologians, notably Dominican and Jesuit, addressed themselves to the serious and pressing political, economic, and social problems of a new age, not always with results pleasing to civil authorities. And they also, as we have seen, attempted to render their moral teaching and solutions to cases of conscience accessible to the parochial clergy, most of whom did not attend University or have much in the way of libraries, and whose general education and formation had been such a source of legitimate concern at Trent.[58]

At the same time, for reasons which we shall explore in the next chapter, morality had come to be seen to a large extent as expressible in legal pronouncements, and could therefore be handled and interpreted according to principles of jurisprudence. From this background the distinction of introducing the moral system known as Probabilism must go to the Spanish Dominican

---

[57] *Supra*, n. 55.   [58] Cf. Angelini and Valsecchi, op. cit., pp. 111–12.

Professor of Theology at Valladolid, and later Salamanca, Bartolomeo de Medina, who expressed the view in 1577 in his *Commentary* on Aquinas that 'if an opinion is probable, . . . it is permissible to adopt it, even if the opposite be more probable'. And if one wishes to know what constitutes a probable opinion, it is one 'stated by wise men and confirmed by very good arguments'.[59] This principle of probabilism, now so clearly expressing what various other theologians had been feeling their way towards, was taken up, developed, and applied to many moral dilemmas by major theologians, notably Bañez, Vasquez, and Suarez.

It was extremely useful in offering a rule which allowed one to escape from doubt and to come to a decision in all those cases to which there were differing moral solutions. In such cases, it was stated, it is permissible to follow that view which seems really probable, even if the contrary view is equally probable or actually more probable. Basically it was simply an application of a more general principle which no one questioned, 'a doubtful law does not oblige one'.[60]

To understand the theme and variations of probabilism as they now developed, it is important to be clear just what moral theologians meant by 'probable' and 'probability'. In English usage to say that something is probable tends to imply that the odds are in its favour, and to say that something is probably the case means that it is more likely than not to be the case. That is exactly what the technical term 'probable' does not mean. In moral parlance 'probable' really means 'proveable' or 'arguable', something for which there is a good argument, or two or more good arguments, irrespective of the merits of any alternative. By contrast, if one balances the arguments for and against a certain line of action as morally permissible and then comes down in favour of the stronger arguments, the moral theologian would consider that an exercise, not of probabilism, but of acting on the 'more probable', or of 'probabiliorism', a line of thought which Medina and other probabilists rejected as expressing the need to have not just a good case, but the better case, in one's moral decision.

Should it happen, however, that the arguments for and against a

[59] 'Si est opinio probabilis (quam scilicet asserunt viri sapientes et confirmant optima argumenta), licitum est eam sequi, licet opposita probabilior sit', quoted ibid., p. 116.
[60] Ibid.

particular decision were not tipped in either direction, but the scales were nicely poised, then, some were to argue, and only then, one could follow either view, adopting the system of 'equal prob- abilities', or 'aequiprobabilism'. And to complete the picture, there was yet a fourth possible line of action. In an important moral matter, on which one's eternal destiny might depend and on which the law, whether God's revealed law or natural law or canon law or civil law, had something to say, even if it might be doubtful in content or in application, was not the safer course to give the benefit of doubt to that law and just obey it, despite any arguments to the contrary? If one espoused this principle of resolution one was adopting the system of 'safer-ism' or 'tutiorism'.[61] Thus, to sum up the different systematic replies elaborated in the sixteenth to the eighteenth centuries to answer the question of what to do when in doubt, the tutiorist would advocate obedience to the law or any other course which was the safer to follow, the probabiliorist would urge doing what seemed the more likely to be right, the aequiprobabilist would judge that either of equally balanced alternatives could be followed, and the simple probabilist would reply that any action was morally justified for which a good case could be made.[62]

Below this elaborate moral shorthand, of course, a fundamentally important moral debate was in fact being conducted on the nature of moral responsibility, the competing claims of truth and security, and the ever-present tension between freedom and responsibility and between freedom and authority, to which we shall return. To complete the setting of the drama which was to ensue, however, on these topics and on the role of the moral theologian it was necessary to consider one further question. It was all very well for probabilists and others to opine that to resolve a case of moral doubt one needed to consider the 'probabilities', or cases for action, but what counted as a probability, or what made for a probable opinion? Medina had defined a 'probable' opinion as 'one that is put forward by wise men and confirmed by very good arguments', a

---

[61] It was to this historical school of thought that Karl Rahner referred in his paradox of advocating for today's Church faced with so many new problems a 'tutiorism of risk', in 'The Theology of Risk', *The Furrow*, 19 (1968), pp. 266–8.

[62] On the 'moral systems', cf. H. Davis, op. cit., vol. i, pp. 77–113. For a modern application, cf. B. Häring, *The Law of Christ* (Cork, 1963), vol. i, pp. 169–89. The most thorough treatment of this whole topic remains the classic article 'Probabilisme' of Th. Deman, OP, in *DTC* 13, coll. 417–619.

fateful order of priority, and Francis Vitoria and others had also taught the legitimacy of following the authority of professional theologians and their opinions in disputed matters.[63] Thus there emerged the division of probability itself into extrinsic probability, that arising from the prestige and authority of the theologians whom one could cite in favour of a certain view, and intrinsic probability, or that coming from the inside, the force of the arguments themselves.

The theory of probabilism, once articulated, spread rapidly through the Catholic Universities and the Church, and acted as an immense stimulant to the development of moral case-studies, which we have already considered.[64] The weighing of the probability, or arguability, of various solutions to a dilemma, and the canvassing and marshalling of the various learned, or grave, authorities, often in serried and opposing ranks, set the scene for what has been called 'the crisis of moral theology' in the seventeenth and eighteenth centuries[65], which was to call in question the teaching authority of theologians and Universities as well as calling in the teaching authority and arbitration of the Holy See. The enormous controversies did not arise simply from the great diversity of opinions put forward on almost every moral question, sometimes seriously and (although this tended to be disregarded) sometimes as pure speculation, but more fundamentally from the underlying principles of method and the atmospheres of thought which they exemplified. The implicit invitation to find good arguments to justify the most bizarre of moral opinions as 'probable', or even to create a doubt where previously there was none, was a challenge which did not go unaccepted. Were the subject-matter not so serious one would be tempted to compare the products of some of the probabilist theologians (in their teaching and not in their mostly irreproachable behaviour) with the fertile imagination and ingenuity of intelligent ten-year-olds. It was not without reason that one moralist became known as the lamb of God because he took away so many of the sins of the world, and another was given the doubtful title of 'prince of laxists'.[66]

---

[63] Vereecke, op. cit., p. 81.
[64] Ibid., p. 84. Cf. Deman, art. cit., coll. 490–4; *supra*. pp. 27–8.
[65] Vereecke, subtitle to Vol. iii.
[66] The Spanish Cistercian Bishop, Caramuel, whose fertile ingenuity earned for him this title from Alphonsus Liguori; cf *DTC* 2, col. 1711.

For that, of course, was the great outcry against the probabilists, that they were minimalists in the moral obligations which they enjoined. They were in effect, it was objected, propagating throughout the Church a movement and an atmosphere of 'laxism', or what today would be termed permissiveness, based on a probabilist system which was bad enough in itself, but which soon degenerated into a principle that in debated questions one could take as a moral norm any opinion which possessed even the least likelihood of being true, or which, however speculative, needed only the extrinsic probability arising from the authority of a single author.[67] And this was the moral climate which confronted Jansenism!

'My dear Father,' I said, 'the world is fortunate indeed to have you as its teachers. These probabilities are most useful. I did not realize why you took so much care to establish that a single doctor, if he is weighty, can make an opinion probable; and that then one can choose, between the "for" and the "against", the one which is more agreeable, even if one does not believe it to be true; and with such security of conscience that a confessor who refused to give absolution on the word of these casuists would be in a state of damnation. I gather from all this that one single casuist can make up new moral rules according to his taste, and dispose as he wishes of all that concerns moral behaviour.' 'What you say', replied the Father, 'requires some qualification . . .'.[68]

The purring irony of Pascal was but the most elegant expression of the vehement Jansenist reaction to laxism and to its principal exponents, the humanist and 'Pelagian' Fathers of the Society of Jesus. Before the Jansenist attacks various works accused of laxism had been placed by Rome on the *Index of Forbidden Books*, and in 1619 the Faculty of Theology at Paris had also censured similar writings.[69] The extreme Augustinianism and supernaturalism of the Jansenists, however, rendered them particularly hostile to any accommodation with humanism or the spirit of the age, and especially prone to the system of tutiorism and a movement of moral rigorism. And Saint-Cyran was instrumental in having Paris condemn further Jesuit writings as 'scandalous, frivolous, and heretical', before Arnaud produced his massive attack on *The*

---

[67] Cf. Angelini and Valsecchi, p. 116.

[68] Pascal, *Les Provinciales*, vi, ed. L. Cognet (Paris, 1965), p. 101. On Jansenism, cf. *supra*, pp. 89–95.

[69] Vereecke, iii, p. 67.

Moral Theology of the Jesuits faithfully extracted from their Books
(1643), which Pascal was to use as his source for the *Provincial
Letters*.[70] The Letters themselves were immediately placed on the
Index by Pope Alexander VII, but the attack of Pascal and formal
censures by the Universities of Louvain and Paris could scarcely be
ignored, not to mention the great scandal being caused throughout
the Church by laxist writers and confessors. And in 1665, 1666,
and 1679 Rome's Holy Office added its own condemnation of
many laxist moral propositions, of which the following may be
considered typical:

A Knight can accept a challenge to a duel so as not to appear a
coward;

An innocent man is permitted to kill a false accuser, false witnesses,
and even the judge about to pass an unjust sentence, if it is the
only way to avoid harm;

If an author is young and modern, his opinion should be judged
probable so long as it is certain it has not been rejected by the
Apostolic See as improbable;

It is not breaking a fast-day to eat little but often;[71]

Generally speaking, one always acts prudently in relying on a
probability, whether intrinsic or extrinsic, however slender, so
long as it does not go outside the bounds of probability;

If anyone, whether alone or in company, whether answering a
question, whether in fun or for any other reason, swears that he
did not do something which he actually did, understanding it in
his mind of something else which he did not do, or which he did
in another way, or some other true [mental] addition, he is not
really lying or committing perjury.[72]

It is permitted to kill another to defend not only one's property but
also one's expectations;

It is licit to procure abortion before the foetus is animated, in order
to prevent discovery leading to death or loss of reputation;

It seems probable that every foetus still in the womb does not have

---

[70] Ibid., pp. 87–8. DTC, 9, coll. 46–9.   [71] DS 2022, 2038, 2047, 2049.
[72] DS 2103, 2126.

a rational soul and begins to possess it only at birth, with the result that 'homicide' is not committed in any abortion;[73]

No one is obliged under pain of mortal sin to restore a large sum, however great, which was stolen in instalments;

It is so obvious that fornication in itself involves no wrongness, and is wrong only because forbidden, that the contrary seems entirely without reason;

The Church's commandment to hear Mass is satisfied by hearing the two halves of it, or even four quarters, said simultaneously by different priests;

It is probably not a mortal sin to make a false charge against someone to defend one's own justice and reputation. And if this is not probable, hardly any opinion in theology will be probable.[74]

The global attack of the Jansenists on the moral teaching of the whole Society of Jesus requires some qualification because, like all other bodies in the Church, it was itself internally split on the subject of probabilism and the other moral systems. Vereecke describes how from 1645 the Society attempted to restrict laxist teachings and how in 1650 its General Congregation declared certain teachings on sexual morality and other topics untenable by Jesuits and imposed a stricter internal censorship on Jesuit publications.[75] Later Jesuit disagreement, with consequences important for showing Rome's attitude to the various systems, centred on the Spanish Tirsio Gonzalez de Santalla who had attacked probabilism, denying that it was official Jesuit doctrine and advocating probabiliorism as the safer course to follow. The Jesuit Superior General, Oliva, refused him permission to publish on the subject, fearing that the Order would be charged with having changed its mind, and Professor Gonzalez appealed from Salamanca to Pope Innocent XI who was known personally to favour probabiliorism. The Pope let it be known through the Holy Office that Father Gonzalez 'should freely and courageously preach, teach, and defend in writing the more probable opinion, and stoutly attack the view of those who assert that between a less probable

[73] DS 2132, 2134, 2135.   [74] DS 2138, 2148, 2153, 2144.
[75] Vereecke, iii, pp. 133–7.

opinion and another known and judged to be more probable it is permissible to follow the less probable'. The Pope also informed the Jesuit General of his wish that all Jesuits and Jesuit Universities should enjoy the same freedom.[76] Six years later, at the wish of Pope Innocent XI, Gonzalez was elected Superior General of the Society of Jesus on the third ballot, and the General Congregation responded to the papal request that it take a strong probabiliorist line by decreeing that those Jesuits who thought an opinion more probable were at liberty to defend it, a conclusion which, Vereecke observes, 'pleased neither the Pope nor the Jesuits'.[77]

It was only four years later, however, in 1690 that under Pope Alexander VIII the most detailed and radical Roman censure on Jansenist and rigorist doctrines was issued, having been sought in reprisal for their gloating over the earlier discomfiture of laxism.[78] Among the errors cited is the view 'that it is not permitted to follow even the most probable of probable opinions', and in the rejection of this position may be seen also the rejection of the principle of absolute tutiorism.[79] With the beginning of the eighteenth century, however, laxism had practically disappeared, leaving the field to the varieties of probabilism and rigorism, with Bossuet, Bishop of Meaux, having probabilism condemned by the Assembly of the French Clergy as 'the source of all moral errors and of laxism'[80] and in Italy Dominican probabiliorists at loggerheads with Jesuit probabilists. 'Moral theology could gain absolutely nothing, either in method or in spirit, from these polemics which descended to personalities. Rather, they encouraged in Italy the double danger of moral decadence congenial to the climate of the century and of Jansenist rigorism which threatened to take root there.'[81]

It was also from Italy, however, that the whole controversy was to be defused and resolved through the genius of Alphonsus of Liguori, whose major influence as a moralist and confessor we have already noted.[82] In the seven successive editions of his *Theologia Moralis* from 1748 Alphonsus was to develop his own moral

---

[76] DS, pp. 466–7.
[77] Vereecke, p. 157. On the Gonzalez case, cf. also Deman, art. cit., coll. 534–7.
[78] DS 2301, proem.
[79] DS 2303.
[80] Cf. E. Amann, art. 'Laxisme', DTC, ix/1, coll. 58–65; Vereecke, p. 164.
[81] Angelini and Valsecchi, p. 120.
[82] Cf. *supra*, p. 26.

system through a development from probabiliorism to probabilism and eventually to aequiprobabilism, acknowledging on the one hand that in principle a doubtful law does not oblige and one may follow a probable opinion, but, on the other, that a law is really doubtful only when the opinions for and against are evenly balanced. Moreover, and perhaps more importantly, in his writings and his treatments of cases Alphonsus came more and more to advance simply a series of personal judgements which did much to quieten disputes without either discouraging the weak or scandalizing the fervent.[83] Not, of course, that Liguori's views did not in various quarters arouse strong opposition, but after his death, with his beatification in 1813 and the strong approbation of a series of Popes culminating in his being declared a Doctor of the Church by Pius IX, the authority of St Alphonsus was assured as a dominant influence in the late eighteenth and subsequent centuries. So much so that, in opposition to some French charges of laxism, Rome affirmed in 1831 that the opinions of Liguori could be 'safely' followed and professed, although without prejudice to the opinions of other 'approved authors'.[84] It is, then, against the whole historical background of the disputes over moral systems and of the crisis which thus befell moral theology that one can best appreciate the remarks of Pope Pius XII in 1950 that the teaching of Alphonsus of Liguori had not only dispelled the darkness of Jansenism but was also 'most thoroughly approved' as a 'safe norm' throughout the Church.[85]

Papal Infallibility in Morals

In the making of moral theology no single event has been more dramatic, and yet in several respects more puzzling, than the solemn definition in 1870 by the First Vatican Council of the infallibility of the Roman Pontiff in his moral teaching. The Vatican definition of papal infallibility in 'matters of faith and morals' was to be the climax of the politically turbulent pontificate of Pope Pius IX which lasted from 1846 to 1878, and it was enacted by a General Council of the Church which was conducted in an atmosphere of Italian and European social and political instability

---

[83] Angelini and Valsecchi, pp. 121–2.   [84] DS 2725–6.
[85] *Supra*, p. 36.

and was abruptly terminated in September 1870 on the occupation of Rome by Italian troops taking advantage of the Franco-Prussian War.[86] The pontificate of Pio Nono and the workings of Vatican I are today the subject of considerable research in a continuing attempt to assess their theological import, but the purpose of this study confines our consideration of both topics to the authority of papal moral teaching and the defining of papal infallibility in this field; that is, to the moral aspects of the two major questions which were to concern the Church and the Council: who possesses infallibility; and in respect of what is it exercised?[87]

At Vatican I no one was in doubt that the Church is possessed of infallibility. The debate and the rancour surrounded the further question to what extent this also applied to the Bishop of Rome. This was the centre of the whole successful move, warmly supported by Cardinal Manning, to reject a preparatory draft decree which had been prepared on the subject of the Church and to replace it with a shorter and much stronger draft on the papacy. In this century, part of the achievement of the Second Vatican Council has been to put the papal teaching of Vatican I back into the context of the whole Church. And it may be said that it was the fear of isolating the papacy from the Church which underlay the considerable opposition at the time of Vatican I, coming partly from those 'inopportunists' who were averse to any appearances of papal absolutism, whether spiritual or temporal, and partly from those who saw in any spiritual or jurisdictional exaltation of the papacy a threat to all the other Bishops of the Church as well as to the legitimate autonomy of national or regional Churches. What was eventually arrived at by the Council Fathers, of whom the majority were always in favour (including the large and dispro-portionate block of Italian bishops), was a decree which was carefully specific in detail and which, if it was not quite so ample as many had hoped, was also not quite so general as others had feared. Of the final form of the Council's Dogmatic Constitution *Pastor aeternus* Schönmetzer comments,

Such a thorny question of papal infallibility had led not a few of the most learned men of the Church to fear that such a definition would open the

---

[86] R. Aubert, *NCE*, xi, p. 407.
[87] In the language of the Council debates and documents these are referred to respectively as the 'subject' of infallibility and the 'object' of infallibility.

way to abuse of the ecclesiastical *magisterium* by insinuating that the Pope could do as he pleased in imposing matters for belief on the faithful without giving careful and serious thought to investigating and proving their truth, and by insisting simply on his charism of infallibility . . . . When Pius IX refused to grant the plea of the minority at the last hour for a change in the definition, many of them left the Council before the decisive Session, in order not to have to subscribe to the decree.[88]

What that decisive Session taught and defined to be 'a dogma divinely revealed'[89] was that

> when the Roman Pontiff is speaking *ex cathedra*, that is, when he is performing the function of pastor and teacher of all Christians and in accordance with his supreme Apostolic authority defining a teaching about faith or morals to be held by the universal Church, then he possesses by the divine assistance promised to him in Saint Peter the infallibility with which the divine Redeemer willed his Church to be equipped in the defining of teaching about faith or morals. Such definitions of the Roman Pontiff are therefore irreformable, not because agreed to by the Church, but in their own right.[90]

It was naturally on the Pope as holder, or 'subject' of infallibility that by far the greater part of the debates and divisions took place, as well as on the various attempts to identify and circumscribe the conditions under which his infallible *magisterium* could be exercised. On the question of the 'object' of infallibility, or the material over which it extended, both general interest and time were lacking for this to be treated with any degree of thoroughness, particularly when papal infallibility was proposed as coterminous with the

---

[88] *DS*, p. 595.

[89] 'Itaque Nos traditioni a fidei christianae exordio perceptae fideliter inhaerendo, . . . sacro approbante Concilio, docemus et divinitus revelatum dogma esse definimus', *DS* 3073. This fourth chapter of the Constitution *Pastor aeternus* in which the Pope 'with the approval of the Council' defined his infallible *magisterium* begins with the summary statement 'Ipso autem Apostolico primatu, quem Romanus Pontifex tamquam Petri principis Apostolorum successor in universam Ecclesiam obtinet, supremam quoque magisterii potestatem comprehendi, haec Sancta Sedes semper tenuit, perpetuus Ecclesiae usus comprobat, ipsaque oecumenica Concilia . . . declaraverunt', *DS* 3065.

[90] 'Romanum Pontificem, cum ex cathedra loquitur, id est, cum omnium Christianorum pastoris et doctoris munere fungens pro suprema sua Apostolica auctoritate doctrinam de fide vel moribus ab universa Ecclesia tenendam definit, per assistentiam divinam ipsi in beato Petro promissam, ea infallibilitate pollere, qua divinus Redemptor Ecclesiam suam in definienda doctrina de fide vel moribus instructam esse voluit; ideoque eiusmodi Romani Pontificis definitiones ex sese, non autem ex consensu Ecclesiae, irreformabiles esse', *DS* 3074.

Church's infallibility in matters of faith and morals. The schema, or draft, which had been prepared on the subject of the Church before the Council opened had dealt in its ninth chapter with the infallibility of the Church and had referred to the object of the Church's infallibility as 'the saving truth of faith and morals'; and when this schema on the Church was quickly rejected in favour of one more explicitly dealing with papal jurisdiction and infallibility the phrase 'faith and morals' was retained.[91]

Not everyone, however, was happy with such a description of the object of papal infallibility, and various alternatives were offered by individual bishops and groups of bishops to the Deputation for the Faith, the papally appointed drafting committee of bishops and theologians, of which Cardinal Manning was a member. He himself suggested, in place of 'faith and morals', describing the purpose of papal infallibility as the duty 'to defend the truth of the faith and by his judgement to define any questions which arise about the faith', and others also were to suggest a general description in terms of 'faith' which made no reference to the subject of morals.[92] Other

---

[91] 'Caput IX. De ecclesiae infallibilitate. Excideret porro ecclesia Christi a sua immutabilitate et dignitate, et desineret esse societas vitae ac necessarium salutis medium, si eadem a salutari fidei morumque veritate aberrare, ac in ea praedicanda atque exponenda falli vel fallere posset', Mansi, Sacrorum Conciliorum nova et amplissima collectio (Arnheim, 1926), vol. li, col. 542. With this, cf. the wording of Trent, 'omnis et salutaris veritatis et morum disciplinae', DS 1501. (supra, n. 43). Later in this same chapter the schema refers to 'Haec autem infallibilitas [sc., Ecclesiae], cuius finis est fidelium societatis in doctrina fidei et morum intemerata veritas, magisterio inest, quod Christus in ecclesia sua perpetuum instituit cum ad apostolos dixit: Euntes ergo docete . . .', ibid., 543. In this same draft, chapter XI, De Romani pontificis primatu, makes no explicit mention of papal teaching on faith and morals, nor of papal infallibility. Cf. ibid., 543–5. Once the decision to concentrate on papal infallibility was taken with about 450 in favour and 137 against in written depositions, but only one against after debate in the aula, papal agreement was also forthcoming, and various new drafts were considered (ibid., 696–701). A chapter to be added to that on papal primacy referred to 'rebus fidei et morum' (ibid., 702), and after lively discussion on the whole schema on the Church, including this additional chapter, this was replaced by a new schema in four chapters dealing exclusively with the primacy and infallibility of the Pope. Cf. Mansi, vol. lii, col. 1. Of this substituted draft the fourth chapter now dealt explicitly with papal infallibility and formed the basis for the final decree. In this draft the operative phrases were 'in rebus fidei et morum' and 'in rebus quae ad fidem et mores pertinent' (ibid., 7).

[92] Manning's proposed formula on papal infallibility says only 'eumque prae ceteris teneri fidei veritatem defendere, et si quae de fide exortae fuerint quaestiones, suo iudicio debere definiri . . . et hanc inerrantiae seu infallibilitatis praerogativam . . . ad idem obiectum semet porrigere, ad quod ambitu suo infallibilitas ecclesiae semet extendit', Mansi li, col. 669. Of this formula the first section above echoes

members of the Council were to offer a variety of amendments: the truth of faith and the goodness of morals; the power of passing laws on faith and morals; the rule of what things are to be believed or loved; the deposit of what things are to be believed and what are to be done; the integrity of morals; matters to be believed and matters to be done; the deposit of faith and good morals; matters relating to faith or to discipline; laws relating to regulations of morals, or to discipline, or to building up the faith.[93]

The Bishop of Orléans, Félix Dupanloup, who may be considered the leader of the opposition to the passing of a decree of papal infallibility, and who was publicly reprimanded for this by Pope Pius IX, claimed to be speaking for others when he voiced general misgivings about the entire project. He complained that God, Christ, and the Church were being set aside 'in order to rush into this question on which we heard almost nothing before the Council except from journalists; to which the Bull convoking the Council made no reference; and on which the draft on the Church contained not a word'. If the subject were pursued he feared he would have serious doubts about the truth itself and also about the freedom of the Council.[94] When he came to comment on the schema itself he was, as might have been expected, no less complaining. The matter was being rushed, and the scriptural and historical arguments adduced were weak for such a conclusion as papal infallibility. 'In the [draft] formula of the definition there are most evident faults and many dangers to be feared'; and he put a series of short, sharp questions about the meaning of various individual words and phrases. On the moral object of infallibility he demanded, 'What

earlier councils, but one of the official theologians considered the second section not erroneous but capable of giving the impression of two infallibilities in 'la mente di chi non è abituato alle profondità teologiche', ibid., 700. For other proposals which do not differentate morals from faith, cf. ibid., 1005, 1014.

[93] 'fidei veritatem, morumque honestatem', ibid., 953; 'de fide moribusque leges ferendi', 973; 'de credendorum vel diligendorum regula', 974; 'tam credendorum quam agendorum depositum', 1004; 'morum integritas', 1005; 'de credendis et agendis ad salutem consequendam necessariis', 1021, cf. 1031; 'quantum fidei depositum bonosque mores custodiendi officium postulat', 823; 'depositum fidei et morum', Mansi, lii, 47; 'de rebus ad fidem vel ad disciplinam spectantibus', ibid., 54; 'leges ad morum regulas, vel ad disciplinam, vel etiam ad fidem adstruendam', ibid., 51.

[94] Ibid., 712–13. For the letter of the Pope to Dupanloup, inviting him to lay aside prejudice and return to the simpler faith of his earlier years, cf., Mansi, lii, coll. 1–3.

are "matters of morals"? There are revealed moral matters, some obvious matters, some obscure, which belong only to philosophy. Where will papal infallibility end? As for the object, "the same object covered by the infallibility of the Church", this is far too vague, and the object of the infallibility of the Church is also vague.'[95]

One of the few other bishops recorded as going into the question of 'morals' in any detail was Archbishop Yusto of Burgos, and his speech discloses an undercurrent which was influencing the progress of the debate when it draws attention to the distinction between truths, or principles, and facts. It was one of the irritating features of Jansenism so far as Rome was concerned that it had tried to wriggle out of the Papal condemnation of the five Jansenist propositions by acknowledging that they could clearly bear a false interpretation, but that, as a matter of fact, in the mind of Jansen himself they did not bear this interpretation. This 'question of fact', maintained by Arnaud, was quickly squashed by another papal Bull asserting that the five propositions excerpted from the *Augustinus* had been condemned 'in the sense intended by' Jansen,[96] but the dispute had the effect of highlighting the question whether the Church's authority and infallibility extended, as a necessary corollary, to cover contingent facts which could not themselves be part of Revelation but whose truth or falsehood was crucial for the practical teaching of revealed truth. To this category of what are known as 'dogmatic facts' Archbishop Yusto added the problem of what he termed 'moral facts', such as the canonization of saints, the Church's approval of the way of life of religious Orders, or even any moral action performed by an individual. He wished to know if 'matters of morals' (*res . . . morum*) was intended to cover all of these.

It would be better, he opined, to refer to principles of morals, or rules of morals. He could give only a few arguments, although many were possible. ' "Matters of morals", as everyone knows, is too broad. They could be moral facts, or disciplinary laws

---

[95] 'Quid *res morum*? Sunt res morales revelatae, aliae evidentes, aliae obscurae, quae ad solam philosophiam pertinent. Ubinam cessabit infallibilitas pontificis? Quoad obiectum: *ad idem obiectum, ad quod infallibilitas ecclesiae extenditur*. Haec sunt vaga nimis; sicut est vagum obiectum infallibilitatis ecclesiae in capite IX', Mansi, li, 995.

[96] DS 2010–12. Cf. *supra*, p. 91.

determining actions to be performed by subjects, or principles or
general rules directing the morals of Christians to attaining a
supernatural end'. It can be 'piously believed' that the Pope is
infallible in judging moral facts, but the Archbishop did not
consider the papal *magisterium* was to be declared infallibly certain
on such moral facts, and most theologians, even those professing
great respect for the Roman Pontiff, openly denied it. It would
mean that the Pope could judge infallibly on every human action,
and most doctors affirmed that it was not a matter of faith that the
Church's infallibility was involved in canonizing saints. 'Moreover,
the reason why theologians affirm that the Church or the Pope are
infallible in matters of morals is because error in matters of morals
would be error in matters of faith since the principles of morals are
revealed.'[97]

Archbishop Yusto was not alone in preferring to describe the
object of papal infallibility as 'matters of faith and principles, or
rules, of morals',[98] but many of the Bishops professed themselves

---

[97] 'Inerrantia seu infallibilitas Romani pontificis iuxta textum schematis effertur
in rebus morum; sed mea sententia haec verba substitui deberent cum his: *in
principiis sive regulis morum*, ita ut pro rebus morum, dum de infallibilitate Romani
pontificis agitur, principia morum generalia intelligantur. Huius variationis rationes
plurimae sunt; at paucas tantum attingam. Res morum, prout omnibus notum est,
nimis late patent; aut enim sunt facta moralia, aut leges disciplinares quibus actus a
subditis ponendi determinantur, aut sunt principia sive regulae generales, quae
mores christianorum dirigere queant ad finem supernaturalem assequendum.

'Iam vero Romanus pontifex, etiam doctoris universalis munere fungens, eritne
praedicandus erroris nescius ex iure divino in his factis moralibus iudicandis? Pie
credi potest: sed utrum vere, utrum certe, et nedum certe sed infallibiliter certe
efferendum sit eius magisterium circa huiusmodi facta moralia, a concilio de fide,
meo iudicio, definiri non potest. Secus enim cum nulla sit actio humana, seu factum
quod morale non sit (nam quodcumque ab homine deliberate agente procedit,
morale factum est), sequeretur quod de his omnibus infallibiliter iudicare posset,
quod neque admittitur neque admitti potest tamquam de fide certum.

'His accedit quod plerique doctores de fide non esse affirment infallibilitatem
ecclesiae in sanctorum canonizatione, licet in hoc casu de moribus et quam
eminenter agatur . . . . Insuper ratio, qua permoti theologi affirmant in rebus morum
ecclesiam sive papam esse infallibilem, est quia error in rebus morum esset error in
rebus fidei, cum morum principia sint revelata. Ergo supponunt obiectum infallibilis
magisterii esse non res morum quascumque, sed morum principia. Reor quidem
libentissime Romani pontificis iudicia de factis moralibus maxima cum reverentia
esse excipienda, sed reor etiam circa ea infallibile non esse eius magisterium . . . .

'Igitur loco verborum "in rebus morum" poni meo iudicio deberet *in principiis
morum* . . . . Alia possem proferre pro mutatione exposita, sed brevitati studens
omitto', Mansi, lii, 853–4, 1132.

[98] 'loco "in rebus fidei et morum" scribatur "in rebus fidei morumque *principiis*,
vel regulis"', ut definitio nostra veritatis limites non transgrediatur', ibid., 1132.

fully content with unqualified reference to 'teaching (doctrine) about', or 'matters of', faith and morals. One explained that the ancients just said the Church is infallible in defining disputes of faith and morals, and so 'the well-used formula "in matters of faith and morals" should be retained'.[99] Another was to refer to the phrase as 'the usual formula of the schools'.[100] Much more to the point, the Deputation for the Faith wanted to leave the phrase itself as general as possible and to specify its detailed content only by identifying it with the area in which the Church itself was infallible. At an early stage in the Council the Jesuit theologians Franzelin and Kleutgen explained in committee that the sense of the formula had been deliberately left indeterminate, so much so that when the theologians suggested substituting 'questions about faith and morals', Manning and others preferred to be more general and refer to 'matters of faith and morals', and the President, Cardinal Bilio, judged that the more general the phrase used the less it would be subject to misinterpretation.[101] So far as concerned reference to the infallibility of the Church, the theologians explained, if the object of the Church's infallibility were determined in another Constitution then the object of papal infallibility would be automatically determined. 'But if no such definition is forthcoming, the object referred to in this decree will have to be judged according to what is now commonly held about the infallibility of the Church: namely,

---

[99] 'Unde sicut auctores schematis in enarrando subiecto infallibilitatis sapienter abstinuerunt ab omni partium enumeratione, sic etiam quoad obiectum usitata formula "in rebus fidei et morum" retinenda, Mansi, li, 815.

[100] 'solitam in scholis formulam "in rebus fidei et morum", Mansi, lii, 1132, 914.

[101] 'quaestiones de fide et moribus', Mansi, liii, 258. 'Priusquam autem a singulis suffragia peterentur, auditus est theologus pater Franzelin, societatis Iesu, qui exposuit emendatum caput quoad rem cum priori prorsus convenire, quoad formam tamen simplicius et generalioribus verbis conceptum esse, ita ut multae difficultates evitentur, quae contra priorem adumbrationem moveri possunt et probabiliter movebuntur. Deinde alter theologus, pater Peters (Kleutgen) societatis Iesu, exposuit . . .', ibid., 259. (Kleutgen had changed his name to Peters for political reasons, ibid., n. 2). 'Quintus, Baltimorensis [Archbishop Spalding], priorem formulam esse praeferendam, cum nova sit vaga, ambigua, indeterminata; et ideo timendum, ne pluribus patribus in congregatione generali displiceat. Contra quae eminentissimus praeses animadvertit, formulam minime esse vagam et ambiguam, sed dumtaxat magis generalem et ideo sinistrae interpretationi minus subiectam', ibid., 259. 'Septimus, Mutinensis, . . . "in rebus fidei et morum" ', ibid. 'Nonus, West-monasteriensis, animadvertit, in formula ipsa pro speciali "quaestiones fidei et morum" ponendum esse generaliter "in rebus fidei et morum" ', ibid. 260. 'Duodecimus, . . . pro "quaestiones de fide etc" ponatur "in definiendis rebus fidei etc" . . . 'rebus fidei et morum' . . . 'decretis fidei et morum', ibid., 261–2.

that it is a "dogma of faith" that the Roman Pontiff cannot be
mistaken when he proposes matters to be believed with divine faith,
and it is "theologically certain" that he is also immune from error
even in declaring other matters.'[102]

The vagueness of appealing to the extent of the Church's
infallibility in order to identify the extent of papal infallibility was
clearly an embarrassment to those enthusiastic for the decree. At
one meeting of the Deputation Cardinal Bilio remarked that they
could not define more about the infallibility of the Pope than was
defined about the infallibility of the Church, that it extended only
to dogmatic definitions strictly so called. He himself considered it
most certain that the Pope was also infallible in the areas of
dogmatic facts, in canonizing saints and other matters of similar
importance, just as the Church was. He would very much like the
Council to define the Church's infallibility not only in dogmatic
definitions but also in dogmatic facts, canonization of saints, and
approval of religious Orders, but at present it would be awkward to
define such papal infallibility before defining the Church's. The
Cardinal President must have been somewhat discomfited to be
informed that although the infallibility of the Church was
obviously a fundamental dogma of faith, it had never actually been
so far defined as such.[103] The determination was there, however, to

---

[102] 'Sensus formulae, quae nunc proponitur, eatenus indeterminatus est, quatenus
quaeri potest, quaenam sit definitio quaestionis fidei, ... Sed huic dubitationi per
ea, quae de obiecto infallibilitatis addita sunt, quantum hic satis est, respondetur. Si
enim in alia constitutione obiectum infallibilitatis ecclesiae determinabitur, eo ipso
etiam obiectum infallibilitatis Romani pontificis declarabitur. Sin vero nulla talis
definitio fiet, de obiecto vi huius decreti iudicandum erit secundum ea, quae nunc
iam de ecclesiae infallibilitate communiter tenentur: nempe dogma fidei esse,
Romanum pontificem non posse errare, cum divina fide credenda proponit, et
theologice certum esse, eum etiam in aliis rebus declarandis ab errore immunem
esse', ibid., 258.

[103] 'Non plus posse definiri de infallibilitate papae, quam definitum sit de
infallibilitate ecclesiae; de ecclesia autem hoc tantum definitum esse, eam esse
infallibilem in definitionibus dogmaticis stricte dictis; ergo quaeritur, inquit, num
proposito schemate infallibilitas papae non nimis extendatur. Non negavit
cardinalis, immo tamquam certissimum asseruit, papam infallibilem quoque esse in
factis dogmaticis, in canonizatione sanctorum aliisque paris momenti rebus, sicut
ecclesia in his infallibilis est. Addidit, se vehementissime cupere, ut in hoc concilio
Vaticano definiretur, ecclesiam infallibilem esse, non solum in definitionibus
dogmaticis stricte sumptis, sed etiam in factis dogmaticis, in canonizatione
sanctorum, in approbatione ordinum. Sed cum nunc de infallibilitate papae
definienda ageretur, antequam actum esset de infallibilitate ecclesiae, illud incom-
modi habere schema, quod plus diceretur, quam oporteret. Ad haec respondebatur,

proceed with defining papal infallibility, and the policy was maintained through all the debates of the Council to retain as the object of such infallibility 'matters of faith and morals' and to provide further precision only by referring generally to the scope of the Church's infallibility.

One spokesman for the schema drafted in these terms, answering the objection that the object was 'indefinite and vague', pointed out that, since the schema described its extent as similar to the Church's infallibility, 'the general proposition "what is to be held in matters of faith and morals . . . " is quite definite and precise', a line of defence which was to be repeated later.[104] Archbishop Deschamps of Mechlin, speaking for the Deputation, was at pains to meet fears shared by many of the minority that the Pope's infallibility was about to be defined in absolute terms, by pointing out that the infallibility in question was not absolute, but 'relative to truths which are contained in the deposit of faith either expressly or implicitly or by an essential and necessary connection'.[105] Another was to explain that since the object of infallibility was matters of faith and morals 'and nothing more', absolute papal infallibility was thus excluded.[106]

It was left to Bishop Gasser to express the official view on the wording and sense of the text of the decree, and to respond to the whole range of comments and emendations, in a long statement which is recognized as of crucial importance for a proper

neque infallibilitatem ecclesiae hucusque ullo modo definitam esse, constare autem apertissime infallibilitatem ecclesiae dogma esse et dogma fundamentale, cum quilibet catholicus actum fidei enuntiando hoc profiteatur: "Credo quod Deus revelavit et ecclesia catholica proponit." Cum igitur fide constet, ecclesiam esse infallibilem, idem de papa definiatur', ibid., 281–2.

[104] 'Animadvertitur . . . *obiectum*, quasi. 1. *indefinita et vaga* sit eius descriptio. Verum cum in schemate expresse dicatur, obiectum illud esse eiusdem omnino extensionis, cuius est ambitus infallibilitatis *ecclesiae*, per hanc declarationem generalis propositio "quid in rebus fidei et morum etc. tenendum sit", definita plane ac determinata evadit', lii, 23. 'Tandem determinari illud infallibilitatis obiectum, et quidem primo generatim, quod significat phrasis "in rebus fidei et morum", deinde specifice verbis asserentibus eundem esse obiecti ambitum, qui assignatur obiecto infallibilitatis ecclesiae', ibid., 36.

[105] 'Nec quaestio est de infallibilitate absoluta summi pontificis, sed de infallibilitate omnino relativa, scilicet relate ad veritates, quae in fidei deposito continentur vel expresse vel implicite, vel connexione essentiali et necessaria', ibid., 66.

[106] '*obiectum* infallibilitatis, hoc est, res fidei et morum, et nihil amplius; igitur excluditur infallibilitas absoluta', ibid., 829.

understanding of the Vatican Council's final statement on the infallibility of the Pope. As Aubert comments, the *Relatio* of Gasser is 'still of prime importance for an understanding of the nuances of the conciliar text'.[107] In a long and detailed speech the Bishop of Brixen carefully explained the purpose of the prerogative of papal infallibility as that of conserving truth in the Church. 'Therefore there is a particular place for such a definition when in some parts of the Church there arise scandals about the faith, dissensions and heresies, which bishops individually or even gathered in provincial councils are unable to deal with, and so are compelled to refer the matter to the holy Apostolic See; or even if the bishops themselves have become sadly infected with error.'[108] Such papal infallibility, he went on, is not absolute, by reason of the restrictions regarding its subject, its object (matters of faith and morals) and the act itself,[109] and he proceeded to analyse and comment upon these various restrictions. With reference to the object, the suggestion had been made to describe this as 'matters of faith and principles of morals'.

But the Deputation for the Faith cannot admit even this emendation, partly because that word would be entirely novel, whereas the term 'matters of faith and morals' and 'doctrine of faith and morals' is extremely well known, and every theologian knows what is to be understood by these words. Moreover, some 'principles of morals' can be merely philosophical principles of natural goodness, which do not belong in every respect to the deposit of faith.[110]

---

[107] R. Aubert (ed.), *The Christian Centuries* (1978), vol. v, pp. 65–6. The *relatio* occupies columns 1204–1230 of Mansi, lii.

[108] 'Finis eiusdem est conservatio veritatis in ecclesia. Talis definitionis ergo tunc est vel maxime locus, cum alicubi in ecclesia scandala circa fidem, dissensiones et haereses exoriantur, quibus reprimendis antistites ecclesiarum singillatim, vel etiam in concilio provinciali congregati impares sunt; ita ut ad sanctam sedem apostolicam hac de causa referre cogantur; vel si ipsi antistites tristi erroris labe infecti fuerint', 1213.

[109] 'Proinde reapse infallibilitas Romani pontificis restricta est ratione *subiecti*, . . .; restricta est ratione *obiecti*, quando agitur de rebus fidei et morum; et ratione *actus*, . . .', 1214.

[110] 'In secunda parte huius emendationis reverendissimus auctor vult, ut pro "rebus fidei et morum" vel *doctrina fidei et morum*, ponatur: *fidei morumque principiis*. Sed etiam hanc emendationem non potest admittere Deputatio de fide et quidem partim quia vox ista esset omnino nova, cum vox *res fidei et morum*, doctrina fidei et morum, sit notissima, et unusquisque theologus scit quid sub his verbis sit intelligendum. Insuper principia morum possunt esse alia mere philosophica naturalis honestatis, quae non sub omni respectu pertinent ad depositum fidei', 1224.

In now presenting the final text, the results of much discussion, which was being unanimously proposed by the Deputation, Gasser commented on the object of infallibility, 'doctrine about faith and morals': 'But not all truths which pertain to the doctrine about faith and Christian morals are of the same kind. And not all are equally required for guarding the integrity of the deposit.' Hence, errors would vary in seriousness accordingly as the truths to which they were opposed belonged more or less to the deposit, which explained the different notes of censure applied to propositions. Infallibility, as he explained, whether in the whole teaching Church or in the Pope, extended to absolutely the same truths, and in the word of God it extended at least to what directly constitutes the deposit of faith, that is, dogmas of faith. There were some other truths which were not revealed as such, but which were required for the complete protection of the deposit, and these included dogmatic facts, on which all Catholic theologians were agreed that the Church is infallible in its definition of them. As to other truths which were not revealed but pertained to protecting the deposit, theologians varied on whether the view concerning them was a dogma or simply theologically certain.[111]

[111] 'Post multas disceptationes, quae in Deputatione de fide hac de re fuerunt agitatae, demum tota Deputatio de fide unanimiter ... hanc formulam novam definitionis infallibilitatis pontificiae congregationi generali proponendam esse censuit. Cum res ista tanti sit momenti, sensum huius novae definitionis aliquibus hic loci exponam .... 4° Continetur in definitione obiectum infallibilitatis. Infallibilitas promissa est ad custodiendum et evolvendum integrum depositum fidei. Hinc universim quidem facile patet, obiectum infallibilitatis esse doctrinam de fide et moribus. At non omnes veritates, quae ad doctrinam de fide et moribus christianis [sic] pertinent, sunt unius modi; nec omnes in uno eodemque gradu ad custodiam integritatis depositi necessariae sunt. Unde etiam consequitur errores contrarios diversis gradibus adversari deposito custodiendo, prout veritates ipsae quibus adversantur magis vel minus ad ipsum depositum pertinent. Qui quidem errorum gradus diversi diversis censurarum notis distinguuntur.

'Iam hic 1° certum est, infallibilitatem a Deo promissam, sive in tota ecclesia docente, cum in conciliis veritates definit, sive in ipso summo pontifice per se spectetur, ad eundem omnino ambitum veritatum extendi; cum idem sit finis infallibilitatis, utrovis modo ea consideretur.

'2° In eo ipso verbo Dei, quo infallibilitas ad custodiam depositi sive pontifici per se spectato, sive ecclesiae docenti promissa est, continetur etiam indubitanter hanc infallibilitatem extendi saltem ad ea, quae per se depositum fidei constituunt, ad dogmata nimirum fidei definienda ....

'At vero 3° cum dogmatibus revelatis, ut paulo ante dixi, veritates aliae magis vel minus stricte cohaerent, quae licet in se revelatae non sint, requiruntur tamen ad ipsum depositum revelationis integre custodiendum, rite explicandum et efficaciter definiendum; huiusmodi igitur veritates, ad quas utique etiam per se pertinent facta

To this explanation of Bishop Vincenz Gasser, speaking on behalf of the Deputation, it is useful to add a later comment of the Jesuit Cardinal Franzelin who had been one of the principal architects of the definition. In the course of his subsequent teaching on the Church he explained of the phrase 'doctrine about faith and morals',

The language of this distinction is consecrated by ecclesiastical usage, and it is not a 'real' distinction but a distinction 'of reason with a basis in reality', in so far as morals are ruled by the revealed divine law which also contains the natural law. The term 'faith', considered as the object of faith, is understood as revealed teaching which is of itself primarily theoretical and to be believed with subjective faith, but many moral obligations follow from it. The term 'morals' here means revealed teaching which is practical, which is, of course, also to be believed with faith, but which also has been provided to command and prohibit acts of morals.[112]

Another, less technical, footnote to the work of the First Vatican Council on papal infallibility in morals is provided by another participant at the Council who was absent from the final voting and who rejected the final formation of the decree, not because he felt it had gone too far but because it had not gone far enough. Cardinal Berardi's objections included the argument that 'the words "doctrine about morals" insinuate that the Roman Pontiff is not immune

dogmatica, quatenus sine his depositum fidei custodiri et exponi non posset, huiusmodi, inquam, veritates non quidem per se ad depositum fidei, sed tamen ad custodiam depositi fidei spectant. Hinc omnes omnino catholici theologi consentiunt, ecclesiam in huiusmodi veritatum authentica propositione ac definitione esse infallibilem, ita ut hanc infallibilitatem negare gravissimus esset error. Sed opinionum diversitas versatur unice circa gradum certitudinis, utrum scilicet infallibilitas in hisce veritatibus proponendis, ac proinde in erroribus per censuras nota haereseos inferiores proscribendis debeat censeri dogma fidei, ut hanc infallibilitatem ecclesiae negans esset haereticus; an solum sit veritas in se non revelata, sed ex revelato dogmate deducta, ac proinde solum theologice certa', 1225–6.

[112] 'Quando revelata doctrina fidei vel morum (1) a Pontifice ex cathedra vel in oecumenico Concilio definitur . . . (1) Haec distinctio usu loquendi ecclesiastico consecrata non est *realis* sed *rationis cum fundamento in re*, quatenus mores lege divina revelata reguntur, qua revelatione etiam lex naturalis continetur. In distinctione enim nomine *fidei* obiectivae nempe, intelligitur revelata doctrina per se primo theoretica et fide (subiectiva) credenda, ex qua tamen multae consequuntur obligationes morales; nomine *morum* vero ibi significatur doctrina revelata practica, quae utique etiam fide credenda, sed ex sese orpinata [ordinata?] est ad imperandos et prohibendos actus morum', Cardinal J. B. Franzelin, SJ, *Theses De Ecclesia Christi Opus Posthumum* (Rome, 1887), p. 54 and note (1).

from error when he makes a judgement on the goodness or badness of some action in the concrete, such as the theft by the Italian Government of the temporal dominion of the Holy See'. Moreover, it could be inferred from this formula that the Roman Pontiff and the whole teaching Church are not infallible in canonizing saints and approving religious Orders, in judging dogmatic facts, and in proposing teaching only connected more or less with dogmas of faith. If this were the case, then the authority of the dogmatic Constitutions *Unigenitus* and *Auctorem Fidei*, and also the authority of the *Syllabus* of errors condemned by Pius IX, would largely collapse, and the ordinary *magisterium* of the Holy See would be deprived of its finest fruits.[113]

Expansion of the 'Ordinary Magisterium'

The definition by the First Vatican Council of papal infallibility in the exercise of the extraordinary, or carefully defined, solemn, *magisterium* in matters of morals did not result in a spate of infallible decisions, but in an enormous increase in papal exercise of its non-infallible ordinary, or day to day, *magisterium* through encyclicals, allocutions, and various interventions in the life and activity of the Church, with effects which might sometimes be described as infallibility by association. The first official papal use of the term 'ordinary' *magisterium* occurs in a letter of Pope Pius IX to the Archbishop of Munich, in 1849, complaining that the recent theological congress presided over by Dollinger was, in its pretensions to academic freedom, undermining the authority of the

---

[113] 'Verba *doctrinam de moribus* insinuant, Romanum pontificem ab errore immunem non esse, quando de honestate vel pravitate alicuius actionis in concreto spectatae decernit; puta de latrocinio temporalis dominii sanctae sedis a gubernio Italico perpetrato . . . . Ex hac definitionis formula pronum cuique esset colligere, Romanum pontificem, atque adeo ecclesiam universam docentem non esse infallibilem (a) in canonizatione sanctorum, et in approbatione ordinum regularium, (b) in iudiciis circa facta dogmatica, (c) in proponendis doctrinis quae plus minusve cum fidei dogmatibus sunt connexae, (d) in profligandis erroribus propius vel longius abhorrentibus a veritatibus revelatis. Quare auctoritas dogmaticarum constitutionum *Unigentius* et *Auctorem fidei*, nec non Syllabi sanctissimi domini nostri Pii IX quoad maximam partem concideret, et magisterium ordinarium sanctae sedis apostolicae potissimo suo fructu frustraretur', Mansi, lii, 1235–6. *Unigenitus* was against Jansenism (cf. *DS* 2400, proem.), while *Auctorem fidei* was aimed at condemning the Jansenist-inspired Synod of Pistoia (cf. *DS* 2600, proem). For Pius IX's *Syllabus of Errors*, cf. *DS* 2901, proem. For Cardinal Berardi's absence, cf. Mansi, lii, 1244. For the full text of his further comments, cf. ibid., 1253–6.

Church and disregarding the revelatory nature of Christianity. He would like to think they did not wish to restrict the obligation of all Catholic teachers (*magistri*) and writers only to matters proposed by the infallible judgement of the Church as dogmas of faith to be believed by all, or that perfect loyalty to revealed truths could be expressed merely by faith and submission to dogmas expressly defined as such by the Church, because 'such submission must also extend to matters which are handed on by the ordinary *magisterium* of the whole Church spread throughout the world as divinely revealed and which are therefore, by universal and constant consent, held by theologians to pertain to faith'.[114]

And since we are dealing with a subjection which binds in conscience all Catholics engaged in the contemplative sciences to contribute new benefits to the Church by their writings, then such groups of men ought to recognize that it is not enough for wise Catholics to receive the dogmas of the Church with reverence, but it is also necessary for them to submit to the decisions of the Pontifical Congregations relating to doctrine, and also to those points of doctrine which are held by common and constant consent of Catholics as 'theological truths' and 'theological conclusions' which are so certain that although contrary opinions could not be termed heretical they would be deserving of theological censure.[115]

John P. Boyle has described summarily how this statement of position by Pius IX was the culmination of years of controversy in the nineteenth century arising from the demise of 'the great

---

[114] DS 2875–80. 'Persuadere Nobis volumus, noluisse obligationem, qua catholici magistri ac scriptores omnino adstringuntur, coarctare in iis tantum, quae ab infallibili Ecclesiae iudicio velut fidei dogmata ab omnibus credenda proponuntur . . . . Nam etiamsi ageretur de illa subiectione, quae fidei divinae actu est praestanda, limitanda tamen non esset ad ea, quae expressis oecumenicorum Conciliorum aut Romanorum Pontificum huiusque Sedis decretis definita sunt, sed ad ea quoque extendenda, quae ordinario totius Ecclesiae per orbem dispersae magisterio tamquam divinitus revelata traduntur ideoque universali et constanti consensu a catholicis theologis ad fidem pertinere retinentur', DS 2987.

[115] 'Sed cum agatur de illa subiectione, qua ex conscientia ii omnes catholici obstringuntur, qui in contemplatrices scientias incumbunt, ut novas suis scriptis Ecclesiae afferant utilitates, idcirco eiusdem conventus viri recognoscere debent, sapientibus catholicis haud satis esse, ut praefata Ecclesiae dogmata recipiant ac venerentur, verum etiam opus esse, ut se subiciant decisionibus, quae ad doctrinam pertinentes a Pontificiis Congregationibus proferuntur, tum iis doctrinae capitibus, quae communi et constanti Catholicorum consensu retinentur ut theologicae veritates et conclusiones ita certae, ut opiniones eiusdem doctrinae capitibus adversae, quamquam haereticae dici nequeant, tamen aliam theologicam mereantur censuram', DS 2880.

university centres of theological learning', and one might view such developments as the filling of a vacuum which had not previously existed when, as Fink commented, the Universities had exercised an ordinary *magisterium* in the Church.[116]

The exercise of the papal teaching authority became more frequent and more insistent from the time of the inaugural encyclical *Mirari vos arbitramur* of Gregory XVI.[117] Papal authority was used to condemn and place on the Index of Forbidden Books an increasing number of works which differed from papal positions or even attacked the exercise of the papal teaching power itself. The Roman Congregations stepped up their activity, and the Holy Office and the Congregation of the Index (distinct congregations until the reform of Pius X) were the instruments of the papal teaching authority and its vigilance over doctrinal matters.[118]

As we have noted, Vatican I concentrated on the extraordinary *magisterium* of the Pope in its infallibility decree, but it had earlier decreed, on the subject of faith and in terms which echo Pius IX's Munich letter, that 'all those things are to be believed with divine and Catholic faith which are contained in God's word, written or handed down, and are proposed for belief by the Church as divinely revealed, whether by a solemn judgement or by its ordinary and universal *magisterium*'.[119] Naturally enough, this 'ordinary and universal' teaching function, which Pius XI was later to describe as the Church's *magisterium* 'exercised every day through the Roman Pontiff and the Bishops in communion with him',[120] was best identified and propounded at the centre of the Church; and its centralization was immensely strengthened when the crisis of Catholic Modernism, diagnosed and treated by Pope Pius X, brought into further relief the function and power of the *magisterum* given by Christ to the 'teaching Church' as contrasted with the

[116] *Supra*, n. 7.
[117] On the dangers of religious indifferentism and rationalism, DS 2730–2.
[118] John P. Boyle, 'The Ordinary Magisterium: Towards a History of the Concept', *Heythrop Journal*, 20 (1979), pp. 380–1.
[119] 'Porro fide divina et catholica ea omnia credenda sunt, quae in verbo Dei scripto vel tradito continentur et ab Ecclesia sive solemni iudicio sive ordinario et universali magisterio tamquam divinitus revelata credenda proponuntur', DS 3011.
[120] 'Etenim Ecclesiae magisterium ... quamquam per Romanum Pontificem et episcopos cum eo communionem habentes cotidie exercetur, id tamen complectitur muneris, ut, si quando aut haereticorum erroribus atque oppugnationibus obsisti efficacius aut clarius subtiliusque explicata sacrae doctrinae capita in fidelium mentibus imprimi oporteat, ad aliquid tum sollemnibus ritibus decretisque definiendum opportune procedat', DS 3683.

'learning Church'.[121] It was only a logical extension of this for Pope Pius XII to stress in 1950 that

> in matters of faith and morals this sacred Magisterium ought to be the proximate and universal norm of truth for any theologian, since Christ the Lord has entrusted to it the whole deposit of faith—Scripture and divine "tradition"—to be guarded, protected, and interpreted . . . . Nor is it to be thought that matters put forward in Encyclical Letters do not of themselves demand assent, on the grounds that in Encyclicals Popes do not exercise the supreme power of their Magisterium. For these matters are taught by the ordinary Magisterium, to which also applies the text 'He that hears you, hears Me' (Luke 10: 16), and for the most part those matters which are proposed and inculcated in Encyclicals already belong to Catholic teaching on other grounds. And if Supreme Pontiffs of set purpose pass judgement in their acts on a matter which has been controverted until then, it is obvious to everyone that that matter, according to the mind and will of the Pontiffs, cannot now be considered a question for free discussion among theologians.[122]

In all these circumstances it is not to be wondered that in this century theologians, including moral theologians, have until quite recently taken up conservative positions on many issues, chastened by Church authority with still vivid memories of both laxist

---

[121] For the papal encyclical, *Pascendi*, which gave a coherent shape to various 'modern' tendencies, cf. *DS* 3475–3500. For the formal condemnation of various 'Errors of Modernists', cf. *DS* 3401–66. Among the latter is to be found the proposition 'In definiendis veritatibus ita collaborant discens et docens Ecclesia, ut docenti Ecclesiae nihil supersit, nisi communes discentis opinationes sancire', *DS* 3406. On the systematic insistence on the 'teaching Church', cf. *supra*, p. 119, and n. 111.

[122] 'Et quamquam hoc sacrum Magisterium, in rebus fidei et morum, cuilibet theologo proxima et universalis norma esse debet, utpote cui Christus Dominus totum depositum fidei—Sacras nempe Litteras ac divinam "traditionem"—et custodiendum et tuendum et interpretandum concredidit, attamen officium, quo fideles tenentur illos quoque fugere errores, qui ad haeresim plus minusve accedant, ideoque "etiam constitutiones et decreta servare, quibus pravae huiusmodi opiniones a Sancta Sede proscriptae et prohibitae sunt" [Code of Canon Law, 1917, 1324], nonnunquam ita ignoratur ac si non habeatur.

'Neque putandum est, ea quae in Encyclicis Litteris proponuntur, assensum per se non postulare, cum in iis Pontifices supremam sui Magisterii potestatem non exerceant. Magisterio ordinario haec docentur, de quo illud etiam valet: "Qui vos audit, me audit"; ac plerumque quae in Encyclicis Litteris proponuntur et inculcantur, iam aliunde ad doctrinam catholicam pertinent. Quodsi Summi Pontifices in actis suis de re hactenus controversa data opera sententiam ferunt, omnibus patet rem illam, secundum mentem ac voluntatem eorumdem Pontificum, quaestionem liberae inter theologos disceptationis iam haberi non posse', Encyclical Letter *Humani Generis*, *DS* 3884–5.

excesses and Jansenist obduracy. Authority of an extrinsic character, as it had been the currency in so many exchanges of probabilities, was still to be a touchstone, but on condition now that it was an 'approved' authority, preferably that of St Alphonsus, whose personal authority alone gave the cachet of at least extrinsic probability to all his opinions, but failing this, the authority of other 'approved authors'. In 1929 the great moralist Vermeersch was to point out, in a review of 'Sixty Years of Moral Theology', that Liguori had become not a guide but a constriction. Rather than now being lighthouses, Aquinas and Alphonsus had become boundary markers.[123] Roman references to other *probati auctores* are to be found regularly in responses of the Sacred Penitentiary, and their role in Canon Law and its interpretation also finds sanction in the Church's Code of Canon Law.[124]

Within the view of the Church's ordinary *magisterium* as it unfolded, the function of the theologian was not only, as Pius IX explained, 'to show how doctrine defined by the Church is contained in the sources' of Revelation,[125] but also, according to Pope Pius XII,

> to indicate how all that is taught by the living *Magisterium* is to be found in Scripture and divine 'tradition', whether explicitly or implicitly .... For along with these sacred sources God gave his Church a living *Magisterium* for the purpose also of illuminating and unfolding what are only obscurely and implicitly in the deposit of faith. This deposit was not entrusted by the divine Redeemer to the individual faithful or even to theologians to be authentically interpreted, but only to the *Magisterium* of the Church, ... whether by the ordinary or extraordinary exercise of this task.[126]

---

[123] A. Vermeersch, 'Soixante ans de théologie morale', *Nouvelle Revue Théologique*, 56 (1929), pp. 875–6.

[124] 'ut probati theologi docent', *DS* 2715; 'verba perpendat S. Alphonsi de Ligorio, . . . Necnon alios probatos auctores consulere non omittat', *DS*, ad 2759s. Cf. *DS*, ad 2726, 3634; *Codex Iuris canonici* (1917), 6, 2.

[125] Writing within days of the closure of the First Vatican Council, at which his papal infallibility had been defined. Cf. Pii IX *Acta*, pars I, vol. v, 260.

[126] 'Verum quoque est, theologis semper redeundum esse ad divinae revelationis fontes: eorum enim est indicare qua ratione ea quae a vivo Magisterio docentur, in Sacris Litteris et in divina "traditione", sive explicite, sive implicite inveniantur .... Una enim cum sacris eiusmodi fontibus Deus Ecclesiae suae Magisterium vivum dedit, ad ea quoque illustranda et enucleanda, quae in fidei deposito nonnisi obscure ac velut implicite contineantur. Quod quidem depositum nec singulis christifidelibus nec ipsis theologis divinus Redemptor concredidit authentice interpretandum, sed soli Ecclesiae Magisterio . . . sive ordinario sive extraordinario eiusdem muneris exercitio', *DS* 3886.

This approach of Pius XII did much to explain the almost innumerable interventions and initiatives with which he reacted to contemporary events in the daily exercise of his *magisterium*. What Hamel describes as 'the multiplication of documents of the magisterium in the moral field which reached its climax under Pius XII' was, he estimates, beneficial on the whole for moral theology, but it also had unforeseen negative results in hampering a critical sense and scientific research as well as engendering a sort of psychological censorship. 'Under Pius XII, the moralist lived in continual expectation, if not under the threat, of a Roman document which could put in question theses and opinions which he was advancing either in his teaching or his writings.'[127]

It can readily be understood how it was to come as something of a change when the Second Vatican Council, in a somewhat different atmosphere from that of its predecessor ninety years previously, was to teach that 'it is for God's people as a whole with the help of the Holy Spirit, and especially for pastors and theologians, to listen to the various voices of our day, discerning them and interpreting them, and to evaluate them in the light of the divine word, so that the revealed truth can be increasingly appropriated, better understood and more suitably expressed.'[128] This recovered view of the whole Church as transcending the nineteenth-century division into teaching and learning Church is also apparent in the affirmation that 'the faithful, clerical as well as lay, have a just freedom of enquiry, of thought, and of humble and courageous expression in those matters in which they enjoy competence'.[129] Welcome precision was also given to the scope of

---

[127] E. Hamel, 'Vari tipi di legittimazione in teologia morale', in *Ortodossia e Revisionismo* (Rome, 1974), pp. 126–7.

[128] 'Totius Populi Dei est, praesertim pastorum et theologorum, adiuvante Spiritu Sancto, varias loquelas nostri temporis auscultare, discernere et interpretari easque sub lumine verbi divini diiudicare, ut revelata Veritas semper penitius percipi, melius intelligi aptiusque proponi possit', *Gaudium et spes.* no. 44; *AAS* 58 (1966), p. 1065.

[129] 'Ut vero munus suum exercere valeant, agnoscatur fidelibus, sive clericis sive laicis, iusta libertas inquirendi, cogitandi necnon mentem suam in humilitate et fortitudine aperiendi in iis in quibus peritia gaudent', ibid., no. 62; *AAS*, p. 1084. On the role of theological faculties, cf. *Gravissimum educationis*, no. 11; *AAS*, ibid., p. 738; 'A scientiarum sacrarum Facultatum operositate plurimum expectat Ecclesia .... Ipsarum Facultatum item est varias sacrarum disciplinarum regiones altius pervestigare ita ut profundior in dies Sacrae Revelationis intellectus obtineatur, patrimonium sapientiae christianae a maioribus traditum plenius aperiatur, dialogus cum fratribus seiunctis et cum non christianis promoveatur atque quaestionibus a doctrinarum progressu exortis respondeatur'.

the Church's teaching authority with the claim and acknowledge-ment that in today's immensely developed world 'the Church, as guardian of the deposit of God's Word, draws religious and moral principles from it, but it does not always have a ready answer to particular questions, wishing to combine the light of revelation with universal experience so that illumination can be forthcoming on the direction which humanity has recently begun to take.'[130] In such an enterprise, however, the Church's pastors are not omni-competent or omniscient. The laity 'should not consider that their pastors always have the expertise needed to provide a concrete and ready answer to every problem which arises, even the most serious ones, or that this is their mission. The laity, as enlightened with Christian wisdom and paying careful attention to the teaching of the *Magisterium*, have their own part to play.'[131]

On the precise role of the hierarchy in the Church and in the exercise of *magisterium*, Vatican II was careful to explain that it was continuing in the footsteps of Vatican I, but it was equally careful to site its teaching in the context of the role of the individual bishop as such and of the collective body of the bishops within the whole Church. This can be seen in the progression of the argument which the Council develops on magisterial teaching about faith and morals. In its *Dogmatic Constitution on the Church* the Council opened with a careful meditation on the mystery of the Church followed by a chapter exploring the nature of the Church as God's People. Only then, in chapter three, did it consider the Church's hierarchical structure as a ministry instituted 'for the good of the whole body'.[132] Within this structure concentration is first fixed on

---

[130] 'Ecclesia, quae depositum verbi Dei custodit, ex quo principia in ordine religioso et morali hauriuntur, quin semper de singulis quaestionibus responsum in promptu habeat, lumen revelationis cum omnium peritia coniungere cupit, ut iter illuminetur, quod humanitas nuper ingressa est', *Gaudium et spes*, no. 33; *AAS*, ibid., p. 1052.

[131] 'Laicis proprie, etsi non exclusive, saecularia officia et navitates competunt. . . . Agnoscentes exigentias fidei eiusque virtute praediti, incunctanter, ubi oportet, nova incepta excogitent atque ad effectum deducant . . . . A sacerdotibus vero laici lucem ac vim spiritualem exspectent. Neque tamen ipsi censeant pastores suos adeo peritos esse ut, in omni quaestione exsurgente, etiam gravi, solutionem concretam in promptu habere queant, aut illos ad hoc missos esse: ipsi potius, sapientia christiana illustrati et ad doctrinam Magisterii observanter attendentes, partes suas proprias assumant', ibid., no. 43; *AAS*, pp. 1062–3.

[132] 'Haec Sacrosancta Synodus, Concilii Vaticani primi vestigia premens, . . .', *Lumen gentium*, no. 18; *AAS* 57 (1965), p. 22. 'Christus Dominus . . . in Ecclesia sua varia ministeria instituit, quae ad bonum totius Corporis tendunt', ibid., p. 21.

the college of bishops in succession to the college of Apostles and on their threefold office to sanctify, teach, and govern.[133] The particular role of the Bishop of Rome within the college then begins to emerge,[134] but immediately a return is made to consider the role of individual bishops each within his own Church and as contributing to the whole Church. It is within this context of the role of the bishop as such that Vatican II takes its first major step on the exercise of *magisterium*.

Bishops are heralds of the faith who lead new disciples to Christ. They are authentic teachers, endowed with the authority of Christ, who preach to the people committed to them the faith which is to be believed and to be put into effect in morals . . . . Bishops teaching in communion with the Roman Pontiff are to be respected by all as witnesses of divine Catholic truth, and the faithful ought to concur in the judgment of their Bishop proposed in the name of Christ about faith and morals, and adhere to it in religious submission of soul.[135]

Once this basic attitude of the faithful to the teaching of their own diocesan bishop on faith and morals has been established, a standard is now available to identify the reception to be given to papal teaching. The same submission is to be shown 'in a special way to the authentic *magisterium* of the Roman Pontiff, even when he is not speaking *ex cathedra*; that is, his supreme *magisterium* should be reverently acknowledged, and the judgements proposed by him should be sincerely adhered to, according to his obvious mind and will, which may be gathered especially from the character of the documents or from his frequent repetition of the same teaching or from his way of speaking.'[136]

---

[133] Ibid., 19–21; *AAS*, pp. 22–5.

[134] Ibid., 22; *AAS*, pp. 25–6.

[135] 'Episcopi enim sunt fidei praecones, qui novos discipulos ad Christum adducunt, et doctores authentici seu auctoritate Christi praediti, qui populo sibi commisso fidem credendam et moribus applicandam praedicant, . . . Episcopi in communione cum Romano Pontifice docentes ab omnibus tamquam divinae et catholicae veritatis testes venerandi sunt; fideles autem in sui Episcopi sententiam de fide et moribus nomine Christi prolatam concurrere, eique religioso animi obsequio adhaerere debent', ibid., 25; *AAS*, pp. 29–30.

[136] 'Hoc vero religiosum voluntatis et intellectus obsequium singulari ratione praestandum est Romani Pontificis authentico magisterio etiam cum non ex cathedra loquitur; ita nempe ut magisterium eius supremum reverenter agnoscatur, et sententiis ab eo prolatis sincere adhaereatur, iuxta mentem et voluntatem manifestatam ipsius, quae se prodit praecipue sive indole documentorum, sive ex frequenti propositione eiusdem doctrinae, sive ex dicendi ratione', ibid., p. 30.

Reflections on Authority

By way of conclusion and comment on this necessarily selective survey of how teaching authority has been exercised and expounded in the making of moral theology, it may be first hazarded that complete clarity has not yet been fully achieved in delineating the Church's commission to teach on moral matters, nor indeed whether that commission has been entrusted to the entire Church or only to a particular section of it. Thus, the rather unilateral teaching of Vatican II's *Dogmatic Constitution on the Church* on the manner in which the faithful are to receive the moral teaching of their Bishop and of the Bishop of Rome, which could still reflect a view of the Church as sharply divided between the teachers and the taught, is considerably softened when read alongside the later and perhaps more mature Conciliar *Pastoral Constitution on the Church in the Modern World*, which recognizes, as we have seen above, a strikingly more than passive role to others in the Church. This we shall consider further in our next chapter.

That the Church has not yet precisely delineated the area of human moral behaviour in which it has a unique competence entrusted to it by Christ appears as an inevitable conclusion to our study of the major magisterial pronouncements on the subject. We have noted how the common term *mores* had a moral connotation long before the Council of Trent, and indeed during and after the Council. But the fact that, as we think very probable, in the dominant and profoundly influential foundation Decree of Trent the term denotes religious and devotional practices could not but have had a distinctly confusing influence on subsequent centuries unaware of this basic ambiguity. In the Bull issued on the eve of the First Vatican Council, in which he invited all Christians to unite with the Catholic Church, Pope Pius IX was obviously quoting the Decree of Trent when he referred to the Church as constituted by God 'with the living authority to teach men especially matters of faith and regulation of morals and to direct and govern them in everything pertaining to eternal salvation'.[137] It is also to be noted that in its Constitution on faith, which preceded the definition of

---

[137] 'Cum enim eiusmodi societates careant viva illa et a Deo constituta auctoritate, quae homines res fidei morumque disciplinam praesertim docet eosque dirigit ac moderatur in iis omnibus, quae ad aeternam salutem pertinent . . .', *DS* 2998. Cf. *supra*, n. 43.

papal infallibility, Vatican I explicitly recalled the teaching of Trent on the interpretation of Scripture, and in renewing it also declared its mind to be 'that in matters of faith and morals which pertain to the building up of Christian doctrine' the true meaning of Scripture is to be considered that held by the Church.[138] Interestingly, however, in the infallibility drafts and decree no attempt was made to use the Tridentine phrase 'regulation of morals' and, as we have seen, the controlling personages were determined to refer only to matters, or doctrine, of morals, despite many misgivings on the part of not a few Bishops who desired some clarification of the idea other than an equally vague comparison with the infallibility of the Church. It may not have helped those who were not familiar with Italian to hear the phrase regularly translated as 'materia di fede e di costumi'.[139] And it was unclear in debates whether the Pope's prerogative was in order to resolve disputes, or 'questions', or whether it extended further; whether it related only to 'principles', that 'novel' term, as Gasser described it, and if so to what kind of principles; or whether it could also descend to contingent particulars; and how all this was to be related to the deposit of faith which Paul had enjoined Timothy to guard well.[140] To attempt to answer, or to quiet, all these legitimate concerns by pointing simply to the infallibility of the Church might go some way to reassuring those haunted by fears of arbitrariness or absolutism in the exercise of papal infallibility, but since the extent, as distinct from the fact, of the Church's infallibility in morals was equally uncertain, little other comfort was to be gained from the identification.

Nor, in the circumstances, was the official *Relatio* on the decree by Bishop Gasser such as to shed light on all these questions, either at the time or today. The amendment 'principles' was rejected on the ground that it would improperly include 'merely philosophical principles of natural morality', but Gasser threw no light on what

---

[138] 'Quoniam vero, quae sancta Tridentina Synodus de interpretatione divinae Scripturae ad coercenda petulantia ingenia salubriter decrevit, a quibusdam hominibus prave exponuntur, Nos idem decretum renovantes hanc illius mentem esse declaramus, ut in rebus fidei et morum ad aedificationem doctrinae christianae pertinentium is pro vero sensu sacrae Scripturae habendus sit, quem tenuit ac tenet sancta mater Ecclesia . . .', DS 3007. Cf. *supra*, n. 44.

[139] In the Italian account of the first meeting of the Deputatio to discuss whether the question of papal infallibility should be proposed to the Council the opening speaker is reported as maintaining papal infallibility 'in materia di fede e di costumi', Mansi, li, 688. Cf. also ibid., 698–700.

[140] Cf. *supra*, nn. 92–3, 95, 97–101, 110–11.

these might be. Moreover, suddenly into the debate was introduced at this final stage a reference to 'the doctrine about faith and *Christian* morals' without any justification or clarification of what this might and might not cover. The crowning touch, however, was to maintain the wisdom of retaining the old well-known term on the grounds that 'every theologian knows what is to be understood by these words'. So much, then, for those Bishops who had laboured for days to offer a more precise alternative wording, or carefully argued for some less ambiguous formulation. And so much for the poor Bishop in one Session who is reported as appealing for 'some declaration which would throw light on what was to be understood by that word *mores*'![141] It is interesting that one theologian, Franzelin, felt it necessary, despite his labours in the Council, to explain afterwards with great care what was to be understood by this distinction 'consecrated by ecclesiastical usage', and to do so in terms which, for a solemn definition of the Church in Council, are of a remarkably technical nature.

It must be concluded that, in this unimpressive section of his official explanation of the Conciliar decree, Gasser was deliberately evading some very real difficulties in a tone which was more dismissive than explanatory. And the supreme irony was that, at the very moment when the 'teaching Church', to which the Bishop alluded, that is, the entire hierarchy, was at a critical juncture in the history of the Church's commission to safeguard the deposit of revelation from error by solemnly defining as a dogma of faith the Pope's official infallibility in the area of moral behaviour, the best, indeed the only, explanation which the Deputation for the Faith could give to the Council Fathers of what precisely was meant by the papal extraordinary *magisterium* in 'morals' was to refer them to the nearest theologian.

In the more than a century since this extraordinary and infallible moral *magisterium* of the papacy was solemnly defined it has never once been manifestly exercised.[142] One explanation of this remarkable sequel may be that the First Vatican Council was too soon in the history of the Church to raise and answer so complex a question definitively, that the time was not ripe (which is very different from

---

[141] 'Optaret alius aliquam declarationem qua, quid per vocem illam *morum* intelligendum sit, clarius constaret', Mansi, li, 1017.

[142] 'Infallibiliter definita nulla intellegitur doctrina nisi id manifeste constiterit', *Codex Iuris Canonici*, 1983, no. 749.3.

saying a definition was inopportune), and that, in any case, the pressures of personalities and events, both inside and outside the Church, did not lend themselves to the patient and dispassionate sifting of evidence and argument which the subject patently required. The time-scale available to the Council, the progressive and introvert centralization of Church affairs on Rome which increased apace throughout the nineteenth century, the enormous popularity and sympathy which the figure of Pius IX attracted from ordinary Catholics throughout the world, the contraction of his temporal authority, his definition in 1854 of the Marian dogma of the Immaculate Conception, and his own views and wishes—all this, humanly speaking, conspired to focus the Council's attention dramatically and, to many, unexpectedly on one single issue, that of papal infallibility.[143] There was a move early in the Council to define it by acclamation, and in all the circumstances it is not really surprising if there was in the Council and in Rome little concern for what has been called, in a slightly different but related context, the small print.[144] It may be surmised that at Vatican I the hidden, perhaps even unconscious, agenda was simply to find a dramatic and perhaps necessary expression of solidarity and loyalty on the part of the Church towards the Holy See and its authority.[145] The most appropriate means to hand turned out to be the Council, and the most natural expression the most solemn act of such a Council. Once that had been achieved at least the immediate purpose and impulse had been satisfied and served.

It is this view which perhaps can make most sense of events following the Council, which highlighted not the extraordinary exercise of the moral *magisterium* of the Pope which had been defined, but the striking increase and expansion of his everyday

[143] On the background, cf. Aubert, op. cit., vol. v. pp. 56–61. On Pius IX's own pre-conciliar views on papal infallibility, cf. *DS* 2781. 'There is a general consensus that non-theological factors played at least as important a role here as the strictly theological ones. Prominent among the former was the widely shared hope that a strong affirmation of the spiritual authority of the Holy See would provide a remedy for the many evils of the day that were looked upon as the fruit of the liberalism and free-thinking stemming from Protestantism and the French Revolution.' F. A. Sullivan, *Magisterium: Teaching Authority in the Catholic Church* (Dublin, 1983), p. 94.

[144] G. Sweeney, 'The primacy: the small print of Vatican I', in A. Hastings (ed.), *Bishops and Writers* (Wheathampstead, 1977).

[145] The formal motivation of the declaration is stressed as countering attacks on papal authority. Cf. *DS* 3072.

teaching function towards 'the learning Church', seen by many to be exercised in an aura of infallibility. The ordinary *magisterium* of the Pope which Vatican II taught should be respected 'in a special way' as compared with the teaching of one's local bishop is today something of a puzzle to theologians. Pope Pius XII left uncontradicted the claim that it was not infallible.[146] The fullest explanation of ordinary *magisterium* in the Church is that given by the Second Vatican Council in the context of the collective teaching of the whole College of bishops dispersed throughout the world, which can in defined circumstances be exercised infallibly.[147] It might be argued that, just as in the exercise of his extraordinary *magisterium* the Pope expresses that of the body of Bishops as if gathered in solemn Council, so in the exercise of his ordinary *magisterium* on a matter of faith or morals the Pope is consciously representative of the whole worldwide episcopate and on that account teaching infallibly. The parallel, however, cannot simply be presumed, and it calls in question the purpose of papal infallibility as such, which appears of its nature to be a charism of an extraordinary quality. By contrast, ordinary *magisterium* in the Church appears to be inherently collective when it has the character of infallibility; so much so that one might conclude that in his ordinary teaching the Pope is infallible if, and only if, his teaching is identical with that of the rest of the episcopate.

Another reflection which arises from this consideration of 'teaching with authority' relates to the status of the moral theologian, whose varied fortunes we have charted in this historical survey, and it may be summed up in the contrast between delegation and subsidiarity. The division of the Church into the teaching Church, or the hierarchy, and the learning Church is, in the history of the Church, an extremely recent one which Congar summed up as '*the* Magisterium becoming autonomous and

---

[146] *Supra*, n. 122. On the papal ordinary magisterium, cf. the study of B. C. Butler, 'Infallibile; Authenticum: Assensus: Obsequium. Christian Teaching Authority and the Christian's Response', *Doctrine and Life* 31 (1981), pp. 77–89, and the comments on Bishop Butler's article by Sullivan, op. cit., pp. 159–173.

[147] 'Licet singuli praesules infallibilitatis praerogativa non polleant, quando tamen, etiam per orbem dispersi, sed communionis nexum inter se et cum successore Petri servantes, authentice res fidei et morum docentes in unam sententiam tamquam definitive tenendam conveniunt, doctrinam Christi infallibiliter enuntiant. Quod adhuc manifestius habetur quando, in Concilio Oecumenico coadunati, pro universa Ecclesia fidei et morum doctores et iudices sunt, quorum definitionibus fidei obsequio est adhaerendum', *Lumen gentium*, no. 25; *AAS* 57 (1965), p. 30.

absolute'.[148] Within such a categorization the role of the theologian is defined as that of obeying and also of justifying totally the pronouncements of the Magisterium, which Congar also described as 'not exactly' in accordance with what nineteen centuries of the Church's life tell us about the function of teacher or doctor in the Church.[149] His study of the role of theologians and of the Universities in earlier centuries argues for at least a softening of that disjunction, whereas a tendency to centralization leads naturally to a viewing of all theological teaching, exploration, and debate as activities carried on only with the permission of superiors and only within certain carefully defined areas in which Rome has not, or not yet, spoken.[150] It is an attitude of mind which can best be summed up in the word delegation, the permitting of theological activity on the part of subordinates only because, or to the degree that, superiors are unable through lack of time to undertake it better themselves. At its most extreme it may even confuse infallibility with omnicompetence or omniscience, or view it as a substitute for critical and historical research.

Subsidiarity is quite other in mentality. As a subject it figures a little in the Church's social teaching, appearing first in the encyclical of Pius XI, *Quadragesimo anno*, as a 'supremely important principle of social philosophy'. Basically it expresses the insight that 'it is unjust and a gravely harmful disturbance of right order to turn over to a greater society of higher rank functions and services which can be performed by lesser bodies on a lower plane. For a social undertaking of any sort, by its very nature, ought to aid the members of the body social, but never to destroy and absorb them.'[151] As a principle of importance in society it was later applied by Pope John XXIII and by the Second Vatican Council in such

---

[148] Art. cit., p. 108.

[149] Ibid., p. 109.

[150] In 1914 Pope Benedict XV circumscribed the areas of discussion for theologians as those in which the Apostolic See had not delivered its own judgement. 'Item nemo privatus, vel libris diariisve vulgandis vel sermonibus publice habendis, se in Ecclesia pro magistro gerat. Norunt omnes, cui sit a Deo magisterium Ecclesiae datum: huic igitur integrum ius esto pro arbitratu loqui, cum voluerit; ceterorum officium est, loquenti religiose obsequi dictoque audientes esse. In rebus autem, de quibus, salva fide ac disciplina,—cum Apostolicae Sedis iudicium non intercesserit— in utramque partem disputari potest, dicere, quid sentiat idque defendere, sane nemini non licet', DS 3625. Cf. Pius XII, *supra*, n. 122.

[151] AAS 23 (1931), p. 203.

areas as education and international economic cooperation.[152] More appropriately to our purpose, however, it appears that this principle of subsidiarity underlies the justification given by Bishop Gasser to the Fathers of Vatican I for the doctrine of papal infallibility: 'There is a particular place for such a definition when in some parts of the Church there arise scandals . . ., dissensions, and heresies, which bishops individually or even gathered in regional councils are unable to deal with, and so are compelled to refer the matter to the holy Apostolic See.'[153] That bishops are not simply delegates of the Pope was a truth to be pressed home by the Second Vatican Council in its teaching that 'they are not to be regarded as vicars of the Roman Pontiff, for they exercise an authority which is proper to them, and are quite correctly called "prelates", heads of the people whom they govern'.[154] It may also be possible to see a similar view of subsidiarity underlying the description by Pope Paul VI in 1967 in an ecumenical context of the papacy as 'the necessary principle of truth, charity, and unity'.[155]

The point of subsidiarity, of course, in contrast to delegation, is that it does not grant limited power or impart carefully circumscribed authority. It recognizes it and respects it as already existing, and only with reluctance and as a last resort does a higher authority or a higher power intervene for a higher good. This, of course, raises the question, if the contrast between delegation and subsidiarity is applied to the status of the theologian in the Church, of what authority is in fact enjoyed by theologians, and in this case moral theologians, within the Christian community. The answer to

---

[152] *AAS* 53 (1961), p. 414; *Gravissimum educationis*, n. 3 (*AAS* 58 (1966), p. 731); *Gaudium et spes*, n. 86 (*AAS*, ibid., p. 1109). On applying the principle in the Church, cf. Pius XII, *AAS* 38 (1946), pp. 144–6; *Codex Iuris Canonici*, 1983, *Praef.*, xxii.

[153] *Supra*, n. 108.

[154] *Lumen gentium*, 27; *AAS* 57 (1965), p. 33. It is interesting to note that, in the aftermath of Vatican I, when the German Chancellor, Bismarck, charged the Vatican with papal totalitarianism and with absorbing the jurisdiction of local bishops, the German hierarchy rejected his interpretation and asserted the general proposition that 'the Catholic Church has no place for the immoral and despotic maxim that the command of a superior always dispenses from personal responsibility'. 'Es ist wahrlich nicht die katholische Kirche, in welcher der unsittliche und despotische Grundsatz, der Befehl des Obern entbinde unbedingt von der eigenen Verantwortlichkeit, Aufnahme gefunden hat', *DS* 3115. Pius IX warmly congratulated the German bishops on their stand against Bismarck and this misinterpretation, *DS* 3112, proem; *DS* 3117. The 'despotic maxim' was to have a sad unfolding in Germany sixty years later.

[155] Sweeney, op. cit., pp. 179–80.

this question must lie partly in considering that there is more than one type of authority, and partly in the realization that to attempt to encompass the mystery of the Church simply in terms of authority structures of superiority and subordination or delegation is either to suspend exploration of the mystery at one particular stage of the Church's history or, what amounts to the same thing, to presume that at any one time or in any one expression the totality of the mystery has been fathomed. There are many different types of authority, of which juridical authority is only one as embodying the exercise of institutional power and the application of sanctions to bring about a desired or agreed end. There is also, in the Church as in any community, the authority of the born leader or in theological language the charismatic figure, such as were the founders of the great religious Orders and movements. There is also the authority of the expert, the individual who is acknowledged as 'an authority' and who commands respect rather than demanding it. And there is also, as we shall consider in our next chapter, the authority of Christian experience, for which there can be no substitute. The flourishing of any community can lie only in the recognition of all such types of authority, in order to achieve a total shared and living authority which will correspond to the nature and needs of the whole community. The challenge to any community is not to introduce an imbalance by stressing one or more expression of authority to the detriment or exclusion of others. Within this spectrum of authorities that of the theologian in the Church, which as a whole is endowed with the teaching commission by Christ, derives in the first instance from his or her incorporation into Christ through baptism, and secondly from such gifts or charisms of the Spirit as are appropriated and expressed through expertise and learning for the good of the Church.

For the correlative of authority is, of course, responsibility. In the case of the moral theologian this includes responsibility to his subject, which is none other than the word and work of God, responsibility to the canons of truth and of scholarship, responsibility to colleagues in the profession of moral theology and to its status in the body of the faithful, and responsibility to that body, the Church including its pastors, and to Christ its head and Master. In the course of this study we have abundant melancholy testimony to irresponsibility on the part of some moral theologians, notably in the period characterized by laxism, both in the wanton silliness of argumentation and in the near-idolatry rendered to extrinsic authorities so different from the twelfth century when, as Southern comments, 'the quoting of authorities was the opening of a debate, not the end of it'.[156]

If the authority of the theological *magisterium*, to use the medieval term, is such, and its responsibilities so grave, so also is the responsibility of the *Magisterium*, in the modern sense of that phrase, in exercising its commission to guard the deposit of faith and to rule, teach, and sanctify the Church of Christ in its participation in the Lord's triple role of priest, prophet, and king. It is interesting to note, however, how in human affairs so admirable a quality as a strongly developed sense of responsibility for something, or for others, can at times transpose into something of a nervous proprietorial attitude towards that thing and a suffocating attitude towards those others. And the *Magisterium*'s responsibility is not just to God for the deposit of faith and for the Church; it is also a responsibility to the Church for which it exists as servant of God's servants and on whose behalf it is to administer its talent, with risk but also with the promise of a hundredfold increase, rather than keep it safe and sterile. Such responsibility to the Church carries with it the obligation to harness all possible resources within and without the Church in its seeking to understand, explain, and develop the saving truth of the Gospel for all men. 'The task, then, for a sharing Church is not to emphasise any one of these authorities to the exclusion of others, but to share the fruits of all within the Church, realizing that no one of them can claim a monopoly of the Spirit.'[157] And within this mutual sharing, the role and function of the theologian would certainly include that of substantiating and clarifying the teaching of the *Magisterium*. But it could also partake of the relationship of artist to patron in producing work which the latter may or may not have commissioned but which, as the product also of skill, vision, and integrity, may also lead to quite surprising results. Such a view of a plurality of complementary authorities in the Church is not easily reconciled with a philosophy or theology of delegation, but it would flourish congenially in an atmosphere of subsidiarity accepted within the society of the Church as well as preached to society outside the Church.

[156] Op. cit., p. 207.
[157] J. Mahoney, 'The Sharing Church', *The Month*, 2nd n.s. 14 (1981), p. 348.

A final, and perhaps the most important, reflection on the theme
of 'teaching with authority' concerns the idea of *magisterium*, or
teaching authority, itself. Fundamental to the entire history and
attitude of the Church to its exercise of moral teaching is the closing
pericope of Matthew's Gospel in which the risen Christ explains to
his Apostles how 'all authority in heaven and on earth has been
given' to him, and commissions them, as a result, to 'make disciples
of all nations, . . . teaching them to observe all that I have
commanded you'.[158] It is of interest, and possibly significance, that
the two key words of this passage, 'authority' and 'teaching', echo
the reaction of the crowds at the end of the major piece of moral
teaching, the Sermon on the Mount, with which in Matthew Jesus
inaugurated his own teaching ministry: 'for he was teaching them
as one having authority'.[159] It is also generally agreed that of the
four Gospels Matthew's is the one most interested, even preoccupied, with Jewish–Christian questions, such as the fulfilment
of the Old Testament prophecies and Law, problems of sabbath
observance and marriage legislation.[160] It appears also to be the
Gospel most interested in the Church as a visible, structured
organization.[161] Given all these factors it is not implausible to see
in the closing scene of Matthew and the commissioning of the

---

[158] Matt. 28: 18–20.

[159] Matt. 7: 29, the Greek terms being *didache* and *exousia*.

[160] Cf. J. L. McKenzie, in *The Jerome Biblical Commentary* (Chapman, 1968),
vol. ii: 'In Mt Jesus is contrasted with the scribes, the teacher of Judaism' (43: 3);
Matthew . . . has been called a Christian scribe or rabbi . . . . there are points of
contact between Mt and the rabbinical writings that are not found in the other
Gospels . . . . Mt reflects not only the rabbinical discussions of Jesus himself, but
controversies of Jewish Christians with their fellow Jews' (43: 7). On Matt. 7: 28–9,
McKenzie comments, 'The Greek word *exousia* translated "authority" means
"authority by commission". Jesus has a commission from the Father to teach—a
commission the scribes do not have' (ibid., 43:53).

[161] The strength of the Gospel of Matthew 'is not in narrative power, literary
appeal, or mystical depth, but in its proved and persistent capacity to shape
Christian thought and church life . . . . The Gospel is the work of a Christian
churchman who writes to serve the needs of the Church and especially its leaders
. . . . His immediate aim is to provide the Church's teachers with a basic tool for
their work.' F. V. Filson, *The Gospel according to Matthew*. Black's New Testament
Commentaries (London, 1960), pp. 2, 4, 20. Cf. McKenzie, op. cit., 'Mt is a Jewish
Gospel, but it is also a Gospel of the Church. The reign of God in Mt is clearly
identified with the community of the disciples' (43: 10). On Matt. 28: 16–20,
McKenzie comments, 'The Church acts in virtue of the commission that Jesus has
received' (43: 206). On the historical background and purpose of Matt., cf. also
G. D. Kilpatrick, *The Origins of the Gospel According to Saint Matthew* (Oxford,
1946).

Apostles as authorized teachers to extend Christ's own teaching a picture emerging from a predominantly Judaeo–Christian community of a juridical, and even rabbinical, authoritative accreditation of Jesus' own personal envoys to the growing Church.

It is not surprising if it was the spirit, as well as the letter, of this Matthaean presentation of moral *magisterium* which proved most attractive and congenial to the whole Western Christian Church, increasingly preoccupied as it was with structures, conditions of membership, the nature of the Church as a perfect society on earth, and a continual series of power struggles within its ranks. And it may be that we have in the moral *magisterium* as it has developed in history a working-out of the Matthaean theology of authoritative moral teaching. It is one in which the great and, on the whole, silent majority of the Church, the laity, who belong not to the teaching but to the learning or listening Church in this picture may be forgiven for feeling that at times they have been caught between the upper and nether millstones of the *Magisterium* and the moral theologian. But Matthew's is not the only theology of the Church to be portrayed in the New Testament, nor is the Matthaean theology of *magisterium* in morals the only scriptural presentation of the Christian's moral life. There is another equally valid, and complementary, theology of moral behaviour and initiative to be found, which starts, as it were, from the inside rather than the outside. When the Second Vatican Council resorted to the traditional phrase with reference to moral behaviour, rather than simply juxtapose its two elements it organically linked them in one passage to refer to 'the faith to be believed and to be put into effect in morals'.[162] In this development of teaching, morality is seen as the practical living out of the Christian's faith, and as such its unfolding and guidance might more appropriately be considered within the Church's sanctifying power rather than its teaching power. Such a non-Matthaean approach is more in keeping with the Johannine and Pauline theologies of moral behaviour, with Christ and his Spirit as internal Teacher, and with the notion of conscience and subjectivity, to which we may now turn. It is a Gospel alternative best summed up in the verse, 'but the anointing which you received from him abides in you, and you have no need that anyone should teach you; as his anointing teaches you about everything, and is true, and is no lie'.[163]

[162] 'fidem credendam et moribus applicandam', *supra*, n. 135.
[163] 1 John 2: 27.

5

SUBJECTIVITY

One of the sharpest distinctions developed in the making of moral theology, and at the same time one of the most challenging, is that between subjective morality and objective morality. Subjective morality refers to the moral goodness or badness of the individual's behaviour as it actually appears to him or her, whereas objective morality refers to the moral goodness or badness of a piece of behaviour considered in itself, whatever the individual subject may think of it. Sometimes the two will coincide, so that, for instance, if it actually is morally bad or morally wrong to introduce children to hard drugs, and yet I make a living out of deliberately doing so, knowing it to be wrong, then one can say that my behaviour is bad both objectively and subjectively. If, on the other hand, I genuinely but mistakenly consider that this man Jesus is a heretic and a menace to my religion and the State, and on those grounds I decide that I am justified in putting him to death, as Abelard speculated, then it could be said that, although objectively bad, my behaviour is subjectively good, since I think I am doing the right thing. Alternatively, if I cannot be persuaded that there is nothing wrong in taking a day off work when I feel unwell, and there actually is nothing wrong in such an action, and yet I act against my conviction, with, in the popular phrase, a guilty conscience, then although my behaviour is not bad in itself, or objectively speaking, nevertheless my action in doing so is subjectively bad. The purpose of this chapter is to trace some of the elements which have contributed to the tradition of evaluating moral behaviour in terms of objectivity and subjectivity, and to offer some observations and reflections on the distinction.

The Raw Material of Behaviour

One of the earliest sustained attempts in the making of moral theology to stress subjectivity is to be found in the writings of Peter Abelard, the turbulent French scholastic, described by Southern as

the 'prince of free-lance teachers', who brought about in the twelfth
century what Rohmer, in his classic study of moral purpose, called
'the crisis of moral subjectivism'.[1] In the philosophical controversy
of his day about the exact status of universal ideas Abelard refused
to regard them as having any reality outside the mind, considering
that the only things which actually existed were individual beings.[2]
With such a predisposition towards what things possessed uniquely,
and against what they might be considered to have in common, it is
not surprising that in his ethics Abelard was equally individualistic,
to the extent of concentrating the morality of good or bad action
not in what was being done, but in the intention with which it was
done. As he argued in his ethical work significantly entitled *Know
Thyself*, 'It is indeed obvious that works which it is or is not at all
fitting to do may be performed as much by good as by bad men
who are separated by their intention alone.'[3] Moral goodness or
badness does not reside in any action considered in itself but derives
only from the intention which produces the action. 'Works in fact,
which as we have previously said are common to the damned and
the elect alike, are all indifferent in themselves and should be called
good or bad only on account of the intention of the agent, not, that
is, because it is good or bad for them to be done but because they
are done well or badly, that is, by that intention by which it is or is
not fitting that they should be done.'[4]

Not only was it the case that 'in an age of objective criteria,
Abeland turned to subjective values',[5] but he also considered the
supreme subjective moral value to be whether in acting one was

---

[1] Southern, op. cit., p. 196. J. Rohmer, *La finalité morale chez les théologiens de
saint Augustin à Duns Scotus* (Paris, 1939), p. 31.

[2] Cf. G. Leff, *Medieval Thought* (London, 1962), pp. 109–11.

[3] Trans. D. E. Luscombe (ed.), *Peter Abelard's 'Ethics'* (Oxford, 1971), p. 29.
'Constat quippe opera quae fieri convenit aut minime eque a bonis sicut a malis
hominibus geri, quod intentio sola separat', ibid., pp. 26–8. Cf. 'Non enim quae
fiunt, sed quo animo fiant pensat Deus, nec in opere sed in intentione meritum
operantis vel laus consistit. Sepe quippe idem a diversis agitur, per iusticiam unius et
per nequitiam alterius, . . . per diversitatem tamen intentionis idem a diversis fit, ab
uno male, ab altero bene', ibid., p. 28; 'Si autem proprie peccatum intelligentes
solum Dei contemptum dicamus peccatum, potest revera sine hoc vita ista transigi,
quamvis cum maxima difficultate', ibid., p. 68.

[4] Ibid., pp. 45–7. 'Opera quippe quae, ut praediximus, eque reprobis ut electis
communia sunt, omnia in se indifferentia sunt nec nisi pro intentione agentis bona
vel mala dicenda sunt, non videlicet quia bonum vel malum sit ea fieri, sed quia bene
vel male fiunt, hoc est, ea intentione qua convenit fieri, aut minime', ibid., pp. 44–6.

[5] Leff, p. 113.

pleasing God or despising him. Sin lies not in feelings or attractions but in consent alone and in 'contempt for God'. God cannot be harmed by us, but he can be despised, 'and so our sin is contempt of the Creator and to sin is to hold the Creator in contempt, that is, to do by no means on his account what we believe we ought to do for him, or not to forsake on his account what we believe we ought to forsake'.[6] It does not appear to be the case, however, that for Abelard what one actually did had no bearing whatsoever on the moral goodness or badness of one's behaviour, and he certainly did not consider that the single factor of obedience to God rendered all good actions equally good any more than contempt of God as the basic factor of sin made all sins equally bad.[7] On the one hand, we can observe him wrestling with the problem of those who executed Christ and persecuted the martyrs in possibly good faith, to conclude that 'we cannot say that they have sinned in this, . . . what contempt of God have they in what they do for God's sake and therefore think they do well, especially since the Apostle says: "If our heart do not reprehend us, we have confidence towards God"?'[8] But on the other hand, he does not consider it sufficient for

---

[6] Luscombe, p. 7. 'Peccatum itaque nostrum contemptus creatoris est, et peccare est creatorem contempnere, hoc est, id nequaquam facere propter ipsum quod credimus propter ipsum a nobis esse faciendum, vel non dimittere propter ipsum quod credimus esse dimittendum', ibid., p. 6.

[7] 'Si ergo non tam pro nostro dampno quam pro Dei offensa debemus cavere peccata, profecto plus ea cavenda sunt in quibus magis offenditur . . . tanto maiori odio quaelibet sunt habenda quanto turpiora in se censentur et ab honestate virtutis amplius recedunt, et naturaliter quoslibet magis offendunt', ibid., pp. 72–4. ' "Quanto eis precipiebat ne dicerent, tanto plus predicabant" [Mark 7: 36] etc. Numquid tales reos transgressionis iudicabis qui contra praeceptum quod acceperant egerunt atque hoc etiam scienter? Quid eos excuset a transgressione nisi quia nichil egerunt per contemptum precipientis, quod ad honorem ipsius facere decreverunt? . . . Fuit bonum precipi, quod non fuit bonum fieri', ibid., p. 30.

[8] 'Si quis tamen querat utrum illi martirum vel Christi persecutores in eo peccarent quod placere Deo credebant, . . . profecto secundum hoc quod superius peccatum esse descripsimus, contemptum Dei vel consentire in eo in quo credit consentiendum non esse, non possumus dicere eos in hoc peccasse nec ignorantiam cuiusquam vel ipsam etiam infidelitatem, cum qua nemo salvari potest, peccatum esse. Qui enim Christum ignorant et ob hoc fidem Christianam respuunt, quia eam Deo contrariam credunt, quem in hoc contemptum Dei habent quod propter Deum faciunt, et ob hoc bene se facere arbitrantur, presertim cum Apostolus dicat, "Si cor nostrum non reprehenderit nos fiduciam habemus apud Deum" [1 John 3: 21]?', ibid., pp. 54–6. 'Non credere vero Christum, quod infidelitatis est, quomodo parvulis vel his quibus non est annuntiatum culpae debeat ascribi non video, vel quicquid per ignorantiam invincibilem fit, cui vel previdere non valuimus, veluti siquis forte hominem quem non videt in silva sagitta interficiat dum feris vel avibus sagittandis intendit', ibid., p. 66.

a good or right intention that one need only believe one is acting well and pleasing God.

An intention should not be called good because it seems to be good but because in addition it is just as it is thought to be, that is, when believing that one's objective is pleasing to God, one is in no way deceived in one's own estimation. Otherwise even the unbelievers themselves would have good works just like ourselves, since they too, no less than we, believe they will be saved or will please God through their works.[9]

Reference to the salvation of the unbeliever serves to remind us that, steeped as he was in the philosophy and the ethical thought of the ancient world, Abelard was theologian as well as logician, and as a Christian thinker he was deeply influenced by the Augustinian stress on true love of God or its absence as the only real determinant of the value of man's actions. 'What seems to characterize Abelard's ethics is the wish to extend to the whole field of the morality of our acts the subjective principle of intention which St Augustine had applied only to the good morality of virtuous actions.'[10] Once this tenet of Augustine was extended with logical and characteristic singleness of purpose to all moral behaviour it was natural enough that it would find expression in a 'concern for the inner point of view in moral discussion, the attitude of a man rather than the nature of his deeds'.[11] The conclusion that all objective human actions were morally in-different, or materially indifferent, was, however, to be rejected by others and to provoke especially from Peter Lombard a deeper consideration of not only subjective but also objective morality.

The author of the *Sentences* was in this regard more faithful to Augustine in viewing some actions as containing an intrinsic morality which made them evil in themselves, and in considering that no intention, however good, could make up for this inherent

---

[9] 'Non est itaque intentio bona dicenda quia bona videtur, sed insuper quia talis est, sicut existimatur, cum videlicet illud ad quod tendit, si Deo placere credit, in hac insuper existimatione sua nequaquam fallatur. Alioquin ipsi etiam infideles sicut et nos bona opera haberent, cum ipsi etiam non minus quam nos per opera sua se salvari vel Deo placere credant', ibid., p. 54.

[10] Rohmer, op. cit., p. 31. Cf. *supra*, pp. 85–8.

[11] Luscombe, pp. xxxi-xxxii. 'Quod et beatus diligenter considerans Augustinus, omne praeceptum vel prohibicionem ad karitatem seu cupiditatem potius quam ad opera reducens . . .', ibid., p. 26.

interior badness.[12] Some actions are bad 'of their type', while others are inherently good although they can become bad through a bad intention.[13] Lombard's successors were to follow this line of analysis of actions being good or bad in their own right, and it was Philip the Chancellor who defined 'good of its kind' as good on account of the 'material' out of which it is made, or by reason of its material object.[14] Thus, in every moral act what was considered was not just the intention or the motive with which it was produced, but, as it were, the raw material from which the act was fashioned. If that stuff, or raw material, is flawed or faulty or quite unsuitable, the same would have to be said of the final product, the subjective use made of the raw material. And it was this raw material which Aquinas was to describe as the 'object' of any action, meaning by this term not the 'objective' or purpose, as the word can sometimes mean in English, but the moral stuff out of which the action is fashioned. 'Any act has a double purpose: the purpose to hand, which is the object, and the further purpose at which the agent is aiming.'[15]

In the philosophical analysis to which Aquinas subjected every moral action he viewed the moral agent as choosing from a range of types, or species, of actions before him and as choosing one of these types in order to clothe and bring about the intention which he has in mind. The individual's action is therefore necessarily coloured or shaped by the qualities inherent in the type of action which he has chosen. Hence the moral evaluation of any individual action must

---

[12] Augustine had been forthright in considering certain acts as such to be sins. 'Cum vero iam opera peccata sunt, sicut furta, stupra, blasphemiae vel cetera talia, quis est, qui dicat causis bonis esse facienda, ut vel peccata non sint, vel, quod est absurdius, iusta peccata sint? quis est, qui dicat: ut habeamus quod demus pauperibus, faciamus furta divitibus aut testimonia falsa vendamus', *Contra mendacium*, 18; *PL* 40, 528. On the difficulties to which this led Augustine in matters of sexual morality, cf. *supra*, p. 64. On Augustine and Abelard, cf. A. M. Meier, *Das peccatum mortale ex toto genere suo* (Regensburg, 1966), pp. 111–12.

[13] Lottin, *Principes*, ii, p. 139.

[14] Ibid., p. 140.

[15] 'Actus aliquis habet duplicem finem: scilicet proximum finem, qui est obiectum eius et remotum, quem agens intendit; et ideo cum bonum ex fine distinguitur contra bonum ex genere, intelligitur de fine remoto quem agens intendit', *In II Sent.* dist. 36, q. 1, a. 5 ad 5; quoted Meier, op. cit., p. 125, n. 2. The distinction between the end 'at hand' and the end 'at a distance', or the proximate and the remote ends, would be analysed further to distinguish between the *finis operis*, the inherent purpose of the act, and the *finis operantis*, the purpose of the agent in performing the act.

take into account not only the *purpose of the agent* in acting, and the *circumstances* in which he acts, but also the material out of which the action is fashioned, its '*object*', with the conclusion that for any act to be morally good it must satisfy the criterion of goodness in each of these three elements.[16] To the question of how one was to satisfy oneself about the inherent morality of the object, or about the quality of the raw material available to one, Aquinas replied that this was the work of reason invoking the law of nature and aided by divine law, enabling man to classify various objects, or types of action, as morally good, morally bad, or morally indifferent. 'One object is reasonable and therefore good of its type, such as clothing the naked. Another is at variance with reason, such as taking other people's property, and therefore bad of its type. A third type is neither reasonable nor unreasonable, such as picking up a straw, etc., and this type is called indifferent.'[17]

The Will of God: Nominalism

The analysis by Aquinas of the moral act into its three components was to become the dominant view in the thirteenth century and

[16] '. . . dicendum quod, sicut dictum est, bonum et malum actionis, sicut et ceterarum rerum, attenditur ex plenitudine essendi vel defectu ipsius. Primum autem quod ad plenitudinem essendi pertinere videtur, est id quod dat rei speciem. Sicut autem res naturalis habet speciem ex sua forma, ita actio habet speciem ex obiecto; sicut et motus ex termino. Et ideo sicut prima bonitas rei naturalis attenditur ex sua forma, quae dat speciem ei, ita et prima bonitas actus moralis attenditur ex obiecto convenienti; unde et a quibusdam vocatur bonum ex genere; puta, uti re sua. Et . . . ita primum malum in actionibus malis est quod est ex obiecto, sicut accipere aliena. Et dicitur malum ex genere, genere pro specie accepto, eo modo loquendi quo dicimus *humanum genus* totam humanam speciem', *STh*, 1a 2ae, q. 18, a 2. 'plenitudo bonitatis [actionis] non tota consistit in sua specie, sed aliquid additur ex his quae adveniunt tanquam accidentia quaedam. Et huiusmodi sunt circumstantiae debitae. Unde si aliquid desit quod requiratur ad debitas circumstantias, erit actio mala', ibid., art. 3. 'Actiones autem humanae, et alia quorum bonitas dependet ab alio, habent rationem bonitatis ex fine a quo dependent, praeter bonitatem absolutam quae in eis existit. Sic igitur in actione humana bonitas quadruplex considerari potest. Una quidem secundum genus, prout scilicet est actio: quia quantum habet de actione et entitate, tantum habet de bonitate, ut dictum est. Alia vero secundum speciem: quae accipitur secundum obiectum conveniens. Tertia secundum circumstantias, quasi secundum accidentia quaedam. Quarta autem secundum finem, quasi secundum habitudinem ad causam bonitatis', ibid., art. 4.

[17] 'Est autem aliquod obiectum quod importat aliquid conveniens rationi, et facit esse bonum ex genere, sicut vestire nudum; aliquid autem obiectum quod importat aliquid discordans a ratione, sicut tollere alienum, et hoc facit malum in genere; quoddam vero obiectum est quod neque importat aliquid conveniens rationi, neque aliquid a ratione discordans, sicut levare festucam de terra, vel aliquid huiusmodi; et huiusmodi dicitur indifferens', *De malo*, q. 2, a. 5.

eventually to be accepted as definitive in classical moral theology. But the balanced relationship which he appeared to have secured between objectivity and subjectivity was radically upset and undermined in the centuries immediately following his. It was all very well to maintain that the natures of things, especially man's, and behind them the creative will of God, gave one a good idea of the stuff of moral behaviour, or of objective morality. But did things actually have natures? And could not God have decided or disposed otherwise, had he so wished? With these radical questions the making of moral theology entered the age of Occam and nominalism which was to shake the hold on objectivity which Aquinas had seemed to secure in the century following Abelard. This he had been enabled to do by a confidence in the power of human reasoning, and especially by an acceptance of the meta-physical concept and analysis of nature which he willingly inherited from Aristotelian thought. But for those who came after Aquinas the lure of Augustine proved stronger than the appeal of Aristotle.

Augustine . . . refused to define natures by reference to the necessary law of essences. Instead, he reduced natures to what God wanted things to be, to the mere objects of God's good pleasure. Thus, giving everything to God, Augustine easily accounted for miracles and for God's personal interven-tion in the world. But his philosophy labours under serious drawbacks: if created natures are not stable principles of action possessed of intrinsic necessity, we are living in the dreamworld of the nominalist philosophers.[18]

Abelard himself had, as Knowles remarks, anticipated 'with strange exactness'[19] the systematic preoccupations of the four-teenth and later centuries with questions of the will, both divine and human, which, of course, had led Paul (Rom. 11) to surrender before the mystery of God's dispensations. In his acceptance of what appears to be for many theologians the ultimate challenge of a commentary on the Epistle to the Romans, Abelard had argued that

however God wishes to treat his creature he cannot be accused of injustice. And what happens in accordance with his will can in no sense be called evil. We can only distinguish good from evil according as it is in agreement with his will and consists in his good pleasure. No one can have the presumption to find fault with what appears to be the worst of reprehensible behaviour when it is done at the Lord's command. Otherwise

[18] J. P. Kenny, in *NCE*, vol. xiii, p. 813.
[19] D. Knowles, *The Evolution of Medieval Thought* (London, 1962), p. 129.

the Hebrews despoiling the Egyptians would have to be seriously accused of theft, etc., ... Our conclusion is that the whole difference between good and bad consists in the decree of God's dispensation which disposes everything excellently for us who are not aware of it; and that nothing should be called well done or ill done except it be in accordance with, or contrary to, his excellent will.[20]

After the death of Aquinas several of his basic theological and philosophical positions were radically questioned almost immediately by the Scottish Franciscan whom Angelini and Valsecchi describe as 'the last great medieval theologian', John Duns Scotus, whose major *Commentary on the Sentences* of Lombard constitutes a 'personal *summa* of theology' and certainly merits for him the admiring title given him by contemporaries of the 'Subtle Doctor'.[21] More attracted to Platonism and Augustinism than to Aristotelianism, Scotus was to lay more stress on the will and on love than on the intellect. And it was within this Franciscan school of thought that the English William of Occam also developed his own theses of a distinctly individualist and personalist nature. For Occam the only things which exist are unique individual beings, which are known to us by direct intuition. Universal ideas do not point to universally shared natures in things, but are merely convenient names, or *nomina*, which we use to classify groups of individuals. The same may be said of human actions, which do not simply exemplify general types of actions, but are to be considered as so many products of single individuals acting in successive, but unconnected, instants. 'The interest of the moralist, then, lies not in cataloguing virtues, but in considering each and every decision in all its precise circumstances.'[22]

---

[20] 'Profiteor, quoquomodo Deus creaturam suam tractare velit, nullius iniuriae potest argui. Nec malum aliquomodo potest dici, quod iuxta eius voluntatem fiat. Non enim aliter bonum a malo discernere possumus, nisi quod eius est consentaneum voluntati, et in placito eius consistit. Unde et ea quae per se videntur pessima, et ideo culpanda, cum iussione fiunt Dominica, nullus culpare praesumit. Alioquin Hebraei spoliantes Aegyptios furti graviter arguendi essent, et qui suos occiderunt proximos cum Madianitis fornicantes, non tam ultores quam homicidae iudicarentur . . . . Constat itaque, ut diximus, totam boni vel mali discretionem in divinae dispensationis placito consistere, quae optime cuncta nobis ignorantibus disponit, nec quidquam bene fieri dicendum aut male, nisi quod eius optimae voluntati consentaneum est aut adversum', *Super Epist. ad Rom.*, lib. 2, 6; *PL* 178, 869; quoted Meier, p. 110, n. 9.

[21] Angelini and Valsecchi, pp. 106–7.

[22] Ibid., p. 108.

Moreover, for Occam and nominalism the idea of what is good or bad is not to be concluded from a close examination of the natures of things, there being none such, nor is it even to be analysed rationally from the order of God's creation. God is absolutely free, and since he could, strictly speaking, have made everything entirely differently, the only ultimately secure basis of morality must lie in the free decision of God's will, who commands exactly as he wills. This stress on the will, or voluntarism, was to result in a positivist morality of commands and of resulting obligations to obey such commands, which even then could not guarantee absolute security or certainty. Although the commonly proposed distinction between God's 'absolute power', according to which he can effect or command absolutely anything, and his 'ordained power', which is to be recognized in the dispensation currently in force, was a distinction which Occam pursued in a largely speculative vein, yet the abolition of 'natures' and the contingent character of the present dispensation of Providence could only introduce into moral theology a provisional and questioning note concerning the moral commandments and laws which God has issued and not so far (or so far as we know) nullified or changed. Morality did not issue from within reality, but was painted on to it from outside, and absolutely speaking it could change colour overnight.

The separation of thought and essence led in theology to a preference for the investigation of all imaginable possibilities on the basis of the *potentia dei absoluta* and to a neglect of the way of salvation which was effectively pointed out and binding in the sources of revelation . . . . In ethics a radical separation of essence and duty and the allied formalism and voluntarism indicated the main features of nominalism.[23]

According to Iserloh,

the beginning of the fourteenth century marked a turning point in philosophy and theology. In general this can be characterized as the dissolution of the universalism and objectivism which had found their imposing expression in the *summae* of High Scholasticism. The philosophical and theological syntheses were supplanted by the critical investigation of individual problems . . . . The individual was more strongly expressed, and the perceiving subject became its own object to a much greater extent.[24]

[23] Iserloh, in Jedin and Dolan, iv, p. 346. [24] Ibid., p. 344.

Occamism and nominalism spread rapidly throughout the European universities despite the protests to the papal court at Avignon of scholars such as John Lutterell, whose objections lost him his chancellorship at Oxford.[25] Their influence throughout the fifteenth and sixteenth centuries was to encourage the fragmentation of theology and the proliferation of disparate casuistry as well as to inculcate an anti-rational, mystical, and pious fideism. 'In moral theology the only thing studied is the problem of obligation. No search is made for the reasons for obligation. It suffices to quote the arguments of authority or of dialectic and to pile up the texts of decrees. The moralist is simply God's lawyer, who proclaims, imposes and interprets God's laws.'[26] It is true that the fifteenth century had also seen a reaction against the 'modern way' of nominalism and its 'extravagant sophistries',[27] and a revival of interest in the 'old way' and in the works of Aquinas. But it was nominalism which characterized the century in such thinkers as John Gerson, chancellor of Paris University, and the thoroughgoing voluntarist and Pelagian Gabriel Biel who had so strong an influence on both Luther and his Catholic opponents.[28] It was also nominalism, with its elimination of natures and of the object, or raw material, of morality as a valid source of moral insight and as the medium for expression in the moral dialogue between God and man, which contributed philosophically to presenting morality more as an immediate encounter, or better, confrontation, between the individual and the will of God. In so doing, it also served to bring into prominence a major feature of subjectivity to which we may now turn—the manner in which the individual appropriates the various commands and laws of God as applying to him and his behaviour and personalizes them in his own conscience.

Conscience and its Functions

The theme of conscience could not but have an important part to play in the making of moral theology, given its frequent appearance

---

[25] Ibid., pp. 346–7. Cf. the philosophical errors which in 1347 Nicholas d'Autrecourt was compelled to disown, *DS* 1028–49, including 'quod Deus potest praecipere rationali creaturae quod habeat ipsum odio, et ipsa oboediens plus meretur quam si ipsum diligeret ex praecepto, quoniam hoc faceret cum maiori conatu et magis contra propriam inclinationem' (*DS* 1049).

[26] Vereecke, i, p. 59.

[27] Jedin and Dolan, iv, p. 594.

[28] Ibid., p. 599.

in the New Testament writings, where it occurs twenty times.[29] The term *syn-eidēsis*, which denotes literally a 'knowing-with', originated in Greek philosophy's identification of the experience of self-awareness in the forming of moral judgements. It indicates an element of identity as well as of diversity, a certain 'over-againstness', which the Roman Stoic, Seneca, expressed in other terms when he wrote of the moral experience as that of 'a sacred spirit seated within us, an observer and guardian of good and evil in us'.[30] In its predominant meaning, first found in the middle of the fifth century BC, as consciousness of one's bad behaviour,[31] the Greek term seems by New Testament times to have become one in popular everyday usage, perhaps not unlike the way in which some of the technical terms of depth-psychology have today acquired common, if simplified, currency. The Latin literal translation, *con-scientia*, became equally common in ethical literature and usage, especially in Seneca and in Cicero, who attributed considerable force to conscience, both in dispelling fear in those who have done nothing wrong and in presenting a continual sanction to those who have sinned.[32]

In Pauline usage, conscience is viewed as a possession of all men by which they evaluate the moral worth of their behaviour in the light of their beliefs, appearing sometimes as witness for the prosecution and at other times as witness for the defence.[33] Sometimes it is mistaken, sometimes corrupted, sometimes good and sometimes weak or wavering.[34] For Paul, Delhaye concludes, conscience 'is therefore not only the witness and interior judge, or the impersonal expression of duty. St Paul goes further and gives the word *syneidēsis* a personal sense, that of the will or the moral

---

[29] Cf. C. Williams, 'Conscience', *NCE*, vol. iv, p. 199.

[30] *Epist.* 41, 1; ibid., 196.

[31] Ibid., 199.

[32] 'Magna vis est conscientiae in utramque partem ut neque timeant qui nihil commiserint, et poenam semper ante oculos versari putent qui peccarint', Cicero, *pro Milone*, 23, 61. On classical usage of the terms συνειδησις and *con-scientia*, cf. Ph. Delhaye, *The Christian Conscience* (New York, 1968), pp. 23–5, 49–50.

[33] Cf. Rom. 2: 15; 9:1; 2 Cor. 1: 12–13. For Delhaye the originality of Paul lay in his positing in men's hearts (Rom. 2: 15) a moral law which did for the Gentiles what the Mosaic law did for the Jews, in informing them of God's will. 'It is no longer merely a question of a reference to God the lawmaker and judge; the law is itself interiorised, it guides the action, it judges it after the fact. It pronounces on the actions of others as an objective norm', ibid., p. 49.

[34] I Cor. 10: 28–9; Titus 1: 15; 1 Tim. 1: 19; 1 Cor. 8: 7, 10, 12.

personality, the centre of the soul where choices are worked out and responsibilities undertaken.'[35] In the two passages in which Paul is most informative on the nature and role of conscience, he indicates that acting according to conscience should be acting according to one's inner convictions, without imposing those convictions or actions on others or criticizing those who believe and act otherwise. We should keep our convictions for between ourselves and God, and fortunate is the man who does not have to criticize himself for what he thinks.[36] The subjective aspect of personal conscience as a norm for behaviour is thus strongly affirmed, while its force is seen to lie in the correspondence between one's perceptions of morality and the objective reality of God and his expectations of man. Nor are these expectations to be found simply and solely in the formal legislation of God presented to man-in-community as from outside the individual. There is also an interior resource which is more than simply a personal reflecting on the law and which contains an element of individual discovery.[37]

Patristic development of the theme of conscience relied heavily upon Paul, stressing the idea he adopted from Old Testament prophetic literature of a moral law written by God on men's hearts.[38] At other times reflection would be expressed in terms of the voice of God speaking interiorly to the individual, reminiscent of the early chapters of Genesis and God's spoken moral injunctions to Adam. Ambrose, for instance, in his reflections on Paradise, observed that it seems natural to us to avoid evil and do good. Everything happens as if we hear the voice of God giving us prohibitions and commands.[39] For Augustine also, the inner resource of moral evaluation and guidance of behaviour could be regarded as 'the law written in hearts', as well as resulting from the

---

[35] Ibid., p. 42.

[36] Thus explicitly of συνείδησις in 1. Cor. 8: 7–13; 10: 23–30. In Romans 14, which deals with the same moral dilemmas, the key term is not συνείδησις, but πίστις, or 'belief', which is apparently used in the moral sense of conviction, or basis for action, rather more than in a religious sense.

[37] Cf. Delhaye, pp. 48–9.

[38] Cf. Augustine, *Conf.*, 2, 4, 9; *PL* 32, 678: 'Furtum certe punit lex tua, Domine, et lex scripta in cordibus hominum, quam ne ipsa quidem delet iniquitas.'

[39] 'Non enim auribus corporis de mandatis coelestibus iudicamus: sed cum esset Dei verbum, opiniones quaedam nobis boni et mali pullularunt; dum id quod malum est, naturaliter intelligimus esse vitandum, et id quod bonum est naturaliter nobis intelligimus esse praeceptum. In eo igitur vocem Domini videmur audire, quod alia interdicat, alia praecipiat', *de Paradiso*, 8, 39; *PL* 14, 292.

fact that 'there is no soul, however perverted, . . . in whose conscience God does not speak'.[40] It was Jerome, however, who was particularly to stimulate medieval and Scholastic analysis of the idea of conscience by his writing of a power of the soul 'which the Greeks call *syntērēsin*, which is the spark of conscience which was not extinguished even in Cain [*sic*] after his expulsion from Paradise, and by which, when we succumb to pleasures or frenzy and are sometimes deceived by a semblance of reason, we still realize that we are sinning'.[41] Paul had used the popular Greek word *syneidēsis* to refer to conscience, but Jerome used another and much more rare Greek term, *syntērēsis*, to refer to the *scintilla*, or spark, of conscience, a power still flickering in man even after sin.[42]

In a typical attempt to do justice to both authorities, later theologians applied the Pauline term to the actual exercise, or judgement, of conscience, while reserving Jerome's term for the idea of conscience as an innate permanent capacity in man, the Scholastic *synderesis*, in the light of which he makes his judgements. Thus, for Aquinas, *synderesis*, or the habit of conscience, is a

[40] 'Nam quando illi valent intelligere, nullam esse animam, quamvis perversam, quae tamen ullo modo ratiocinari potest, in cuius conscientia non loquatur Deus?' *de serm. Dom. in mont.*, 2, cap. 9; *PL* 34, 1283.

[41] Commenting on Ezekiel's vision of the four creatures in human form (Ezek. 1: 4–12), Jerome writes, 'Plerique, iuxta Platonem, rationale animae, et irascitivum, et concupiscitivum, quod ille λογικόν et θυμικόν et ἐπιθυμητικόν vocat, ad hominem, et leonem ac vitulum referunt . . . . Quartamque ponunt quae super haec et extra haec tria est, quam Graeci vocant συντήρησιν, quae scintilla conscientiae in Cain quoque pectore, postquam eiectus est de paradiso, non extinguitur, et qua victi voluptatibus, vel furore, ipsaque interdum rationis decepti similitudine, nos peccare sentimus', *Comm. in Ezech.*, I, 1; *PL* 25, 22.

[42] On the 'spark' of conscience, cf. Augustine, *supra*, p. 84. Jerome's συντήρησις has baffled many commentators. Cf. Lottin, *Psychologie et morale aux XIIe et XIIIe siècles* (Louvain, 1948), vol. ii, 1, pp. 103–5. Delhaye (pp. 107–10) argues that it is a copyist's error for συνείδησις, but this does not explain why Jerome should consider it necessary to draw attention to such a common Scriptural term. As a noun derived from the verb συντηρῶ, meaning 'to keep, preserve, or observe strictly', συντήρησις would appear to be capable of expressing moral control or sensitivity, and instances of its usage in Greek papyri of a late period are to be found. Cf. Liddell and Scott, *A Greek–English Lexicon* (ed. 1925), vol. ii, *s.v.* συντηρέω. This would bear out the suggestion of T. C. Potts, *Conscience in Medieval Philosophy* (Cambridge, 1980), pp. xiii, 10–11. Moreover, G. W. H. Lampe, *A Patristic Greek Lexicon* (Oxford, 1961), *s.v.*, cites usages by Gregory Nazianzen, Gregory of Nyssa and others which have the meaning of preservation, maintenance, or conservation, whether by the soul of the body, or of creation, or of the commands of Christ. This general sense of holding together in some sort of control seems to fit precisely the function assigned by Jerome to συντήρησις as being 'above' the three other elements of the soul, *supra*. n. 41.

habitual, intuitive grasp of the first principles for action, the precepts of the law of nature, which 'prompts us to good and complains at what is bad'.[43] Not that we always have the precepts of natural law in mind, any more than we are always actually speaking. But just as we have a grasp of the rules of grammar, so we have a habitual grasp of the basic rules of morality.[44] And conscience 'in the strict sense' is the action of applying such knowledge to our past or contemplated actions.[45] The action of conscience, then, is no more and no less than an ordinary act of human reason applying the various principles of morality to individual situations. As such it is not, of course, the originating source of moral principles but only the medium, or 'image', of God's eternal reason, or eternal law, which, as we have seen in an earlier chapter, is the primary and supreme rule of human behaviour. This being so, when human reason is defective for any reason, Aquinas argued, recourse should be had to the eternal reason which is to some extent made known to us either through our natural reason or by some additional revelation.[46]

Two aspects of conscience to which Aquinas gave particular

---

[43] 'Unde et synderesis dicitur instigare ad bonum, et murmurare de malo, inquantum per prima principia procedimus ad inveniendum, et iudicamus inventa. Patet ergo quod synderesis non est potentia, sed habitus naturalis', *STh* 1, q. 79, a. 12.

[44] 'Non est autem idem quod quis agit, et quo quis agit: aliquis enim per habitum grammaticae agit orationem congruam . . . . Alio modo potest dici habitus id quod habitu tenetur: sicut dicitur fides id quod fide tenetur. Et hoc modo, quia praecepta legis naturalis quandoque considerantur in actu a ratione, quandoque autem sunt in ea habitualiter tantum, secundum hunc modum potest dici quod lex naturalis sit habitus', *STh*, 1a 2ae, q. 94, a. 1.

[45] 'Conscientia, proprie loquendo, non est potentia, sed actus . . . . Dicitur enim conscientia testificari, ligare vel etiam instigare, et etiam accusare vel remordere sive reprehendere. Et haec omnia consequuntur applicationem alicuius nostrae cognitionis vel scientiae ad ea quae agimus . . . . Unde proprie loquendo, conscientia nominat actum. Quia tamen habitus est principium actus, quandoque nomen conscientiae attribuitur primo habitui naturali, scilicet syndersi . . . .' *STh* 1, q. 79, a. 13. '. . . ab habitu primorum principiorum, qui dicitur synderesis. Unde specialiter hic habitus interdum conscientia nominatur', ibid., ad 3.

[46] 'Quod autem ratio humana sit regula voluntatis humanae, ex qua eius bonitas mensuretur, habet ex lege aeterna, quae est ratio divina . . . . Unde manifestum est quod multo magis dependet bonitas voluntatis humanae a lege aeterna, quam a ratione humana: et ubi deficit humana ratio, oportet ad rationem divinam recurrere', *STh*, 1a 2ae, q. 19, a. 4. 'Licet lex aeterna sit nobis ignota secundum quod est in mente divina; innotescit tamen nobis aliqualiter vel per rationem naturalem, quae ab eo derivatur ut propria eius imago; vel per aliqualem revelationem superadditum', ibid., ad 3. Cf. ibid., q. 21, a. 1.

consideration and which were to play a significant part in the
making of moral theology were the deductive manner in which
increasingly detailed objective moral principles are derived from
more general principles, and the consequences for man of error in
his subjective grasp and application of such principles. Objectively
speaking, the conclusions of natural law principles are not all
universally applicable, since the more one descends in reasoning
from the general to the particular, and the more qualifications one
builds into the principles, then the more circumstances and counter-
qualifications will also enter into consideration and affect the
reaching of particular conclusions. Thus Aquinas argued that
although the first principles of natural law cannot change, the
secondary precepts, which have the nature of conclusions drawn
from these principles, are subject to change in a minority of
practical applications according to circumstances.[47] This flexibility
of conclusion and application, which later moral theology was not
to accept in any whole hearted manner, is also expressed in
definitional terms by Aquinas in his statements that underlying

---

[47] 'Ad legem naturae pertinent ea ad quae homo naturaliter inclinatur; inter quae
homini proprium est ut inclinetur ad agendum secundum rationem. Ad rationem
autem pertinet ex communibus ad propria procedere, ut patet ex I *Physic.* Aliter
tamen circa hoc se habet ratio speculativa, et aliter ratio practica. Quia enim ratio
speculativa praecipue negotiatur circa necessaria, quae impossibile est aliter se
habere, absque aliquo defectu invenitur veritas in conclusionibus propriis, sicut et in
principiis communibus. Sed ratio practica negotiatur circa contingentia, in quibus
sunt operationes humanae: et ideo, etsi in communibus sit aliqua necessitas, quanto
magis ad propria descenditur, tanto magis invenitur defectus . . . . Apud omnes enim
hoc rectum est et verum, ut secundum rationem agatur. Ex hoc autem principio
sequitur quasi conclusio propria, quod deposita sint reddenda. Et hoc quidem ut in
pluribus verum est: sed potest in aliquo casu contingere quod sit damnosum, et per
consequens irrationabile, si deposita reddantur; puta si aliquis petat ad impugnandam
patriam. Et hoc tanto magis invenitur deficere, quanto magis ad particularia
descenditur, puta si dicatur quod deposita sunt reddenda cum tali cautione, vel tali
modo: quanto enim plures conditiones particulares apponuntur, tanto pluribus
modis poterit deficere, ut non sit rectum vel in reddendo vel in non reddendo. Sic
igitur dicendum est quod lex naturae, quantum ad prima principia communia, est
eadem apud omnes . . . . Sed quantum ad quaedam propria, quae sunt quasi
conclusiones principiorum communium, est eadem apud omnes ut in pluribus . . . :
sed ut in paucioribus potest deficere . . . quantum ad rectitudinem, propter aliqua
particularia impedimenta', S*Th* 1a 2ae, q. 94, a. 4. 'Quantum ad prima principia
legis naturae, lex naturae est omnino immutabilis. Quantum autem ad secunda
praecepta, quae diximus esse quasi quasdam proprias conclusiones propinquas
primis principiis, sic lex naturalis non immutatur quin ut in pluribus rectum sit
semper quod lex naturalis habet. Potest tamen immutari in aliquo particulari, et in
paucioribus, propter aliquas speciales causas impedientes observantiam talium
praeceptorum', ibid., a. 5.

moral principles always make such actions as murder, theft, or adultery unalterably wrong as a matter of natural law, but that what will vary according to circumstances is whether individual situations really satisfy the definition of what constitutes such actions.[48] The consequences of this approach to morality by way of circumstances altering cases and of considering exceptional situations readily lent itself to an encouragement of casuistry and to a theology of doubt such as we have already seen and shall consider further in the next chapter. It was another aspect of conscience, to which Aquinas devoted somewhat less attention in considering the subjective element of knowledge and error in one's grasp of natural law and its practical implications, which was to have even more impact in the development of moral theology.

In considering the universal character of natural law Aquinas was concerned not only with the extent to which it applied in the multiplicity of human moral situations, but also with the degree to which it was self-evident, particularly as it became more detailed either in content or in application. In moral reasoning, the more one descends from the general to the particular the more possible it is for human reason to be unduly influenced by feelings, or by one's environment and culture, or by fallen nature.[49] It is true, he argued, that the fundamental tendencies built by God into human nature and experienced by individuals generate moral principles, as we have seen.[50] It does not follow, however, that all human natural inclinations, such as the desire for pleasure or for honour, generate such natural law conclusions, but only those which are ordered in accordance with reason.[51] And reason does not always act as it should. Again, it is true that some very common or general precepts

---

[48] 'Sic igitur praecepta ipsa decalogi, quantum ad rationem iustitiae quam continent, immutabilia sunt. Sed quantum ad aliquam determinationem per applicationem ad singulares actus, ut scilicet hoc vel illud sit homicidium, furtum vel adulterium, aut non, hoc quidem est mutabile', *STh* 1a 2ae, q. 100, a. 8. ad 3. Like so many of the early moralists, Aquinas was preoccupied with the instances in the history of Israel when God had commanded apparently immoral behaviour at variance with his own commandments forbidding killing, theft, and adultery. On how he explained such events, cf. J. Mahoney, *Seeking the Spirit* (London, 1981), pp. 55–9.

[49] *STh* 1a 2ae, q. 94, a. 4 (*Supra*, p. 106, n. 128.)

[50] *Supra*, p. 79.

[51] 'Sicut ratio in homine dominatur et imperat aliis potentiis, ita oportet quod omnes inclinationes naturales ad alias potentias pertinentes ordinentur secundum rationem. Unde hoc est apud omnes communiter rectum, ut secundum rationem dirigantur omnes hominum inclinationes', *STh* 1a 2ae, q. 94, a. 4 ad 3.

of natural law are known to all men, and can never as such be entirely expelled from their hearts. But their application in particular instances can be impeded if reason is itself clouded by the emotions.[52] And even secondary and more particular general precepts as such, which render the common precepts more specific, can be driven from men's hearts whether through wrong convictions or cultural influences.[53]

Man's conscience, then, in so far as it is a 'dictate of reason', can be simply mistaken in its reasoning, presenting as bad something which is really and objectively good, or the reverse. Aquinas was clear that not to follow one's conscience in such circumstances would be wrong, because it would be tantamount to disregarding what one considered to be true and as deriving ultimately from God.[54] If we knew, of course, that what human reason was commanding was also against a commandment of God, then there would be no obligation to follow reason, although in this case our reason would not be completely and totally mistaken since it is only through it that we are also aware of God's commands.[55] No one is morally bound by any precept except through the medium of his knowledge of the precept. And since conscience is simply the application of knowledge to an action, then 'conscience is said to

[52] 'Ad legem naturalem pertinent primo quidem quaedam praecepta communissima, quae sunt omnibus nota: quaedam autem secundaria praecepta magis propria, quae sunt quasi conclusiones propinquae principiis. Quantum ergo ad illa principia communia, lex naturalis nullo modo potest a cordibus hominum deleri in universi. Deletur tamen in particulari operabili, secundum quod ratio impeditur applicare commune principium ad particulare operabile, propter concupiscentiam vel aliquam passionem', *STh* 1a 2ae, q. 94, a. 6.

[53] 'Quantum vero ad alia praecepta secundaria, potest lex naturalis deleri de cordibus hominum, vel propter malas persuasiones, eo modo quo etiam in speculativis errores contingunt circa conclusiones necessarias; vel etiam propter pravas consuetudines et habitus corruptos; sicut apud quosdam non reputabantur latrocinia peccata, vel etiam vitia contra naturam, ut etiam Apostolus dicit, *ad Rom.* I, [24 sqq]', ibid. Cf. ibid., q. 77, a. 2.

[54] 'Non solum enim id quod est indifferens, potest accipere rationem boni vel mali per accidens; sed etiam id quod est bonum, potest accipere rationem mali, vel illud quod est malum, rationem boni, propter apprehensionem rationis . . . . Unde dicendum est simpliciter quod omnis voluntas discordans a ratione, sive recta sive errante, semper est mala . . . iudicium rationis errantis licet non derivetur a Deo, tamen ratio errans iudicium suum proponit ut verum, et per consequens ut a Deo derivatum, a quo est omnis veritas', *STh* 1a 2ae, q. 19, a. 5 et ad 1.

[55] 'Si aliquis homo cognosceret quod ratio humana dictaret aliquid contra praeceptum Dei, non teneretur rationem sequi: sed tunc ratio non totaliter esset errans', ibid., ad 2.

bind by force of the divine precept'.[56] This remains true even when
conscience is mistaken in its reasoning, as it often can be. For 'when
a reason which is in error proposes something as a command of
God, then to dismiss the dictate of reason is just the same as
dismissing the command of God'.[57]

It is a well-known feature of Aquinas's teaching, however, that
although he considered one was bound to follow one's erroneous
conscience and would do wrong in not obeying it, he did not
therefore consider that such conscientious behaviour was automatically always good. Everything depended on why conscience
was mistaken in the first place, and on the degree of negligence or
guilt which might accompany such a state. If conscience acts from a
lack of knowledge which one ought to possess, then the error is
culpable and so also is the conscientious behaviour resulting from
it. The ignorance in question could be 'ignorance of the law of
God', that is, of a divine commandment, whether revealed or
attainable by reason, 'which one is obliged to know', and as such it
would be culpable ignorance on Aquinas's terms. It could also be,
however, 'ignorance of some circumstance' in its application to a
particular situation, and this can happen 'without any negligence'.[58]

---

[56] 'Unde, cum conscientia nihil aliud sit quam applicatio notitiae ad actum,
constat quod conscientia ligare dicitur vi praecepti divini', *De Veritate*, q. 17, a. 3.

[57] 'Sed quando ratio errans proponit aliquid ut praeceptum Dei, tunc idem est
contemnere dictamen rationis, et Dei praeceptum', *STh* 1a 2ae, q. 19, a. 5 ad 2.

[58] 'Respondeo dicendum quod, sicut praemissa quaestio [art. 5; cf. *supra*, nn.
54–5, 57] eadem est cum quaestione qua quaeritur utrum conscientia erronea liget;
ita ista quaestio eadem est cum illa qua quaeritur utrum conscientia erronea excuset.
Haec autem quaestio dependet ab eo quod supra [q. 6, a. 8] de ignorantia dictum est
. . . . Si igitur ratio vel conscientia erret errore voluntario, vel directe, vel propter
negligentiam, quia est error circa id quod quis scire tenetur; tunc talis error rationis
vel conscientiae non excusat quin voluntas concordans rationi vel conscientiae sic
erranti, sit mala. Si autem sit error qui causet involuntarium, proveniens ex
ignorantia alicuius circumstantiae absque omni negligentia; tunc talis error rationis
vel conscientiae excusat, ut voluntas concordans rationi erranti non sit mala. Puta, si
ratio errans dicat quod homo teneatur ad uxorem alterius accedere, voluntas
concordans huic rationi erranti est mala: eo quod error iste provenit ex ignorantia
legis Dei, quam scire tenetur. Si autem ratio erret in hoc, quod credat aliquam
mulierem submissam, esse suam uxorem, et ea petente debitum, velit eam
cognoscere; excusatur voluntas eius, ut non sit mala; quia error iste ex ignorantia
circumstantiae provenit, quae excusat, et involuntarium causat', *STh* 1a 2ae, q. 19,
a. 6. The difference is between 'ignorance of law' and 'ignorance of fact'.

[59] 'Supposito errore rationis vel conscientiae qui procedit ex ignorantia non
excusante, necesse est quod sequatur malum in voluntate. Nec tamen est homo
perplexus: quia potest ab errore recedere, cum ignorantia sit vincibilis et voluntaria',
ibid., ad 3. Cf. *de Veritate*, q. 17, a. 4 ad 3, 'conscientia erronea errans in his quae

And so, to the dilemma that if one declines to follow a mistaken conscience one is doing wrong and that if one decides to follow such a conscience one is also doing wrong, Aquinas's reply is that if the mistake is not itself blameworthy, then the subsequent action is not subjectively bad, whereas if it is blameworthy then the dilemma as such vanishes 'because the agent can correct his mistake, since his ignorance is vincible and voluntary'.[59]

Ignorance and Salvation

The distinction invoked by Aquinas between ignorance which is vincible, and which is therefore blameworthy since it can be overcome and corrected, and ignorance which is invincible and therefore guiltless, was given impetus, by his authority, to become in the making of moral theology the sanctuary and refuge of non-sinners, and the major escape clause in objective morality. If one acted from ignorance which was incorrigible and could not in any way be dispelled then one could not be judged morally blameworthy, whether by men or God, for one's actions, however wrong they might be in themselves. Medieval theologians, however, tended to see all ignorance as a sequel to the fall of man, and as in some way partaking of sin. Accordingly, they were not particularly disposed to exonerate from all personal guilt individuals who acted out of ignorance, although they were compelled to admit that such factors as environment, habit, and prejudice could not be so easily dismissed from moral evaluation and categorized simply as personal sin.[60] Perhaps the most striking application and develop-

sunt per se mala, dicat contraria legi Dei; sed tamen illa quae dictat, dicit esse legem Dei. Et ideo transgressor illius conscientiae, transgressor efficitur legis Dei; quamvis conscientiam sequens, et eam opere implens, contra legem Dei faciens mortaliter peccat; quia in ipso errore peccatum erat, cum contingeret ex ignorantia eius quod scire debebat.'

[60] Cf. M. Bévenot, 'St Thomas and the Erroneous Conscience', in *Thomistica Morum Principia*, ii, (Rome, 1961), pp. 107–13. It may be significant that Aquinas, while granting that action which proceeds from invincible ignorance is not sinful, appears to shrink from describing it as actually good. In *STh* 1a 2ae, q. 19, a. 6, for instance, the introductory question to be discussed is 'Utrum voluntas concordans rationi erranti, sit bona', but Aquinas begins by rephrasing the question as 'utrum conscientia erronea excuset', *supra*, n. 58. The three preliminary objections which preface the article all conclude 'Ergo voluntas concordans rationi (etiam) erranti, est bona', and Aquinas's approach is invariably to take up a different position from such preliminaries, even if only nuanced. The first consideration draws from him the response based on Pseudo-Dionysius that for an act to be good it must be so in every

ment of this thinking over the centuries has been that concerning the eternal fate of unbelievers and the way in which the Church has understood the maxim that 'there is no salvation outside the Church'.

Originating in a letter of the third-century African bishop Cyprian on the Catholic Church's attitude to heretics and schismatics, the phrase became part of the Church's theological armoury in combating heresy.[61] The necessity of Church membership was graphically described by the seventh-century sixteenth Council of

---

respect, although it can be bad as a whole from only one defect. 'Et ideo ad hoc quod dicatur malum id in quod fertur voluntas, sufficit sive quod secundum suam naturam sit malum, sive quod apprehendatur ut malum. Sed ad hoc quod sit bonum, requiritur quod utroque modo sit bonum.' And yet, according to Aquinas, no particular human act can be morally indifferent. On invincible ignorance in Abelard, (cf. *supra*, n. 8), Luscombe, observes, (op. cit., p. 62, n. 1), 'A certain "objectivization" of mediaeval moral theology brought many authors to think that in the case of the natural law, ignorance was not guiltless', and he quotes the influential principle of Gratian, 'ignorantia iuris naturalis omnibus adultis damnabilis est', ibid., pp. 155–6.

[61] In common with Tertullian and the bishops of Asia Minor, and even against the judgement of Pope Stephen, Cyprian maintained that heretical baptism was not valid, and that heretics entering the Church must be baptized. It was in this vein that he wrote in his *Epistola ad Iubaianum*, to a fellow bishop representing the contrary view, that seventy-one bishops of Africa and Numidia 'hoc idem denuo sententia nostra firmavimus, statuentes unum baptisma esse quod sit in Ecclesia catholica constitutum, ac per hoc non rebaptizari, sed baptizari a nobis quicumque ab adultera et profana aqua veniunt abluendi et sanctificandi salutaris aquae veritate', *PL* 3, 1110. Not even martyrdom would save a heretic who was outside the Church. 'Quod si haeretico nec Baptisma publicae confessionis et sanguinis proficere ad salutem potest, quia salus extra Ecclesiam non est, quanto magis ei nihil proderit, si in latebra et in latronum spelunca adulterae aquae contagione tinctus, non tantum peccata antiqua non exposuerit, sed adhuc potius nova et maiora cumulaverit? Quare Baptisma nobis et haereticis commune esse non potest, cum quibus nec Pater Deus, nec Filius Christus, nec Spiritus sanctus, nec fides, nec Ecclesia ipsa communis est. Et ideo baptizari eos oportet qui de haeresi ad Ecclesiam veniunt', ibid., 1123–4. Cf. also his dogmatic statement, 'Habere iam non potest Deum patrem, qui Ecclesiam non habet matrem. Si potuit evadere quisquam qui extra arcam Noe fuit, et qui extra Ecclesiam foris fuerit evadit. Monet Dominus et dicit: Qui non est mecum, adversus me est; et qui non mecum colligit, spargit (Matt. 12: 30). Qui pacem Christi et concordiam rumpit, adversus Christum facit. Qui alibi praeter Ecclesiam colligit Christi Ecclesiam spargit', *De unitate Ecclesiae*, cap. 6; *PL* 4, 503–4. The strong Matthaean statement, 'He who is not with me is against me, and he who does not gather with me scatters', appears in accord with that Gospel's stress on organizational identity, as we have earlier suggested (pp. 173–4) and is put to good use by Cyprian. It would be more difficult to take so intransigent a view if one were faced with the Marcan answer of Jesus to John, 'he that is not against us is for us' (Mark 9: 38–40).

Toledo,[62] and asserted in Cyprian's terms in the twelfth-century Creed prescribed for the Waldensians,[63] to find its fullest formal expression in the thirteenth century, in the Creed of the Fourth Lateran Council directed against the Albigensian heretics: 'There is one universal Church of the faithful, and outside it absolutely no one is saved.'[64] This was spelt out by the Council of Florence in its decree for the Jacobites which professed the belief that 'no one who is outside the Catholic Church, not just pagans, but Jews, heretics, and schismatics, can share in eternal life'.[65]

By the eighteenth century the absolute necessity of Church membership for one's eternal salvation was given fresh application by its being directed not just against dissident Christians but now against the religious indifferentism of the age. It underlies the condemnation by Pope Leo XII of the view that 'God has given full liberty to everyone to embrace or adopt without danger to salvation whatever sect they please according to their private judgement'.[66] And it was again asserted in 1832 by Pope Gregory XVI in his attacks on freedom of conscience as 'absurd' and on the view that any profession of faith can lead to the soul's eternal salvation provided right and good morals are required by it. Augustine himself had demanded, what worse death could the soul suffer than 'the freedom of error'?[67]

---

[62] 'atque omnes, qui nunc in [Ecclesia] minime consistunt sive constituerint aut ab ea recesserunt ... perpetuae damnationis sententia ulciscentur atque in fine saeculi cum diabolo eiusque sociis ignivomis rogis cremabuntur', *DS* 575.

[63] 'Corde credimus et ore confitemur unam Ecclesiam non haereticorum, sed sanctam Romanam catholicam, apostolicam, extra quam neminem salvari credimus', *DS* 792.

[64] 'Una vero est fidelium universalis Ecclesia, extra quam nullus omnino salvatur', *DS* 802. On the anti-heretical nature of the Creed, cf. F. Vernet, 'Latran, IV^c Concile oecuménique du', *DTC* tom. viii, col. 2659.

[65] 'Firmiter credit, profitetur et praedicat, nullos extra catholicam Ecclesiam exsistentes, non solum paganos, sed nec Iudaeos aut haereticos atque schismaticos, aeternae vitae fieri posse participes; sed in ignem aeternum ituros', *DS* 1351. In the previous century the famous Bull of Boniface VIII, 'Unam sanctam', which gave official sanction to St Bernard's 'two-swords theory', one wielded by the Church and the other for the Church, opened with the ringing statement 'Unam sanctam Ecclesiam catholicam ... extra quam nec salus est nec remissio peccatorum', and developed Cyprian's comparison (*supra*, n. 61) with Noah's ark, *DS* 870.

[66] 'docens amplam unicuique libertatem a Deo factam esse, ut quae cuique secta iuxta suum privatum iudicium vel opinio arriserit, eam quisque sine salutis periculo amplecti vel adoptare valeat', *DS* 2720.

[67] 'pravam illam opinionem, ... qualibet fidei professione aeternam posse animae salutem comparari, si mores ad recti honestique normam exigantur ....

It was Pope Pius IX who first qualified the rigour of Cyprian's phrase in official Church teaching. In an 1854 allocution he explained, 'It must be held by faith that no one can be saved outside the Apostolic Roman Church . . . , but it must equally be considered certain that those who are in ignorance of the true religion, if it is invincible, are not guilty of this in the eyes of God.'[68] Shortly afterwards, in an encyclical on religious indifference to the bishops of Italy, Pio Nono deplored the serious error of some Catholics who considered that people living in errors and alienated from the true faith and Catholic unity can reach eternal life, a view which was completely at variance with Catholic teaching.[69] He went on, however,

We and you know, that those who are in invincible ignorance about our most holy religion, and who carefully observe the natural law and its precepts inscribed in everyone's heart by God, who are prepared to obey God and who lead a good and correct life, can by the power of God's light and grace gain eternal life, since God, who clearly sees, examines and knows the minds, hearts, thoughts and habits of all, would never in his supreme goodness and mercy allow anyone to be punished with eternal torment if he was not guilty through his own fault.

But it is also very well known as a Catholic dogma that no one can be saved outside the Catholic Church and that those who are stubbornly resistent to the authority and definitions of that Church and are pertinacious in their division from its unity and from the successor of Peter, the Roman Pontiff, to whom the Saviour has entrusted guardianship of the vineyard, cannot attain to eternal salvation.[70]

Atque ex hoc putidissimo indifferentismi fonte absurda illa fluit ac erronea sententia seu potius deliramentum, asserendam esse ac vindicandam cuilibet libertatem conscientiae . . . . At "quae peior mors animae, quam libertas erroris?" inquiebat Augustinus', DS 2731.

[68] 'Tenendum quippe ex fide est, extra Apostolicam Romanam Ecclesiam salvum fieri neminem posse . . . ; sed tamen pro certo pariter habendum est, qui verae religionis ignorantia laborent, si ea sit invincibilis, nulla ipsos obstringi huiusce rei culpa ante oculos Domini', DS pp. 570–1.

[69] 'gravissimum errorem, in quo nonnulli catholici misere versantur, qui homines in erroribus viventes et a vera fide atque a catholica unitate alienos ad aeternam vitam pervenire posse opinantur. Quod quidem catholicae doctrinae vel maxime adversatur', DS 2865.

[70] 'Notum Nobis vobisque est, eos, qui invincibili circa sanctissimam nostram religionem ignorantia laborant, quique naturalem legem eiusque praecepta in omnium cordibus a Deo insculpta sedulo servantes ac Deo oboedire parati, honestam rectamque vitam agunt, posse, divinae lucis et gratiae operante virtute, aeternam consequi vitam, cum Deus, qui omnium mentes, animos, cogitationes habitusque plane intuetur, scrutatur et noscit, pro summa sua bonitate et clementia minime patiatur, quempiam aeternis puniri suppliciis, qui voluntariae culpae reatum non habeat.

Invincible ignorance thus formally becomes the literally saving clause in applying what had hitherto tended to be seen as the absolute necessity of boarding the Catholic Church as the one and only ark of salvation from a surrounding sea of sin.[71] There may also have been, with Pius IX, the stirrings of an awareness that other Christians outside the Catholic Church might be in a slightly better condition than unbelievers when it came to prospects of salvation, with a corresponding shift from the absolute necessity of the Church to the uncertainty or insufficiency of other means outside that Church. It is true that in his *Syllabus* he listed as errors not only the views that any religion can be a road to eternal salvation and that there is at least good hope for the salvation of all who are not in the true Church, but also the view that Protestantism is a version of Christianity as pleasing to God as Catholicism, thus following the original aim of Cyprian's shaft.[72] However, on the eve of the First Vatican Council, in a letter inviting all non-Catholics to enter the Church, he argued that the only true successor to the Church founded by Christ was that which possessed 'that living and God-given authority which teaches men especially matters of faith and discipline of morals, and directs and governs them in everything related to eternal salvation'. And he urged those who did not possess the unity and truth of the Catholic Church to welcome the occasion of the Council to respond to the needs of their hearts 'and strive to extricate themselves from that state in which they cannot be certain of their salvation'.[73]

'Sed notissimum quoque est catholicum dogma, neminem scilicet extra catholicam Ecclesiam posse salvari, et contumaces adversus eiusdem Ecclesiae auctoritatem, definitiones, et ab ipsius Ecclesiae unitate atque a Petri successore Romano Pontifice, cui vineae custodia a Salvatore est commissa, pertinaciter divisos aeternam non posse obtinere salutem', DS 2866–7.

[71] Cf. *supra*, nn. 61, 65.

[72] 'Homines in cuiusvis religionis cultu viam aeternae salutis reperire aeternamque salutem assequi possunt . . . . Saltem bene sperandum est de aeterna illorum omnium salute, qui in vera Christi Ecclesia nequaquam versantur . . . . Protestantismus non aliud est quam diversa verae eiusdem christianae religionis forma, in qua aeque ac in Ecclesia catholica Deo placere datum est', DS 2916–18. Cf. *supra*, n. 61.

[73] 'Cum enim eiusmodi societates careant viva illa et a Deo constituta auctoritate, quae homines res fidei morumque disciplinam praesertim docet eosque dirigit ac moderatur in iis omnibus, quae ad aeternam salutem pertinent, . . . Quamobrem ii omnes, qui Ecclesiae catholicae unitatem et veritatem non tenent, occasionem amplectantur huius Concilii, . . . ac indigentiis eorum cordis respondentes ab eo statu se eripere studeant, in quo de sua propria salute securi esse non possunt', DS 2998–9.

In an encyclical on the unity of the Church and on the need for a visible expression of such unity, Pope Leo XIII, Pius IX's successor, explored 'not how the Church *could* be one, but how its Founder *willed* it to *be* one'.[74] If Pius IX had been prepared to entertain the possibility of salvation in other Christian bodies, however uncertain, Leo XIII (who utterly rejected the validity of Anglican ordinations)[75] appears to have been more forthright in concluding from an analysis of the concept of the Church as the mystical body of Christ that separated and dispersed limbs, or members, cannot form one body with the head, and that those who are separate from the Church 'are wandering away from the will and command of Christ the Lord and abandoning the road to salvation to end in ruin'.[76]

Fifty years later, Pope Pius XII devoted an encyclical to the Church as the mystical body of Christ, in which he explored further the theme of 'salvation outside the visible Church'.[77] and introduced a new consideration. He repeated Pius IX's appeal to non-Catholic Christians to embrace the security of the Catholic Church, but he also began to blur the 'frontiers' of that Church by attempting to explain how it is that salvation can come only through that Church. 'Even if by some unconscious wish and desire they are related (*ordinentur*) to the mystical body of the Redeemer, they are missing the many great heavenly gifts and aids which can be enjoyed only in the Catholic Church.'[78] To the invincible ignorance which his predecessors had seen as not depriving those outside the Church of eternal salvation, Pius XII now added a more positive attempt to explain how such people are in fact saved, by an unconscious desire which somehow connects them, albeit imperfectly and tenuously,

---

[74] 'exquirendumque non sane, quo pacto una esse Ecclesia *queat*, sed quo unam esse *is voluit, qui condidit*', DS 3302.

[75] Cf. DS 3315–19.

[76] 'Dispersa membra atque seiuncta non possunt eodem cum capite, unum simul effectura corpus, cohaerere .... Quamobrem dispersa a membris ceteris siqua membra vagantur, cum eodem atque unico capite conglutinata esse nequeunt .... Est igitur Ecclesia Christi unica et perpetua: quicumque seorsum eant, aberrant a voluntate et praescriptione Christi Domini relictoque salutis itinere ad interitum digrediuntur', DS 3304.

[77] 'De salute hominum extra visibilem Ecclesiam', DS 3821.

[78] 'quandoquidem, etiamsi inscio quodam desiderio ac voto ad mysticum Redemptoris Corpus ordinentur, tot tamen tantisque caelestibus muneribus adiumentisque carent, quibus in Catholica solummodo Ecclesia frui licet', ibid.

with the Church. Such latitude, however, was not acceptable to those Catholics including the American Jesuit, Leonard Feeney, who wished to apply with all logical rigour the Church's express traditional belief in the statement of Cyprian that 'outside the Church there is no salvation'. And in the statement of Rome's Holy Office against Feeney we find both the traditional recourse to invincible ignorance and an elucidation of the new idea of 'membership of desire' (if one may so describe Pius XII's explanation) as an application at a more general level of the traditional development in Sacramental theology whereby in certain circumstances the simple wish to receive one of the Church's Sacraments is considered as effective as actual reception.

The letter of the Holy Office is notable not for pointedly maintaining that it is the role of the Church's *magisterium* and not of 'private judgements' to explain what is contained in the deposit of faith, but for its statement that the necessity of Church membership for salvation is an 'infallible pronouncement', and for the way in which it now proceeds to provide an authoritative explanation of that pronouncement.[79] 'No one will be saved who knows that the Church has been divinely instituted by Christ and who nevertheless refuses to subject himself to the Church or denies obedience to the Roman Pontiff, the vicar on earth of Christ.'[80] But God has instituted various helps to salvation which can sometimes be obtained simply by a wish or desire for them, as the Council of Trent taught in the case of baptism and penance. And the same can be said of the Church as a general help to salvation.

For someone to obtain eternal salvation it is not always required that he actually be incorporated in the Church as a member. What is at least required is that he belong by wish and desire. And this desire need not always be explicit as it is in the case of catechumens. When a person is in invincible ignorance God also accepts an implicit desire, which is so called

---

[79] 'Inter ea autem, quae semper Ecclesia praedicavit et praedicare numquam desinet illud quoque infallibile effatum continetur, quo edocemur "extra Ecclesiam nullam esse salutem". Est tamen hoc dogma intelligendum eo sensu, quo id intelligit Ecclesia ipsa. Non enim privatis iudiciis explicanda dedit Salvator noster ea, quae in fidei deposito continentur, sed ecclesiastico magisterio', *DS* 3866.

[80] 'Quare nemo salvabitur, qui sciens Ecclesiam a Christo divinitus fuisse institutam, tamen Ecclesiase sese subiicere renuit vel Romano Pontifici, Christi in terris vicario, denegat oboedientiam', *DS* 3867.

because it is contained within the good disposition of the soul with which a person would desire that his will be conformed to the will of God.[81]

When the Second Vatican Council came to consider the mystery of the Church, it acknowledged in detail the Roman Catholic Church's many links with other Christians and in this Christian context made no reference to Cyprian's famous maxim.[82] In its decree on ecumenism the element of the Church's gradual qualification of Cyprian which found expression was not the necessity of Catholic membership but, in the wake of Pius IX and Pius XII, the security to be derived from such membership through full access to all the means of salvation instituted by Christ. In a shift of concept from biological incorporation into the body of Christ to the more social and personal idea of communion the Council described those non-Catholics who believe in Christ and have been properly baptized as 'constituted in an imperfect communion with the Catholic Church' and as possessing many rites which 'open the way to the communion of salvation'. It remains true, however, that 'it is only through the Catholic Church of Christ, which is the general aid to salvation, that the whole fullness of the means of salvation can be obtained'.[83] It was only when it turned to consider the status of non-Christians, including adherents

---

[81] 'Infinita sua misericordia Deus voluit, ut illorum auxiliorum salutis, quae divina sola institutione, non vero intrinseca necessitate, ad finem ultimum ordinantur, tunc quoque certis in adiunctis effectus ad salutem necessarii obtineri valeant, ubi voto solummodo vel desiderio adhibeantur . . . . Idem autem suo modo dici debet de Ecclesia, quatenus generale ipsa auxilium salutis est. Quandoquidem ut quis aeternam obtineat salutem, non semper exigitur, ut reapse Ecclesiae tamquam membrum incorporetur, sed id saltem requiritur, ut eidem voto et desiderio adhaereat. Hoc tamen votum non semper explicitum sit oportet, prout accidit in catechumenis, sed ubi homo invincibili ignorantia laborat, Deus quoque implicitum votum acceptat, tali nomine nuncupatum, quia illud in ea bona animae dispositione continetur, qua homo voluntatem suam Dei voluntati conformem velit', *DS* 3869–70. Thus what had for centuries been a formal condition of personal salvation had now become a theological explanation of personal salvation.

[82] Addressing fellow Roman Catholics, the Council stated in modified Cyprian terms the need to remain in the Church. 'Ad fideles ergo catholicos imprimis Sancta Synodus animum vertit. Docet autem, Sacra Scriptura et Traditione innixa, Ecclesiam hanc peregrinantem necessariam esse ad salutem. Unus enim Christus est Mediator ac via salutis, qui in Corpore suo, quod est Ecclesia, praesens nobis fit . . . . Quare illi homines salvari non possent, qui Ecclesiam Catholicam a Deo per Iesum Christum ut necessariam esse conditam non ignorantes, tamen vel in eam intrare, vel in eadem persevare noluerint', *Lumen gentium*, 14; *AAS* 57 (1965), p. 18.

[83] 'Hi enim qui in Christum credunt et baptismum rite receperunt, in quadam cum Ecclesia catholica communione, etsi non perfecta, constituuntur . . . . Non paucae etiam christianae religionis actiones sacrae apud fratres a nobis seiunctos

of other religions, that the themes of invincible ignorance and of an implicit desire contained in a general wish to obey whatever might be God's will were invoked to provide the fullest to date explanation of how the Roman Catholic Church is to understand its role in man's salvation.

Those who without blame are ignorant of the Gospel of Christ and of his Church, and yet who seek God with a sincere heart, and try in their behaviour, under the influence of grace, to fulfil his will as they acknowledge it through the dictate of conscience, can attain to eternal salvation. And divine Providence does not deny the aids needed for salvation to those who through no fault of their own have not yet arrived at an express acknowledgement of God, but who by the help of his grace try to lead a good life.[84]

Nothing more strikingly illustrates the late emergence in the Church's moral teaching of a respect for moral subjectivity than the manner in which the severe objectivism of Cyprian's third-century shaft against the heretics of his day, which became a regular weapon in the Church's continuing campaign against heresy, schism, and unbelief, has come to be dramatically blunted only within the past hundred years. It is instructive not only for our subject but also for the development of doctrine in general how this

peraguntur, quae . . . aptae dicendae sunt quae ingressum in salutis communionem pandant . . . . Attamen fratres a nobis seiuncti, sive singuli sive Communitates et Ecclesiae eorum, unitate illa non fruuntur . . . . Per solam enim catholicam Christi Ecclesiam, quae generale auxilium salutis est, omnis salutarium mediorum plenitudo attingi potest', *Unitatis redintegratio*, 3; *AAS*, ibid., pp. 93–4. In the earlier *Lumen gentium*, reviewing the ecclesial activities of other Christians, the Council concentrated on the many common links, ibid., 15.

[84] 'Ii tandem qui Evangelium nondum acceperunt, ad Populum Dei diversis rationibus ordinantur . . . . Qui enim Evangelium Christi Eiusque Ecclesiam sine culpa ignorantes, Deum tamen sincero corde quaerunt, Eiusque voluntatem per conscientiae dictamen agnitam, operibus adimplere, sub gratiae influxu, conantur, aeternam salutem consequi possunt. Nec divina Providentia auxilia ad salutem necessaria denegat his qui sine culpa ad expressam agnitionem Dei nondum pervenerunt et rectam vitam non sine divina gratia assequi nituntur', *Lumen gentium*, 16; *AAS* 57 (1965), p. 20. In the decree, *Ad gentes*, on the Church's missionary activity among non-Christians, the Council quoted *Lumen gentium*, 14, on ignorance as the only saving factor (*supra*, n. 82), and continued, 'Etsi ergo Deus viis sibi notis homines Evangelium sine eorum culpa ignorantes ad fidem adducere possit, sine qua impossibile est Ipsi placere (Heb. 11: 6), Ecclesiae tamen necessitas incumbit (cfr. 1 Cor. 9: 16), simulque ius sacrum, evangelizandi, ac proinde missionalis activitas vim suam et necessitatem hodie sicut et semper integram servat', *Ad gentes*, 7; *AAS* 58 (1966)), p. 955.

stark and 'infallible' proposition, which ineluctably implies the absolute objective obligation of entering the Roman Catholic Church, has been glossed and interpreted in two directions. By an explanation in an ecumenical context, to which we shall return, that other Churches do possess positive resources for salvation and that 'the brethren who believe in Christ are Christ's disciples, reborn in baptism, sharers with the People of God in very many riches',[85] the Second Vatican Council signalled a major shift from dwelling on the deficiencies for salvation of other Christian bodies to a recognition of their positive qualities, even if they do not possess the 'complete fullness' of the means to salvation. And in a moral context the continued recourse to the principle of invincible ignorance, that no one can be damned by a good God except through his own fault, was likewise given a more positive turn by the recognition that fidelity to what is perceived by the individual in his conscience as what morality requires, whether or not he believes in God, will eventuate in eternal salvation, since it implicitly includes a willingness to believe in God and to adhere to the Church which his Christ founded. It is true, of course, that the explanatory letter of the Holy Office on the subject cautioned that only a desire informed by 'perfect [supernatural] charity' and accompanied by supernatural faith would effect this connection with the Church, but this condition is fulfilled by the Council's assertion that to a man trying to lead a good life with the help of grace God does not deny the helps needed for salvation.[86] With this evolution in the Church's understanding of how the Church figures in the divine scheme of universal salvation we are not far from anonymous Christianity, or, for that matter, from anonymous Roman Catholics.

Subjectivity and 'Situation Ethics'

If ignorance, however, was viewed as the escape clause in a thoroughly objective approach to morality which prevailed in

---

[85] 'aestiment fratres in Christum credentes esse Christi discipulos, baptismate regeneratos, perplurium bonorum Populi Dei consortes', ibid., 15; *AAS*, p. 964.

[86] 'Neque etiam putandum est, quodcumque votum Ecclesiae ingrediendae sufficere, ut homo salvetur. Requiritur enim, ut votum, quo quis ad Ecclesiam ordinetur, perfecta caritate informetur; nec votum implicitum effectum habere potest, nisi homo fidem habeat supernaturalem', *DS* 3872. With which compare *Lumen gentium*, 16; *supra*, n. 84.

moral theology for centuries, it proved inadequate in this century not only to do justice to the positive insights of ecumenism and genuine attempts at fidelity to conscience, but also to cope with the growing influence of existentialist and personalist ways of thought which brought to a head dissatisfaction with the pre-eminently objective and unreflective manner in which moral theology had been conducted in the nineteenth and early twentieth centuries. Such advances as the science might be considered to have made were heavily dependent on recourse to Rome for the appropriate line to take on new moral problems as they arose, and on the steady and almost invariably negative pronouncements from Rome couched in terms of condemning various types of behaviour as intrinsically and objectively wrong. Hamel shows how alongside the contented acceptance of authoritative interventions by the *Magisterium* there was little attempt made by moral theologians to enquire into scientific justification for the positions adopted. 'For example, they affirm as certain the intrinsic malice of all fornication and all sexual activity outside marriage, but at the same time they confess the inadequacy of the arguments used to prove it. Speaking of premarital intercourse, Ballerini confessed, "it is certainly forbidden, but we are still looking for convincing arguments to prove it".'[87]

In a new European philosophical atmosphere of change and spontaneity which reacted against fixed essences and natures and complete moral predictability, man's moral conscience came to be seen as 'no longer a function applying a general principle to a particular case by an automatic syllogism, but more as a faculty which under the guidance of the Spirit of God is endowed with a certain power of intuition and discovery which allows it to find the original solution appropriate to each case'.[88] Beginning in the Church in Germany, with similar stirrings in France, this post-war existentialist mood began to raise fundamental questions which the science of moral theology was not equipped to answer concerning the objectivity of moral values based on a stable human nature and the subordination of the subject to an impersonal morality imposed from outside him.[89] The answer was to come authoritatively from

[87] Hamel, 'Vari tipi', p. 126. Vermeersch, art. cit., also strongly deplored the lack of critical reasoning in moral theology.
[88] R. Aubert, op. cit., p. 76.
[89] Cf. ibid., pp. 76–8.

Rome in strong reactions from Pope Pius XII in 1952 and again in
1956 against 'situation ethics' and what he considered a radical
rejection of moral objectivity and of the traditional doctrine of
conscience.[90]

The writers who follow this system consider that the decisive and ultimate
norm for action is not the objective right order, which is determined by the
law of nature and known with certainty from this law, but some interior
mental judgement of each individual, a light by which he knows what he
should do in the concrete situation. According to them, this final decision is
not the application of the objective law to the particular case with due
attention and weight to the particular features of the 'situation' according
to the laws of prudence, as is taught by the tradition of objective ethics
followed by more important authors, but it is an immediate inner
illumination and judgement. In many matters at least, this judgement is
ultimately not measured or measurable or to be measured in its objective
rightness and truth by any objective norm outside man and independent of
his subjective conviction. It is fully self-sufficient.[91]

According to these authors the traditional concept of 'human nature' is
inadequate, and reference should be made to a concept of 'existing' human
nature, which in very many respects does not have any objective absolute
validity but is relative only and therefore changeable, apart perhaps from
some few elements and principles which refer to metaphysical (absolute
and unchangeable) human nature. The same purely relative validity is
applied also to the traditional concept of 'the law of nature'; and a great
many matters which are today proposed as absolute requirements of
natural law are, in their view, . . . based on the concept of 'existing

---

[90] *AAS* 44 (1952), 270–8; 413–19; 48 (1956) 144–5, *De Ethica situationis.* The
1956 Instruction of the Holy Office resumes and develops more systematically the
papal allocutions of 1952, and its essentials are contained in *DS* 3918–21.
[91] 'Auctores, qui hoc systema sequuntur, decisivam et ultimam agendi normam
statuunt non esse ordinem obiectivum rectum, naturae lege determinatum et ex hac
lege certo cognitum, sed intimum aliquod mentis uniuscuiusque individui iudicium
ac lumen, quo ei in concreta situatione posito innotescit quid sibi agendum sit. Haec
igitur hominis ultima decisio secundum eos non est, sicut ethica obiectiva apud
auctores maioris momenti tradita docet, legis obiectivae ad particularem casum
applicatio, attentis simul ac ponderatis secundum regulas prudentiae particularibus
"situationis" adiunctis, sed immediatum illud internum lumen et iudicium. Hoc
iudicium saltem multis in rebus ultimatim nulla norma obiectiva extra hominem
posita atque ab eius persuasione subiectiva independente, quoad suam obiectivam
rectitudinem ac veritatem est mensuratum neque mensurandum neque mensurabile,
sed sibi ipsi plene sufficit', *DS* 3918.

nature', and are therefore only relative, changeable and always adaptable to each situation.[92]

Taking these principles and applying them, they say . . . that men who judge in their own consciences what they should do in the present situation by a personal intuition through the medium of that inner light, and not above all according to objective laws, are saved, or are easily freed, from many ethical conflicts which are otherwise insoluble.[93]

This powerful intervention of Pope Pius XII, who was then at the peak of his regular and frequent teaching activity on moral matters, concluded that 'many elements of this system of "situation ethics" are contrary to truth and the dictate of sound reason, show traces of relativism and modernism, and are far removed from the traditional Catholic teaching of centuries . . . '.[94] His condemnation of 'situation ethics' has dominated moral theology until very recently and still does in many quarters. The dark references to relativism and especially to 'modernism' have contributed to an emotional atmosphere in the Church surrounding the whole system of 'situation ethics' which is reminiscent of the bitter crisis which overtook all intellectual endeavour earlier this century in the fields of biblical and dogmatic study and which resulted in a period of artificial and enforced tranquillity. Not many members of the Church are clear on exactly what is meant by 'situation ethics', but most are sure that it should be avoided like the plague. In reflecting now on the whole theme of this chapter, that of subjectivity, we may usefully begin, therefore, with this major papal teaching which

[92] 'Secundum hos auctores "naturae humanae" conceptus traditionalis non sufficit, sed recurrendum est ad conceptum naturae humanae "exsistentis", qui quoad plurima non habet valorem obiectivum absolutum, sed relativum tantum ideoque mutabilem, exceptis fortasse illis paucis elementis atque principiis, quae ad humanam naturam metaphysicam (absolutam et immutabilem) spectant. Eiusdem valoris tantum relativi est traditionalis conceptus "legis naturae". Perplura autem, quae hodie circumferuntur tamquam legis naturae postulata absoluta, nituntur secundum eorum opinionem . . . in dicto conceptu naturae existentis, ideoque non sunt nisi relativa et mutabilia atque omni semper situationi adaptari queunt', *DS* 3919.

[93] 'Acceptis atque ad rem deductis his principiis dicunt . . . homines in sua quisque conscientia non imprimis secundum leges obiectivas, sed mediante lumine illo interno individuali secundum intuitionem personalem iudicantes, quid ipsis in praesenti situatione agendum sit, a multis conflictibus ethicis aliter insolubilibus praeservari vel facile liberari', *DS* 3920.

[94] 'Multa, quae in huius "Ethicae situationis" systemate statuuntur, rei veritati sanaeque rationis dictamini contraria sunt, relativismi et modernismi vestigia produnt, a doctrina catholica per saecula tradita longe aberrant', *DS* 3921.

strongly affirms the claims of objectivity and of its crucial role in the workings of conscience. To what exactly was Pope Pius XII objecting?

Two distinct themes occupy his analysis and condemnation: one to do with the objectivity of human nature and natural law; and the other to do with moral decision-making. On human nature he complains of those who reject a static and absolute concept of nature in favour of a concept of an existing and partly changing human nature, and who therefore conclude that the moral 'law of nature' should reflect this view of nature and accordingly be changing and adaptable to each existing situation. This he describes as akin to relativism and a rejection of objectivity in morals. Now, objectivity in morals, as we have seen in considering the 'raw material' of morality, means deriving moral standards from things as they are, and not just as I think them to be, or would like them to be. And if things and situations are by their nature fluid and changing, then it is not a lack of objectivity so to describe them. On the contrary, if one were to see that as well as a stable factor or element, human nature as it is found and experienced has also a fluid element and one were to deny that, such a judgement would be flying in the face of objectivity. Moreover, to espouse a relatively changeable view of objective human nature obviously entails a corresponding adaptability in the objective moral conclusions to be derived from such a nature. And it is less than accurate to condemn such conclusions with the emotional charge of relativism as if they were not based on objective data. In effect, the whole gravamen of Pope Pius XII's complaint about a partial rejection of the objective absolute validity of human nature stands or falls by whether or not one conceives nature metaphysically and a priori as being objectively static and absolutely unchangeable, or whether it is conceived of historically and culturally as well as metaphysically.

The other suspect theme, savouring of modernism, which Pius XII condemned in situation ethics relates to moral decision-making. He refers several times to an interior and immediate illumination and judgement, an intuition which suffices to inform the individual in each situation what he should do without having to go through the traditional process of conscience applying the objective law to each situation.[95] In thus emphatically stressing the rational process

---

[95] *Supra*, nn. 91, 93.

of arriving at a moral judgement and decision, Pius was undoubtedly in the mainstream of traditional moral theology as it had evolved scientifically. But it is interesting to compare this rationalist tradition, pursued in systematic isolation from doctrinal and spiritual theology, with a more intuitive approach to knowledge by way of experience and insight which these other branches of theology have pursued and developed, and which indeed is a fundamental element in the moral teaching of Aquinas, although not of neo-Thomism.[96] And it is difficult to reconcile the neo-Thomist approach of Pius XII with what appears to be the teaching of the Second Vatican Council, that some form of interior intuitional judgemental activity is part of normal Christian living.

As the Council explained, the Spirit of truth arouses and sustains in all the faithful who have received his anointing a supernatural 'sense of faith', which is not exercised only in matters of dogma and doctrine but also in morals, enabling the People of God as a whole to penetrate the faith more deeply by accurate judgement and apply it more thoroughly to life.[97] That this is not simply conscience as traditionally understood seems clear from the Council's later teaching, in concluding its treatment of marriage and the family in contemporary society, that a valuable contribution to the solving of modern difficulties in this area can be made by 'the Christian sense of the faithful and the upright moral conscience of men'.[98] It appears, then, that at least the Christian has more within him in the way of moral resources than just the conscientious use of reason. And indeed, many years previously, Pope Pius XI had explained in

---

[96] Cf. J. Mahoney, 'The Spirit and Moral Discernment in Aquinas', in *Seeking the Spirit: Essays in Moral and Pastoral Theology* (London, 1981).

[97] 'Universitas fidelium, qui unctionem habent a Sancto Spiritu (cf. 1 John 2: 20, 27), in credendo falli nequit, atque hanc suam peculiarem proprietatem mediante supernaturali sensu fidei totius populi manifestat, cum "ab Episcopis usque ad extremos laicos fideles" universalem suum consensum de rebus fidei et morum exhibet. Illo enim sensu fidei, qui a Spiritu veritatis excitatur et sustentatur, Populus Dei sub ductu sacri magisterii, cui fideliter obsequens, iam non verbum hominum, sed vere accipit verbum Dei (cf. 1 Thess. 2: 13), semel traditae sanctis fidei (cf. Iud 3), indefectibiliter adhaeret, recto iudicio in eam profundius penetrat eamque in vita plenius applicat', *Lumen gentium*, 12; *AAS* 57 (1965), p. 16.

[98] 'Christifideles, praesens tempus redimentes atque aeterna a mutabilibus formis discernentes, bona matrimonii et familiae . . . diligenter promoveant . . . . Ad quem finem obtinendum sensus christianus fidelium, recta hominum conscientia moralis necnon sapientia ac peritia eorum qui in sacris disciplinis versati sunt magno auxilio erunt', *Gaudium et spes*, 52; *AAS* 58 (1966), p. 1074.

his encyclical on marriage how Christian married couples receive from the Sacrament of matrimony a grace which so increases and perfects their natural resources 'that they do not just understand by reason, but have an intimate "taste" for . . . whatever belongs to the married state and its ends and duties'.[99]

It is interesting to note how it appears to be particularly in moral questions connected with marriage that this tenuous theme of Christian 'feeling' supplementing or sometimes substituting for rational argumentation is to be found. In his encyclical on contraception, Pope Paul VI maintained that the arguments which he proposed in support of his teaching were not more compelling grounds for acceptance of that teaching than the light of the Holy Spirit which he enjoyed in propounding it.[100] In the same vein Pope John Paul II described his predecessor's teaching as a 'deeply wise and loving intuition' in which he had been successful in 'voicing the experience of many married couples'.[101] He also referred to it as 'a truly prophetic proclamation . . . regarding marriage and regarding the transmission of life', and in acknowledging that it was difficult for many to understand in modern society, he urgently called on theologians to 'provide enlightenment and a deeper understanding' of it.[102]

Such official statements on an interior resource which is not identical with reason logically applying objective universal principles point to something akin to a distinction between insight and argumentation, and to a view that in at least some areas of morality one's spiritual reach may be beyond one's intellectual grasp. In Shaw's *Saint Joan* the distinction is dramatically exemplified in the exchange between Joan and Dunois, the Bastard of Orleans who admires the country Maid but is baffled by her claims to be directed by heavenly voices of the saints and the ringing of church bells:

---

[99] 'ut coniuges non ratione tantum intelligere, sed intime sapere firmiterque tenere, efficaciter velle et opere perficere valeant quidquid ad statum coniugalem eiusque fines et officia pertinet', *AAS* 22 (1930), p. 555.

[100] 'Vos [sacerdotes] primi in ministerio vestro perfungendo exemplum sinceri obsequii edite, quod interius exteriusque ecclesiastico Magisterio tribuendum est. Etenim nostis tali vos obsequio devinciri non potius illis de causis, quae allatae sunt, quam ob Sancti Spiritus lumen, quo praecipue Ecclesiae Pastores in explananda veritate fruuntur', *Humanae Vitae*, 28; *AAS* 60 (1968), p. 501.

[101] *Familiaris Consortio*, CTS (London, 1981), no. 33; *AAS* 74 (1982), p. 122.

[102] Ibid., nos. 29, 31; *AAS*, ibid., pp. 115, 117–8.

Dunois: Then, Joan, we shall hear whatever we fancy in the booming of
the bell. You make me uneasy when you talk about your voices;
I should think you were a bit cracked if I hadn't noticed that you
give me very sensible reasons for what you do, though I hear you
telling others you are only obeying Madame Saint Catherine.

Joan (crossly): Well, I have to find reasons for you, because you do
not believe in my voices. But the voices come first; and I find the
reasons after: whatever you may choose to believe.[103]

'The voices come first; and I find the reasons after.' For Joan, it
appears, the heavenly guidance was sufficient for herself, and the
reasons she worked out to justify the teaching were for other
people. What the Church and moral theology have always regarded
with reserve, and rightly, is subjectivism, or the view that whatever
the individual thinks is morally right on any matter is in fact
(objectively) right and for that very reason. Hence the importance
of 'reasons' as well as insights or intuitions and the clear and
continual need to maintain the difference between reasoning and
rationalizing. Even traditional spiritual theology would be rather
more cautious than the Maid and would view reasoning and
'reasons' as playing some part in the delicate task of authenticating
insights or, in more biblical language, in 'discerning the spirits'.[104]
But at least she is represented as recognizing a role for reasons as an
almost indispensable medium in society, if not for probing, at least
for communicating moral insights, however inadequately.

In this sense, the dispute over situation ethics is at least in part an
enquiry into moral communication, not only within the individual
subject but also with other human subjects in the Church. What
Pius XII's analysis and condemnation did not sufficiently take into
account was that situation ethics raises a fundamental issue about
the relation of insight to argument which cannot be settled by
simply dismissing one or the other as of no account. There is
considerably more to moral decision-making than the reasoned
application to particular situations of what are considered objective
moral norms. Essential though it is for insights and moral intuitions
to be subjected as far as possible to the bar of reason, when that is
done all is not necessarily said or expressed. The moral 'feel' for a

[103] George Bernard Shaw, *Saint Joan*, scene V.
[104] 1 Cor. 12: 10. Cf. Mahoney, 'Discernment of Spirits', in *Seeking the Spirit*,
pp. 118–34, and 'Moral Reasoning in Medical Ethics', in *The Month*, 2nd n.s. 18
(1985), pp. 293–9.

situation which Christians are considered to possess by reason of their personal adhesion of faith may be unashamedly of the character of insight in search of arguments or, in terms more generally applicable to theology as a whole, of Christian experience seeking understanding.

False Religions or Ecumenism?

In its strongly a priori and deductive approach to moral situations the science of moral theology has traditionally accorded negligible acknowledgement to the role and the weight of experience as a subjective contribution to the examination of particular issues. And in this context the recent revolution in the Roman Catholic Church's attitude to other Christians may be seen as such a triumph of experience over selective logic, and as exemplifying the priority of a fresh grasp of objective reality over reasoned arguments which then seek to elucidate, refine, and justify that new perception. It can also be seen as a striking instance of a shift in the moral evaluation of actions hitherto considered objectively bad whatever the circumstances.

We have already seen how the Church's understanding of its infallible teaching that there is absolutely no salvation outside the Church has had to be refined and qualified. Being outside the Catholic Church is not such an absolute and unmitigated evil and disaster as it was for centuries considered, and not just by reason of invincible subjective ignorance and divine goodness. God is now acknowledged more freely to be at his saving work also outside the Church and particularly among other Christian bodies, through what were until comparatively recently considered the depraved practices and cultures of benighted pagans and the heretical and false religious ceremonies of Protestants and others. Modern controversy on the Church's teaching about moral absolutes has concentrated mainly on such topics as contraception, sterilization, divorce, and abortion, with claims for historical illumination from such other subjects as traditional teaching on usury and slavery. One area of moral doctrine which evidences much more recent development in this regard and which is also more enlightening for other fields of theology, notably ecclesiology, is that which is part conclusion and part exemplification of God's universal salvific will, ecumenical worship.

At the First Vatican Council one of the bishops present publicly objected that he did not think all the ills of modern thought, rationalism, free-thinking, liberalism, and so on, should be so freely blamed on Protestantism. He did not go so far as to commend Protestant 'subjective judgement', but he did observe that he thought many Protestants were in good faith. For this observation he was shouted down by fellow-bishops with cries of 'Luther' and 'Lucifer'.[105] This deplorable behaviour was but an extreme

[105] Bishop Strossmayer's speech addressed itself to the revised schema *De fide catholica*, which in its final form as the Dogmatic Constitution *Dei Filius* was promulgated on 24 April 1870 (Mansi, li, 429–37). Among the points to which Strossmayer took exception was the document's account of the progressive religious decline which followed upon the Council of Trent. 'Hic sermo est, reverendissimi patres, de protestantismo; et venerandi episcopi, qui huic schemati corrigendo insudarunt, omnium malorum et omnium errorum, qui inde a concilii Tridentini temporibus usque ad nostra tempora mundum inundarunt, omnium inquam errorum et malorum fontem et originem protestantismum esse putant' (ibid., 74). This was not fully in accord with the truth and certainly not in accord with charity. The Protestants had certainly done great wrong in subjecting matters of faith 'subiectivo rationis iudicio et arbitrio', and this had opened floodgates. But humanism and laxism pre-existed Protestantism, and the latter could not be blamed for the eighteenth-century excesses of Voltaire and the Encyclopaedists which had emerged from within Catholic France. Moreover, continued Strossmayer, there were many important Protestants, including Leibniz, who were as concerned as the Council was about many of the errors of the times, and Guizot's writings against Renan were such as Catholics could usefully study (ibid., 74–5). At this, as the account of the General Session of the Council reports, there was a *murmur* among his listeners, which was repeated when he went on to state, 'Ego quidem existimo dari in medio protestantium magnam turbam, quae virorum illorum in Germania, Anglia et America vestigia premens et Dominum nostrum Iesum Christum adhuc amans meretur, ut ad eam applicentur illa magni Augustini verba: Errant, errant, sed bona fide (*murmur*) errant: haeretici sunt, haeretici, sed nullus pro haereticis habet' (75). There followed altercation between the bishop and the Cardinal presiding, who asked Strossmayer, 'precor, reverendissime pater, ut abstineas a verbis quae scandalum in nonnullis patribus excitant' (ibid.). Strossmayer insisted, 'ego existimo dari in protestantismo non unum alterumve hominem, sed turbam hominum qui adhuc Iesum Christum amant' (76), and he did not wish the Council to place any limits to God's action among them. It may have been the speaker's prolixity which also exhausted the patience of his listeners, but when at last, having moved on to another point, he was ruled out of order and retired in protest at all the interruptions, the objections appear to have been mainly directed at his favourable reference to Protestants. 'Descendit orator et indignabundi patres e subselliis egrediuntur, singuli pro se varia obmurmurantes. Alii dicebant: . . . *Lucifer est iste, anathema, anathema. Alii vero: Alter Lutherus est iste, eiiciatur foras.* Omnes autem clamabant: *Descende, descende. Orator autem semper dicebat:* Protestor, protestor, *et descendit*', ibid., 77. On this conciliar episode, cf. Cuthbert Butler, *The Vatican Council* (London, 1930), vol. i, pp. 270–3, 275. J. J. Hennessy, in *The First Council of the Vatican: The American Experience* (New York, 1963), p. 147, records the comment of an American bishop emerging from the Council to Lord Acton, 'There is certainly one assembly in the world rougher than the American Congress.'

instance of the deep suspicion and disfavour with which in those
days Rome regarded all attempts at a Christian *rapprochement* and
of the completely negative attitude which the Church and moral
theology maintained in its teaching on *communicatio in sacris*, or
any sharing in religious activities with non-Catholics. Some years
before the Council the Roman Congregation of the Holy Office had
written disapprovingly to the English hierarchy on the subject of
Catholic participation in a move to seek Christian unity based on
the 'branch theory' that the three communions, Roman Catholic,
Greek, and Anglican, together comprised the Catholic Church. The
Holy Office was firm on the need 'to teach the faithful not to be led
by heretics to join this Society with heretics and schismatics'. It was
completely unacceptable that the faithful and clergy should pray for
Christian unity on the initiative of heretics and, what was worse,
with an intention polluted and infected with further heresy.[106]

The uncompromising character of this absolute refusal to share
in any act of worship with heretics or schismatics was upheld for
the universal Church with the promulgation in 1917 of the Code of
Canon Law, which laid down that it is 'illicit for Catholics in any
way to assist actively or take part in sacred worship of non-
Catholics'. The canon in question also made provision for 'passive
or merely material presence' under certain conditions and in certain
circumstances such as civic or family duties; and it is enlightening
to note how this distinction between 'active' and 'passive' attendance at non-Catholic worship was explained in the most influential
English-language Commentary on the Code of Canon Law, that of
T. L. Bouscaren. Even in the case of being simply physically present
at such occasions, he observes, 'it is conceivable that even merely
passive presence might be accompanied by an internal intention to
approve, assent to, or encourage the non-Catholic worship; if that
were true it would be formal co-operation in an evil act, and
forbidden by the natural law'. The stringent conditions which alone
would permit such passive presence indicate that 'though not
intrinsically wrong by reason of its object (the thing being done)', *as*

---

[106] 'At quod Christifideles et ecclesiastici viri, haereticorum ductu, et quod peius
est, iuxta intentionem haeresi quam maxime pollutam et infectam, pro christiana
unitate orent, tolerari nullo modo potest', *DS* 2887. For the explicit instructions of
the Holy Office, cf. also *AAS* 11 (1919), pp. 309–16.
[107] *Codex iuris canonici* (1917), 1258: '1. Haud licitum est fidelibus quovis
modo active assistere seu partem habere in sacris acatholicorum. 2. Tolerari potest
praesentia passiva seu mere materialis, civilis officii vel honoris causa, ob gravem

active and formal participation would be, 'it is likely to be wrong by reason of its circumstances and consequences'.[107]

In 1919 the Holy Office reissued its 1864 condemnation of Catholic participation in the London society for seeking Christian unity with the comment that it applied to all meetings and public and private committees convened by non-Catholics with a view to achieving Church unity. And as late as 1948 it was to recall once more the Church's teaching, as expressed in its law, that any sharing in worship with non-Catholics was 'entirely forbidden'.[108] It came, then, as a very considerable shock to moral theologians and others when in the following year Pope Pius XII gave very guarded permission to Roman Catholics to engage in ecumenical discussions, and even allowed that such meetings could begin and end with shared prayer.[109] In England the influential moralist Canon E. J. Mahoney, who had for years been keeper of the clergy's conscience in his regular column in *The Clergy Review*, and who had also advised the hierarchy on relations with other Christians, including public association with 'heretical religious worship', commented on this Catholic volte-face, 'the more common view, in this country at least, has regarded *communicatio in sacris . . .* as wrong in itself', on the grounds that 'there is always implied in the action, it would seem, at least an external approval of heretical worship'.[110] In making a public recantation of the advice he had been giving regularly for years on the subject in loyalty to Rome's teaching, Mahoney permitted himself the pained observation, 'The instructions of the Holy Office and Propaganda on the subject, some of them extremely difficult to explain on any other principle . . . have led one to believe that, for all practical purposes, this outlook has been favoured by the Holy See . . . . Accordingly in this journal the solutions offered so far have been based on the view that a united prayer is wrong of its nature.'[111]

---

rationem ab Episcopo in casu dubii probandam, in acatholicorum funeribus, nuptiis similibusque sollemniis, dummodo perversionis et scandali periculum absit.' Cf. T. L. Bouscaren, *Canon Law: A Text and Commentary* (Milwaukee, 1963), p. 708.

[108] *AAS* 11 (1919), p. 309; 40 (1948), p. 257.

[109] *AAS* 42 (1950), pp. 142–7.

[110] *Clergy Review* 33 (1950), pp. 398–9. On Mahoney's influence, cf. M. J. Walsh, 'Ecumenism in Wartime Britain (1)', *Heythrop Journal* 23 (1982), p. 249.

[111] Art cit., p. 400. Bouscaren, *supra*, had taken the same line in his view that active participation would be 'intrinsically wrong'.

The rapid and cumulative developments which followed upon Pius XII's rejection of the teaching that actively sharing in prayer with other Christians is always and everywhere intrinsically and objectively wrong require no chronicling here except to point to the culmination to date of this papal opening to ecumenism. In a highly dramatic and symbolic religious service in Canterbury Cathedral in May 1982, Pius's successor, Pope John Paul II, took part with leaders of the Anglican Communion and of other Churches in an event which the Pope described as 'this historic day which centuries and generations have awaited'.[112] Much enlightenment on the subject and official encouragement of the ecumenical movement was provided by the Second Vatican Council, especially in its Decree on Ecumenism *The Restoration of unity among all Christians*, from which the following points relevant to our study may be noted. Even with the careful qualifications personally added by Pope Paul VI the document is refreshingly positive in its appreciation of non-Catholic Christianity.[113] Looking to the remote and immediate past it recognized that 'at times men on both sides were to blame' for the major separations in history from full communion with the Catholic Church. As for the ecumenical future, it acknowledged not just that the Church is continually in need of 'reformation' but also that it needed to rectify 'any deficiencies in morals, Church discipline or even the manner of formulating doctrine', as distinct from the actual deposit of faith.[114] This was the closest the Council Fathers came to adverting to the Church's complete change in attitude to other Christians, whether individually or corporately, and to sharing with them in worship. In its treatment of the latter, however, it may be seen to have brought some refinement to the understanding of the traditional phrase *communicatio in sacris*, which had hitherto been understood generally of any active sharing with other Christians in any form of joint prayer or worship.

[112] *AAS* 74 (1982), p. 920.

[113] On Pope Paul's last minute alterations, cf. W. M. Abbott, *The Documents of Vatican II* (London, 1966), p. 338.

[114] 'quandoque non sine hominum utriusque parte culpa', *Unitatis Redintegratio*, no. 3; *AAS* 57 (1965), p. 93; 'Ecclesia in via peregrinans vocatur a Christo ad hanc perennem reformationem qua ipsa, qua humanum terrenumque institutum, perpetuo indiget; ita ut, si quae, pro rerum temporumque adiunctis, sive in moribus, sive in ecclesiastica disciplina, sive etiam in doctrinae enuntiandae modo – qui ab ipso deposito fidei sedulo distingui debet—minus accurate servata fuerint, opportuno tempore recte debiteque instaurentur', ibid., no. 6; *AAS* ibid., pp. 96–7.

On joint ecumenical prayer the Council simply disowned previous practice by stating that 'in certain special circumstances . . . it is allowable, indeed desirable, that Catholics should join in prayer with their separated brethren' as a means to obtain the grace of unity and as 'a genuine expression of the bonds uniting Catholics with their separated brothers'.[115] Where it stopped short, however, appears to have been in connection with sharing in formal denominational worship, as distinct from ecumenical, although the distinction may sometimes be a difficult one to apply in practice. Explicit reference was not made to full Eucharistic participation, but it appears to be this which the Council had primarily, if not exclusively, in mind as in many respects the nerve-centre of ecumenism which had its own particular difficulties connected with ministry,[116] and to which it now seemed to reserve the phrase *communicatio in sacris*. Even here, however, it was not absolutely rigid, contenting itself with stating, after its encouragement of ecumenical prayer,

But *communicatio in sacris* may not be considered as a means to be used indiscriminately for the restoring of Christian unity. Such communication rests largely on two principles: expressing the unity of the Church; and sharing in the means of grace. The expression of unity for the most part forbids communication. The grace to be sought sometimes commends it. Practical decisions in the light of all the circumstances of time, place and persons should be made prudently by local episcopal authority unless the Episcopal Conference according to its statutes, or the Holy See, determine otherwise.[117]

---

[115] 'In quibusdam peculiaribus rerum adiunctis, cuiusmodi sunt precationes quae "pro unitate" indicuntur, atque in oecumenicis conventibus licitum est immo et optandum, ut Catholici cum fratribus seiunctis in oratione consocientur', ibid., no. 8; *AAS*, p. 98.

[116] 'Communitates ecclesiales a nobis seiunctae, quamvis deficiat earum plena nobiscum unitas ex baptismae profluens, et quamvis credamus illas, praesertim propter Sacramenti Ordinis defectum, genuinam atque integram substantiam Mysterii eucharistici non servasse, tamen . . .', ibid., no. 22; *AAS*, p. 106.

[117] 'Attamen communicatio in sacris considerare non licet velut medium indiscretim adhibendum ad Christianorum unitatem restaurandam. Quae communicatio a duobus principiis praecipue pendet: ab unitate Ecclesiae significanda, et a participatione in mediis gratiae. Significatio unitatis plerumque vetat communicationem. Gratia procuranda quandoque illam commendat. De modo concreto agendi, attentis omnibus circumstantiis temporum, locorum et personarum, prudenter decernat auctoritas episcopalis localis, nisi aliud a conferentia episcopali, ad normam propriorum statutorum, vel a Sancta Sede statuatur', ibid., no. 8; *AAS*, p. 98.

'Practical decisions' are not matters of principle, but are a discerning application of principles which may often be in conflict in particular situations. Of the two principles mainly in question where *communicatio in sacris* is concerned, the Council opted 'for the most part' against sharing, on the grounds that it would appear to express a unity within the Church which did not yet exist. But it was prepared to allow it 'sometimes' and not 'indiscriminately', in view of the access to God's grace which it had to offer. As a matter of absolute objective principle, then, the Council did not rule out *communicatio in sacris*, even in the more specific sense in which it understood it.[118] From this particular salutary development of doctrine and its moral implications, which is still in process, many lessons may be learned for moral theology. One is that it be wary of being too dogmatic in its utterances, whether in applying the dogmas of the Church in too sweeping a manner to cover areas which, with hindsight or reflection, it perceives do not come within the ambit of such dogmas; or of being so confident that it always knows what is objectively right and objectively wrong, or good and bad *per se*. Another is that it be wary of assessing the objective morality of various types of behaviour by concentrating moral attention on only certain features of such behaviour, whether in the abstract or in actual practice. So long as non-Catholic Christians were regarded as simply and solely heretics and schismatics for having separated themselves from the true Church, then, of course, any truck with them could have no redeeming features either for Catholics or for them. One might try to deliver them from the error of their ways and the darkness of sin and perdition by taking them back on board the one ark of salvation which, as Pope Boniface VIII argued, could have only one captain and ruler, Christ and his Vicar, the Roman Pontiff, submission to whom was absolutely necessary for salvation.[119]

The situation must be otherwise, however, once it begins to be appreciated that charges of heresy and schism are far from being a complete and adequate description and evaluation of the status in God's eyes of the reality of non-Catholic Christian life and experience. At Vatican I an attempt was made by one bishop to

[118] On the background to the Council's decision, cf. H. Vorgrimler (ed.), *Commentary on the Documents of Vatican II* (London, 1967–9) vol. ii, pp. 105–8.
[119] *DS* 870–2. Cf. *DS* 875, 'Porro subesse Romano Pontifici omni humanae creaturae declaramus, dicimus, diffinimus omnino esse de necessitate salutis.'

recognize subjective good faith, but by Vatican II the Church had taken a much more measured approach to the objective facts of the case. 'Very many of the most significant elements or endowments which together go to build up and give life to the Church herself can exist outside [*extra*] the visible boundaries of the Catholic Church'; and, what is more, although only through the Catholic Church can 'the fullness of the means of salvation' be obtained, nevertheless many religious 'sacred actions' in other Churches 'can be rightly described as capable of providing access to the community of salvation'.[120] The shift of attention which this betokens is not unlike that between the attitude of a pessimist who judges a bottle half-empty and an optimist who judges it half-full. Objectively, its contents remain the same, but one's attention to them is selective, although not, it should be noted, completely subjective. And moral theology must allow systematically in many other fields of human behaviour than inter-Christian worship for a shift from a pessimistic dwelling, if a further homely comparison is appropriate, on the hole in a doughnut to a positive appreciation of what nourishing qualities it may also possess!

How can such a shift, or preparedness for possible shift, be brought about? One precondition would be the sort of mental humility described above. Another must be an openness to simple Christian experience and to that 'Christian sense' which we have also already considered. It was this in the field of Christian co-operation which simply came to resist an over-conceptual and over-rational consideration of non-Catholic Christian reality and a negatively selective evaluation of it born of hostility and polemic. Experience of such reality, often by laity before the more isolated or protected clergy, when reflected upon with some theological common sense, introduced a human and Christian sense of proportion which frequently strained against the confines of theological niceties, until the rest of the Church came to recognize the release of the Spirit, and official teaching was correspondingly adjusted. And it is in this context particularly interesting to note

---

[120] 'Insuper ex elementis seu bonis, quibus simul sumptis ipsa Ecclesia aedificatur et vivificatur, quaedam, immo plurima et eximia exstare possunt extra visibilia Ecclesiae catholicae saepta: ... Non paucae etiam christianae religionis actiones sacrae apud fratres a nobis seiunctos peraguntur, quae ... aptae dicendae sunt quae ingressum in salutis communionem pandant', *Decree on Ecumenism*, no. 3; *AAS* ibid., p. 93.

that when the Archbishop of Canterbury and Pope John Paul undertook to proceed further with joint deliberations towards unity they appealed to the members of their two communions not only to work and pray for ecumenism but to share in ecumenical experience.[121] It is from the continuing dialectic, for the Church as for all believers, between belief and experience that there results what theology has come to term the development of doctrine. 'It is, if we may so express it, a matter of trying to make faith-sense of experience and at the same time of making experience-sense of faith; of finding an overall context of a meaning and purpose to life within which to locate all our ordinary experiences and interrelate them, and at the same time of continually checking such a vision of life against each new experience as it arises.'[122]

Road-Maps and Acorns

This developmental dialectic between the objective and the subjective in moral matters can be glimpsed in the work of the Church's major moral theologian, Thomas Aquinas, in the tension to be observed between his treatise on external law and his treatise on *beatitudo*, or internal fulfilment, and we shall be exploring the theme of law in morality in our next chapter. The tension is not dissimilar from a view of the moral life which would regard it as a road mapped out ahead of the individual as contrasted with a more internal view of morality in terms of the development of the moral subject, with which we may close this chapter.

The objective, or road-map view, considers every moral action of man as potentially a step towards, or away from, his final goal in life and in eternity. And every step counts. Morality is basically a matter of how each step fits into that movement. If it carries man forward it is morally good and if it takes him down a side-road or even backwards then it is disordered and morally bad. Everything depends, apparently, on where the person puts his feet in his moral odyssey. And individual acts in the abstract are to be viewed as so many stepping-stones surrounding man. Some will carry him forward, others backwards, and yet others off at an angle. Each stepping-stone has to be carefully considered for its capacity to

---

[121] *AAS* 74 (1982), p. 925.
[122] J. Mahoney, *Bioethics and Belief* (London, 1984), p. 112.

advance man or to retard him in his journey. And so not only does every step count, but even more every stone counts. Whatever takes man a step closer to God is by definition objectively a morally good act, and whatever causes him to waver or falter on the way is venial sin, in contrast to mortal sin, which is a deliberate striking out in a new direction, objectively away from God. What is more, God himself has mapped out the way ahead for man, and leads him along 'the right path', by indicating in his law which are the right and which are the wrong steps for man to take, which stepping-stones to choose and which stones at all costs to avoid if he is to reach his heavenly goal and destiny.

Such a depicting of morality as a 'way' and as a journey of return to source has both biblical and Neoplatonist warrant. It exploits the metaphorical language and imagery of movement, direction and pilgrimage, and its simple pictorial attractiveness is evident. But in its very objectivity, as a kind of bird's-eye view of the moral causeway along which man must pick his way with care, it also contains inherent weaknesses. One such is that it makes no allowance for man's getting innocently lost, or for his mistakenly taking the wrong stepping-stones by choosing moral acts which are 'objectively' bad. It could be argued, of course, that if man does put a foot wrong it is his own fault, that his ignorance is sinful in being either a deliberate wandering off the right path or culpable negligence in not consulting and trusting the road map provided. But moral theology came to realize, albeit slowly, as we have seen, that human ignorance could not be so lightly disposed of as sinful. The notion of incorrigible, or invincible, ignorance was to develop systematically as a refuge for such 'wandering sinners', as they would otherwise have to be classified, and as a neat category to explain many a puzzle in moral experience whenever the objective map of the moral life was seen not to coincide neatly with the steps actually traced by some individuals and societies.

But the refuge of invincible ignorance was only itself a staging post in the journeying of moral theology. It did not explain how those who were recognized as 'suffering' from it eventually reached their destination, nor how this could be, as Vatican II taught, the same destination held out before all men. The further and more positive step, as we have seen in the illuminating history of the Roman Catholic attitude to other Christian bodies, to ecumenism and to *communicatio in sacris*, was to be a closer scrutiny of some of the stones laid out before man and a dawning awareness that some which had hitherto been classified as untrustworthy, or at least insecure, could in fact bear the weight of man and lead him in a forward-moving direction. Such a re-evaluation in other areas of morality might disclose that other stepping-stones hitherto considered treacherous can bear some weight, or the weight of some individuals. It will also tend to shift this directional approach to morality from one where a detailed map is provided to one where a destination and a compass will prove more helpful and more realistic for individuals, at least in default of a built-in sense of direction or as a confirmation of that gift of the Spirit.

Once one systematically allows, then, for error in good faith and even more for a variety of moral perceptions of reality by individuals, the road-map view of morality is seen as being of only limited value. An alternative view which exists in the moral tradition—particularly of Aquinas—but which the moral teaching of the Church or of subsequent theologians has found less congenial, approaches morality from within the subject rather than presenting it to him from outside. It is a view of the moral development of the individual which is more organic than mechanical, and more cumulative than successive in its approach, exploiting now the theme and the language of self-realization. Rather than view the moral agent like an arrow in flight and on course towards the centre of the target, it considers him more in terms of an acorn growing into an oak tree, and, what is more, of this acorn growing into a particular oak tree. For this way of viewing the moral life proceeds by a capitalizing of personal resources, or in more Aristotelian terms, by the fulfilment of one's human potentialities towards happiness, or Aquinas's beatitude. Moral acts are not steps. They are now stages of personal growth, more like rings in a tree. The emphasis moves away from the series of more of less connected acts and objective stepping-stones along which one must move to the agent performing the acts or, to be more accurate, to the person who is becoming more, or less, himself in and through his actions. Morality is ultimately in this view not about actions but about the acting subject.

It is this approach, of course, which makes more sense of the whole approach to morality by way of the moral virtues, which are not to be seen simply as moral skills enabling one the more easily to follow the moral road-map, and choose and perform the right actions. They are perfections and liberations of the person, who now not only acts virtuously, but actually is, or is becoming, really judicious, fair-minded, self-controlled, and courageous. It is this way of viewing morality, also, which makes more sense of those areas where objectivity and subjectivity appear to be in conflict or contradiction—actions which another tradition has considered bad in themselves, or in their 'object', but which the subject may honestly not see in that light. In the oak tree approach such actions can be absorbed by the subject as real stages of internal growth if the subject genuinely considers them to be such. And the basic reason for this appears to be the fact that underlying all man's moral decisions for action is the basic disposition, or fundamental option, by the subject of himself towards what he perceives as good and therefore, at least implicitly, towards objective good, or God.

We may recall how it was Pope Pius XII who linked the moral man to the Church by an unconscious or implicit desire contained within the good dispositions of the soul.[123] It was also he who described how 'the grandeur of the human act consists precisely in its transcending the very moment when it is performed, to commit the whole orientation of one's life, to lead it to adopt a stance in relation to the absolute'.[124] If that be true, then it appears even more the case that the grandeur of the human subject consists in his being able in and through such a single act to transcend the co-ordinates of space and time and even the 'objective' matter of the act to commit himself in a radical personal choice for or against God, and to grow or diminish in that option throughout life.[125]

An obvious objection, of course, to such an approach which attempts to do more justice to subjectivity, is that it places too much credence in the moral resources of the individual and in the last resort discounts the amount of objective wrong and harm which the individual may perpetrate in his singleminded pursuit of self-fulfilment. The answer to such serious objections must lie,

---

[123] *Supra*, p. 200.

[124] 'La grandeur de l'acte humain consiste précisément à dépasser le moment même où il se pose pour engager toute l'orientation d'une vie, pour l'amener à prendre position vis-à-vis de l'absolu', *AAS* 48 (1956), p. 470.

[125] Cf. J. Fuchs, *Human Values and Christian Morality* (Dublin, 1970), ch. 4, 'Basic Freedom and Morality', pp. 92–111. The theme of the 'fundamental option' is discussed by the Sacred Congregation for the Doctrine of the Faith in its 1975 *Declaration on certain questions concerning sexual ethics*, no. 10; *AAS* 68 (1976), pp. 88–90; and also by Pope John Paul II in his 1984 exhortation *Reconciliatio et Paenitentia*, CTS (London, 1984), pp. 63–4; *AAS* 77 (1985), p. 223.

however, in considering the individual not just as a moral agent but as a moral subject, and a subject within a kingdom of subjects. It is this stress on the individual as reflecting subject, and not just as agent in danger of being a moral automaton, which enables him to contribute to the moral experience and collective wisdom of the Christian community, and at the same time requires him to respect the experience and wisdom of other individuals in the community, as well as of the community as a whole. It is this view of the individual as moral and reflecting subject which also is more Johannine than Matthaean, as we have suggested, and which is required as a balance, if not a corrective, to the comparatively recent distinction within the community of Christ's disciples between the 'teaching' Church and the 'learning' Church which may be seen as a logical and historical outcome of stressing the Matthaean theology of teaching authority.[126] As a complete description of the Church's Christian moral awareness the distinction is quite inadequate in its implication that the 'teaching' Church has nothing to learn from the 'learning' Church, and that the latter has nothing to teach the former. The reality is that the Spirit of truth is imparted to the entire Church logically prior to being conferred on any group or individual within the Church, and that no one in the Church possesses a monopoly of the Spirit of Christ who is, in the lovely medieval phrase, Christ's dowry to his bride.

The Johannine role of the Spirit as internal teacher of all the faithful (and, indeed, of all men) was one from which the Catholic Church was to move away in the aftermath of the Reformation and the controversy over 'private judgement'. It has not been wholly lost, however, and most recently traces of it are to be found in the statement of Pope Paul VI about the role of the Spirit in the exercise of moral teaching within the Church. In his encyclical on contraception the Pope observed that 'while the Holy Spirit of God assists the *Magisterium* as it puts forward correct teaching, he is internally enlightening the hearts of the faithful and is inviting them to give their assent' to that teaching.[127] What is stressed here is, as had become customary, a purely receptive and passive role for the faithful under the interior guidance of the Spirit; although it might

---

[126] *Supra*, p. 174.

[127] The clergy are to propound the encyclical's teaching with confidence, 'pro certo habentes, Sanctum Dei Spiritum, dum adest Magisterio rectam proferenti doctrinam, intus corda fidelium illustrare eosque ad assentiendum invitare', *Humanae Vitae*, no. 29; *AAS* 60 (1968), p. 502.

be observed that, to the extent that the faithful are not found to give their assent to a particular piece of moral teaching by the *Magisterium*, to that extent the force of the teaching may be open to question. But if to this acknowledgement of the interior role of the Spirit be added the more positive and active characteristics which we have noted in the teaching of Pius XI and the Second Vatican Council,[128] then more justice is done to the individual believer as moral subject, and more warrant is given to his or her Christian experience and perception of moral reality.

What such respect for the moral subject also brings out is a further consideration on the question of teaching authority which occupied our previous chapter, in which we considered not only the authority of the Church's hierarchical magisterial activity but also the inherent authority of the theologian within the Church. To these must now be added, for a full picture of the Spirit's work in and on his Church, at least one other authority, that of Christian personal experience. This is the unique contribution of the participant rather than the spectator, the voyager and the eye-witness rather than the armchair traveller, the one who 'speaks from experience', and with the authority of a direct, immediate connection with events. Not, of course, that such experiential authority is necessarily self-authenticating, far less infallible. It needs probing and testing, as do other forms of authority. But it cannot be substituted for in its contribution to the total harmony of diverse authorities which together go to make up the human expression of the fundamental authority of the Spirit of Christ within his Church.[129]

To this question of a rounded picture of Christian morality which will do more justice to subjectivity within the community there must, of course, be added the question of moral communication between subjects, and between God and his Church, and of how that communication is expressed and mediated. In the making of moral theology the outstanding medium and expression of moral communication has been in terms of law, whether eternal, natural, divine, positive, canon, or civil law. Accordingly, our next chapter will turn to consider the role of law and the language of law in Christian morality.

[128] *Supra*, nn. 97–9.
[129] Cf. ' "The Church of the Holy Spirit" in Aquinas', in Mahoney, *Seeking the Spirit.*

6

THE LANGUAGE OF LAW

Any consideration of Christian morality and of the making of moral theology must acknowledge that the idea and the connotations of law are all-pervading and appear all but indispensable to the subject. Our normative documents of the Bible are permeated with the Hebrew theme of *Torah*, translated as *nomos* and *lex*. The Ten Commandments are a central feature of the Mosaic treaty struck by God with his people, Israel, as is the Johannine 'new commandment' of the New Covenant. And the Matthaean portrayal of Jesus shows him as carefully respecting and 'perfecting' the Law, as the new Moses of God's new people.

The prophets had promised a 'new law', not now engraved on stone tablets but to be written on men's hearts. From Paul, the rabbi, and from Graeco-Roman philosophy and jurisprudence the Fathers and the Scholastics were to develop the creational doctrine of a 'law of nature' which binds all men in its precepts, and which is confirmed and supplemented by the divine moral law revealed in Scripture. Human societies, as well as the 'perfect society' of the visible Church,[1] are viewed as regulating a whole variety of human activities by positive law and are regarded as aiming to express the general laws of human nature in particular determinations which will vary as seems appropriate to times, people, and places.

Behind all this deployment of law in its many manifestations and

---

[1] What had been the 'two cities' of Augustine, the city of God and the city of men, gave a spur to Counter-Reformation theologians such as Bellarmine, and to the papacy opposed to the political dissolution of the nineteenth century, to develop a theology of the Roman Catholic Church as a distinct society fully self-sufficient to achieve its own purposes. As Pope Leo XIII explained, 'Haec societas, quamvis ex hominibus constet, non secus ac civilis communitas, tamen propter finem sibi constitutum atque instrumenta, quibus ad finem contendit, supernaturalis est et spiritualis: atque ideo distinguitur ac differt a societate civili: et, quod plurimum interest, societas est genere et iure perfecta, cum adiumenta ad incolumitatem actionemque suam necessaria voluntate beneficioque Conditoris sui, omnia in se per se ipsa possideat. Sicut finis, quo tendit Ecclesia, longe nobilissima est, ita eius potestas est omnium praestantissima, neque imperio civili potest haberi inferior aut eidem esse ullo modo obnoxia', *DS* 3167.

excursions into human life there exists, as its source and archetype, the 'eternal law' of God, which Augustine defined as 'the divine reason or the will of God commanding the natural order to be preserved and forbidding its disruption'.[2] The purpose of this chapter of our study is to consider how the whole theme and idea of law in morality have been understood in the making of moral theology and to offer some observations on the language of law. For this purpose a convenient starting-point can be found in Augustine's reference to the eternal law as 'the divine reason or the will of God'.

Morality as Law: Voluntarism

In Augustine's definition of eternal law there are two major elements, God's reason and God's will. And the eternal law, as it works out in history, is viewed as the expression of God's intellect and will at work conjointly. It is possible, however, to stress one of these two factors, not to the complete exclusion of the other, but almost inevitably to the detriment of the other. And one of the major tendencies in the historical working out of moral theology has been to place a great emphasis on morality as the fulfilling of God's will as he legislates for his creatures. Such stress on the will of God may go hand in hand with a view of man himself which gives a priority to his will over his power of reasoning, and which may find expression in a priority of love over contemplation. Of this predilection we can see signs in Augustine and in his influence on succeeding centuries. It emerges strongly in Abelard with his view of morality as strongly subjective and as determined above all, not by how one perceives reality, but by how one freely chooses to direct one's activities in relation to God and by how God himself through his laws wills us to behave. It was to reappear, firmly and increasingly strongly, in the Franciscan reaction to Aquinas and his more intellectual approach and to culminate in the work of William of Occam and nominalism. In this approach morality is to be expressed entirely in terms of God's law, behind which the major force is his sovereignly free will according to which he need not, absolutely speaking, have decreed thus and thus for men, but which he has simply chosen to express in this manner in this particular

[2] Cf. *supra*, p. 74.

dispensation of his divine providence. As Gabriel Biel, one of the most influential of the late medieval nominalists, explained, 'all justness and rightness of the rational creature consists in its conformity to the will of God . . . . Therefore our justice consists in our will, which is weak and not right in itself, being conformed to the rule of the divine will, which is essentially right.'[3]

We can observe this stress on the role of will, or voluntarism, pervading the whole thought of the highly influential Spanish Jesuit theologian, Francisco Suarez, whose work in the sixteenth and seventeenth centuries was to play a dominant part in determining the later course of moral theology, and particularly in its stress on the will. As Vereecke points out, in the theology of Suarez we find a new emphasis on God as personal, but we also find a strong emphasis on his will as expressed in all his laws. For Suarez, 'the supreme norm of rightness of action is the law. Thereby the whole of law is introduced into moral theology, since all laws derive from divine authority if they are authentic'.[4] And behind all this deployment of laws as expressive of the radical voluntarism of Suarez lies his basic understanding of law, whether God's or man's, as an expression of the will. He defines law as 'the act of a just and right will, by which a superior wills to oblige an inferior to do this or that'. And he explains that in substance a law is 'an order proceeding from the will of a competent party which is able to impose obligation'.[5]

---

[3] Quoted in H. E. Oberman, *The Harvest of Medieval Theology* (Cambridge, Mass., 1963). p. 104, n. 48. On the Franciscan move towards voluntarism F. C. Copleston concludes, 'It would seem, then, that Scotus occupies a position midway, if one may so put it, between St Thomas and Occam. He agrees with the former that there are moral principles which are unalterable and he does not teach that the entire moral law depends on the arbitrary decision of God's will. On the other hand, he attributed a much greater degree of prominence to the divine will in the determination of the moral order than St Thomas had done, and he appears to have held that obligation, at least in regard to certain commandments, depends on that will as distinct from the divine intellect. While, then, if we look at Scotus's philosophy by itself, we must allow that his moral doctrine is not that of arbitrary divine authoritarianism, we must also allow, if we look at the historical development of thought, that his moral doctrine helped to prepare the way for that of Occam, in whose eyes the moral law, including the whole decalogue, is the arbitrary creation of the divine will', *A History of Philosophy*, vol. ii (London, 1950), p. 550.

[4] Vereecke, ii, p. 107.

[5] In his treatise *De Legibus et Legislatore Deo* (*Opera Omnia*, ed. Berton (Paris, 1856), vol. v), Suarez follows Aquinas (*STh* 1a 2ae, qq. 90–109) and his expositors (ibid., p. XI), but frequently develops his own positions. Thus, in discussing the nature of law and the parts played in it by the mind and the will of the lawmaker, he

It is this view of morality as expressed predominantly in terms of law and the centrality of the will, both God's and man's, which lies at the centre of the whole controversy surrounding probabilism which we have already considered.[6] For Suarez, and indeed for the medievals contemplating the round assertion of Paul that 'what does not proceed from conviction is sin' (Rom. 14: 23), the problem of the doubtful conscience was a seriously practical one. And the Spanish moralists who developed the theory of probabilism were looking to solve a variety of moral dilemmas by the elaboration of one moral principle which could confer both clarity and peace of soul. Given their view of morality as essentially compliance with laws of various kinds, and given also their view of law as primarily the expression of the will of the lawmaker to oblige his subjects to certain types of behaviour, it was natural enough that they should view moral dilemmas as problems of doubt, either doubt about the law itself, as to its meaning or extent, or doubt of fact, as to whether this particular situation or case was one actually covered by a particular law. Once a moral problem had been so defined it was possible to invoke the formal principle of jurisprudence which underpinned the whole age of probabilism, *lex dubia non obligat*, 'a law which is doubtful is not binding'. Hence, in any situation in which a clear doubt existed (or could be made to

first exposes the view of Aquinas, Cajetan, and other Thomists that it is an act of the intellect (Book I, cap. 6, 1–7; pp. 17–18), and then the view of John Major, Occam, Bonaventure, and Scotus, that it is an act of the will (ibid., 8–19; pp. 18–21), to reach his own conclusion that law in the lawmaker 'esse actum voluntatis iustae et rectae, quo superior vult inferiorem obligare ad hoc vel illud faciendum' (24; p. 22). It is this which leads Suarez (cap. 12, 4; p. 54) to prefer Aquinas's reference to law as 'commune praeceptum' (so capitalizing on his authority from *STh* 1a 2ae, q. 96, a. 1 ad 2) to the definition to which Thomas himself had carefully argued (ibid., q. 90, a. 4), 'et sic ex quattuor praedictis potest colligi definitio legis, quae nihil est aliud quam quaedam rationis ordinatio ad bonum commune ab eo qui curam communitatis habet promulgata'. Proceeding to consider the purpose of law, Suarez claims to agree with Aquinas that this is 'to make men good'. But whereas the latter explains this in terms of the peculiarity of the law being to induce subjects to their own peculiar virtue ('manifestum est quod hoc sit proprium legis, inducere subiectos ad propriam ipsorum virtutem', ibid., q. 92, a. 1), Suarez is of the opinion that the main efficacy of the law in making men good is its obligatory force: 'Praecipua efficacia legis ad faciendos homines bonos est eius obligatio, quae videtur esse maxime intrinsecus effectus eius', cap. 14, 1; p. 56. Thus he concludes 'ex dictis de substantia legis: est enim imperium procedens a voluntate efficaci obligandi eius qui potestatem habet', ibid., 3; p. 57. Cf. Book VI, chap. 8, 7 (vol. vi, p. 37): 'verba enim legis secundum se tantum sunt ad ostendendam voluntatem legislatoris tanquam signum expressum eius'.

[6] Cf. *supra*, pp. 135–8.

exist) either about the wording or import of the law in question or about its applicability to the facts of the case the law, whether divine revealed law or natural law, ecclesiastical law or civil law, lost its binding force on men's consciences and was to be considered as not obligatory. Hence also the preoccupation with analysis of the precise wording and understanding of the terms of these legal 'precepts' which was to remain such a central feature of casuistry.

In the course of the controversy surrounding probabilism, however, its major axiom—that a doubtful law does not oblige—came itself under scrutiny. Why should a doubtful law *ipso facto* have no claim upon men's consciences? The answer to this question was a relatively simple one for thinkers such as Suarez and Vasquez who devoted much of their expertise to considering the morality of expeditions of conquest in the East and in the New World. It was to be found in the field of property law and in the establishment of titles to ownership. 'In a case of doubt the one in possession has the better case'; or possession is nine points of the law. If, then, there is any doubt about which has a claim to ownership or dominion over man's conscience and behaviour, a law coming to man from outside, or his innate freedom of choice and action, clearly on the basis of this legal maxim personal freedom is in possession and the law has no *locus standi*.[7]

With this stress on individual moral freedom as primary, and on morality as law requiring firm justification to encroach on that freedom, Suarez, Vasquez, and others held a view of freedom which was thoroughly Occamist in character, that human freedom is the great undetermined, and the will is totally spontaneous to act or not to act.[8] For Occam, man's greatness lies in his freedom as the

---

[7] On *lex dubia*, cf. Angelini and Valsecchi, p. 116. On the deeper principle, cf. Suarez, Treatise on Goodness and Badness of Human Acts, Disputatio 12 (on conscience), sec. 5, 7 (*Opera*, vol. iv, p. 448), 'Circa dubium iuris est advertendum variis modis posse contingere: primo, quia simpliciter dubitatur de tota lege quoad exercitium: id est, an lata sit, necne. Et tunc generalis regula est non obligare: ratio peti potest ex illo principio, quod in dubiis melior est conditio possidentis; homo autem continet libertatem suam'. Cf. *De Legibus*, Book VI, chap. 8, 10 (*Opera*, vol. vi, p. 38), 'ergo nunquam licet cum illo dubio agere contra verba legis, quia operari cum conscientia practice dubia semper est malum. Denique tunc lex possidet ius suum, et in aliis melior est conditio possidentis'; ibid., chap. 8, 11 (p. 38), 'Item in casu dubio praesumptio est pro lege, quia verba eius per se sufficiunt ad obligationem, unde ad minimum se habet tanquam possidens in casu dubio cuius melior est conditio.' 'Cet usage du "principe de possession" sera bientôt l'un des traits caractéristiques du probabilisme', Deman, *DTC*, XIII, col. 475.

[8] Vereecke, iii, pp. 49–50.

created image of the supremely unfettered God and law is then seen
as something external to man's will and as potentially threatening
to invade and conquer that will. For the Spanish theologians,
freedom is absolute indeterminism, and so, with this major stress
on subjectivity, 'conscience is analysed in its internal coherence
without reference to anything outside itself. The result is a
continual tension between objectivism and subjectivism, intrinsicism
and extrinsicism, between an ethics of intention and an ethics of
law'.[9] Conscience thus becomes the cockpit where one's freedom
and another's law face each other as antagonists, and where it is the
individual who judges whether or not his freedom must yield to
law.

It was inevitable, of course, that one's theological view of man
since the Fall would influence and colour one's attitude to the
importance or preference to be attributed to the freedom of the
individual. Indicative of this was the Jesuit stress on human
freedom within the mysterious action of God's grace over against
the Bañezian and Dominican preference for divine physical pre-
motion to safeguard God's initiative. It was also the Jesuit spirit of
renaissance and humanist optimism about the considerable natural
resources still available to man even after the original sin which
evoked continual charges of Pelagianism, and which underlay their
clear preference as a body for probabilism.[10] Equally, the Jansenist
fury at probabilism, and not just at laxism, can be seen as the
reaction of an extreme Augustinism in the conviction that all that
man can produce from his own resources is sinful pride and a
spurious autonomy and self-sufficiency. To assert that man in his
puny freedom has claims over conscience which can be superior to
the claims of the laws of the divine majesty could only be, in such a
view, sheer blasphemy.

The Theory of Purely Penal Law

Alongside the basing of probabilism on morality conceived as law
and on the voluntaristic view of law, it is instructive to consider
another important instance of the voluntarist current in moral
theology as the science addressed itself to the further question
whether in fact all laws, including civil laws, do morally oblige and

---

[9] Ibid., p. 52.   [10] Cf. *supra*, pp. 141–2.

bind their subjects in conscience. The widespread social problems which were to raise that question as a matter of principle and of practical urgency have been most usefully treated by the Australian Jesuit moralist, Daniel, in his study of the 'purely penal law' theory in the Spanish theologians from Vitoria to Suarez. As he explains, 'the anonymous current of purely penal law theory' arose from social and legal conditions in sixteenth century Spain. 'In certain areas of positive law, where all Catholics were agreed that the state might make laws binding in conscience, the belief was prevalent that the presence of a penalty relieved the subject of obligation in conscience. Of these perhaps the most common were laws regulating the use of the fruits of nature, such as wood, pasture, or game, sumptuary laws controlling the luxurious habits of the nobility or would-be nobility, regulations of trade to control the flow of money or produce from the Kingdom, and taxation laws'.[11]

One instance of this view was to be seen as arising from the national policy of maximizing the raising of sheep and wool export by widespread deforestation, which also resulted in a scarcity of wood for building and fuel and, as a consequence, led to severe and absolute laws forbidding the taking of wood even from common-land. 'Naturally the people concluded that these laws did not oblige them in conscience, and it was left to the theologians to find a way out of the situation for them.'[12] Another major social problem of the age was that arising from the imposition of sales taxes of up to more than ten per cent on all transfer of property or goods, with the aim of swelling the royal exchequer to finance wars and engage in other kingly pursuits, as well as of filling the pockets of the middlemen to whom the collecting of taxes was farmed out.[13] The moral questions raised by these wood laws and tax laws appeared to be those of stealing or fraud, the duty of restitution, and payment of the fine imposed on those unfortunates who were apprehended. Some theologians were to see underlying such laws fundamental issues about ownership, public property, and the common good as providing the basis of just laws.[14] Others, however, were reluctant to consider declaring that certain royal laws were simply unjust,

---

[11] W. Daniel, *The Purely Penal Law Theory in the Spanish Theologians from Vitoria to Suarez* (Rome, 1968), p. 130.

[12] Ibid., p. 132.

[13] Ibid., pp. 139–40.

[14] Ibid., pp. 134–8, 144–6, 150–8.

and rather than discuss justice they preferred to speculate on obedience.[15] The line of argument which was to prevail was that the lawmaker did not intend that the laws themselves should oblige in conscience, but only payment of the penalties imposed for their infringement, as an alternative source of revenue. Thus, not without objections, the view was 'commonly taught by preachers and confessors, and adopted by a grateful laity, that tax laws do not oblige in conscience to payment or restitution because they are penal', that is, carry a penalty.[16]

The moral theory of the 'purely penal law' which was thus elaborated and perfected, especially by Suarez, attempted to explain and justify in theological terms the common persuasion that some of society's laws could not possibly bind subjects in conscience. In its development the theory found considerable encouragement in the Rules of various religious Orders which did not themselves oblige under pain of sin but nevertheless could carry a penalty for infringement, as also in the various ecclesiastical disqualifications, or 'irregularities', which could be incurred by actions which were not in themselves wrong or forbidden.[17] The popularity of the theory was to last into the twentieth century, with further elaboration of the reasons justifying it.[18] What lay at its base initially was the considerable hardship involved in the observance of some laws of society coupled with a prevailing respect for the authority of the lawmaker in society. The dilemma was to be resolved by recourse to a theory based on divining the real intention of the lawmaker in formulating his laws, and on concluding that it was his will that some laws did not in themselves bind in conscience, but only payment of the fine or penalty upon apprehension and conviction.

Epicheia

Concentration on the intention and the will of the lawmaker, which was formalized in the theory of purely penal laws, also underlies the

[15] Ibid., pp. 143, 147.
[16] Ibid., p. 144.
[17] Ibid., pp. 9–37.
[18] Cf. H. Davis, *op. cit*, vol. i, pp. 144–8; M. Zalba, *Theologiae Moralis Compendium* (Madrid, 1958), vol. i, pp. 255–62. The theory of purely penal law received its long overdue *congé* from moral theology in the teaching of the Second Vatican Council on the need for Christians to avoid an individualistic morality in favour of the social virtues, *Gaudium et spes*, no. 30; *AAS* 58 (1966), pp. 1049–50.

highly influential Suarezian doctrine of *epicheia* in the observance of laws, which in turn further reinforces the legal approach to morality in its voluntarist expression. The problem which was here addressed was that of coping with difficult or unforeseen situations which a particular human law did not appear to have envisaged. In such circumstances Suarez and those who followed him saw the need for interpretation of the law in question, and they expressed this in terms of understanding or of attempting to construct what was, or would be, the mind and the will of the person who had framed the legislation in the first place. For Suarez, then, the process by which this mental exercise takes place, termed *epicheia*, is a justification for not obeying the literal sense of the law based on 'the presumed intention and equity of the legislator'. It is a matter of 'conjecturing' his mind.[19] The stress on the lawmaker is evident in the explanation of a modern commentator who writes, '*Epieikeia* is not strictly an interpretation of law, nor is it presumed dispensation from it, but it is rather the interpretation of the mind and will of him who made the law. It is therefore not a violation of law.'[20]

In this Suarezian approach we can again note the respect for authority which was evident in the theory of purely penal law, and it appears coupled with an element of presumed benignity on the part of authority. The idea of such benign consideration, akin to kindness or even indulgence in certain conjectural situations, may be considered as providing a clue to a whole mental attitude to law in general which is not just Suarezian or nominalist or even specifically Christian. A reawakening of interest in the subject of *epicheia* as it has figured in moral theology under the influence of Suarez has shown that it has strong affinities with a Platonic approach to law and its apparent exceptions.[21]

---

[19] 'Alia differentia est, quod in lege positiva, quando interpretatio fit per epiikiam, non fit circa actum prohibitum per legem nec circa obscuritatem verborum eius. sed potius supponitur illum esse actum prohibitum secundum speciem suam, et comprehendi sub verbis legis spectatis in sua proprietate: tota vero interpretatio et coniectura fit circa intentionem legislatoris, quod non fuerit mens eius comprehendere talem casum, seu actum illum pro tali opportunitate. Et haec est propria epiikia quae dicitur emendatio legis, utique secundum speciem verborum, iustificando illam (ut sic dicam) per intentionem et aequitatem praesumptam legislatoris', *De Legibus*, Book II, ch.16, 13 (*Opera*, vol. v, p. 158).

[20] Davis, op. cit., i, p. 188.

[21] In what follows use is made of the author's 'Obedience: Consent or Conformity?', Supplement no. 6 (May, 1968) to *The Way*, pp. 5–19. Cf. also, E. Hamel, 'Fontes graeci doctrinae de epikeia', *Periodica* 53 (1964), pp. 169–185; 'L'usage de l'épikie', *Studia Moralia*, vol. iii (Rome, 1965), pp. 48–81.

Plato is generally regarded as having viewed the world in which we live as a pale and deficient imitation of an ideal world, and this way of considering earthly reality influenced his views on the nature and function of laws. In some of his works he realized that written laws were too universal in their formulation to cover all possible contingencies and eventualities, and he considered that it was much better to have a community governed by a wise individual superior to all written laws who would personally legislate for each individual situation as it arose. In the absence of such a benevolent dictator and as the best alternative he was of the view that absolute obedience should be required to the written laws of society.[22] In his later works, however, Plato had come to see that the best society in practice was one based on positive legislation,

[22] On the Platonic doctrine of forms, cf. Copleston, op. cit., vol. i, pp. 163 ff., esp. pp. 175–7, 179, 201. '[Plato] was hostile to life and this world, only in so far as they are disordered and fragmentary, out of harmony with or not expressing what he believed to be stable realities and stable norms of surpassing value and universal significance', ibid., p. 205. In *The Statesman* Plato develops his famous and influential political argument that the ideal form of government is to be found in a small group or an individual legislating wisely for each individual case, and that written, and necessarily general, laws are a poor substitute. Given such a body of legislation, however, it is essential for the state that the laws be always observed, whatever the circumstances. 'It is clear that lawmaking belongs to the science of kingship; but the best thing is not that the laws be in power, but that the man who is wise and of kingly nature be ruler .... Because law could never, by determining exactly what is noblest and most just for one and all, enjoin upon them that which is best; for the differences of men and of actions and the fact that nothing, I may say, in human life is ever at rest, forbid any science whatsoever to promulgate any simple rule for everything and for all time .... But we see that law aims at pretty nearly this very thing, like a stubborn and ignorant man who allows no one to do anything contrary to his command, or even to ask a question, not even if something new occurs to some one, which is better than the rule he has himself ordained .... And so we must believe that the lawmaker who is to watch over the herds and maintain justice and the obligation of contracts, will never be able by making laws for all collectively, to provide exactly that which is proper for each individual .... But he will, I fancy, legislate for the majority and in a general way only roughly for individuals, whether he issues written laws or his enactments follow the unwritten traditional customs .... Assuming that the form of government we have described is the only right form, don't you see that the other forms must employ its written laws if they are to be preserved by doing that which is approved of nowadays, although it is not perfectly right ... that no citizen shall dare to do anything contrary to the laws, and that he who does shall be punished by death and the most extreme penalties. And this is perfectly right and good as a second choice, as soon as you depart from the first form of which we were just speaking .... Therefore the next best course for those who make laws or written rules about anything whatsoever is to prohibit any violation of them whatsoever, either by one person or by a greater number .... Such states, then, it seems, if they are to imitate well, so far as possible that true form of government—by a single ruler who rules with science—

since only thus could society be protected against the excesses and abuses of a bad ruler. But it was even more important in such a situation that the laws be observed by all, including the ruler. In the concrete, of course, allowance must be made for the frailty and weakness of men. But any weakening or diminution of the law must be considered a concession and an indulgence, a departure from the perfect and the ideal, and a wounding of the law which sapped its strength. It would be much to be preferred that all men without distinction observe the law with equal fidelity, and it was to be regretted if not all were capable of doing so.[23]

must never do anything in contravention of their existing written laws and ancestral customs', 294a–300c; Loeb trans., pp. 133–55. Cf. Copleston, op. cit., pp. 233–4. As Hamel, 'Fontes', p. 175, crisply sums up, 'omnipotentia regis, ut solutio idealis, omnipotentia legis, ut solutio secundaria practica'.

[23] 'The selection of officials that is thus made will form a mean between a monarchic constitution and a democratic; and midway between these our constitution should always stand . . . . There is an old and true saying that "equality produces amity", which is right well and fitly spoken; but what the equality is which is capable of doing this is a very troublesome question, since it is very far from being clear. For there are two kinds of equality which, though identical in name, are often almost opposites in their practical results. The one of these any State or lawgiver is competent to apply in the assignment of honours . . . by simply applying the lot to give even results in the distribution; but the truest and best form of equality is not an easy thing for everyone to discern . . . for it dispenses more to the greater and less to the smaller, giving due measure to each according to nature . . . . Indeed, it is precisely this which constitutes for us "political justice", which is the object we must strive for . . . . And whoever founds a State elsewhere at any time must make this same subject the aim of his legislation,—not the advantage of a few tyrants, or of one, or of some form of democracy, but justice always; and this consists in what we have just stated, namely, the natural equality given on each occasion to things unequal. None the less, it is necessary for every State at times to employ even this equality in a modified degree, if it is to avoid involving itself in intestine discord, in one section or another,—for the reasonable and considerate (τὸ γὰρ ἐπιεικὲς καὶ ξύγγνωμον), wherever employed, is an infringement of the perfect and exact, as being contrary to strict justice; for the same reason it is necessary to make use also of the equality of the lot, on account of the discontent of the masses, and in doing so to pray, calling upon God and Good Luck to guide for them the lot aright towards the highest justice (πρὸς τὸ δικαιότατον). Thus it is that necessity compels us to employ both forms of equality; but that form, which needs good luck, we should employ as seldom as possible. The State which means to survive must necessarily act thus, my friends, for the reasons we have stated. For just as a ship when sailing on the sea requires continual watchfulness, both by night and day, so likewise a State, when it lives amidst the surge of surrounding States and is in danger of being entrapped by all sorts of plots, requires to have officers . . . above all, in view of the manifold innovations that are wont to occur constantly in States, to prevent if possible their occurrence, and in case they do occur, to ensure that the State may perceive and remedy the occurrence as quickly as possible', *Laws*, Book 6, 756e–758d; Loeb trans., vol. i, pp. 411–7.

We can thus see how Plato's view of the individual as an imperfect realization of the universal and the ideal led him to regard departures from the written laws of society as a lowering of ideals and as a necessary but undesirable exercise of benignity and clemency. We can see also in Suarez and the tradition following him a similar view of the exceptional case as something which calls for the presumed benignity or human clemency of the lawmaker. On such occasions the legislator could, strictly speaking, demand that his law be observed, but in the circumstances one judges that such would not be his will.[24] There is in the tradition more than a hint of a grudging and suspicious concession to human weakness, an undesirable falling away from the norm and a need to justify such a decline from observance of the law in terms of physical or moral impossibility, or of human frailty and forgiveness.

The Rational Basis of Law

Underlying the three historical developments which we have been considering, the controversy over probabilism, the theory of purely penal law, and the Suarezian doctrine of *epicheia*, there is to be found a preoccupation with law couched in voluntarist terms, giving a preponderant importance to the will and to the wishes of the lawmaker which has profoundly influenced the whole course and conduct of moral theology until comparatively recent times. Some shift in approach, however, may be beginning to take place which can be briefly characterized as a reassertion of reason and of the particular, reminiscent of the approach, not now of Plato, but of his pupil, Aristotle.

Aristotle shared with his master the view that written laws are too universal in their formulation and scope to cover all possible contingencies and eventualities, and he explained that any lawmaker must confine himself only to what happens in the great majority of cases and legislate for them. But Aristotle differs radically from Plato in his view of exceptional cases and emergencies. For Plato the exception is a deviation and a deficiency, due

---

[24] 'Chez Suarez, c'est la personne du législateur, sa *mens*, son vouloir surtout, qui domine. Il s'agit moins de réaliser la justice et d'assurer le bien commun, que d'agir *ad mentem legislatoris*. La fonction de l'autorité n'est pas tant d'organiser le bien commun au nom de tous, que de diriger les sujets, en leur imposant des lois, en liant leur conscience dans la mesure où c'est nécessaire,' Hamel, 'L'usage', p. 66.

to the imperfect way in which worldly reality embodies and represents the ideal, whereas for Aristotle the exception, far from weakening the law, actually improves and corrects it. For Aristotle it is the law itself which is inherently weak and imperfect, precisely because it is universal and general in its formulations. Worldly reality is too rich and varied to be comprehended by a general law, with the result that on occasion the general law has to be corrected and improved in order to bring it into line with real life. This correction and improvement of the law in a minority of cases is done simply by the individual's ignoring what the law says, and by his contravening the letter of the law in order to observe the spirit and above all the true purpose of the law.[25]

Such an Aristotelian correction and improvement of the law in

---

[25] The key section in Aristotle is Book 6, ch. 10, of his *Nicomachean Ethics*, Loeb trans., pp. 313–7. 'We have next to speak of Equity and the equitable (ἐπιειϰείας ϰαὶ τοῦ ἐπιειϰοῦς), and of their relation to justice and to what is just respectively. For upon examination it appears that Justice and Equity are neither absolutely identical nor generically different . . . . For equity, while superior to one sort of justice is itself just: it is not superior to justice as being generically different from it. Justice and equity are therefore the same thing, and both are good, though equity is the better (ταὐτὸν ἄρα δίϰαιον ϰαὶ ἐπιειϰές, ϰαὶ ἀμφοῖν σπουδαίοιν ὄντοιν ϰρεῖττον τὸ ἐπιειϰές). The source of the difficulty is that equity, though just, is not legal justice, but a rectification of legal justice. The reason for this is that law is always a general statement, yet there are cases which it is not possible to cover in a general statement. In matters therefore where, while it is necessary to speak in general terms, it is not possible to do so correctly, the law takes into consideration the majority of cases, although it is not unaware of the error this involves. And this does not make it a wrong law; for the error is not in the law nor in the lawgiver, but in the nature of the case: the material of conduct is essentially irregular. When therefore the law lays down a general rule, and thereafter a case arises which is an exception to the rule, it is then right, where the lawgiver's pronouncement because of its absoluteness is defective and erroneous, to rectify the defect by deciding as the lawgiver would himself decide if he were present on the occasion, and would have enacted if he had been cognizant of the case in question. Hence, while the equitable is just, and is superior to one sort of justice, it is not superior to absolute justice, but only to the error due to its absolute statement. This is the essential nature of the equitable: it is a rectification of law where law is defective because of its generality. In fact this is the reason why things are not all determined by law: it is because there are some cases for which it is impossible to lay down a law, so that a special ordinance becomes necessary. For what is itself indefinite can only be measured by an indefinite standard, like the leaden rule used by Lesbian builders: just as that rule is not rigid but can be bent to the shape of the stone, so a special ordinance is made to fit the circumstances of the case.' Cf. Aristotle, *Rhetoric*, I, xiii, 13, τὸ γὰρ ἐπιειϰὲς δοϰεῖ δίϰαιον εἶναι, ἔστι δὲ ἐπιειϰὲς τὸ παρὰ τὸν γεγραμμένον νόμον δίϰαιον. *Epicheia* is justice regardless of the written law. The Greek 'παρὰ νόμον' will be invariably translated by the Scholastics as '*praeter legem*'.

some cases cannot in his view of reality be described as a weakening or a benign relaxation of the law. As Édouard Hamel observes, 'what defect there is, is to be found not in concrete reality, as Plato held, but in the positive law which is too abstract and indeterminate'.[26] It is true, of course, that the law has some purchase upon reality, but only in most instances and in the normal course of events. In other instances, however, it is for the individual, by exercising the virtue of *epicheia*, to correct the limitations inherent in the law, rather than the role of law being to condone the limitations of the individual. In this view of Aristotle we can see his concentration on worldly reality and on the inherent value of individual things, as contrasted with Plato's view of the individual and of this life as only shadows of the ideal.

The Aristotelian view of law and of the supplementing importance of *epicheia* was introduced into Christian philosophy when his *Nicomachean Ethics* was translated into Latin in 1245 by the bishop of Lincoln, Robert Grosseteste, and seized upon by the encyclopaedic Dominican scholar, Albert the Great, later bishop of Regensburg. For Albert the matter is summed up in his statement that 'one must respect the continual variability of the real, and not attempt to locate all human actions under one and the same universal rule. The real must not be bent to the rule; it is the rule which must be adapted to the real.'[27] The analogy of the 'rule', which both Aristotle and Albert use, is not, of course, that of a wooden rule, or rigid rod, which is snapped or broken on occasions, but that of a flexible measuring-line, or tape, which can follow both straight and undulating surfaces alike, and is sufficiently flexible to be able to do so without strain. It was this flexibility inherent in the law because of its universal and abstract character which both Aristotle and Albert recognized, as also did Albert's student and fellow-Dominican, Thomas Aquinas, when he wrote,

Laws are made for human actions. But such actions are individual and concrete situations, and they are infinitely variable. Hence, it is impossible to establish a ruling of law which is never defective. Lawmakers consider what normally happens and draw upon that to frame a law; but in certain cases the observance of that law would be against justice and against the common good which is what the law aims at .... In such cases ... it would be bad to follow the law laid down, but on the other hand it would

---

[26] 'Fontes', pp. 181–2.   [27] Quoted Hamel, 'L'Usage', p. 51.

be good to ignore the wording of the law in order to do what is called for by justice and the common benefit. And this is what *epicheia* is for.[28]

What Aquinas found so congenial about 'the virtue which Aristotle terms *epieikeia*' was that it was so eminently reasonable. To act according to this virtue is not to abandon justice, nor is it opposed to severity in applying a law, nor indeed is it to pass judgement on the law itself, or even to take it upon oneself to interpret the intention of the lawgiver in a matter considered doubtful. On the contrary, *epicheia* is itself an act of justice which in fact directs legal justice as 'a kind of higher rule of human acts' and which indicates when the wording of the law should not be followed in cases when to do so would be wrong.[29] The context of Aquinas's remarks here is that of the general theme of justice and its many parts and applications. Elsewhere in the *Summa*, in his formal treatise on law, he delivers the same judgement in terms which take us beyond *epicheia* as a form of justice to consider, in the light of exceptional cases, the whole purpose and function of law.

I have already explained that every law is directed to the common good of men. This is what gives it the force and character of law; and to the degree that it falls short of this it loses its power to oblige . . . . It often happens that to observe something is conducive to the common good in most instances, but extremely harmful to it in some instances. Since the lawmaker cannot foresee every single case he legislates for what occurs in most cases, directing his intention to the general benefit. So, if a case occurs where observing such a law would be detrimental to the common good, it is not to be observed. In a city under siege a law might decree that the city

---

[28] 'Quia humani actus, de quibus leges dantur, in singularibus contingentibus consistunt, quae infinitis modis variari possunt, non fuit possibile aliquam regulam legis institui quae in nullo casu deficeret: sed legislatores attendunt ad id quod in pluribus accidit, secundum hoc legem ferentes; quam tamen in aliquibus casibus servare est contra aequalitatem iustitiae, et contra bonum commune, quod lex intendit . . . . In his ergo et similibus casibus malum esset sequi legem positam: bonum autem est, praetermissis verbis legis, sequi id quod poscit iustitiae ratio et communis utilitas. Et ad hoc ordinatur epicheia', *STh* 2a 2ae, q. 120, a. 1,

[29] Cf. Aquinas, *Commentary on Aristotle's Ethics*, Bk 5, lect. 16. 'epieikes non deserit iustitiam simpliciter, sed iustum quod est lege determinatum. Nec etiam opponitur severitati, quae sequitur veritatem legis in quibus oportet: sequi autem verba legis in quibus non oportet, vitiosum est', *STh.*, ibid., ad 1. 'Ille de lege iudicat qui dicit eam non esse bene positam. Qui vero dicit verba legis non esse in hoc casu servanda, non iudicat de lege, sed de aliquo particulari negotio quod occurrit', ibid., ad 2. 'Nam legalis iustitia dirigitur secundum epieikeiam. Unde epieikeia est quasi superior regula humanorum actuum', ibid., a. 2.

gates remain closed, which is helpful to the common good on the whole. But if it happens that the enemy are pursuing some citizens whose services are necessary to saving the city, it would be ruinous to the city if the gates were not opened for them. Thus, in such a case the gates should be opened, contrary to the wording of the law, to preserve the common good as the lawmaker intends.[30]

Such behaviour would not be presuming to judge the law, but only the individual case; it would be following the intention of the lawmaker 'in a case where it is manifest from the obvious harm that the lawmaker intended otherwise'.[31]

It is to be noted, of course, that Aquinas here, as elsewhere, respects the authority and the intention of the lawmaker, and he would allow for personal initiative only in obvious emergencies and necessities, which are not subject to law.[32] Possibly his thought is more liberal by the time he comes to treat more systematically and more explicitly of *epicheia*,[33] but whenever he explains the correct attitude to be taken with respect to law in the event of exceptional circumstances, he makes it quite clear that the intention of the

---

[30] 'Sicut supra dictum est, omnis lex ordinatur ad communem hominum salutem, et intantum obtinet vim rationem legis; secundum vero quod ab hoc deficit, virtutem obligandi non habet . . . . Contingit autem multoties quod aliquid observari communi saluti est utile ut in pluribus, quod tamen in aliquibus casibus est maxime nocivum. Quia igitur legislator non potest omnes singulares casus intueri, proponit legem secundum ea quae in pluribus accidunt, ferens intentionem suam ad communem utilitatem. Unde si emergat casus in quo observatio talis legis sit damnosa communi saluti, non est observanda. Sicut si in civitate obsessa statuatur lex quod portae civitatis maneant clausae, hoc est utile communi saluti ut in pluribus: si tamen contingat casus quod hostes insequantur aliquos cives, per quos civitas conservatur, damnosissimum esset civitati nisi eis portae aperirentur: et ideo in tali casu esset portae aperiendae, contra verba legis, ut servaretur utilitas communis, quam legislator intendit', *STh* 1a 2ae, q. 96, a. 6.

[31] 'ille qui in casu necessitatis agit praeter verba legis, non iudicat de ipsa lege: sed iudicat de casu singulari, in quo videt verba legis observanda non esse', ibid., ad 1. 'Ille qui sequitur intentionem legislatoris, non interpretatur legem simpliciter; sed in casu in quo manifestum est per evidentiam nocumenti, legislatorem aliud intendisse', ibid., ad 2.

[32] 'Sed tamen hoc est considerandum, quod si observatio legis secundum verba non habeat subitum periculum, cui oportet statim occurri, non pertinet ad quemlibet ut interpretetur quid sit utile civitati et quid inutile: sed hoc solum pertinet ad principes, qui propter huiusmodi casus habent auctoritatem in legibus dispensandi. Si vere sit subitum periculum, non patiens tantam moram ut ad superiorem recurri possit, ipsa necessitas dispensationem habet annexam: quia necessitas non subditur legi', ibid., a. 6.

[33] Cf. *STh* 2a 2ae, q. 120, a. 1 ad 3, 'Interpretatio locum habet in dubiis, in quibus non licet, absque determinatione principis, a verbis legis recedere. Sed in manifestis non est opus interpretatione, sed executione.'

lawmaker himself must ever be to contribute to the general good and benefit of the community. Indeed, no law has power to oblige except to the degree that it does, or will, in fact preserve or contribute to the general good. And this is fully in accord with the famous definition of law given by Aquinas which stresses that it is pre-eminently an expression of reason, not of will. It is not concerned so much with orders as with order, with recognizing in reality, or introducing into reality, an order of events or of behaviour within an overall view to general utility and the benefit of all. In considering the essence of law, the first question which Aquinas raises for consideration is its connection with reason; and he argues that for the commands of a will to take on the character of law that will has itself to be regulated by reason, on pain of being an injustice rather than a law.[34] In essence, then, law is an act of the reason which establishes order for the benefit of the community.[35]

With this Thomistic rational view of law, whether human or divine, we are moving in quite a different intellectual world from that of Occam and nominalism, as also from that of Suarez and the more voluntarist attitude to morality. Suarez, to be sure, is not a pure voluntarist, recognizing as he does that 'the intellect has an important part to play in assessing the various courses open to the lawgiver, but the final act of choice is an act of the will, and the motive force of the law (as it originates in the lawgiver) belongs to the will. The will is the source of movement, not only for the person in whom it resides but also for others whom he is to command'.[36] On his side, Aquinas also acknowledged the important part played by the will, but as Daniel observes, comparing the Suarezian and Thomist approaches, 'in the former it is the will that moves the subject, person to person, and in the latter it is the intellect that lays down a rule of action that leads to an end, namely, the common good, which dominates the whole process, whether of lawmaking or of the fulfilment of the law by the subject'.[37]

---

[34] 'Circa legem autem in communi tria occurrunt consideranda: primo quidem, de essentia ipsius; . . . Circa primum quaeruntur quatuor. Primo: utrum lex sit aliquid rationis', *STh* 1a 2ae, q. 90, proem. 'Ex hoc enim quod aliquis vult finem, ratio imperat de his quae sunt ad finem. Sed voluntas de his quae imperantur, ad hoc quod legis rationem habeat, oportet quod sit aliqua ratione regulata. Et hoc modo intelligitur quod voluntas principis habet vigorem legis: alioquin voluntas principis magis esset iniquitas quam lex', ibid., ad 3.

[35] 'quaedam rationis ordinatio ad bonum commune', ibid., q. 90, a. 4.

[36] Daniel., op. cit., p. 88.

[37] Ibid., p. 95.

The Suarezian voluntaristic view of *epicheia* was developed within a context of civil law, but there have not been lacking moral theologians, including the great Alphonsus Liguori, who would apply the doctrine to various other forms of law, including natural law itself. In principle, and to the extent that morality is conceived and expressed in legal terms, such application is quite legitimate and it is mistaken to argue, as Davis did, that 'natural law and divine law do not admit of the use of *epieikeia*, since the Divine Author of such law has foreseen every contingency'.[38] God's foresight of, and provision for, every contingency is precisely what is traditionally meant by the eternal law, whereas the commands of revealed divine law and the precepts of natural law are not identical with eternal law, but provide only partial and generalized expressions of this law. They still have to be applied in particular cases, and it is at that level that both Aquinas and Suarez locate the functioning of *epicheia*. Equally, Zalba's attempts to explain away the teaching of Liguori on *epicheia* in natural law are rendered unncessary to the extent that one follows a Thomist rationalist view of law which views it as essentially the authoritative exercise of reason orientating behaviour to the common good. It is characteristic of all morality that it is action in accordance with reason, and whether or not one invokes the Aristotelian concept of *epicheia* the ethical system of Aquinas contains a strong element of the need to adapt the application of general moral commands and laws to the infinite variety of contingent circumstances.[39]

The same rational approach to law gives its long overdue *congé* to the theory and intricacies of 'purely penal law', and at the same time provides a much more coherent theory for the social problems and the popular practical solutions which led theologians to elaborate and espouse that theory. 'The theory of purely penal law stands or falls with the voluntarist theory of law',[40] as an attempt to read in the wording of the law, as in a crystal ball, what would be the true mind of the lawmaker, and what the consequent fortunes, for good or ill, of his subjects. The nature of law is not simply that the individual be subject directly to the will of the governing powers, but that both are subject to the requirements of the good of society. It is that alone which gives moral import to law, lacking

---

[38] Op. cit., p. 189. [39] Cf. Zalba, op. cit., vol. i, p. 309, n. 53.
[40] Daniel, p. 207.

which there is no just or true law. It was complaisance with the social conditions of the time and an unduly reverential attitude to authority which led theologians to seek practical solutions to social ills in a consideration of the nuances of obedience rather than in a critical appraisal of those ills in the light of justice. And the systematic development of the theory of purely penal law was to lead to a moral individualism and social unconcern verging at times on irresponsibility and dishonesty which has hindered rather than fostered a healthy development of moral theology, well meriting the implied rebuke in the teaching of the Second Vatican Council which criticizes an individualistic attitude towards society and a minimizing attitude towards its laws and the everyday norms of social life.[41]

Within the Church, also, of course, the intellectualist approach to law is the only one truly consonant with human dignity, and one which may well turn out to be crucial in the reception given by the Church at large to its new Code of Canon Law.[42] It is an approach which scrutinizes above all what is the purpose of any law and to what extent the application of any particular law in a given situation is conducive to the attainment of that purpose, the common good of the society in question. *Epicheia*, in the teaching of Aristotle and Aquinas, is a virtue, and as such it is a quality of human judgement to be cultivated rather than, as in the more Platonic and Suarezian approach, a regrettable necessity to be carefully hedged about and constrained. It is the acknowledgement that reality cannot all be pigeonholed, that what distinguishes a thing is not necessarily an imperfection or a deviation, but frequently that which gives it a particular dignity; that general laws are good and necessary for the functioning of any social organization, but that occasions can, and do, arise which they have not foreseen and in which it is not good that a law be observed in a purely literal compliance with its requirements. It requires considerable moral maturity to acknowledge that such cases can arise with respect to any legal formulation, and it is the refusal or reluctance to countenance even such a possibility which has been branded as literalism or legalism, the attitude that at all costs the letter of the law must be observed. Not many individuals perhaps would openly

---

[41] Cf. *Gaudium et spes*, no. 30; *AAS* 58 (1966), pp. 1049–50.
[42] Promulgated on 25 January 1983, with effect from Advent 1983.

and explicitly profess such an attitude, but as a mentality and as an implicit presupposition it appears not uncommon in many areas and walks of life, not excluding the religious aspects of life. At times, also, it may betoken simply a failure of moral nerve. It is, after all, sometimes easier to take refuge with relief in a literal observance of the law and to find peace of mind, or better, security in simple obedience, particularly if this latter is widely extolled as eminently desirable and akin at times even to loyalty to the institution.

In our fourth chapter we considered the varying moral systems elaborated in the sixteenth century and later to resolve the moral dilemmas arising from cases of doubtful conscience,[43] and it will be clear that what is being rejected here is the system proposed as tutiorism, or opting for the safer approach.[44] When in doubt about a particular moral precept, either in its wording or in its applicability in the present situation, this theory would maintain, the safer line is to follow the precept. From the rational approach to law which we have been more recently considering it emerges that tutiorism is subject at least to three inherent defects. One is that it makes security the moral norm at the possible expense of truth, and either engenders or reinforces a corrosive self-mistrust. It could be argued against this criticism, of course, and frequently is, that 'no one is a judge in his own case', and that man is incorrigibly prone to self-deception or self-interest. This retort, in turn, however, raises questions about the fundamental reliability not only of human reasoning and man's other resources but also of God's grace. And more immediately to the point, it is a defence of tutiorism which revealingly relies once again and heavily on an entirely legal approach to matters of morality.

The second weakness of an attitude of opting for the 'safer' line of action is that, as we have already noted, it appears radically voluntaristic. It accepts that the existence and terms of the law are of more significance and import than their purpose, both in general and even in every particular instance. It enjoins a respect for power—and even for possible sanctions not intrinsically connected with the purpose of the law—rather than for the purpose of law as reasonably furthering the common good and shared interests and to that extent open to scrutiny and evaluation. And this consideration

---

[43] Cf. *supra*, p. 136.   [44] *Supra*, p. 137.

in turn leads to the third defect of this particular moral system or mental attitude—that at heart it implies that the most important moral stance and the only moral virtue which really counts for salvation, is obedience to, and compliance with, the will of another, and ultimately with the will of God, conceived quite separately from the mind of God who is ultimate reason. Voluntarism in general, and tutiorism in particular, cannot hold in balance the two elements which entered into Augustine's definition of the eternal law, 'the divine reason or the will of God', and they are expressive of a radical bias towards the latter, to the neglect of reason which Aquinas, for instance, clearly considered to be of the essence of all law.[45]

To reject tutiorism, however, whether as a moral system or as a disquietingly prevalent attitude, is not necessarily to espouse the other moral system which it was at pains to combat, that of probabilism, or the view that, given the support of several 'grave' authorities and sufficiently good reason, one would be at liberty to disregard the law.[46] For this other product of the sixteenth century suffers from the same defect of being thoroughly voluntaristic. The definition of a probable opinion proposed by Medina which was to carry such weight ominously placed the extrinsic authority of theologians before the intrinsic force of argument.[47] More fatally, however, the systematic justification of probabilism, especially as propounded by Suarez, in terms of a doubtful law possessing no obligatory force and of man's personal freedom being 'in possession' of his conscience until ousted by a superior force of law, presents a view of morality characterized by conflict and antagonism between wills.[48] Vereecke, in his study of the various moral systems, presents an eloquent defence of the advocates of probabilism as attempting to adapt the older traditional and static moral teaching in a flexible manner to the many new situations and problems affecting sixteenth-century society. And he makes the

---

[45] 'Lex aeterna nihil aliud est quam ratio divinae sapientiae, secundum quod est directiva omnium actuum et motionum', *STh* 1a 2ae, q. 93, a. 1. In this rational approach Aquinas makes good use of Augustine's other description of eternal law, 'lex aeterna est summa ratio, cui semper obtemperandum est', *De libero arbitrio*, 6; PL 32, 1229, quoted *STh* ibid., *sed contra*.

[46] Cf. *supra*, p. 136.

[47] 'Si est opinio probabilis (quam scilicet asserunt viri sapientes et confirmant optima argumenta), licitum est eam sequi', Angelini and Valsecchi, op. cit., p. 116.

[48] Cf. *supra*, p. 228.

revealing statement, 'accustomed to regard the Gospel law as an external law, in the juridical sense, they did not consider they had the right to impose an obligation of which they were not absolutely certain'.[49] Such has continued to be the mental approach of probabilism at its best and it has often given witness to an admirable and genuinely pastoral concern for individuals in the complexity of their lives. It also, as Vereecke observes, placed great emphasis on the goodness and mercy of God, opposing a religion of fear, obligation, and law with a religion of God's love and a conviction that, strange as it may appear, salvation is easy and severity not necessarily a component of the moral life.[50]

While safeguarding individuals against a tyrannical view of law and authority, however, probabilism was still couched in legal and voluntarist terms. And if Suarez and others could be understood as struggling on behalf of the individual and his rights against the claimed omnipotence of law and of the lawgiver such an approach could, and did, degenerate into a power struggle between two wills, that of the lawgiver (including God) to dominate the subject, and that of the subject to be free from the demands of the lawmaker, including God. Paradoxically, however, it is the rationalist approach to law and to morality which most respects and enhances the dignity of the individual for which Suarez argued, and which gives a proper context to the function and exercise of his freedom, since it is not centred on a possible conflict of wills but on the harmonious use of reason on the part of both the lawmaker and the individual, and on their joint and complementary subordination to the common good.

What Sort of God?

It is also the rationalist rather than the voluntarist approach to law which does more justice to God, or at least less injustice to him. Man's concept of God and of his attributes lies at the theological heart of the whole subject of the role of law in moral theology. The predilection for the will and the power rather than the mind of God, which is to be found by and large in Scripture, as in Augustine, Abelard, and the Franciscan tradition of Scotus and Occam, may be seen as in some sense an attempt to glorify the

---

[49] Vereecke, iii, pp. 58–9.   [50] Ibid.

transcendence and majesty of God, and his supreme freedom of activity. One consequence of this is to view the divine–human relationship as a continual series of border incidents and demarcation disputes. The more one accords to man, the more is being subtracted from God; and tragically, the more one immerses man in the filth of his own sins and corruption, the more one is aiming at exalting the divine mercy and goodness in his deigning to extricate and save man.

By contrast, an approach to God by way of considering the divine mind and reason serves to make God less opaque and inscrutable and to diminish the gap between God and his human creature. Much, if not all, of Christian theology is a theology *ex convenientia*, of exploring the fittingness and the intrinsic coherence of why God is as he is and why he has acted in history as he has done. It is an act of faith in the ultimate intelligibility and self-consistency of God, and a stumbling attempt to comprehend something of the mystery which one believes is not at heart an intellectual absurdity or sheer caprice. The corresponding danger here, of course, is of reducing God to human categories of thinking, and of worshipping false idols of the true God; of losing the sense of transcendence and mystery (which is not, however, aloofness) and neglecting the *via negativa*, the way of negation of the mystics, which must be a continual corrective to any such intellectualist approach. What makes individuals prefer one way to the other is matter for conjecture. It may also be a matter of metaphysics. Augustine, for all his splendid rhetoric, could conceive of divine and human action as only in competition (and this possibly was the radical flaw of Jansenism); and he therefore was unable ever to give a satisfactory answer to his puzzled question about Paul's forthright statement that God's sons are driven by God's Spirit (Rom. 8: 14). If God's sons are driven, or actuated, by God's Spirit, how can they themselves be active?[51] What is at issue is the analogy of being, which does not posit created being as a threat to, or a trespassing upon, uncreated being. And in particular what appears to be at issue is the question of causality. The biblical mentality,

---

[51] E.g., 'Non qui spiritu suo aguntur: sed, *quotquot Spiritu Dei aguntur, hi filii sunt Dei*. Dicit mihi aliquis: Ergo agimur, non agimus. Respondeo: Imo et agis, et ageris; et tunc bene agis, si a bono agaris. Spiritus enim Dei qui te agit, agenti adiutor est tibi . . . . Prorsus si defuerit, nihil boni agere poteris', *Serm.* 156, 10–11; PL 38, 855–6. Cf. *de corrept. et gratia*, 2; PL 44, 918.

and especially the Old Testament, is largely occasionalist, as is Augustine, attributing very little to the reality and activity of secondary causes under God, and viewing all human activity as predominantly the theatre of God's activity. It was Aquinas's great contribution, based on Aristotle and probably influenced by John Damascene, to exploit the idea of instrumental causality in theology, including Christology, and so to view God and man as not acting on the same plane of being, where demarcation disputes are inevitable, but on different planes of being, with God as principal agent and man as his free instrument with his own real but subordinate contribution to make. The difference may be seen as that between two oarsmen rowing a boat together and a sail driving a boat under the power of the wind.[52]

Is God, then, a jealous God or a generous God, to phrase the question in over-simple terms? The very fact, and sharing, of divine revelation to man appears to indicate some priority of mind over will, in God as also in man, or at least indicates that will cannot be stressed to the exclusion or the total incapacitation of God's and man's reason. Naked will, or totally undetermined freedom, is neither what God is nor what he created and restored in man. What he is in himself is reason and will identified, and what he created in man is the rational will, and the freedom of choice to act or not, in this way or that, in accordance with reason.

In thus attempting to identify the character of God, which is essentially love, and in which will and reason coincide, we may by way of conclusion consider that it is a remarkable, if largely unremarked, fact that it should have been thought that in depicting God as a moral lawmaker anything like the full truth of the matter had been reached. In the opening chapter of this study of the making of moral theology it was pointed out how the Sacrament of Penance has suffered for centuries from an over-conceptualized and rigorously univocal pursuit of the idea of God as judge and of the sinner's encounter with him as taking place within some sort of

---

[52] 'Semper enim actio magis attribuitur principali agenti, quam secondario, puta si dicamus quod securis non facit arcam, sed artifex per securim. Voluntas autem hominis movetur a Deo ad bonum. Unde supra 8, 14 dictum est: *Qui Spiritu Dei aguntur, hi sunt filii Dei*. Et ideo hominis operatio interior non est homini principaliter, sed Deo attribuenda', Aquinas, *Comm. in Rom.*, cap. 9, lect. 3. 'Humanitas Christi est instrumentum divinitatis, non quidem sicut instrumentum inanimatum, quod nullo modo agit sed solum agitur: sed tanquam instrumentum animatum anima rationali, quod ita agit quod etiam agitur', *STh* 3, q. 7, a. 1 ad 3.

court of law.[53] And it appears that moral theology as a whole, unconsciously or at least unreflectively, has done something similar and at a much deeper level with the whole idea of morality, expressing it almost entirely in the language of law as enacted, promulgated, and sanctioned by God as the supreme legislator. And yet such language is purely analogical, ascribing to God the words and ideas of human everyday experience raised to the highest power of which they are capable.

No doubt such 'analogical' considerations had no place in Israel, which saw itself as essentially and literally a theocratic society, established as such by God's personal intervention in history to make with his people a solemn and binding legal covenant which incorporated a basic criminal code. In the prophets, as also in the New Testament and particularly in the rabbinical and casuistical mind of Paul, the concepts and terminology of the Jewish theocratic legal system, such as justice, law, commandment, punishment, are still in use, but they are increasingly like old wineskins, creaking with paradox and the new wine of the Gospel. The justice of God is revealed as mercy (Rom. 1: 17), the perfect law is 'the law of liberty' (Jas. 1: 25), and 'the law of the Spirit of life in Christ Jesus has set me free from the law of sin and death' (Rom. 8: 2). It is a law still 'engraved', to be sure, but now on human hearts rather than on stone (Heb. 8: 10).

Patristic theorizing on conscience, with its Pauline aspects of accusation or exculpation, was at times to depict it as the voice of God in a way which appears influenced by God's interrogation of and sentence on Adam's sinful behaviour in the early chapters of Genesis.[54] At other times it was to take on board, as we have seen, the whole Stoic construct of nature as a cosmic expression of law with resulting human obligations—to be spelt out in increasing detail in 'natural law'.[55] And perhaps a further influential factor in the increasingly systematic expression of all morality in legal terms is to be identified in the ease with which developing Christian moral thought viewed all religious and moral activity as dominated by, and falling within the framework of, a relationship of justice towards God.

The cause of this last inevitably impoverishing phenomenon lay

---

[53] Cf. *supra*, p. 34.
[55] Cf. *supra*, pp. 72–83.

[54] Cf. *supra*, p. 186.

in Christian thinking simply accepting as gospel the Platonic and Aristotelian quartet of political moral virtues channeled to it especially through the writings of Cicero, Ambrose, Augustine, and Gregory, with some encouragement from the Book of Wisdom.[56] The four virtues of temperance, justice, prudence, and fortitude, considered as cardinal, or on which all other virtues turn, were to become and remain in moral theology what Pope St Gregory the Great described as the foundations of the whole building of good behaviour.[57] As such they were enormously furthered by the work of Aquinas, who uses them systematically in his *Summa* of theology

[56] The first appearance of the quartet occurs in *The Republic*, where Plato has Socrates conclude that 'justice . . . is the remaining virtue in the state after our consideration of soberness, courage, and intelligence' (δικαιοσύνη, σωφροσύνη, ἀνδρεία, φρόνησις), Bk 4, 10 (433); Loeb trans., p. 369. On the parallel between a human community and the human soul it follows that 'whereby the state was wise (σοφός) so and thereby is the individual wise . . . and as the individual is brave (ἀνδρεῖος), thereby, and so is the state brave . . . a man is in the same way in which a city was just (δικαία)', ibid., chap. 16 (441C–D; p. 407). To be brave (ἀνδρεῖος), wise (σοφός), sober (σώφρων), and just (δίκαιος) are, therefore, desirable moral characteristics, ibid., 442B–D; pp. 409–11. Cf. *Laws*, 631. The tradition is taken up by Cicero (*Tusculan Disputations*, 3, 17) envisaging being exhorted by 'Pythagoras or Socrates or Plato' to arouse the virtues which may be dormant in him. 'Iam tibi erit princeps fortitudo . . . ; aderit temperantia, . . . Ne iustitia quidem sinet te ista facere. . . . Prudentiae vero quid respondebis docenti virtutem sese esse contentam . . .' Thus, Ambrose, 'Et quidem scimus virtutes esse quatuor cardinales, temperantiam, iustitiam, prudentiam, fortitudinem', *Expos. Evang. sec. Luc.*, Bk 5, 62; *PL* 15, 1653. Augustine is somewhat dismissive, perhaps in view of his attitude to pagan 'virtues' (cf. *supra*, pp. 85–8). 'Virtutem quoque deam [Romani] fecerunt. . . . Quando quidem virtutem in quatuor species distribuendam esse viderunt, prudentiam, iustitiam, fortitudinem, temperantiam . . . . Cur temperantia dea esse non meruit . . .? Cur denique fortitudo dea non est . . .? Quare prudentia, quare sapientia nulla numinum loca meruerunt? an quia in nomine generali ipsius virtutis omnes coluntur? . . . Has deas non veritas, sed vanitas fecit: haec enim veri Dei munera sunt, non ipsae sunt deae. Verumtamen ubi est virtus et felicitas, quid aliud quaeritur? Quid ei sufficit, cui virtus felicitasque non sufficit? Omnia quippe agenda complectitur virtus; omnia optanda, felicitas', *de civitate Dei*, 4, 20–1; *PL* 41, 127–8. The Alexandrian author of the Greek Book of Wisdom (1st century BC) adopted Hellenistic thought to portray God as teaching 'self-control and prudence, justice and courage' (Wis. 8: 7, RSV).

[57] 'In quatuor vero angulis domus ista consistit, quia nimirum solidum mentis nostrae aedificium, prudentia, temperantia, fortitudo, iustitia sustinet. In quatuor angulis domus ista subsistit, quia in his quatuor virtutibus tota boni operis structura consurgit', *Moralia*, 2, 49; *PL* 75, 592. Gregory, as was his wont, was allegorizing on 'the four corners of the house' which was struck by the wind and collapsed upon Job's children (Job 1: 19). The same penchant for allegory led both Ambrose and Augustine to seize upon the four cardinal virtues as intimated by the four rivers branching out from the garden in Eden (Gen. 2: 10), and thus to give them pride of place in Christian moral thinking. Cf. Augustine, *de civ. dei*, 13, 21; *PL* 41, 315,

as the four major moral categories within which all moral activity is classified, or as the skeletal structure of man's entire moral enterprise. At one point in his treatment, it is true, Aquinas almost appears to be struggling against the framework imposed upon him by Christian and classical tradition, but his final comment against a series of objections is 'this is how many people speak of these virtues, both sacred doctors and also philosophers'.[58]

It is a peculiar feature of this comprehensive analysis of all human moral behaviour under four key headings or 'principal' virtues that three of them, prudence, temperance, and fortitude, have to do with man's internal moral strategy, while only one relates outside himself to other individuals and to God, that of justice, or of rendering to each person what is his due, or is owing to him. As Aquinas explains, by the other three cardinal virtues man brings order (*ordo*) into his interior life, whereas by justice he brings order into his relationships with others.[59] Prudence controls his practical thinking, temperance controls his sensuality, and fortitude controls his aggressiveness.[60] It is only by justice, and the various component parts of justice, that a man controls his relationships with others.[61] And these 'others' include God. For the

'Nemo itaque prohibet intelligere paradisum, vitam beatorum: quatuor eius flumina, quatuor virtutes, prudentiam, fortitudinem, temperantiam, atque iustitiam; et ligna eius, omnes utiles disciplinas; . . .' He ends by saying, however, that such exegesis is permissible provided we also accept the historical accuracy of the account.

[58] 'Et sic multi loquuntur de istis virtutibus, tam sacri doctores quam etiam philosophi', *STh* 1a 2ae, q. 61, a. 3. Aquinas's general treatment of the moral virtues occurs in *STh* 1a 2ae, qq. 58–61. The quartet of cardinal virtues provides the systematic structure of his detailed moral theology in *STh* 2a 2ae, qq. 47–170, following upon the theological virtues of faith, hope, and charity.

[59] 'iustitia inter omnes virtutes morales praecellit, tamquam propinquior rationi. Quod patet et ex subiecto, et ex obiecto . . . . Secundum autem obiectum sive materiam, quia est circa operationes, quibus homo ordinatur non solum in se ipso, sed etiam ad alterum', *STh* 1a 2ae, q. 66, a. 4.

[60] 'Inter alias autem virtutes morales, quae sunt circa passiones . . . fortitudo, quae appetitivum motum subdit rationi in his quae ad mortem et vitam pertinent, . . . temperantia, quae subiicit rationi appetitum circa ea quae immediate ordinantur ad vitam, vel in eodem secundum numerum, vel in eodem secundum speciem, scilicet in cibis et venereis', ibid. 'Prudentia non solum dirigit virtutes morales in eligendo ea quae sunt ad finem, sed etiam in praestituendo finem', ibid., a. 3 ad 3.

[61] Faced with the objection, as against both the view of Aristotle that justice is the outstanding virtue (*Ethics*, v. 1, 15; *STh* ibid., a. 4) and the reference by Ambrose to this and the other three as 'cardinal' or 'principal' virtues (ibid., q. 61, a. 1), that surely this should be reserved to the theological virtues of faith, hope, and charity,

unfortunate fact was that through this complete absorption of the Platonic system of virtues the whole religious relationship of man to his God was categorized by Aquinas as primarily a subdivision of the virtue of justice. Religion consists simply in giving to God what is his due.[62] As a matter of justice God has dominion over us and we are his servants—owing reverence and honour to his supreme transcendence and subjecting ourselves to him who is our superior.[63] It is only a logical consequence of this mental straitjacket that Aquinas should then develop as so many expressions of justice towards God the activity of prayer and other 'duties' of religion, and should complete his treatise on justice[64] with an

Aquinas adopts the somewhat lame approach that the latter are not strictly human virtues, but 'super-humanae, vel divinae', ibid., ad 2. It is this basic Aristotelian nature-orientated philosophy which leads him to create a superstructure of divinely infused moral virtues emanating in the individual from the theological virtues. 'Unde oportet quod his etiam virtutibus theologicis proportionaliter respondeant alii habitus divinitus causati in nobis, qui sic se habent ad virtutes theologicas sicut se habent virtutes morales et intellectuales ad principia naturalium virtutum', ibid., q. 63, a. 3. Cf. ibid., ad 3; art. 4.

[62] 'Quia vero iustitia ad alterum est, . . . omnes virtutes quae ad alterum sunt possunt ratione convenientiae iustitiae annecti . . . . Sunt enim quaedam virtutes quae debitum quidem alteri reddunt, sed non possunt reddere aequale. Et primo quidem, quidquid ab homine Deo reditur, debitum est: non tamen potest esse aequale, ut scilicet tantum ei homo reddat quantum debet', *STh* 2a 2ae, q. 80, a. 1. It may be noted that Aquinas' major sources for his consideration of the virtue of religion are Aristotle and Cicero (cf. ibid.), in whom can be discerned the Platonic influence of the *Euthyphro*, 12, d–e, explaining that 'holiness is a part of the right (μόριον γὰρ τοῦ δικαίου τὸ ὅσιον)', and that 'the part of the right which has to do with attention to the gods constitutes piety and holiness (εὐσεβές τε καὶ ὅσιον)' (Loeb. trans., p. 47).

[63] 'Cum servus dicatur ad dominum, necesse est quod ubi est propria et specialis ratio dominii, ibi sit specialis et propria ratio servitutis. Manifestum est autem quod dominium convenit Deo secundum propriam et singularem quandam rationem . . . . Et ideo specialis ratio servitutis ei debetur', *STh* 2a 2ae, q. 81, a. 1 ad 3. 'Bonum autem ad quod ordinatur religio est exhibere Deo debitum honorem. Honor autem debetur alicui ratione excellentiae. Deo autem competit singularis excellentia: inquantum omnia in infinitum transcendit secundum omnimodum excessum. Unde ei debetur specialis honor', ibid., a. 4. 'Per hoc quod Deum reveremur et honoramus, mens nostra ei subiicitur, et in hoc eius perfectio consistit; quaelibet enim res perficitur per hoc quod subditur suo superiori', ibid., a. 7.

[64] *STh* 2a 2ae, qq. 83–91. 'Deinde considerandum est de praeceptis iustitiae . . . utrum praecepta decalogi sint praecepta iustitiae', ibid., q. 122 et art. 1. 'Praecepta decalogi sunt prima praecepta legis . . . . Manifestissime autem ratio debiti, quae requiritur ad praeceptum, apparet in iustitia, quae est ad alterum . . . . Et ideo praecepta decalogi oportuit ad iustitiam pertinere. Unde tria prima praecepta sunt de actibus religionis, quae est potissima pars iustitiae; quartum autem praeceptum est de actu pietatis, quae est pars iustitiae secunda; alia verio sex dantur de actibus iustitiae communiter dictae, quae inter aequales attenditur', ibid., a. 1.

examination of the Ten Commandments, 'precepts of justice' which are naturally also 'first precepts of law'.[65]

The location of all interpersonal morality and of man's religious relationship to God within the categories of justice and of law obviously has a certain verbal and conceptual justification from Scripture, as we have seen, and from reason, as well as from a whole-hearted acceptance of classical schemes of morality. But to consider that this non-Christian, indeed, atheistic, category of justice can be an adequate and completely enlightening means of conceptualizing and expressing the reality of man's relationship to the God of Israel and to Jesus Christ is both a travesty of the Gospel and an ignoring of the fact that all our discourse about God (and here the voluntarists have a point) is severely limited. Moral theology has in this respect considered itself exempt from the limiting axiom of all theology, that of analogical predication about God and all his activities—that is, the inherent limitations of applying directly to God terms and ideas which are in the first instance derived from more mundane human experience. If, then, to speak of God as lawmaker, and of the expressions of his reason and will as so many just laws, precepts, and commandments, is, in accordance with the axiom of analogy, potentially true but also potentially false, then this latter qualification is something which moral theology has on the whole not considered, simply proceeding blissfully on its way of pushing to the ultimate logical rigour and implication the concepts of law and lawmaker as if they were merely univocal ideas which could apply to God in all respects.[66] This is the ultimate literalism and legalism of moral theology and it is, in that respect at least, profoundly untheological.

How is this centuries old near-monopoly of law and legal terminology in articulating the moral enterprise to be countered

---

[65] Cf. our earlier observations on the univocal pursuit into literal detail of the forensic analogy of the Sacrament of Confession, pp. 35–6. Within the analogy of God as legislator, cf. particularly the debated questions on how his various laws are promulgated, it being of the essence of legal obligation that the existence and content of any law be known by those whom they affect. 'Unde promulgatio necessaria est ad hoc quod lex habeat suam virtutem', *STh* 1a 2ae, q. 90, a. 4.

[66] In other words, just as the view of the Church as a 'perfect society' (*supra*, p. 224), modelled at times in alarmingly Levitical terms on ancient Israel, generates a strong legal and authoritative approach to man's conduct towards his fellows and towards the governing head of that society, so other concepts of the Church will lead to other correspondingly appropriate ways of viewing moral behaviour, none entirely adequate in itself, but all acting as counterpoint to each other.

and corrected? Partly, it may be suggested, by cultivating a proper sense of humility and diffidence, and by not claiming such unwarranted clarity and distinctness for the compelling nature of moral conclusions in terms of legal command and obligation. Partly also by acknowledging that such developments as the doctrines of probabilism and of *epicheia*, whether in the Thomist or the Suarezian sense, were a laudable attempt to mitigate the rigours of a full-blown legal approach to morality and yet at the same time, ironically, provided a reinforcement to viewing morality from the point of view of law and justice. And partly by distinguishing more clearly between moral instruction or teaching on the one hand, which is couched most frequently in categorical absolutes with distinct voluntaristic overtones, and moral education on the other hand, which seeks to probe and disclose the reality, both divine and human, which is both the source and the purpose of such teaching.

More positively, what moral theology has come to require as a matter of urgency is the development of other theologies of the moral life as supplements and correctives to that thoroughly explored for centuries in terms of law. As well as the themes of legal enactment and imposition the Bible also contains themes of invitation and attraction; of calling as well as sending; of Abraham as well as Moses. As well as morality being couched in terms of due submission to the all-powerful will of a legislating God, it can also be explored as the story which God is narrating in action, or as pilgrimage, or 'way', or co-creation with man as a participant in divine providence. It can also be explored in terms of art. The pervasive intellectual order of the cosmos can in a true sense, as it has been traditionally, be read as the expression of divine reason and divine law. But it can also be appreciated, as Augustine and others in the mystical tradition have appreciated it, with a sense of beauty and wonder for the grandeur of things, as well as for their tears. There appear to be close affinities between the moral sense which has so often eluded rational dissection—that 'Christian sense of the faithful' to which Vatican II referred and which we have considered in the previous chapter—and the aesthetic sense.[67] A geometrical theorem can be not only true but beautiful, and of two equally successful lines of mathematical proof, one may be preferred for its elegance. In spiritual and mystical theology there

---

[67] Cf. *supra*, pp. 207–10.

are currents, not so much of reason and reasoning about God and human behaviour, as of affinity with God and the things of God—whether this finds expression in the Pauline theme of moral discernment on the part of 'the spiritual man' (1 Cor. 2: 14–15), or in the more elaborate treatment by Aquinas of knowledge by connaturality.[68] And to the extent that moral theology, after centuries of separation, is now drawing closer to the Church's spiritual and mystical traditions, to that extent it is experiencing a healthy corrective to its former preoccupation with law, commandment, and sin.

In like manner, it is possible to conceive of moral initiative as proceeding from obligation and compulsion laid upon man from outside, as it were, in the way of which law is a typical expression. But it can also be conceived as impulsion, as a movement welling up from within man to seek expression in behaviour, as in the experience of the artist or the prophet responding to stimuli or situations. Such, of course, in terms of fundamental human tendencies, is the ground of Aquinas's elaboration of natural law. But it can take other expressions such as prophecy, whether in speech, or in creative action, or as artistic expression. 'The Lord God has spoken; who can but prophesy?' (Amos 3: 8.) And the artistic urge of the poet, or composer, or painter, is experienced as an inarticulate force welling up within, and as an impelling urge which is not just an 'I ought' but an 'I must' in terms of external expression.

This, interestingly, is rather how Aquinas completes his systematic treatise on law in analysing 'the Law of the Gospel', a vital section of his *Summa* which subsequent moral theology was to ignore in its concentration on Aquinas the moral philosopher, and perhaps also in its concern to give nothing away to Protestant individualism and private judgement. After having established the essence of law in general and considered in turn the eternal law, the natural law, human law, and the Mosaic Law, Aquinas came finally, in a totally original treatment, to what he termed 'the evangelical law, which is called the New Law'.[69] In this new law he posited a fundamental and radical distinction between what he called its primary and secondary elements. The secondary element comprises all the

---

[68] Cf. J. Mahoney, 'The Spirit and Moral Discernment in Aquinas', *Seeking the Spirit*, pp. 63–80.

[69] 'De lege Evangelii, quod dicitur lex nova', *STh* 1a 2ae, q. 106.

teaching of Scripture, the documents of faith, and the precepts which put order into human reactions and human behaviour—all of which have one simple function, either to dispose man to receive the primary element of the new law or to help man express that primary element.[70] And the primary element of the Gospel law is nothing other than the presence of the Holy Spirit within man. 'The major characteristic of the law of the New Testament, in which its whole power consists, is the grace of the Holy Spirit which is given through faith in Christ . . . . As Augustine said, . . . "What are the laws of God written by God himself in our hearts, if not the very presence of the Holy Spirit".'[71]

Thus for Aquinas the idea of law which began as an act of reason directing actions in order to the common good has by the end of his treatise become in the Christian dispensation simply the working in us of a person, the Holy Spirit of God. His pervasive presence and activity in our minds and hearts, prompting us to act, is so intimate to us and impelling in us as to be the supreme moral initiating force. And to call this a 'law', as Aquinas was constrained to do by prophetic and Pauline usage and by the march of his argument, is to strain to the very limit, and beyond, the element of paradox in such Christian moral language. It is scarcely justifiable, but may be justified on traditional grounds only if 'law' is recognized to be, where God is concerned, a thoroughly analogical, and therefore potentially very misleading concept.

All these considerations do not constitute an argument that the role of law or even the language of law in moral theology are false, but only that they have very considerable inherent limitations which have not been taken into account in the making of moral theology. Within the analogy of law there is much truth struggling

---

[70] 'In scriptura Evangelii non continentur nisi ea quae pertinent ad gratiam Spiritus Sancti vel sicut dispositiva, vel sicut ordinativa ad usum huius gratiae . . . . Usus vero spiritualis gratiae est in operibus virtutum, ad quae multipliciter scriptura Novi Testamenti homines exhortatur', ibid., a. 1 ad 1. 'Habet tamen lex nova quaedam sicut dispositiva ad gratiam Spiritus Sancti, et ad usum huius gratiae pertinentia, quae sunt quasi secundaria in lege nova, de quibus opportuit instrui fideles Christi et verbis et scriptis, tam circa credenda quam circa agenda. Et ideo dicendum est quod principaliter lex nova est lex indita, secundario autem est lex scripta', ibid., a. 1.
[71] 'Id autem quod est potissimum in lege novi testamenti, et in quo tota virtus eius consistit, est gratia Spiritus Sancti, quae datur Christi fidelibus . . . . Unde et Augustinus dicit, in libro *de Spiritu et Littera* [21; PL 44, 222], . . . "Quae sunt leges Dei ab ipso Deo scriptae in cordibus, nisi ipsa praesentia Spiritus Sancti" ', ibid.

for expression, and it is truth which is much more accurately expressed in the rational view of law than in the voluntarist tradition, not least because in human interaction there are times when even the voluntarist must appeal to something beyond and above the claims of the lawmaker. 'Voluntarism can ignore or minimize the objective rule of the common good, living on the borrowed capital of an objectivist tradition, but refusing to acknowledge its debt until in a crisis of misuse of authority it is forced to turn to the objective standards of natural law and the common good to overrule the expressed will of the lawgiver.'[72] The language of law, whether of the rationalist or the voluntarist persuasion, has played a highly significant part in the making of moral theology, and will no doubt continue to play a part, if only as one human manner of seeking to give articulation and expression to the ways of God for man. In such a limited role, it remains important to be mindful not only of the differing views of law and the diverging conclusions to be derived from them, but more fundamentally of the mentalities underlying them—neither particularly Christian, but one of which is considerably more consonant with the character of God and the personal dignity of man. One may identify the two mentalities as Platonic and Aristotelian, or one may content and delight oneself in witnessing them at work in two more recent thinkers, Wordsworth and Robert Frost.

In his *Ode to Duty* Wordsworth extols this 'Stern daughter of the Voice of God' for being a light and a rod, and for being 'victory and law When empty terrors overawe', as well as for calming 'the weary strife of frail humanity'. In his youthful past the poet had neglected the 'mandate' of duty, 'But thee I now would serve more strictly, if I may'. He is, in fact, weary of the spontaneity of youth, and in the key verses of the poem he sighs,

> Me this unchartered freedom tires;
> I feel the weight of chance desires:
> My hopes no more must change their name,
> I long for a repose that ever is the same.

In Stoic mood, he continues,

> Stern Lawgiver! . . .
> Thou dost preserve the stars from wrong;
> And the most ancient Heavens, through Thee, are fresh and strong.

[72] Daniel, op. cit., p. 51.

And he concludes,

> The confidence of reason give;
> And in the light of truth thy bondsman let me live!

In so describing the weary burden of human freedom Wordsworth may be thought to have certain affinities with Dostoevsky's Legend of the Grand Inquisitor: moral freedom is, when all is done, too heavy a burden and task for most people to bear. With law, at least you know where you are; and 'me this unchartered freedom tires'. By contrast, another nature poet, Robert Frost, writes of some power elemental in life which will not be subject to neat categories and controls or be suppressed by unreasoning force.

> Something there is that doesn't love a wall,
> That sends the frozen-ground-swell under it,
> And spills the upper boulders in the sun.

In the piece *Mending Wall*, he explains how this recurs every year, and how he and his neighbour then arrange to meet and walk the length of the wall, each picking up and replacing the dry stones which have fallen on his side, the neighbour saying sententiously, 'Good fences make good neighbours'. Frost continues,

> Spring is the mischief in me, and I wonder
> If I could put a notion in his head:
> '*Why* do they make good neighbours? Isn't it
> Where there are cows? But here there are no cows.
> Before I built a wall I'd ask to know
> What I was walling in or walling out,
> And to whom I was like to give offence.
> Something there is that doesn't love a wall,
> That wants it down'.

But to no avail.

>   I see him there
> Bringing a stone grasped firmly by the top
> In each hand, like an old-stone savage armed.
> He moves in darkness, as it seems to me,
> Not of woods only and the shade of trees.
> He will not go behind his father's saying,
> And he likes having thought of it so well
> He says again, 'Good fences make good neighbours'.[73]

[73] *Mending Wall*, from *The Poetry of Robert Frost* ed. E. C. Lathem (London, 1971). Quoted with permission.

The one thing which a voluntarist approach to morality and to authority cannot handle is the question, *Why?* And yet this is the consideration at the heart of the rational approach to law and to morality, as it is at the heart of Frost's poem. 'But here there are no cows.' The 'something' which doesn't love a wall, which may be the same power which prompts the poet's mischievous, yet serious, question, is not an antinomian force. There is a place for walls, so long as one can answer a few questions first, and so long as the neighbour can 'go behind his father's saying'. The effect of Frost's reflections is to put law firmly in its proper place. In considerably more prosaic terms, the aim of this chapter has been to consider the potent influence which the analogy and language of law have had in the making of moral theology, and to 'go behind' them in an attempt to cast light on their genesis and development, as well as on their advantages and limitations.

7

THE IMPACT OF *HUMANAE VITAE*

In the course of this study of the making of moral theology we have had occasion to consider the importance of outstanding thinkers such as Augustine and Aquinas; the currents and developments of thought such as Stoicism and voluntarism; the sway of ideas such as 'natural' and 'supernatural'; and the influence of Councils such as Trent and Vatican I. The scope and the purpose of our study have not permitted detailed consideration of any one event, although in the concluding chapter particular attention will be given to the Second Vatican Council and to the fresh brief which it gave to the discipline of moral theology. Of individual historical occurrences, however, which have contributed to the present state of moral theology in almost all its aspects none can rival, it can be argued, the letter which Pope Paul VI addressed to the Roman Catholic Church in July 1968. The letter was *Humanae Vitae* and its subject was contraception. This chapter is not, however, on the topic of contraception nor even on Pope Paul's encyclical letter. It is a study of the impact of, or the events brought about in the Church and in moral theology by, *Humanae Vitae*. After a brief narrative of events leading to the issuing of the encyclical, it will offer an analysis of the impact of the letter and some theological reflections on the whole phenomenon.

Events Preceding the Encyclical

It was the major chemical innovation in the 1950s in the control of female fertility which so dramatically opened up to scrutiny the traditional Roman Catholic moral condemnation of contraception.[1] This had been most vehemently summed up a generation previously by Pope Pius XI in his encyclical letter, *Casti Connubii*, which was directed at both the surgical operation of sterilization and any

[1] Cf. A. Valsecchi, *Controversy: The Birth-control Debate 1958–1968* (London, 1968), pp. 1–8.

interference with the act of intercourse itself.[2] Now it was possible, in effect, to regulate fertility for shorter or longer periods without affecting the act of intercourse and without the surgical intervention condemned as self-mutilation. This medical development was to lead moral theologians, and Pope Pius XII, into a series of casuistical considerations about morally permissible or morally

---

[2] The asseveration of the traditional teaching, from which the Lambeth Conference of the Anglican Communion had recently and partially retreated, occupies only a few paragraphs of the papal disquisition on the many contemporary attacks on the institution of 'Chaste Marriage' (cf. *supra*, p. 59): 'De prole sit sermo, **quam** multi molestum connubii onus vocare audent, quamque a coniugibus, non per honestam continentiam (etiam in matrimonio, utroque consentiente coniuge, permissam), sed vitiando naturae actum, studiose arcendam praecipiunt . . . . At nulla profecto ratio, ne gravissima quidem, efficere potest, ut, quod intrinsece est contra naturam, id cum natura congruens et honestum fiat. Cum autem actus coniugii suapte natura proli generandae sit destinatus, qui, in eo exercendo, naturali hac eum vi atque virtute de industria destituunt, contra naturam agunt et turpe quid atque intrinsece inhonestum operantur . . . . Cum igitur quidam, a christiana doctrina iam inde ab initio tradita neque umquam intermissa manifesto recedentes, aliam nuper de hoc agendi modo doctrinam sollemniter praedicandam censuerint, Ecclesia Catholica, cui ipse Deus morum integritatem honestatemque docendam et defendendam commisit, in media hac morum ruina posita, ut nuptialis foederis castimoniam a turpi hac labe immunem servet, in signum legationis **suae** divinae, altam per Nostrum extollit vocem atque denuo promulgat: quemlibet matrimonii usum, in quo exercendo, **actus**, de industria hominum, naturali sua vitae procreandae vi destituatur, Dei et **naturae** legem infringere, et eos qui tale quid commiserint gravis noxae labe commaculari', *AAS* 22 (1930), pp. 559–60. The claim to a doctrine 'passed on from the beginning' rests on Augustine's exegesis of Gen. 38: 8–10 (ibid.). This and the denunciatory language, as well as the Tridentine teaching on the possibility of obeying the commandments (*supra*, p. 54), are not to be found in *Humanae Vitae*, but the basic arguments and terminology are repeated. The teaching of Pius XI on sterilization occurs in the context of eugenics and of the move in some quarters to prevent certain individuals from marrying, or to sterilize them whether they be willing or not. Genetic counselling might often be called for, the Pope judged, but no more. As for sterilization, 'publici vero magistratus in subditorum membra directam potestatem habent nullam; ipsam igitur corporis integritatem, ubi nulla intercesserit culpa nullaque adsit cruentae poenae causa, directo laedere et attingere nec eugenicis nec ullis aliis de causis possunt unquam . . . . Ceterum, quod ipsi privati homines in sui corporis membra dominatum alium non habeant quam qui ad eorum naturales fines pertineat, nec possint ea destruere aut mutilare aut alia via ad naturales functiones se ineptos reddere, nisi quando bono totius corporis aliter provideri nequeat, id christiana doctrina statuit atque ex ipso humanae rationis lumine omnino constat', ibid., pp. 564–5. Thus was enunciated the 'principle of totality', which Pope Pius XII was later to deploy against organ transplantation from living donors but whose extension he **was** to reject when applied to the 'totality' of the person, or even of a marriage, in justification of contraceptive sterilization, whether of a surgical nature or of a temporary and medically induced nature. Pius XI's teaching on sterilization as a contraceptive measure was spelled out some years later by the Holy Office, *DS* 3760–5.

forbidden recourse to the anovulant pill for a variety of reasons on the part of married and unmarried women.[3] Despite papal rejection in 1958 of the use of 'the pill' for contraceptive purposes on the ground that it brought about a direct sterilization, even if only temporary, the debate waxed into the 1960s, particularly with contributions from the Louvain theologian, Professor L. Janssens, and from the study of the American gynaeocologist, Dr John Rock, entitled *The Time Has Come*.[4] With the publicizing of these and other contributions debate became widespread among Roman Catholics on the validity of the Church's official teaching, and ranged from the difficulties experienced by married couples and their families to the growing international debate on the population explosion and the economic and ecological consequences of world over-population.[5]

In 1963, shortly before his death, Pope John XXIII set up a small and confidential international commission to consider the threat of over-population, and in the following year and on subsequent later occasions this papal commission was considerably enlarged as it became clear that the underlying basic issue was the Church's whole stance on marital sexuality.[6] In 1964 Pope Paul VI referred to the findings of the commission to date and promised that its conclusions would soon be delivered. 'Meanwhile,' he observed,

We say frankly that so far we do not have sufficient reason to consider the norms given by Pope Pius XII on this matter as out of date and therefore as

---

[3] Cf. Valsecchi, pp. 1–8.

[4] Pope Pius XII, *AAS* 50 (1958), p. 734. For reactions to his interventions, cf. Valsecchi, pp. 9–26. Janssens had first written in 1958 and continued to contribute to the debate, Valsecchi, pp. 4, 24, 38–41. Rock's *The Time Has Come* (London, 1963) was important as a contribution from a layman and an expert in human fertility studies. An impressive study by the distinguished American Jesuit moralists, John C. Ford and Gerald Kelly, attempted to combine fidelity to the papal *magisterium* with delicate moral analysis presented 'in a way which will be useful to priests, theologians, theological students, and others who have a professional interest in the problems chosen for discussion', *Contemporary Moral Theology, Vol. ii; Marriage Questions* (Cork, 1963), p. [v].

[5] Contribution to the debate on the part of married couples was typified by M. Novak (ed.), *The Experience of Marriage*, (London, 1965). On population and economic considerations, cf., e.g., Rock, pp. 3–27. On the debate in Britain prior to *Humanae Vitae*, much useful documentation is to be found in Leo Pyle (ed.), *The Pill and Birth Regulation* (London, 1964).

[6] Cf. Peter Harris *et al.*, *On Human Life* (London, 1968), pp. 10–11. See *Informations catholiques internationales*, Suppl. au No. 317–18 (August 1968), pp. iii–vi, for a brief history of the Vatican II debate and the papal commission.

not binding. They must be considered as valid, at least until We feel obliged in conscience to change them. In a matter of such seriousness it seems well that Catholics should wish to follow one single law, that which the Church puts forward with authority. It therefore seems opportune to recommend that, for the present, no one take it upon himself to make pronouncements in terms which differ from the prevailing norms.[7]

This papal statement, of course, only fuelled the debate. The very fact that a papal commission did not consider the matter open and shut confirmed suspicion and surmise on the subject, to the extent that the traditional law might be considered doubtful and therefore subject to 'probabilism', with not only considerable arguments being marshalled against it but also the authority of numerous theologians of international repute.[8] In the circumstances it was not in the least surprising that the view gained ground that individuals might in good conscience act contrary to the traditional teaching. In 1963 the Dutch hierarchy had expressed a hope that when the Second Vatican Council, first convened by Pope John XXIII, resumed its work it would be able to consider questions about use of the contraceptive pill 'in a broader context'.[9] And in 1964, in London, Archbishop Thomas Roberts, the Jesuit retired Archbishop of Bombay, also looked forward to the Council's third session, 'where, it is expected, this question will be raised', since for him it

[7] 'La questione è allo studio, quanto più largo e profondo possibile, cioè quanto più grave ed onesto dev'essere in materia di tanto rilievo. È allo studio, diciamo, che speriamo presto concludere con la collaborazione di molti ed insigni studiosi. Ne daremo pertanto presto le conclusioni nella forma che sarà ritenuta più adeguata all'oggetto trattato e allo scopo da conseguire. Ma diciamo intanto francamente che non abbiamo finora motivo sufficiente per retinere superate e perciò non obbliganti le norme date da Papa Pio XII a tale riguardo; esse devono perciò retinersi valide, almeno finché non Ci sentiamo in coscienza obbligati a modificarle. In tema di tanta gravità sembra bene che i Cattolici vogliano seguire un'unica legge, quale la Chiesa autorevolmente propone; e sembra pertanto opportuno raccomandare che nessuno per ora si arroghi di pronunciarsi in termini difformi dalla norma vigente', *AAS* 56 (1964), pp. 588–9. The diplomatic tone of the last sentence, 'recommending' that at present no one make a statement diverging from the traditional teaching, may be explained by the context of a papal address to Cardinals and by the awareness that a number of bishops and cardinals, including the Dutch hierarchy, felt the need for some flexibility in the matter. Cf. Pyle, pp. 32–4. It may also be noted that Archbishop Roberts's article expressing his disquiet about the Church's teaching had appeared only a few weeks previously. Cf. the further documentation contained in Leo Pyle (ed.), *Pope and Pill* (London, 1968), pp. 8–12.
[8] Cf. Pyle, *The Pill*, pp. 221–4, *Pope and Pill*, pp. 24–6. On the repercussions caused in England by statements of the highly popular Redemptorist moralist, Bernard Häring, cf. Pyle, *The Pill*, pp. 150–64. (On probabilism, cf. *supra*, pp. 227–9).
[9] Ibid., p. 33.

was only the Church's authority and not its arguments from natural law which carried weight at present.[10] 'We certainly may and must press for the acceptance by the General Council of the "challenge" to justify by reason our own challenge to the world made in the name of reason.'[11] A different expectation of the Council was expressed by Cardinal Heenan and the English hierarchy, namely, that it would 'reassure and comfort those bewildered by current attacks on the traditional teaching about Christian marriage'.[12] The suggestions that the Council might produce a change in teaching were irresponsible, for the teaching traditional since Augustine and restated by Popes Pius XI and XII was 'the plain teaching of Christ' who warns against false leaders and 'calls for sacrifice and self-denial'.[13]

When it did meet, however, for its third session the Council was not to debate the subject, far less decide on it, except to conclude in the most general terms that in harmonizing married love with respect for human life married people could not depend simply on sincerity and a weighing of motives, but must assess their conduct on 'objective criteria, drawn from the nature of the person and his acts'. Nor was it permissible for children of the Church to take measures for controlling birth which were condemned by the Church's *Magisterium*.[14] The reason for this conciliar silence on contraception, as the Council Fathers explained in their general teaching on marriage and responsible parenthood, was that 'some questions which require further and more detailed investigation have been entrusted at the command of the Supreme Pontiff to a commission for the study of population, family, and childbirth, so that when it completes its task the Supreme Pontiff may deliver judgement. With the teaching of the *Magisterium* in this state, this

[10] Ibid., pp. 86–7.
[11] Ibid., p. 90.
[12] Ibid., p. 96.
[13] Ibid.
[14] 'Moralis igitur indoles rationis agendi, ubi de componendo amore coniugali cum responsabili vitae transmissione agitur, non a sola sincera intentione et aestimatione motivorum pendet, sed obiectivis criteriis, ex personae eiusdemque actuum natura desumptis, determinari debet quae integrum sensum mutuae donationis ac humanae procreationis in contextu veri amoris observant; quod fieri nequit nisi virtus castitatis coniugalis sincero animo colatur. Filiis Ecclesiae, his principiis innixi, in procreatione regulanda, vias inire non licet, quae a Magisterio, in lege divina explicanda, improbantur', *Gaudium et spes*, no. 51; *AAS* 68 (1966), p. 1072.

holy Synod does not intend immediately to propose specific solutions'.[15]

Pope Paul had, in fact, informed the Council of his wish that the problem of contraception be left to the papal commission which was still in session, but this did not prevent several of the Bishops from expressing strong views on the subject.[16] Cardinal Leger, Archbishop of Montreal, publicly referred to a 'fear with regard to conjugal love which has paralysed our theology for such a long time', and Cardinal Suenens of Malines–Brussels offered some observations for the benefit of the papal commission, although his suggestion that a commission be also appointed by the Council to collaborate with the Pope's commission was not taken up.[17] Later, Pope Paul enlarged the fifty-strong membership of the commission to include a body of sixteen cardinals, archbishops, and bishops, with Cardinal Ottaviani as president and Cardinal Heenan of Westminster as vice-president.[18] From remarks of the Pope later that year it appears that he was at the time personally conscious of his responsibility to make a final decision, but unclear as to what it should be.[19] In a public address the following year (October 1966),

[15] 'Quaedam quaestiones quae aliis ac diligentioribus investigationibus indigent, iussu Summi Pontificis, Commissioni pro studio populationis, familiae et natalitatis traditae sunt, ut postquam illa munus suum expleverit, Summus Pontifex iudicium ferat. Sic etiam doctrina Magisterii, S. Synodus solutiones concretas immediate proponere non intendit', ibid., note 14; *AAS*, p. 1073. On various unsuccessful attempts to influence the Council to endorse the teaching of *Casti connubii* and to perpetuate the reference to procreation as the 'primary end' of marriage, cf. Pyle, *Pope and Pill*, pp. 41–8, 68–70; Harris, op. cit., pp. 16–18. This occasioned what *Informations catholiques*, ibid., pp. iii-iv, termed 'une des batailles les plus rudes du concile'. In the event, the Conciliar footnote 14 (*supra*) simply referred the reader to *Casti connubii*, the address of Pius XII to Midwives (October 1951), and the allocution of Pope Paul to the College of Cardinals (*supra*, n. 7).

[16] Cf. Harris, pp. 12–13; Pyle, *Pope*, pp. 27–34.

[17] Pyle, ibid., p. 29; Harris, p. 13.

[18] Harris, p. 14; *Inf. cath.*, ibid., p. iv.

[19] Addressing a conference of Italian women on 12 February 1966, Pope Paul described how the recent Council had given a 'synthetic view' of the problems concerning the family, and continued, 'Non è stata possibile in sede conciliare una trattazione esauriente della materia, specialmente circa il grave e complesso problema sulle norme relative alla natalità. Non è ancora possibile sciogliere la riserva enunciata nel Nostro discorso del giugno 1964; ma in attesa di poter dare più precisi insegnamenti, crediamo opportuno da parte Nostra dire in proposito una parola di esortazione pastorale . . . . Non tutti i problemi, dicevamo, sui quali gli sposi e i genitori cristiani attendono e desiderano una parola, hanno potuto essere affrontati: alcuni di essi, per la loro complessità e delicatezza, non potevano venire discussi facilmente in una assemblea numerosa; altri richiedevano e richiedono studi approfonditi, per i quali è stata costituita, com'è noto, una speciale Commissione

in the course of a eulogy on woman, he repeated what he had said more than two years previously, and commented that the conciliar teaching on parenthood was 'most useful' but did not alter the 'substantial elements' of Catholic doctrine on the regulation of births.[20]

Eventually, in 1966, Pope Paul informed the world that the 'broad, varied, and extremely skilled international commission' had now presented its findings, but, he added, 'they cannot be considered definitive' without consideration of their serious doctrinal and pastoral implications. On this the Pope was now engaged, and would be 'for some time yet'. In the meantime, he continued, the traditional norm 'cannot be considered as not binding, as if the *magisterium* of the Church were in a state of doubt at the present time, whereas it is rather in a moment of study and reflection concerning matters which have been placed before it as worthy of the most attentive consideration'.[21] What followed,

---

pontificia, la quale è stata incaricata di approfondire lo studio di questi problemi nei loro vari aspetti: scientifici, storici, sociologici e dottrinali, avvalendosi anche di larghissime consultazioni di Vescovi e di esperti. Noi invitiamo ad attendere i risultati di questi studi, accompagnandoli con la preghiera: il Magistero della Chiesa non può proporre norme morali, se non quando è certo di interpretare il volere di Dio; e per raggiungere questa certezza la Chiesa non è dispensata dalle ricerche, né dall'esame delle molte questioni da ogni parte del mondo proposte alla sua considerazione: operazioni queste talvolta lunghe e non facili', *AAS* 58 (1966), pp. 218–19. Pyle, *Pope and Pill*, p. 59, records an interview of Pope Paul which appeared in *Corriere della Sera* (4 October, 1965), and in which he is reported as saying, 'The world is wondering what we think and we must give an answer. But what? The Church has never in her history confronted such a problem . . . . There is a good deal of study going on; but we have to make the decision. This is our responsibility alone. Deciding is not as easy as studying. But we must say something. What? . . . God must truly enlighten us.'

[20] 'Ricorderemo qui soltanto ciò che abbiamo esposto nel Nostro discorso del 23 giugno 1964; e cioè: il pensiero e la norma della Chiesa non sono cambiati; sono quelli vigenti nell'insegnamento tradizionale della Chiesa. Il Concilio Ecumenico, testé celebrato, ha apportato alcuni elementi di giudizio, utilissimi ad integrare la dottrina cattolica su questo importantissimo tema, ma non tali da cambiarne i termini sostanziali . . . . Con ciò la nuova parola, che si attende dalla Chiesa, sul problema della regolazione delle nascite, non è ancora pronunciata, per il fatto che Noi stessi, avendola promessa e a Noi riservata, abbiamo voluto prendere in attento esame le istanze dottrinali e pastorali, che su tale problema sono sorte in questi ultimi anni . . . .' *AAS* 58 (1966), pp. 1168–9.

[21] 'Ciò è parso essere Nostro dovere; e abbiamo cercato di compierlo nel modo migliore, incaricando un'ampia, varia, versatissima Commissione internazionale; la quale, nelle sue diverse sezioni e con lunghe discussioni, ha compiuto un grande lavoro, ed ha a Noi rimesso le sue conclusioni. Le quali, tuttavia, a Noi sembra, non

almost inevitably, was widespread debate on when a state of doubt is not a state of doubt, with all the probabilist implications of that term, but only a state of study and reflection which could not therefore be pointed to as a basis for a legitimate variety of practical solutions.[22]

The situation could only be exacerbated when the final report of the papal commission was unofficially made public, and it also became known that 'the four theologians of the minority group acknowledged they could not demonstrate the intrinsic evil of contraception on the basis of natural law and so rested their case on Authority and the fear of possible consequences of change both to Authority and to sexual morality'.[23] In its final report, comprising eight short chapters, the papal commission distinguished between a selfish and sinful 'contraceptive mentality', and intervention in physiological processes as an application of objective moral criteria; and it concluded 'it is impossible to determine exhaustively by a general judgement and ahead of time for each individual case what these objective criteria will demand in the concrete situation of a couple'.[24] The cardinals and bishops of the papal commission prefaced the technical report with a pastoral introduction in which the Church's *magisterium* was described as 'in evolution' on the subject. This approach was unacceptable to the small number of dissentients in the commission, whose views were expressed in a document immediately dubbed the 'Minority Report' by the media, but which had in fact been a position paper produced for the commission and arguing in favour of retaining the Church's

possono essere considerate definitive, per il fatto ch'esse presentano gravi implicazioni con altre non poche e non lievi questioni, sia d'ordine dottrinale, che pastorale e sociale, le quali non possono essere isolate e acantonate, ma esigono una logica considerazione nel contesto di quella posta allo studio. Questo fatto . . . impone alla Nostra responsabilità un supplemento di studio . . . . È questo il motivo che ha ritardato il Nostro responso, e che lo dovrà differire ancora per qualche tempo. Intanto, come già dicemmo nel citato discorso, la norma finora insegnata dalla Chiesa, integrata dalle sagge istruzioni del Concilio, reclama fedele e generosa osservanza; né può essere considerata non vincolante, quasi che il magistero della Chiesa fosse ora in stato di dubbio, mentre è in un momento di studio e di riflessione su quanto è stato prospettato come meritevole di attentissima considerazione', ibid., pp. 1169–70.

[22] Cf. Pyle, *Pope*, pp. 71–73.
[23] Dr John Marshall, a member of the Papal Commission from its first appointment, in a letter to *The Times*, 3 August 1968 (Pyle, *Pope*, pp. 83–5).
[24] Pyle, pp. 263, 266.

traditional doctrine.[25] It claimed to uphold 'a teaching which until the present decade was constantly and authentically taught by the Church', and it observed that 'for the Church to have erred so gravely in its grave responsibility of leading souls would be tantamount to seriously suggesting that the assistance of the Holy Spirit was lacking to her'.[26] After exploring various lines of philosophical argument the paper concludes that 'the question is not merely or principally philosophical. It depends on the nature of human life and human sexuality, as understood theologically by the Church.'[27] The *magisterium* and its authority are being viewed by some in modern times as providing broad clarifications and not specific edicts issued once for all. But the Holy See has never viewed matters in this manner.[28]

Eventually, five years after the original small commission had been appointed by Pope John XXIII, four years after Pope Paul VI had predicted that the commission's results would soon be forthcoming, and two years after it had finally submitted its report, Pope Paul VI issued, on 25 July 1968, his encyclical letter 'on the right ordering of propagating human offspring'.[29] Its message (in extremely summary form) was that the conclusions of the papal commission did not exonerate the Pope from a personal examination of the whole matter. Those conclusions had not been unanimous, and in particular certain approaches and arguments had emerged which deviated from the Church's firm traditional teaching.[30] After

---

[25] Cf. Harris, pp. 20, n. 19; 165; Pyle, pp. 193–4, recording the statement of Cardinal Heenan with reference to 'the minority report which, although I presided at many meetings of the Pontifical Commission, I had not seen before it appeared in *The Tablet*. It was not signed by any of the cardinals or bishops. I assume that the priests who signed sent their views privately to the Pope. This does not constitute what in England we would call an official minority report.' In giving the text of the document, Pyle, p. 272, reports that the four theologians who signed it were Frs Ford, Visser, Zalba, and de Lestapis. For the contrary 'position paper' arguing for 'evolution' in Church teaching, and submitted by Frs Fuchs and Sigmond and Canon Delhaye to be 'approved by a majority of the theologians on the commission,' cf. Pyle, pp. 296–306.

[26] Pyle, pp. 276, 296.

[27] Ibid., p. 280.

[28] Ibid., pp. 282–4.

[29] *Litterae Encyclicae . . . de propagatione humanae prolis recte ordinanda, AAS* 60 (1968), pp. 481–503. In accordance with custom the letter is referred to by its opening words, 'Humanae vitae tradendae munus gravissimum . . .'.

[30] 'Attamen conclusiones, ad quas Coetus pervenerat, a Nobis tales existimari non poterant, quae vim iudicii certi ac definiti prae se ferrent quaeque Nos officio liberarent, tam gravis momenti quaestionem per Nosmetipsos consideratione

careful reflection and prayer Pope Paul himself concluded that the Church's traditional rejection of contraception and sterilization must be upheld as following from the basic principles of the human and Christian doctrine of marriage and as part of God's moral law. He closed by recalling his reliance on 'the firm doctrine of the Church which the Successor of Peter faithfully guards and interprets along with his brothers in the Catholic episcopate', and he repeated the need for man, if he is to attain to the true happiness for which he longs, to observe the laws which God has built into his nature to be wisely and lovingly respected.[31]

Six days after the publication of *Humanae Vitae*, at his weekly summer audience at Castelgandolfo, Pope Paul reflected on his encyclical and disclosed his own tortured feelings in the course of its preparation and in the making of his final decision. First and foremost was the continual awareness of the weight of his enormous responsibility, which had caused him great spiritual suffering, to respond to the Church and to all humanity against the background of tradition and the teaching of his immediate predecessors, as well as of the Council. He was predisposed to accept so far as he could the conclusions and the consultative nature of the papal commission, but at the same time to act prudently. He was fully aware of the impassioned discussions going on, of the media and of public opinion, and of the appeals of

expendendi; his vel etiam de causis, quod in Coetu plena sententiarum consensio de normis moralibus proponendis afuerat, quodque praesertim quaedam quaestionis dissolvendae viae rationesque exstiterant, a doctrina morali de matrimonio, a Magisterio Ecclesiae firma constantia proposita, discendentes', ibid., no. 6; pp. 484–5.

[31] 'Verumtamen Ecclesia, dum homines commonet de observandis praeceptis legis naturalis, quam constanti sua doctrina interpretatur, id docet necessarium esse, ut *quilibet matrimonii usus* ad vitam humanam procreandam per se destinatus permaneat', ibid., no. 11; p. 488. 'Quare primariis hisce principiis humanae et christianae doctrinae de matrimonio nixi, iterum debemus dicere, . . .', no. 14; p. 490. 'Ecclesia autem . . . non idcirco iniunctum sibi praetermittit officium, totam legem moralem, cum naturalem tum evangelicam, humiliter ac firmiter praedicandi. Cum Ecclesia utramque hanc legem non condiderit, eiusdem non arbitra, sed tantummodo custos atque interpres esse potest, eique numquam fas erit licitum declarare, quod revera illicitum est, cum id suapte natura germano hominis bono semper repugnet', ibid., no. 18; p. 494. 'Vos . . . nunc advocamus, firmissima freti Ecclesiae doctrina, quam Petri Successor, una cum catholici episcopatus Fratribus, fideliter custodit atque interpretatur . . . siquidem homo ad veram felicitatem, quam totis sui animi viribus affectat, pervenire nequit, nisi leges observat, a summo Deo in ipsius natura insculptas, quae sunt prudenter amanterque colendae', ibid., no. 31; pp. 502–3.

countless less powerful troubled individuals. He had frequently felt submerged in a sea of documents, and humanly overwhelmed at the apostolic duty of pronouncing on them all. Often he had trembled before the dilemma of simply yielding to current opinion or of delivering a judgement which would be ill received by contemporary society or might be an arbitrary imposition on married couples.

He had, Pope Paul continued, consulted many experts. He had prayed for light from the Holy Spirit and placed his conscience at the full disposal of the voice of truth, seeking to interpret the divine rule he saw emerging from the interior demand of authentic human love, from the essential structures of the institution of marriage, from the personal dignity of married people, from their mission to serve life, and from the holiness of Christian marriage. He had reflected on the factors established by the traditional doctrine of the Church, and especially on the teaching of the Council. He had weighed the consequences of one decision and the other. And he had had no further doubt on his duty to speak as he had done.

Throughout all this concern, he had been continually also guided by a second feeling, that of love and pastoral sensitivity for married people. He had been happy to follow the Council's personalist approach to marriage, thus giving first place 'in the subjective evaluation of marriage' to the love which creates and nourishes a marriage. And this had led him to accept all the pastoral, medical, and educational suggestions which would ease the observance of the ruling which he had reaffirmed.

The Pope's final feeling in preparing the encyclical had been one of hope. In spite of the diversity of widespread opinions and in spite of the difficulties which the way he had indicated would entail for those who wished to commit themselves faithfully to it, as for those who ought to teach it, his hope was that the encyclical would be well received for its own force and its human truth, and that educated people especially would be able to discover in it its connection with the Christian view of life which authorized the Pope to make his own St Paul's statement, 'we have the mind of Christ' (1 Cor. 2: 16). He also hoped that Christian couples would understand that, however severe and hard his words could appear, they were aimed at interpreting the genuineness of their love which was called to be transfigured in the love of Christ for his mystical spouse, the Church. His final wish to his audience was that, as he had attempted to deal with the subject truthfully and lovingly, so they would consider *Humanae Vitae* with respect and in the light of the Christian life.[32]

A more technical official commentary on the encyclical had been presented by Monsignor Lambruschini to the world's press on the occasion of its publication. He was professor of moral theology at Rome's Lateran University, and as well as being chosen as official spokesman of the Vatican on this occasion he had been a member of the commission and was obviously familiar with the whole debate and its history.[33] He described how the commission had worked as four interconnected groups of experts in various fields: doctors and research scientists; demographers: married couples, mostly doctors; and theologians. This last group had a certain prominence and guiding role, while the others provided expertise from their various fields of competence. 'In fact the conclusions of the commission were proposed by the theologians who, nevertheless, had not reached a full concordance of judgements concerning the norms to be proposed. While the theologians of the minority found a common platform in the line of the preceding *magisterium*, those of the majority were not unanimous in their attempt at explaining up to what point of the renewal of that *magisterium* its continuity would be compromised. And it was not just a matter of shades of meaning but of rather profound dissent'.[34]

---

[32] Unusually, the text of this allocution was subsequently printed in *AAS* 60 (1968), pp. 527–30. One interesting feature is that reference is made (p. 528, n. 1) to the study *Amour conjugal et renouveau conciliaire* of the French Jesuit theologian, G. Martelet, whom many considered a prominent collaborator in the composing of *Humanae Vitae*. As a candid baring of the soul, the allocution is a remarkable event. 'A voi diremo semplicemente qualche parole non tanto sul documento in questione, quanto su alcuni Nostri sentimenti, che hanno riempito il Nostro animo nel periodo non breve della sua preparazione. Il primo sentimento è stato quello d'una Nostra gravissima responsabilità . . . Non mai abiamo sentito come in questo congiuntura il peso del Nostro ufficio' (p. 528). . . 'Quante volte abbiamo avuto l'impressione di essere quasi soverchiati da questo cumulo di documentazione' (p. 529). . . . 'E finalmente un sentimento di speranza ha accompagnato la laboriosa redazione di questo documento; la speranza ch'esso, quasi per virtù propria, per la sua umana verità, sarà bene accolto, nonostante la diversità di opinioni oggi largamente diffusa . . .' (p. 530).

[33] On Lambruschini's membership of the commission from its inception, cf. Harris, p. 260. Harris also reports (p. 166) that Lambruschini declined in the course of the final plenary meeting of the commission to participate in drafting a theological report, 'although earlier he had seemed to favour the majority view'. The text of his press statement is reproduced in part in Pyle, pp. 101–5.

[34] Pyle, p. 102.

The most important point which Lambruschini had to make in his lengthy background statement concerned the status of Pope Paul's encyclical as a teaching document of the papal *magisterium*. After observing that study of the encyclical did not suggest that it was an infallible statement, but that nevertheless its authenticity was reinforced by its continuing the teaching of the Church's *magisterium*, he went into the question of how it was to be received.

The pronouncement has come. It is not infallible, but it does not leave the questions concerning birth regulation in a condition of vague problematics. Assent of theological faith is due only to definitions properly so-called, but there is owed also loyal and full assent, interior and not only exterior, to an authentic pronouncement of the *magisterium*, in proportion to the level of the authority from which it emanates—which in this case is the supreme authority of the Supreme Pontiff—and to its object, which is most weighty, since it is a matter of the tormented question of the regulation of births. In particular, it can and must be said that the authentic pronouncement of the *Humanae Vitae* encyclical prevents the forming of a probable opinion, that is to say an opinion acting on the moral plane in contrast with the pronouncement itself, whatever the number and the hierarchical, scientific, and theological authority of those who considered in the past few years that they could form it for themselves. The pretext of a presumed doubt in the Church because of the Pope's long silence has no substance and is in conflict with the renewed pontifical and conciliar appeals to observe previous and always valid directives of the *magisterium*.[35]

Reactions to the Encyclical

One thing at least, then, seemed clear, and that was that Pope Paul's teaching on contraception did not claim to be given infallibly, although a press conference may be considered a strange, almost casual, way of informing the Church on such a matter. But events were to demonstrate that little else appeared clear or settled. The hopes which Pope Paul had expressed about the reception of his encyclical were to be sadly disappointed in the completely unprecedented and violent reactions which it aroused, both outside and within the Roman Catholic Church. One of the signatories to the final commission report described the immediate aftermath of the encyclical's appearance as 'the month of theological anger'.[36]

[35] Ibid., p. 104.
[36] After the August holidays, 'Septembre, par contre, fut le mois de la "colère théologique" ', Philippe Delhaye (ed.), *Pour relire Humanae Vitae* (Gembloux, 1970), p. 9. On Delhaye's position in the papal commission, cf. *supra*, n. 25.

One French periodical commented that 'the first reactions, ranging from enthusiasm through indifference and stupefaction to outright rejection, highlight the place of the contraception controversy in the postconciliar Church and also how much interest the encyclical has aroused outside the Church'.[37] And it was in a context of conflicting reactions within the Church, from individuals, lay, clerical, and scientific, including members of the papal commission, and from professional groups as well as from innumerable periodicals, that the next major development took place—the gradual responses of all the regional and national hierarchies throughout the world to the papal teaching on contraception. In a preliminary letter to all the bishops of the Church, Pope Paul had requested them to present the encyclical in its true 'positive and beneficent aspect',[38] and in the encyclical itself he also requested that bishops discharge their most important responsibility and give a lead to their clergy and people in safeguarding the sanctity of marriage.[39] In the more than thirty episcopal statements which resulted from these two requests we thus have a body of widely-based literature which views *Humanae Vitae* from the standpoint of local churches and is also in a position to comment on the widespread critical reactions to the encyclical.[40]

It is of interest to note that although no local hierarchy took

[37] *Information cath. intern.*, p. xiii. In its editorial the French periodical commented that the encyclical raised the question, not of faith in Christ and its formulation, but of 'some great moral truths'. This was the value of the 'debate' which *Humanae Vitae* was inaugurating, ibid., p. i.

[38] E. Hamel, 'Conferentiae episcopales et Encyclica "Humanae Vitae" ', *Periodica* 58 (1969), p. 327; John Horgan, *Humanae Vitae and the Bishops* (Ireland, 1972), p. 112. Horgan's work and that of Delhaye (*supra*, n. 36) are valuable for providing collections of the various episcopal statements, as well as for their comments and background explanations. Hamel's is a useful factual and theological analysis of the statements.

[39] *Humanae Vitae*, no. 30; *AAS*, ibid., p. 502. Hamel points out that the Belgian hierarchy also referred to the encyclical's statement (no. 28; p. 501) on 'the light of the Holy Spirit enjoyed especially by the Church's pastors in explaining the truth', art. cit., p. 328.

[40] Pyle, *Pope and Pill*, pp. 105 ff., provides much general and editorial reaction, mainly in Britain. Although it reprints a few statements of individual bishops the work evidently went to press before the 'Statement of the Bishops' Conference of England and Wales' was issued in September 1968. (For this, cf. Horgan, op. cit., pp. 112–18). It may also be noted that the translation of the encyclical in Pyle, pp. 239–56 (and in Valsecchi) reproduces the Vatican English version, in which, as the author pointed out in the *Tablet* at the time, the final two sentences of paragraph 29 of the encyclical had been omitted. Cf. Pyle, p. 255, Valsecchi, p. 228, with *AAS*, ibid., p. 502 (infra, n. 59).

public issue with the substantial teaching of the encyclical, some more than others are to be seen struggling with it in an attempt to explain it and to bring its general teaching closer to the real lives, difficulties, and anxieties of their own people. Thus the feature most common to many of these episcopal statements is a sympathetic attempt to help married couples to come to terms with *Humanae Vitae* in the intimacy of their family lives and personal circumstances, and particularly in the light of preoccupations and characteristics peculiar to various regions, countries, and localities. The diversity of the Church is witnessed to, for instance, in the crises of population growth and widespread poverty in under-developed countries noted by the hierarchies of Ceylon and Puerto Rico,[41] or in the fact of being a small minority in an almost completely secular sophisticated society as evidenced in the Scandinavian statement.[42] The confident historical tradition of German and Belgian theological reflection may be sensed in the pronouncements of these hierarchies,[43] and may be contrasted with the stress on tradition and conservation contained in others.[44] The blend of speculation and pragmatism in the context of France[45] may be interestingly compared with the recognition of individual conscience and of the emergence of an articulate laity in England, the land of John Henry Newman,[46] or with the awareness of a powerful theological establishment in the Universities and Colleges of the United States.[47] And the frank and participatory character of

---

[41] Cf. Horgan, pp. 88–9, 231–3.

[42] Cf. the remarks of Horgan, pp. 26–8, on the Scandinavian Church.

[43] The West German Bishops issued two statements (Horgan, pp. 303–4, 305–12) in a Church where public reaction to the encyclical 'was extraordinarily vocal' (ibid., p. 14), and were also in the enviable position of being able to refer to a Letter which they had issued the previous year on 'the necessity and the degree of obligation of decisions of the Church on moral questions' (ibid., p. 304). For the Belgian text, cf. Delhaye, pp. 123–7.

[44] E.g., Italy (Horgan, pp. 163–8), Spain (246–52), India (130–1), Scotland (242–5), Ireland (138–9, 140–62).

[45] French text, adopted 'à la quasi-unanimité', in Delhaye, pp. 149–57, with commentary of Cardinal Renard, pp. 158–61.

[46] 'It must be stressed that the primacy of conscience is not in dispute . . .', Horgan, pp. 112–8 at p. 116.

[47] Horgan, pp. 262–3, 264–302, with extensive quotation from Cardinal Newman (p. 273), and reference to other issues which were disquieting American Catholics, including abortion, the arms race, and the Vietnam War. On this last, the hierarchy wrote positively on the role of dissenting conscience and observed that 'the war in Vietnam typifies the issues which present and future generations will be less willing to leave entirely to the normal political and bureacratic processes of national decision-making' (p. 299).

the Dutch Pastoral Council, including its nine bishops, is evident in its finding the arguments unconvincing,[48] in marked contrast to several episcopal statements elsewhere in the Church which stress the traditional religious values of self-mistrust and the need for authoritative guidance.[49]

From these statements, and from all the other literature evoked by *Humanae Vitae*, it is evident that controversy in the Church at large over the encyclical concentrated on three particular topics: the manner in which Pope Paul had reserved the final judgement and statement to himself; the intrinsic force of the arguments from natural law and tradition which were adduced to justify the Pope's conclusion despite the findings of the papal commission; and the binding force of that conclusion on members of the Church. In the remainder of this chapter we shall offer some reflections on these three topics before concluding with some more general reflections on the impact of the encyclical in the making of modern moral theology.

Collegiality in the Church

Among the episcopal reactions to Pope Paul's initiative were also letters written directly to him by hierarchies or groups of their members. Some unreservedly thanked him for the step which he had taken,[50] but one of the most forthright came from thirty of the thirty-one Indonesian bishops, some of whom were Dutch missionaries. They professed their obedience, but also observed that some of them had difficulties of conscience in not being entirely convinced by the arguments of the encyclical. They expressed a

---

[48] Horgan, pp. 191, 192. 'The assembly considers that the encyclical's total rejection of contraceptive methods is not convincing on the basis of the arguments put forward' (192).

[49] E.g., Columbia (Horgan, pp. 92–4), Portugal (pp. 220–9), Yugoslavia (pp. 313–32).

[50] Addressing the Latin-American Episcopate in the month following his issuing of the encyclical, Pope Paul observed, 'La gran mayoría de la Iglesia la ha recibido favorablemente con obediencia confiada', AAS 60 (1968), p. 649. The subsequent CELAM meeting, held at Medellín, described the teaching of the encyclical as 'clear and unequivocal' and observed that 'the mutual help which married couples derive from meeting together, aided by professional experts and by priests, could give incalculable help to those who in spite of difficulties are trying to reach the ideal proposed' (Horgan, p. 85). On the encyclical's teaching interpreted as an 'ideal', cf. *infra*, p. 284.

wish that 'in so delicate a matter touching the life of the Christian community and all men so intimately, the college of bishops had been expressly consulted'. They also viewed the subsequent world-wide discussion as a witness to Christian vitality and to a continual desire to deepen the meaning of marriage and exalt its sacramental dignity. If there was to be, as intimated, a further encyclical on marriage as a whole, they would respectfully and frankly consider it more consonant with the spirit of Vatican II and of the times for the entire episcopate first to express their opinions in a collegial manner, and they would hope for more precise and solid arguments to be forthcoming, with clearer criticism of contrary positions.[51]

This fraternal reminder of the Church's doctrine of episcopal

---

[51] 'Saint-Père, . . . Certains d'entre nous considèrent la doctrine contenue dans *Humanae Vitae* comme une délivrance . . . . D'autres, en revanche, se sentent accablés dans leur conscience par l'encyclique; . . . ils ne se sentent pas entièrement convaincus par l'argumentation de l'encyclique; et ils auraient préféré que, dans une matière aussi délicate, qui touche si intimement à la vie de la communauté chrétienne, voire de l'ensemble du genre humain, le collège des évêques eût été consulté de façon expresse . . . . Nous avons été informés de l'intention qu'aurait votre Sainteté, après la présente encyclique sur le planning familial et la régulation des naissances, d'en rédiger une autre sur le mariage. Il nous semble que nous ne manquerions nullement à la fraternelle obéissance que nous devons a l'autorité apostolique, si nous exprimions humblement, main en toute franchise le vœu suivant. A l'heure actuelle, il serait—à ce qu'il paraît—plus conforme encore à l'esprit du concile Vatican II et de notre temps, que tous nos frères dans l'épiscopat disséminés dans le monde entier puissent, avant que la doctrine chrétienne sur le mariage soit exposée dans l'encyclique que nous attendons, émettre leur opinion plus explicitement sur ces problèmes, puisqu'ils sont, en tout cas, appelés à agir collégialement (voir *Lumen Gentium*, no. 22 *in fine*) . . .', trans. from the Dutch, in Delhaye, *Pour relire*, pp. 87–8. In a letter to the Indonesian clergy, the bishops referred to their personal communication to Pope Paul and drew attention to his courage and sincerity in 'listening to the voice of his conscience', while also acknowledging a possible *conflictus conscientiae* for many others. 'Il est compré-hensible—et on peut les approuver—que, pour sauvegarder leur amour réciproque et le bien de leur famille, l'homme et la femme puissent, dans une situation déterminée, aboutir à une conclusion qui diffère de la doctrine de l'encyclique' (Delhaye, pp. 89–91). The public statement of the Indonesian hierarchy is not in Delhaye, but cf. Horgan, pp. 132–7, where the bishops advise distressed couples to approach their priests who 'will be able to help husbands and wives in settling their difficulties in peace of mind before God' (136). The further encyclical of Paul VI on marriage to which the Indonesian hierarchy refers did not materialize, although he had said in his allocution following the publication of *Humanae Vitae*, 'non è la trattazione completa di quanto riguardo l'essere umano nel campo del matrimonio, della famiglia, dell'onestà dei costumi, campo immenso nel quale il magistero della Chiesa potrà a dovrà forse ritornare con disegno più ampio, organico e sintetico' (*AAS*, ibid., p. 527.) The project was, instead, to be taken up years later by the Roman Synod of Bishops, to result in Pope John Paul II's apostolic exhortation, *Familiaris Consortio, AAS* 74 (1982), pp. 81–191.

collegiality—the joint responsibility of the entire 'college' of bishops in the Church for the wellbeing of the Church at large— gave theological weight and expression to the widespread reaction that Pope Paul need not, or should not, have felt it necessary to restrict final reflection and action to himself. The anguish felt by him at the heavy responsibility he experienced, as described above, in having to give a definitive judgement on contraception gave eloquent witness to his nobility and strong sense of personal duty, which no one questioned. But the question which did have to be asked, in the view of many, was whether that final lonely eminence was necessary in view of the doctrine of episcopal collegiality which had been recently affirmed in Vatican II as a balancing development of the concentration by Vatican I on the role and function of the papacy.[52] In his encyclical Pope Paul vindicated the competency of the Church's *magisterium* to interpret the natural moral law in the communication by Christ of his divine power 'to Peter and the other apostles . . . . as the authentic guardians and interpreters of the whole moral law'.[53] But in the event matters had proceeded in a way which is perhaps best summed up in the simple phrase 'old habits die hard'.

Nevertheless, it is possible to argue that developments following the issuing of *Humanae Vitae* can be viewed as a cumulative expression of episcopal collegiality in the Church. One commentator on the various episcopal statements notes the degree to which they may be considered as 'primarily pastoral in purpose and tone', some of them not content with repeating the 'general principles' of the encyclical but applying them to particular questions about the binding force of the encylical and the situation of those who cannot

[52] Cf. *Lumen gentium*, 22; *AAS* 57 (1965), pp. 26–7, 'Collegium hoc quatenus ex multis compositum, varietatem et universalitatem Populi Dei, quatenus vero sub uno capite collectum unitatem gregis Christi exprimit. In ipso, Episcopi, primatum et principatum Capitis sui fideliter servantes, propria potestate in bonum fidelium suorum, immo totius Ecclesiae funguntur, Spiritu Sancto organicam structuram eiusque concordiam continenter roborante . . . . Eadem potestas collegialis una cum Papa exerceri potest ab Episcopis in orbe terrarum degentibus, dummodo Caput Collegii eos ad actionem collegialem vocet, vel saltem Episcoporum dispersorum unitam actionem approbet vel libere recipiat, ita ut verus actus collegialis efficiatur.'

[53] 'Haud namque dubium est—ut saepenumero Decessores Nostri pronunti-averunt—Christum Iesum, cum Petrum ceterosque Apostolos divinae potestatis suae participavisset, eosque ad omnes gentes praeceptis suis docendas misisset, illos ipsos totius de moribus legis certos custodes interpretesque instituisse', no. 4; *AAS* 60 (1968) p. 483.

accept it, whether in theory or in practice. He is of the opinion that at times an interpretation given amounts, in effect, to a rejection in that respect of the encyclical's prohibition.[54] A more promising theological line, however, is taken by another commentator who views many of the episcopal statements as complementing the doctrine of the encyclical by placing it 'in a higher synthesis which includes the traditional doctrine on Christian conscience and its duties and responsibilities, as well as principles for assessing culpability'.[55] And he goes on to make the important theological point that the various bishops' joint statements on the encyclical are also exercises in episcopal collegiality and acts of the ordinary *magisterium* of the Church.[56]

In other words, it is misleading and an undervaluing of such pronouncements to view them simply as pastoral or executive applications of the Church's doctrine, and not as also magisterial exercises of episcopal doctrinal teaching in continuity with the papal teaching and providing an organic development of that teaching. Thus, the teaching of the Church's ordinary *magisterium* on contraception is not to be considered as *Humanae Vitae* alone, but *Humanae Vitae* in the light of all other more particular episcopal statements. The total result, then, may be regarded as collegiality after the event, a gradual building up of episcopal collegial teaching in the Church over the months following the promulgation of the encyclical.

Had there been such full consultation and such an exercise of episcopal co-responsibility before the whole Church's hierarchical *magisterium* pronounced on the subject—as the Indonesian bishops at least would have wished—and assuming that the whole episcopate would have actually agreed on a statement being issued, it is impossible to say what the outcome would have been in terms of the arguments marshalled and the nature of the final conclusion. It is not implausible to consider that the collegial teaching which

[54] A. Flannery, in Horgan, pp. 351–67 at pp. 356–7.

[55] Hamel, 'Conf. Episc.', p. 329.

[56] Ibid., p. 331, 'Plerique declarationes natae sunt ut fructus laboris et reflexionis communis, cui participaverunt omnes Episcopi uniuscuiusque nationis . . . . En opus vere collegiale quod perfecerunt Episcopi secundum proprias nationes adunati, suam solidaritatem communionemque cum successore Petri semper affirmantes, sed suam responsabilitatem pastoralem erga proprium gregem assumentes. Unde talia documenta, qua testimonia fidei et veritatis, maius pondus habent quam studium theologorum privatorum. Vere sunt actus ipsius magisterii ordinarii Ecclesiae.'

eventually materialized was the more realistic and effective for being a slow accumulation in response to the way in which the original encyclical was being received. The nuances to be found in various episcopal statements would not necessarily have been built into an earlier joint statement, since many of these qualifications and glosses were found to be a necessary consequence of, and accommodation to, widespread critical reactions to the encyclical from laity, clergy, and theologians throughout the rest of the Church. Perhaps one conclusion to be drawn from this consideration is that a doctrine even of episcopal collegiality, while clearly providing a broader theological context for the exercise of papal responsibility, is still in danger of continuing the sharp distinction between the 'teaching' Church and the 'learning' Church which we examined in an earlier chapter.[57] The painful experience of the reactions to *Humanae Vitae* in the Church as a whole points, rather, to the need for more thorough consideration and broadening of the sources of consultation and co-responsibility in the Church. In the body of episcopal teaching, comprising the encyclical and the resulting episcopal pronouncements which the Pope had invited in its support, it is possible to see a further expression of the Matthaean theology of authoritative teaching which we have already considered, with little reference to the positive functioning of what Vatican II also referred to as 'the Christian sense of the faithful' having a contribution to make to the solution of difficulties of family life.[58] It is true, of course, that Pope Paul referred to the influence of the Holy Spirit in the minds and hearts of the faithful, but the role of the Spirit is seen by him as simply confirming what was being proposed by the papal *magisterium* rather than as making any more positive contribution to the contents of that proposal.[59]

[57] *Supra*, p. 222.
[58] Cf. *supra*, p. 207.
[59] 'Fiduciae autem pleni loquamini, dilecti Filii, pro certo habentes, Sanctum Dei Spiritum, dum adest Magisterio rectam proferenti doctrinam, intus corda fidelium illustrare eosque ad assentiendum invitare', no. 29; *AAS*, p. 502. (This was one of the sentences omitted in the Vatican English translation of the encyclical—cf. supra, n. 40—the other, immediately following and completing paragraph 29, being 'Coniuges vero necessariam precandi viam edocete, apteque instituite, ut saepius magna cum fide ad Eucharistiae et Paenitentiae sacramenta accedant, neque umquam pro sua infirmitate animos demittant' (ibid.). Paragraphs 28–9 are addressed to priests.) On this merely confirmatory role of the Spirit, cf. *supra*, p. 222.

Besides pointing to the need not only for episcopal collegiality but for a collegiality which accords with the gift of the Spirit to the entire Church as a mutually teaching and learning community, the event of *Humanae Vitae* in the Church may contain the seed of another theological development concerning the nature of the Church. As we have seen, both before and in the encyclical Pope Paul requested his brothers in the world-wide episcopate to commend the papal teaching to their people, and this the various episcopal conferences and groupings did, with the various comments which we have been considering. In the invitation and production of these several statements it is possible to see, in germ at least, a practical acknowledgement of the reality of the 'local Church' which Vatican II had begun to rescue from the obscurity of history, but to which it had been able to provide only general pointers for further reflection.[60] In addressing episcopal conferences Pope Paul may also be considered as, perhaps unknowingly, addressing himself not just to Christian individuals within the universal Church—whether episcopal or otherwise, and possessing various degrees of jurisdiction or teaching authority—but to Christian communities in the persons of their pastors. And the responses of those pastors, in taking particular account of local reactions and peculiarities, may also be seen as expressing in some measure and in however inchoate a manner the responses of the local Churches as such to the papal encyclical. The development of the theology of the local Church in more recent years, then, may be considered to provide a context, in the light of *Humanae Vitae*, within which further papal pronouncements might be considered more explicitly as directed not to souls but to Churches at various levels of regional or national self-identity. To that extent they would constitute not simply authoritative decisions but the initiation of dialogue, with a view to eliciting and identifying the mind of the whole Church which Christ founded. In this interpretation of the past which provides a project for the future, the role of not only the episcopacy but also the papacy may be theologically clarified as rooted in, and emerging from, the body of all the faithful which they exist to serve.

---

[60] 'Haec Christi Ecclesia vere adest in omnibus legitimis fidelium congregationibus localibus, quae, pastoribus suis adhaerentes, et ipsae in Novo Testamento ecclesiae vocantur. Hae sunt enim loco suo Populus novus a Deo vocatus, in Spiritu Sancto et in plenitudine multa (1 Thess. 1: 5)', *Lumen gentium*, no. 26; *AAS* 57 (1965), p. 31.

And in such a theological context it is not in the least fanciful to consider not only episcopal documents (as recently in the United States of America) but also papal ones as partaking of something of the nature of a parliamentary White Paper—at least in the area of disputed moral questions—which considers and sifts all relevant facts and arguments and reactions before a final judgement is formulated.

Reasoning, Prophecy, and Intuition

It was the force of the encyclical's arguments, both those intrinsic from human reasoning, and those extrinsic from tradition and the assistance of the Holy Spirit to the *magisterium*, which formed the second basic issue to which *Humanae Vitae* gave rise. It is interesting for a historically-minded theologian to compare the reaction of Pope Paul to moves to modify the Church's traditional teaching on contraception with the reaction of Pope Pius XII and the earlier encyclical *Humani Generis* to similar moves to modify the Church's traditional teaching on the descent of all men from a single parent, Adam. In the former there is to be found an uncompromising reiteration of the need for any exercise of marriage to remain inherently orientated to reproduction.[61] In the latter case Pius XII was more circumspect with regard to the view that the human race is descended from more than one original human being. 'This view cannot be held by Christians . . . . since it is not at all clear how this kind of view can be reconciled with what is stated about original sin by the sources of revealed truth and the actions of the Church's *magisterium*.'[62] Pius commented that it was not clear how new thinking could be reconciled with traditional teaching; Paul stated of the findings of his papal commission that some of its approaches 'deviated from' the Church's traditional teaching.[63]

The difference between these two approaches is one of more than words. The former is a reasoned and reasonable hesitancy which

---

[61] *Supra*, n. 31.

[62] 'Cum nequaquam appareat quomodo huiusmodi sententia componi queat cum iis quae fontes revelatae veritatis et acta Magisterii Ecclesiae proponunt de peccato originali . . .', DS 3897.

[63] *Supra*, n. 30.

almost implies an invitation to those concerned and competent to continue their endeavours and to try to make it clear how such a position could come to be reconciled with traditional Church teaching. The latter is a flat rejection. In *Humanae Vitae* it was the confident tone of the conclusions following on what appeared very spare or outmoded arguments which baffled many readers. They found the arguments lacking in force, particularly since the papal commission on the subject had concluded, by a large majority, in favour of change. Probably the most highly respected theologian in the Church, Karl Rahner, felt it instructive to offer a theological analysis of the striking phenomenon of strong, rapid, and wide-spread disagreement with the non-infallible teaching of the encyclical and particularly with its arguments, which he himself found more the adopting of a particular attitude to contraception than an explanation or proof of that attitude. 'It hardly goes beyond the actual statement of the thesis.'[64] And despite the warnings of Monsignor Lambruschini at the Vatican Press Conference, aimed at forestalling any attempt to cast theological 'doubt' on the Pope's teaching, one of the most influential moral theologians in the Church, the American Richard McCormick, who wrote from within a highly experienced American Jesuit tradition in medical ethics, concluded regretfully that 'at least very many theologians will agree that there are serious methodological problems, even deficiencies, in the analysis used to support this conclusion', and that the teaching reiterated in the encyclical 'remains a teaching subject to solid and positive doubt.'[65]

That these were not just the reactions of a few aberrant theologians, and that in the years following the issuing of the encyclical there continued to be widespread dissatisfaction among Church members with the case against contraception, emerged clearly in 1980 when the recently established Synod of Bishops met in Rome to 'act in the name of the whole episcopate' and 'give more effective help to the supreme pastor of the Church', as the Council

---

[64] 'On the Encyclical "Humanae Vitae" ', *Theological Investigations*, vol. xi (London, 1974), p. 277. Cf. ibid., p. 265, where Rahner identifies some of 'the basic assumptions underlying the papal position' which are 'in the encyclical itself so fleetingly indicated' but which 'do need to be discussed'. The article first appeared in *Stimmen der Zeit* 182 (1968), pp. 193–210, and was reprinted in other publications and languages (ibid., p. 324).

[65] *Theological Studies* (29 (1968), pp. 731, 737.

document *Christus Dominus* described its function.[66] The discussions in Synod on the theme of the family today contained
numerous requests for a clearer explanation of the teaching of
Humanae Vitae if it was to have the desired effect. It was in the
light of these pressing requests that Pope John Paul II addressed
himself to the subject of contraception in his Apostolic Exhortation,
issued the following year, on the role of the Christian family in the
modern world; and what he had to say is of great importance for
moral theology for several reasons. He explained first how 'in
continuity with the living tradition of the ecclesial community
throughout history, the recent Second Vatican Council and the
magisterium of my predecessor Paul VI, expressed above all in the
encyclical *Humanae Vitae*, have handed on to our times a truly
prophetic proclamation, which reaffirms and reproposes with
clarity the Church's teaching and norm, always old yet always new,
regarding marriage and regarding the transmission of human life'.
It was this, he continued, which had led the Synod to reaffirm the
teaching of Vatican II and of *Humanae Vitae*, 'particularly that love
between husband and wife must be fully human, exclusive, and
open to new life'.[67]

Having, however, referred to the teaching of Pope Paul VI as 'a
truly prophetic proclamation' his successor also acknowledged how
difficult this was to understand in modern society with its quite
widespread 'anti-life mentality' and the many complex problems,
including population growth, which affected married couples.[68]
The Church maintained, however, that all these problems really
reconfirmed the importance of 'the authentic teaching on birth
regulation reproposed in the Second Vatican Council and in the
Encyclical *Humanae Vitae*'. This was why he and the Synod Fathers
felt it their duty to call on theologians to help the hierarchical
Magisterium make this teaching 'truly accessible to all people of
good will' by 'illustrating ever more clearly the biblical foundations,

---

[66] 'Episcopi e diversis orbis regionibus selecti, modis et rationibus a Romano
Pontifice statutis vel statuendis, Supremo Ecclesiae Pastori validiorem praestant
adiutricem operam in Consilio, quod proprio nomine *Synodus Episcoporum*
appellatur, quae quidem, utpote totius catholici Episcopatus partes agens, simul
significat omnes Episcopos in hierarchica communione sollicitudinis universae
Ecclesiae participes esse', *Christus Dominus*, no. 5; *AAS* 58 (1966), p. 675.
[67] *Familiaris Consortio*, CTS (London, 1981), no. 29; *AAS* 74 (1982), p. 115
('Propheticum vere nuntium'). On the Council's approach, cf. *supra*, pp. 263–4.
[68] Ibid., no. 30; *AAS*, pp. 115–16.

the ethical grounds and the personalistic reasons behind this doctrine'. And he concluded, 'in fulfilment of their specific role, theologians are called upon to provide enlightenment and a deeper understanding, and their contribution is of incomparable value and represents a unique and highly meritorious service to the family and humanity'.[69]

The previous pastoral experience of Pope John Paul II had, of course, made him aware of what he here termed 'the many complex problems' which affected married couples and which contributed to the difficulty of appreciating the prophetic nature of the Church's repeated teaching. Not only had he been a participant, as Archbishop of Cracow, at the Second Vatican Council but he had also been one of the members of the hierarchy appointed by Pope Paul to the papal commission in its final stage, although he was not in Rome during the crucial days when the commission discussed and voted on its final report.[70] An article had also been published in the Vatican publication, l'*Osservatore Romano*, in January 1969, by Cardinal Wojtyla which strongly supported the argumentation of *Humanae Vitae* in characteristically personalist terms.[71]

Two lines of reflection are suggested by Pope John Paul's remarks concerning reasons, the prophetic nature of *Humanae Vitae*'s teaching, and the function of moral theologians. The first is that in offering 'a pressing invitation to theologians to collaborate with the hierarchical *Magisterium*' the Synod is clearly justified in viewing this ecclesial role as essential to the function of moral theologians. And in specifying that such collaboration take the form of a search for a more cogent explanation of the teaching of *Humanae Vitae* the bishops envisage this contribution along the lines laid down by Pope Pius XII when he described the function of theologians as 'indicating how what the living *Magisterium* teaches is found, either explicitly or implicitly in Scripture and divine tradition'.[72] It cannot be deduced, of course, from this specific expectation of the Synod of Bishops that they would view the entire role of theologians as exclusively supportive in this way, important as this function undoubtedly is. Most theologians would consider their contribution to the mind and teaching of the Church as more

---

[69] Ibid., no. 31; pp. 117–18.
[70] Cf. Harris, pp. 162, 165–7.
[71] A French translation is to be found in Delhaye, pp. 185–93.
[72] DS 3886. Cf. *supra*, p. 160.

than one of apologetics, particularly in an area where the teaching in question, which many people have found incomprehensible, is not proposed infallibly and is therefore in principle capable of refinement or reform. Theologians have frequently been considered—most publicly in the workings of many Ecumenical Councils and indeed in the papal commission itself—as providing a contribution which is more than simply a confirmation of the current state of the question, and which may also include, in the spirit of what Vatican II had to say of the entire people of God, an exploring of what from the Word of God the Church is trying to articulate to itself and the world. In this perspective it is not, then, inappropriate, as we have already suggested, to compare the relationship between hierarchy and theologians with that existing between the patron and the artist whose work he commissions but whose final product may be in some respects not quite what the patron originally had in mind.[73]

The second line of reflection concerns prophecy. As we have seen, Pope John Paul II described *Humanae Vitae* as 'a truly prophetic proclamation', but in view of other remarks in his Apostolic Exhortation the sense of 'prophecy' intended here cannot be that proposed by some commentators at the time when the encyclical appeared. Some invoked the term in what was in effect a softening interpretation of the papal teaching, as in the suggestion that 'perhaps the document should be read as one that points in a general direction and prophetically defends the great values of life and marital love. In other words, perhaps it can be read as delineating an ideal towards which we must work.'[74] But Pope John Paul firmly rejected this prophetic-ideal approach when he observed that married people 'cannot look on the law as merely an ideal to be achieved in the future: they must consider it as a command of Christ the Lord to overcome difficulties with constancy'.[75]

How, then, is one to understand 'prophetic' in this context?

---

[73] 'Totius populi Dei est, praesertim pastorum et theologorum, adiuvante Spiritu Sancto, varias loquelas nostri temporis auscultare, discernere et interpretari easque sub lumine verbi divini diiudicare, ut revelata Veritas semper penitius percipi, melius intelligi aptiusque proponi possit', *Gaudium et spes*, 44; *AAS* 58 (1966), p. 1065, Cf. *supra*, p. 172

[74] McCormick, art. cit., pp. 736–7, recording, but doubting, this interpretation of the encyclical.

[75] *Familiaris Consortio*, no. 34; *AAS* 74 (1982), p. 123.

Another possible approach could be by way of considering a particular feature of the role of the prophet in any community. As we find the prophet active in Scripture and in society today, it may be suggested, he or she can be seen as adopting a personal position in some area of activity which is an extreme one and which is not one necessarily to be imitated or adopted to the same degree by everyone else. The prophetic stance is often one which, by its extremity, other people are made incapable of ignoring or of avoiding completely in their own personal scheme of things. In a sense, and in his need to make an impact, or even a dent, in the minds and lives of others, the prophet is compelled by his very nature or vocation to simplify, and even to over-simplify, the complexities of life. It is often a feature of life in any society that one can gain a hearing only with a dramatic headline and rarely with a distinction. The penchant for prophets to over-simplify is not far removed in this respect from heresy, which is the selection of only one aspect of truth to the systematic exclusion of all others. Perhaps the difference is that the heretic insists that there are no other aspects which fall to be considered, while the prophet is more concerned that the aspect on which he concentrates should never be lost sight of in the whole.

Such an interpretation of prophecy may appear a novel one in characterizing it as an apostolic over-simplification in order to have an effect on the lives of others, but it does offer a hypothesis which fits a variety of prophetic statements and actions. Must one really put no trust whatsoever in princes, or just keep a wary eye on them? Must one always, and without exception, give to absolutely anyone who asks? Or offer no resistance of any kind, not even restraint, to evil-doers? The prophetic role in society and in the Church of religious vowed to the evangelical counsels of poverty, chastity, and obedience has been given fresh impetus and meaning by the Second Vatican Council in its general treatment of charisms, but the prophetic function of such a life is not to induce everyone else to adopt that state. It is to make them seriously aware of the need for some presence in their lives of what religious profess in an extreme form and which could not as such be sustained by all, or by society in general. Again, the spectrum of simplified prophetic stances often adopted by individuals honoured as saints in the course of history is not proposed as a set of attitudes to be universally adopted to the same degree of thoroughness, but as rebukes or reminders to the Church and the society of the day that the values which are in vogue stand in need of balancing and correcting.[76]

Within this understanding of 'prophecy', then, the traditional teaching of the Church on contraception becomes one which is not a charge (or even an 'ideal') laid on all, but an invitation, or vocation, extended to some within the Church and society, with the aim of stressing certain values which are in danger of being submerged or overlooked in the many complex problems of married life. Trust in God and his foresight, which is a central insight in all biblical prophecy; the incomparable dignity of being selected by God to collaborate in his creation at its peak—the emergence of a new human person; the sacrificial element which is central to all genuine love: these and other values may be considered the prophetic dimension in the Church's traditional refusal to permit married couples to express their love for each other in ways which systematically block off that expression from one of its normal consequences. To insist that this consequence should never be impeded in order to highlight the values which such insistence betokens can be seen as prophetic, as a trumpet call from within an orchestral score containing many other melodies. But if it is prophetic teaching in the sense analysed above, then it is over-simple as a complete or sufficient portrayal of Christian married life and all its values and moral requirements. And if it is prophetic action, then it is a vocation offered only to some and perhaps similar in this respect to the teaching of Jesus on permanent celibacy—that it is not for all, 'but only those to whom it is given' (Mat. 19: 11)—or to the teaching of Paul on marriage that 'each has his own special gift from God, one of one kind and one of another' (1 Cor. 7: 7).

It must be obvious, however, that this view of prophecy as a necessarily over-simplified statement or style of life for apostolic purposes is, if applied to Church teaching on contraception, not compatible with the teaching of Pope John Paul, who insists in terms more of a theology of law that the message of *Humanae Vitae* gives married couples 'the norm for the exercise of their sexuality'.[77] What, then, is the sense of the term 'prophetic' which he ascribed to

---

[76] A secular counterpart may be seen in the social and political function of single-issue pressure groups.

[77] *Familiaris Consortio*, no. 34; *AAS*, p. 124.

the encyclical of his predecessor? In the rather popular meaning of 'prophecy', the term can apply to a statement about the future which cannot be substantiated at the time, but which events will show to have been true. The progress of time may enter into the meaning of the term here, not simply in the sense of prediction, but in the sense that a time will come when, looking back, it will be possible to say the teaching was true in spite of the difficulties which men and women had in accepting it, and particularly in accepting the arguments and reasons proposed to justify it. In other words, we may have here an instance of an insight in search of explanation or articulation, some moral truth which the mind can reach but which it cannot, or not yet, fully grasp. In an earlier chapter we considered how Shaw's Saint Joan first heard her voices and the reasons came afterwards, and how (*pace* Pius XII) there is an element in the Church's moral and spiritual tradition which partakes more of intuition than of rational argument.[78] We may recall also how Pope John Paul referred to Pope Paul's 'intuition' in his encyclical, which reflected the experience of many married couples.[79] If to these considerations we add the Pope's request to theologians to provide more enlightening arguments for the teaching on contraception, then it does appear that 'prophetic' in this context is pointing to a quality of immediacy, almost of inspiration, which has not to date been captured or communicated in rational considerations.

This apparently intuitive element of Christian experience is one to which Rahner has referred as 'a moral instinct of faith', a Christian capacity to form moral judgements, whether in particular instances or on more general topics, which cannot be adequately expressed or justified by purely rational considerations, however much the attempt is, and must be, made.[80] As Rahner wrote of *Humane Vitae*, after concluding that it had adopted rather than proved a particular stance in its arguments, the rationale which is clear in the encyclical is adherence to the traditional doctrine of Pius XI and Pius XII; but this factor undoubtedly has considerable theological importance, especially since a global 'instinct' in particular moral questions can be genuine, even if a pope cannot

---

[78] *Supra*, pp. 208–10.

[79] *Supra*, p. 208; *Familiaris Consortio*, no. 33; AAS 74 (1982), p. 122.

[80] 'The problem of genetic manipulation', *Theological Investigations*, Vol. ix, pp. 238–43, 251.

explain himself right up to the final rational and reflective detail.[81]
It appears, then, that this is the sense to be ascribed to Pope John
Paul's statement that *Humanae Vitae* was 'a truly prophetic
proclamation'. In Scripture, prophecy has the quality of being a
direct utterance claiming to originate in God, and in the New
Testament particularly of being a charismatic utterance imparted
by the Spirit of Christ for the building up of the Church. Its
authenticity and its content cannot really be adequately proved or
disproved by rational argument. They can only be 'discerned', and
in some sense authenticated or otherwise by their fruits, or their
working out in history. Nevertheless, the challenge continually
exists to explore, analyse, and commend such utterances in more
prosaic and rational terms, with varying degrees of success. This it
may be said Pope Paul attempted to do, with arguments which
many found opaque or inconclusive and which he himself wrote
were not to be considered as of more importance than the guidance
of the Spirit which he believed he had received in finally deciding to
uphold the traditional attitude of the Church to contraception.[82]

If there is, however, an element of immediacy and of inarticulate-
ness in solely rational terms about any moral insight or intuition,
then the difficulty of expression can affect not only arguments
adduced to prove it, but also statements attempting to express and
define it. Just how the teaching of Pope Paul was to be understood
and accepted by individuals in the Church at large leads us to

---

[81] Art.cit. (*supra*, n. 64), p. 266. 'In all respects we shall surely have to say that on
these questions a specific position has indeed been adopted, but this is merely stated
rather than explained or proved in any effective sense. It becomes clear in the
encyclical itself that the real and primary reason for adhering to this position is the
need that is felt to hold firm to the traditional teaching of Pius XI and Pius XII. This
fact certainly carries a not inconsiderable theological weight, the more so since in
individual moral questions a certain global 'instinct' can be right even when it is
incapable of being explicitated to the utmost at the level of rational theory and
speculation. Yet in view of the fact that *according to the encyclical itself* what is in
question here is not simply a divine revelation of a moral norm, but rather a
principle of the "natural law", it would have been desirable for the material grounds
for holding the papal thesis to have been justified by more precise arguments.'
[82] 'Etenim nostis tali vos [sacerdotes] obsequio devinciri non potius illis de causis,
quae allatae sunt, quam ob Sancti Spiritus lumen, quo praecipue Ecclesiae Pastores
in explananda veritate fruuntur', no. 28; *AAS*, p. 501. Some translators and
commentators have taken this sentence as an assertion that the guidance of the Spirit
is more important than the arguments advanced, but logically they could be of equal
importance. Cf. J. Mahoney, 'Understanding the Encyclical: Six Pastoral Questions',
The Month 40 (1968), pp. 243–4.

consider the third topic around which controversy and dissent flowed in the aftermath of the encyclical.

The Witness of Conscience

The impact of *Humanae Vitae* on the traditional moral doctrine of conscience was considerable. The encyclical itself stated that 'a right conscience is the true interpreter of the objective moral order instituted by God'.[83] It also asserted that 'the interpretation of the natural moral law pertains to the Church's *Magisterium*'.[84] And this inevitably raised the question of the relationship between the individual's conscience and the hierarchical *magisterium* of the Church. It was not simply a speculative question but one which, as events have shown increasingly, has been an actual and agonizing one for many, accentuated perhaps in being depicted frequently, if only implicitly, in terms of a voluntarist confrontation between the freedom of the individual and the binding force of the Church's ordinary non-infallible *Magisterium*. In the previous chapter we saw how the long voluntarist tradition in moral theology led to an adversarial, or conflict, approach to the subject of conscience, in which moral decisions have often been depicted as a complying with, or a repulsing of, the dictates of a more powerful authority. It may be enlightening to pursue these reflections in the context of the application within the Church of *Humanae Vitae*.

One of the revealing signs of the presence of an adversarial attitude of opposing wills in the interpretation of conscience appears to be the arousal of strong feelings and emotions, even to the pitch of anger. Confrontation is the order of the day, with debate conducted in terms of freedom of conscience on the one 'side', and on the other a demand for the respectful obedience which is due to legitimate authority. On the whole, conscience, like human rights, emerges into prominence only when it is felt to be threatened, or to be a threat; and the controversial atmosphere is not one which lends itself to a dispassionate consideration of the

---

[83] 'Porro ea, de qua loquimur, conscia paternita praecipue aliam eamque intimam secum fert rationem, pertinentem ad ordinem moralem, quem obiectivam vocant, a Deoque statutum, cuius recta conscientia est vera interpres', no. 10; *AAS*, p. 487.

[84] 'Nemo sane christifidelium eat infitias, ad Ecclesiae Magisterium interpretationem legis moralis naturalis spectare', no. 4; *AAS*, p. 483.

subject. In point of fact, much of the controversy over conscience is misplaced if it is viewed as a struggle for supremacy between competing powers at odds with each other, for then it can engage individuals in often rancorous dispute rather than in reasonable debate. Those who claim the authority of conscience in such dispute can appear to be in a much stronger, even in an impregnable, position when they say 'my conscience tells me', or 'my conscience would not allow me', than if they were to say simply 'in my view', or 'my personal belief'. It is a move to appeal to the apparently supreme authority of an all-controlling conscience, to whose dictates the only possible reaction on the part of an adversary is to retreat in some confusion at having had the temerity to attempt to impose on another's conscience.

Moreover, the court-of-appeal attitude to conscience does bring out cogently the idea of the duty to follow one's conscience and of having a responsibility towards one's conscience. What it can ignore, however, is that as well as being responsible *to* conscience, the individual is also responsible *for* his conscience—for the quality of its judgements, the range and seriousness of its enquiries, and the respect accorded to it in other areas of his life. It is this personal responsibility for conscience which underlies the emphasis placed, usually by those in authority, upon the need for formation, or education, of conscience, and it can be summed up in the crisp computer maxim, 'garbage in, garbage out'. It also appears to underlie the statement of Vatican II that respect for the dignity of an individual's conscience cannot be automatically extended to a person who shows little concern in searching for truth and goodness, or whose conscience has slowly grown blind as a consequence of his behaviour.[85]

If conscience, however, has a much humbler, more pedestrian, and less exalted function than many people appear to suppose and if it is simply, as Aquinas argued, the result of thinking hard, honestly, and practically on a particular issue and canvassing aid from wherever possible, rather than being an impersonal internal oracle, then from where does its real authority derive? From two sources, it may be suggested, from the dignity and personal

---

[85] 'Non raro tamen evenit ex ignorantia invincibili conscientiam errare, quin inde suam dignitatem amittat. Quod autem dici nequit cum homo de vero ac bono inquirendo parum curat, et conscientia ex peccati consuetudine paulatim fere obcaecatur', *Gaudium et spes*, 16; *AAS* 58 (1966), p. 1037.

vocation of the individual person; and from the claims of reason to attain to God's truth for that individual. Such a view may be seen to cast some light on much of the controversy after *Humanae Vitae* which appeared to centre in voluntaristic terms on the legitimacy or otherwise of claims to personal freedom of conscience, for it indicates that the issue was not really and basically about freedom or licence. At its best the issue is about the exercise of moral responsibility and about the extent to which an individual moral subject may surrender the responsibility which he experiences as personal and in some respects unique, and abdicate it to be discharged for him by another claiming such authority. It was Sir Thomas More, in the Tower of London, who rejoined that he would not pin his soul at another man's back.[86] And in post-Nuremberg or post-Vietnam society the claim to be justified by works of obedience needs to be extremely carefully nuanced. If, then, a person genuinely believes that one line of action rather than another is God's objective expectation of him and that his personal and inalienable moral responsibility lies in this direction then it becomes a matter of saying, not that he is free to follow conscience, but that he is bound to follow conscience.

Where, then, does the hierarchical *magisterium* find its place in such considerations? Or, in the terms of the debate following the issuing of Pope Paul's encyclical, is dissent from non-infallible teaching a morally legitimate option for a member of the Church? If respect is paid to the moral tradition of the Church and to the teaching of many conferences of bishops in the aftermath of *Humanae Vitae*, there are really only three possible answers to this question. The short answer is, yes. A less short answer is, yes but. And the long answer is, yes provided that certain conditions are adequately fulfilled.[87] And the far point of all these answers is not

---

[86] Cf. R. W. Chambers, *Thomas More* (London, 1938), p. 309.

[87] Although a very few episcopal statements, e.g., New Zealand (Horgan, pp. 193–4), Australia (p. 57), and Mexico (Delhaye, pp. 73–6), leave either no, or very little, room for individual conscience to dissent from the encyclical, by far the larger number consider the possibility in full seriousness. Hamel makes the valid point that, in the nature of the case, statements issued quickly in response to the encyclical could not be the result of long and maturing reflection on the pastoral implications and reactions. 'Immediate post encyclicam scribentes, non potuerunt, tempore deficiente, suo documento eandem praecisionem, eadem complementa doctrinae dare, quam si fuisset longius maturatum', art. cit., p. 333. No statement, however, rules out explicitly the possibility of conscientious dissent, and some almost amount to a 'crash course' on the subject. Of marked world-wide interest were the statements

just that even a mistaken conscience must be obeyed, or that to act from invincible ignorance is not something for which one can be held morally guilty. The ultimate theological point of these answers is that in dissenting one may very well be correct, even although in thus going against Church teaching one is undertaking a serious risk of being wrong. That risk, and responsibility for it, have to be assessed and weighed against the counter-claims of any other competing personal responsibilities in the religious solitariness of man's heart, where he is ultimately, as Vatican II taught, 'alone with God'.[88]

The complexity of conscientious dissent in this, as in other areas

from the Canadian bishops (Horgan, pp. 76–83), the Philippines (pp. 195–210), and France (Delhaye, pp. 149–57). This last was issued only on 8th November 1968, on which the Episcopate commented 'ce délai leur a permis de procéder à de larges consultations auprès des prêtres et des laïcs, notamment des foyers; de nombreux théologiens leur ont fait part de leurs réflexions, ainsi que des experts de diverses disciplines' (ibid., p. 149). Particular interest centred on the advocacy in this statement of choosing the lesser evil when there is a conflict of duties, although it was not always appreciated, perhaps, that the context of this advice was that of subjective, and not necessarily objective, morality. 'La contraception ne peut jamais être un bien. Elle est toujours un désordre, mais ce désordre n'est pas toujours coupable. Il arrive, en effet, que des époux *se considèrent* en face de véritables conflits de devoirs . . . D'une part, ils sont *conscients* du devoir de respecter l'ouverture à la vie de tout acte conjugal; . . . D'autre part, ils *ne voient pas*, en ce qui les concerne, comment renoncer actuellement à l'expression physique de leur amour sans que soit menacée la stabilité de leur foyer (*Gaudium et spes*, 51, 1). A ce sujet, nous rappellerons simplement l'enseignement constant de la morale: quand on est dans une alternative de devoires où, quelle que soit la décision prise, on ne peut éviter un mal, la sagesse traditionelle prévoit de rechercher devant Dieu quel devoir, en l'occurrence, est majeur. Les époux se détermineront au terme d'une réflexion commune menée avec tout le soin que requiert la grandeur de leur vocation conjugale', ibid., pp. 154–5 (italics added). For the Vatican's denial of reports that this interpretation of the encyclical was welcomed in Rome, cf. Hamel, art. cit., p. 337, n. 6. On the traditional (subjectively) 'perplexed conscience', cf. ibid., pp. 342–3.

[88] 'Conscientia est nucleus secretissimus atque sacrarium hominis, in quo solus est cum Deo, cuius vox resonet in intimo eius', *Gaudium et spes*, 16; *AAS* 58 (1966), p. 1037. As the conciliar text notes, this description of conscience owes much to a broadcast of Pope Pius XII on the subject of educating the consciences of the young against the 'new morality' of handing over all moral criteria to the individual conscience and disregarding the central role of Christ's Church in its education. 'La coscienza è come il nucleo più intimo e segreto dell'uomo. Là egli si rifugia con le sue facoltà spirituali in assoluta solitudine: solo con se stesso, o meglio, solo con Dio— della cui voce la coscienza risuona—e con se stesso. Là egli si determina per il bene o per il male . . . . La coscienza è quindi, per dirla con una immagine tanto antica quanto degna, un *adyton*, un santuario, sulla cui soglia tutti debbono arrestarsi; anche, se si tratta di un fanciullo, il padre e la madre. Solo il sacerdote vi entra come curatore di anime e come ministro del Sacramento della penitenza . . .', *AAS* 44 (1952), p. 271.

of the Church's moral teaching, is that it involves three distinct factors: the intrinsic *rational* factor of the arguments proposed to justify the teaching; the extrinsic *religious* factor of hierarchical authority; and the *social* factor of the combined search for truth and the effect of this on others. Problems first arise when the first factor, the intrinsic force of the arguments, is found to be not compelling, or even not coherent, or simply not understandable. And this must be for God's rational creatures a highly significant factor. Pope Paul considered that 'the men of our day are particularly suited to perceive how this teaching is in harmony with human reasoning', and for good measure he added that 'a consideration of the consequences of contraception could lead responsible men to become even more convinced of the truth of this teaching'.[89] If, then, the individual cannot find it in himself or herself to accept these rational considerations, whether in general or in their application to a particular situation, and if, indeed, he has good reason to judge to the contrary, then this throws a considerable strain on the second factor mentioned, the extrinsic religious element. Despite, and not because of, rational considerations the matter becomes one of naked religious belief that the Holy Spirit is at work in the statement of the papal *magisterium*. The strain then is one not just created by the absence of a persuasive rational factor; it is the additional strain of the failure of this first factor despite the claims made for it, and the subsequent need for faith to bear a weight which it was not really intended to bear even by the Church's teaching authority. As Monsignor Lambruschini explained in introducing the encyclical, 'assent of theological faith is due only to definitions properly so-called', a quality which he was far from ascribing to *Humanae Vitae*.[90] Given, then, this sense of failure and additionally the pull of rational and perhaps urgent personal considerations in a contrary direction, it cannot be a matter for surprise if the strain placed on belief also in some cases casts doubt on the way in which

---

[89] 'Putamus nostrae aetatis homines aptissimos esse ad perspiciendum, quam haec doctrina sit humanae rationi consentanea', 12; *AAS* 60 (1968), p. 489. 'Probi homines satius etiam sibi persuaderi possunt de veritate doctrinae, quam Ecclesia hac in re proponit, si mentem convertant ad ea, quae secutura sunt vias rationesque, ad natorum incrementa artificio coercenda adhibitas', 17; *AAS*, p. 493. On the possibility of a too facile appeal to consequences to confirm moral positions reached by another route, cf. J. Mahoney, *Bioethics and Belief*, pp. 18–20.

[90] *Supra*, p. 271.

Pope Paul envisaged the Holy Spirit as at work. In asking priests to accept and commend his teaching he refers both to his rational arguments and to the personal aid he has received from the Holy Spirit, and he contrasts these two factors in a call for internal and external obedience to the Church's *magisterium* on the part of priests as an example to all. 'You know that you are bound to such obedience not more on account of the arguments proposed than on account of the light of the Holy Spirit enjoyed especially by the Pastors of the Church in expounding the truth.'[91]

The motive of obedience and trust in the Church's *magisterium* is here contrasted with the suasive force of intrinsic reasoning, with a judgement that the latter is not an overriding factor and that the former is of at least equal, and possibly greater, relevance in influencing the attitude of priests to the papal teaching. In their pastoral ministry, as described by the Pope, however, a new factor is introduced. They are to speak with confidence, 'in the certainty that while the Holy Spirit of God is present to the *Magisterium* as it proposes correct teaching, he is interiorly enlightening the hearts of the faithful and inviting them to give their assent'.[92] In thus referring to the work of the Spirit intimately and individually in 'the hearts of the faithful' Pope Paul introduces an activity of the Spirit which is complementary to the assistance given to their pastors, and moves beyond the motive of obedience which he has commended to priests. But by appealing to what is in effect the patristic (and Thomist) doctrine of the Holy Spirit as internal teacher of all Christians the Pope was introducing a theme which leads to consideration of what we have suggested is a third factor in analysing the complex psychological and theological phenomenon of dissent—the social implications, disquieting to some, of a shared ecclesial search for truth.[93]

The Spirit and the Church

The work of 'enlightenment' among the faithful—which Pope Paul identified as characteristic of the Holy Spirit inviting them to give assent to the teaching of the *Magisterium*—can be understood only in terms of illumination and clarification leading to an understanding of, and agreement with, the rational considerations

[91] Cf. *supra*, n. 82.
[92] Cf. *supra*, n. 59.
[93] Cf. J. Mahoney, ' "The Church of the Holy Spirit" in Aquinas', in *Seeking the Spirit*, pp. 97–117.

advanced by the encyclical, and not in terms of simply accepting on trust by an act of the will—which is more an act of consent than of assent. The process might almost be described as one of reception by the Church at large of an exercise of the papal *magisterium*, a recognition of the truth contained in moral teaching of the Pope's ordinary *magisterium*. In matters of solemn definitions of dogmas as contained in some sense in 'the deposit of revelation' the Church's hierarchy is extremely sensitive to any suggestion that their truth or intrinsic force is in any sense dependent on 'reception' by the body of the faithful.[94] But in the case of *Humanae Vitae*, which does not claim to be propounding revelation in any sense, and which makes no claim to infallibility, Pope Paul may appear to imply that the reception of his teaching by the Church at large will have, through the complementary influence of the Spirit, at least a confirmatory value in establishing the truth of his teaching. The possibility cannot be ruled out, however, that in such non-infallible teaching on a matter which is not contained in revelation the response of the body of the faithful will be less than whole-hearted in agreeing with the papal teaching and the considerations underlying it. For the influence of the Holy Spirit in the hearts of the faithful, as described by Pope Paul, is envisaged purely as disposing them to be receptive, whereas it might be a more positive one of refining, qualifying, or even correcting the papal teaching.[95]

---

[94] Cf. the Vatican I definition of papal infallibility which included as a very late addition the statement that 'eiusmodi Romani Pontificis definitiones ex sese, non autem ex consensu Ecclesiae, irreformabiles esse', *DS* 3074. This apparently solitary statement was commented on at Vatican II, 'Quare definitiones eius ex sese, et non ex consensu Ecclesiae, irreformabiles merito dicuntur, quippe quae sub assistentia Spiritus Sancti, ipsi in beato Petro promissa, prolatae sint, ideoque nulla indigeant aliorum approbatione, nec ullam ad aliud iudicium appellationem patiantur', *Lumen gentium*, 25; *AAS* 47 (1965), p. 30.

[95] 'The teaching authority in the Catholic Church, and above all in those cases in which it does not produce any definitorial pronouncement (and in many cases it is quite incapable of doing so) is an important and essential element for the discovery of truth and the development of doctrine in the Church. But it is not the sort of official body which acts in isolation and in every respect in total independence of other real elements in the Church, and so presides over this discovery or development of doctrine in a totalitarian manner . . . . On any true understanding there is, even in the Catholic Church, an open "system" in which the most varied factors (the "instinct" of the faithful, fresh insights on the part of individual Christians and theologians, fresh situations that arise in a particular age, the new questions to which these give rise and much else besides) work together to throw fresh light upon the Church's own awareness of her faith, and to produce a development of doctrine', Rahner, *Theological Investigations*, xi, p. 286.

Such a more positive, or innovatory, work of the Spirit on the body of the faithful is at variance, of course, with any sharp disjunction within the Church between those who teach and those who are taught, the *Ecclesia docens* and the *Ecclesia discens*, which we have already considered in discussing the nature of teaching authority and of *magisterium*.[96] And it appears, in recognizing that the Spirit may blow where he wills, to do more justice to the fuller and rounder picture of the Church which receives the Spirit of Christ as a whole and logically prior to the diversification of gifts within the Christian community. Moreover, in adopting a truly complementary attitude towards those gifts, rather than a simply confirmatory one on the part of the 'learning' Church, this view of the Spirit's influence also makes room for the doctrine of moral discernment on the part of all the faithful, and notably on the part of married people whose 'Christian sense' was acknowledged in moral problems by the Second Vatican Council but not referred to in any way by Pope Paul in his encyclical.[97]

Within this more complex description of the work of the Spirit in the Church which, through a variety of channels, is ever leading the community towards the 'whole truth',[98] not only is disagreement wellnigh inevitable, but it is almost essential, or at least normal. It appears to be the case that the tranquillity which appeared to be a characteristic of the Church in the first half of this century, and which for many has been so rudely shattered in the ferment following the Council, was really abnormal, an imposed serenity resulting from the spirited Roman campaign against anything savouring of 'modernism'.[99] For many in the Church this must be a disquieting conclusion, and one which appears to have scant regard either for the authority of the Church's hierarchical *magisterium*, or for the destructive effects of dissent within the Christian body. On the question of teaching authority we have already reflected at

---

[96] Cf. *supra*, pp. 119, 174, 278.

[97] Cf. *supra*, p. 207.

[98] John 16: 13.

[99] 'Whatever the situation may have been over the last hundred years from the psychological point of view in the awareness of the average Catholic with regard to his attitude towards the Church, it is not true to suggest that the Catholic Church either has understood herself in the past, or understands herself now as a Church in which everything that is important is already clear from the outset, and already possessed as a matter of absolute certainty; or as a Church in which every fresh discovery of truth takes place solely and exclusively through the pronouncements of her supreme official teachers', Rahner, ibid.

some length, in an attempt to broaden its base within the Church as a whole and in the process to take into account the subjective moral experience of various individuals within the community.[100] The social effects of dissent, however, call for consideration in this study of the impact of *Humanae Vitae* as part of the third major topic for reflection which we have identified—after collegiality and the method of the encyclical—as being of importance in the recent making of moral theology.[101]

The effect and the influence on others of one's moral actions is a factor which moral theology has traditionally considered of great importance. It could scarcely be otherwise given the strong and explicit teaching of Jesus and Paul on the subject of scandal, or constituting a 'stumbling block' to others.[102] From such New Testament teaching classical moral theology was to elaborate a doctrine of scandal which would distinguish between 'active' and 'passive' scandal (giving, or receiving bad example); and between the Gospel and Pauline 'scandal of the weak' (or those who are vulnerable in conscience) and 'pharisaical scandal', self-evidently referring to others determined to misconstrue whatever one did.[103] In having a care for the effects on others of one's personal decisions and behaviour there was no necessity to take into account the quite predictable reactions of those who would 'pharisaically' take offence at anything, or, indeed, the likelihood of setting bad example to thoroughly good or thoroughly bad people, in accordance with the maxim, *coram sanctis et sceleratis nullum scandalum* (saints and scoundrels cannot take scandal). All the problems concerned the 'weak', or those whom Paul described as 'weak in faith' (Rom. 14: 1): those whose grasp of the Gospel and its behavioural implications was uncertain or immature, and who would not be helped by any diversity in behaviour or controversy between different groups within the community. In such circumstances Paul preached a strong doctrine of mutual tolerance and sensitivity, with particular stress on the responsibilities towards their 'weaker brethren' of those who were 'knowledgeable' and

---

[100] Cf. *supra*, p. 223.
[101] *Supra*, p. 274.
[102] Cf. Luke 17: 1–2 and parallels; Rom. 14: 1–15: 2; 1 Cor. 8.
[103] The Gospel bias for Pharisaical scandal was found in Luke 13: 14–17; Matt. 11: 18–19. Moralists were also to identify 'diabolical scandal' as a deliberate setting out to corrupt others by one's behaviour.

correspondingly 'strong' in their ability to exercise moral freedom of choice (Rom. 15: 1), concluding with the ringing principle, 'Only take care lest this liberty of yours somehow become a stumbling block to the weak' (1 Cor. 8: 9).

One historical consequence of Paul's apparently uncompromising criterion of concentrating on the needs of the 'weak' within the community may be seen in the clinging to conservative attitudes and positions on the grounds of not 'offending pious ears' or not 'disturbing the simple faithful', without adverting to the fact that this was only one element in Paul's pastoral policy. Alongside it needs to be placed his continuous and urgent plea for mutual tolerance and respect. And both these have to be seen within the long-term strategy of Paul to educate the less knowledgeable out of their ignorance and weakness, as we see him doing in spelling out his own views on the questions disputed in the early Church.[104] Moreover, in any concentration on care for the 'weaker brethren' there is a presumption that they can be identified within the community, but this can be done only by selecting and concentrating on certain features within a situation of controversy. For there can also be, paradoxically, a 'scandal of the strong', a weakening of the faith and adherence of even the 'knowledgeable' and the 'mature' as a consequence of uncompromising and insensitive insistence on the universal applicability of traditional teaching. All believers are vulnerable and 'weak' in some sense, whether in their ignorance or credulity or in their erudition and self-confidence.

Another difficulty which arises from attempting to apply Paul's teaching on scandal to later controversies within the Church, such as that over contraception, is that casting some as the 'weak' and others as the 'strong' is in danger of being tendentious and patronizing, and, more fundamentally, is raising the issue of what limits there may be to community tolerance, as we shall have cause to explore in our next chapter. Within our present consideration of internal dissent over *Humanae Vitae* what may be observed is that perhaps the greatest danger for the Church which has emerged is a stratification, or polarization, between differing theologies, whether of marriage or of the Church's *magisterium*, or of the Church itself, which may result in, or betray as a presupposition, the view that justification is by theology alone. This would be to introduce once

---

[104] Cf. Rom. 14: 22–3.

again an element of Gnosticism into Christianity, a distinction between the élite initiates and the unsophisticated *rudes*, or unskilled, of classical moral theology. On a natural level, it would be to confuse intelligence with education; and in moral matters it would be to confuse insight with articulation, as we have explored that distinction. For, if, as we have suggested, the Church, or its hierarchical *magisterium*, can be identified at times as possibly stretching towards a moral insight which it cannot, or cannot yet, fully articulate either to itself or to others, then in principle there is no reason why the same possibility cannot, or should not, be also recognized in the case of even the 'simplest' of the faithful. In the matter of possible dissent, then, and its social repercussions, there appears no ultimately satisfactory answer other than the Pauline appeal to mutual respect and tolerance within his continual efforts to strengthen and unite all the faithful in their personal, subjective appropriation of the Gospel.

The Wider Impact

Thus far in this examination of the impact of *Humanae Vitae* we have identified the three major elements which emerged as collegiality in the Church; the function of reason, prophecy, and moral insight; and questions of conscience and dissent; together with the implications of all these for moral theology. By way of conclusion we may now consider some more general features of the aftermath of the encyclical and their implications for the Church and moral theology.

It may not be too much to say that to the outside world and for the first time the Roman Catholic Church was seen to be composed of ordinary human beings. Pope Paul had anguished—and even hesitated—over his decision in a way which appeared very far removed from the seemingly effortless, or apparently uncaring, decision-making of some of his predecessors. And the resulting emotions also astonished the world. To outsiders, possibly, the credibility of the so-called institutional Church was diminished (although this had possibly never been very great). But by the same token, the moral integrity and credibility of many in the Church, both those for and those against the encyclical, were respected increasingly and admired by many, even if the occasion was a subject which other churches and society in general considered no longer in dispute. And within the Church the experience was a searing one for all, irrespective of which 'side' they happened to support. In its own way, the controversy was exemplifying the teaching of the Council on the inevitability of the pilgrim Church's suffering pains and difficulties from within as well as from without, as it journeys through history and attempts to engage in honest dialogue with modern society.[105]

Moreover, the Church was seen not to be a monolith. Quite apart from all the reactions of individuals, and of groups of theologians and others, the statements of national and regional hierarchies were compared and contrasted in their nuanced local applications and teaching. And, as we have suggested, not only was a first hesitant step being taken towards collegial initiative, at the Pope's invitation, but at the same time the individual characteristics of local churches were also finding expression and some recognition. Notable also in such statements was a deep and genuine pastoral concern as the hierarchy strove, with varying degrees of success, to identify with married couples as those most affected by the encyclical. Such concern began, of course, with Pope Paul himself, not only as he described his feelings in coming to a final decision, as we have seen,[106] but also in the encyclical, which was strikingly different in temper and language from *Casti Connubii* and almost regretful, if firm, in tone, stressing prayer and the sacramental life as well as a largely overlooked positive theology of married love.[107] And this pastoral concern was shared and extended by many bishops and priests suffering with their people, again irrespective of which 'side' they supported.

Above all, however, *Humanae Vitae* constituted the first major test for the post-conciliar Church and for the various 'openings' which the Second Vatican Council had introduced to the Church's thinking and activity. The encyclical was a catalyst which, to adopt a well-worn but valid phrase, did most to bring about the crisis of identity within the Church which had been imminent since the closing of the Council. The ecclesiological question, which is probably the major theological issue of this century, in terms of the Church's self-perception, found expression in such areas as

---

[105] 'afflictiones et difficultates suas, internas pariter et extrinsecas,', *Lumen Gentium*, no. 8; *AAS* 57 (1965), p. 12.

[106] *Supra*, pp. 268–70.

[107] *On Casti Connubii*, cf. *supra*, p. 260.

authority and dissent, conscience and obedience, the *sensus fidelium* and moral responsibility. Apart from those members who, tragically, left the Church or felt expelled from it, many others took a half step back from it and began perhaps for the first time to take a somewhat more detached view of it than they had hitherto as the entire Church was being forced to examine itself and to follow through the practical and theological implications of events.

Finally, so far as the discipline of moral theology itself was concerned, the impact of *Humanae Vitae* was, and continues to be, considerable. The official status and authority of theologians was weakened and the media, or popular, status of some was considerably inflated to a degree which has given to theological publication and even professional discussion, however tentative, a quite unhealthy publicity and on occasion a quite unwarranted if now unofficial authority. Probabilism was dealt an official blow from which it is unlikely to recover its former legalistic vigour, if only because the category of 'approved authors' was considerably diminished and tended rather to be replaced by an unofficial category of suspect authors. The entire methodology of moral theology was in question, and the relationship between the theologian and the *Magisterium* became the subject of innumerable conferences and statements. Parties and advocates began to compete for attention and influence as the moral authority of Rome was considered diminished. Out of this considerable disarray of moral theology, as part of the impact of *Humanae Vitae*, it may be that what was struggling to emerge was a deeper insight into the function of moral theology and a glimpse of theological pluralism behind the diversity of moral behaviour. One thing appears incontrovertible. The Church, and with it moral theology, have been changed immeasurably by Pope Paul's letter. But the seeds of such change had been sown by the Second Vatican Council, and *Humanae Vitae* was but the first major testing of the renewal of moral theology demanded by the Council. That demand and the pattern of that renewal we shall consider in our final chapter.

8

A PATTERN IN RENEWAL?

In the previous chapter exploring the impact of *Humanae Vitae* and its implications for moral theology the suggestion was made that Pope Paul's encyclical constituted the first real testing of the Church and of moral theology in the aftermath of the Second Vatican Council. The Council itself was the major event of this century in the Church's life and the most momentous exercise to date of the Church's hierarchical *magisterium* in all its history, not only for the extent and the depth of the subjects with which it dealt, but also for the overall orientation which it gave to the Church's life and activity. What Newman wrote of Augustine, as the Western Church of the fifth century struggled to face the realities of a new European age, can be applied with even more appropriateness to the work and hesitant application of Vatican II in a new era of world history, that it has produced a new edition of the Catholic Tradition,[1] even if it may not necessarily be the final edition.

Among its many accomplishments the Council gave a strong impetus and a new direction to moral theology in ways which are still being explored and to which it would be impossible to do full justice in a single chapter of this historical study. We shall accordingly consider first what the Council had to contribute to the making of moral theology, and then venture to survey the whole sweep of post-conciliar moral theology, attempting to identify what elements of a pattern may emerge in much the same way as the previous chapters of this study have attempted to identify developing themes and to reflect upon them. Our conclusion will be that in the renewal of moral theology as it has begun to take shape in the past twenty years two features in particular may be discerned; a drive towards totality and an attempt to recognize diversity. We shall conclude that what both features require for completion and understanding, as well as for a more rounded characterization of moral theology, is a recovery of mystery.

[1] Cf. *supra*, p. 40.

The Second Vatican Council: A Call for Renewal

In the course of its three years of reflection and discussion (1962–1965) the Council convened by Pope John XXIII had much to say about the moral behaviour of the Church's members, and about the role of the Church and its hierarchy in guiding that behaviour. If one had to single out any conciliar sentence as summing up the general temper of the Council's thinking, notwithstanding its firm teaching on numerous moral topics as we shall see shortly, it would be difficult to overlook the statement from its final and hard-fought *Pastoral Constitution on the Church in the Modern World*, 'The Church safeguards the deposit of God's Word, from which religious and moral principles are drawn. But it does not always have a ready answer to individual questions, and it wishes to combine the light of revelation with the experience of everyone in order to illuminate the road on which humanity has recently set out.'[2]

On the subject of moral theology itself the Council had some terse and sharp comments which any schoolteacher would recognize as of the 'could do better' variety. In discussing the educational and vocational formation of men for the priestly ministry and for the tasks which were to emerge for them from the Council, the Bishops of the Church also had an opportunity to identify the nature and function of the various branches of theology which they themselves had studied and upon which they had called in order to formulate their conciliar pronouncements. It was in this context that they delivered the rebuke, 'Special attention should be given to the improvement of moral theology. Its scientific exposition should be nourished more by the teaching of Scripture, and it should throw light on the exalted nature of the calling of the faithful in Christ, and on their obligation to produce fruit in love for the life of the world.'[3]

The record of the Council shows the background out of which this new programme for moral theology emerged, but from the point of view of the discipline itself perhaps the most enlightening,

---

[2] *Gaudium et spes*, no. 33; *AAS* 58 (1966), p. 1052.

[3] 'Specialis cura impendatur Theologiae morali perficiendae, cuius scientifica expositio, doctrina S. Scripturae magis nutrita, celsitudinem vocationis fidelium in Christo illustret eorumque obligationem in caritate pro mundi vita fructum ferendi', *Optatam totius*, no. 16; *AAS* 58 (1966), p. 724.

and certainly the most influential, commentary on the Council's observations so far as they affected the future of moral theology was an article written shortly afterwards by Josef Fuchs, Professor of Moral Theology in Rome's Gregorian University, in which he analysed the current state of moral theology in the Church and the steps required to improve it.[4] The Council had singled out moral theology for special treatment, not because of its centrality (which was accorded to the Bible as 'the soul of all theology'), nor because of its pre-eminence (which was accorded to dogmatic theology), but because 'it left much to be desired'. As Fuchs observed, 'moral theology must be a genuine theological discipline, drawing its doctrine from divine revelation and expounding it in the light of faith and under the guidance of the Church's *magisterium*'.[5]

Such moral theology should be Christocentric, focusing on the response of the individual Christian to the call of Christ. A morality of law, and especially of natural law, is not thereby ruled out, but it is seen to be 'much too abstract and inadequate', involving 'only one element in the full and rich relationship between God and man-subsisting-in-Christ', which is found portrayed especially in Paul.[6] Neither moral theology 'designed primarily as a code of precepts and obligations imposed upon the Christian', nor the presentation of moral theology as 'Christian ethics' in the context of the Enlightenment, viewing Jesus mainly as a moral teacher, does justice to God's gracious calling of individuals to a life commensurate with their salvation in Christ, or to the quality of their response to that call.[7] And taking up the theme of Rahner and others on the morality of non-Christians and the supernatural existential which affects all men, as we have earlier considered it, Fuchs concludes that 'there are many grounds for supposing that even those who in all sincerity declare themselves atheists may encounter God, on occasion, in their inmost consciousness'.[8]

---

[4] The article first appeared as 'Theologia moralis perficienda; votum Concilii Vaticani II', *Periodica de re morali, canonica, liturgica*, Rome, 55 (1966), pp. 499–548. The passages quoted here are from the English translation, 'Moral Theology According to Vatican II', in J. Fuchs, *Human Values and Christian Morality* (Dublin, 1970), pp. 1–55. For the views of the Council bishops on the state and needs of traditonal moral theology, cf. *Acta Synodalia Concilii Vaticani II*, vol. iv/4, Rome, 1978, pp. 23, 43, 113–14.

[5] Ibid., p. 2.

[6] Ibid., pp. 3–4.

[7] Ibid., pp. 8–11.

[8] Ibid., pp. 13–15. Cf. *supra.* pp. 100–2.

This positive and attractive note in an improved, Christocentric, and biblically inspired moral theology will do justice, Fuchs considers, to the effects hoped for by the Council, seen as the Johannine fruits in the lives of the faithful incorporated into the vine which is Christ (cf. John 15: 2–5), with a sharing in his saving love as the life force at work in them. It is this consideration which enables Fuchs to stress the social dimension in all Christian moral behaviour, in contrast to a past individualistic view, as well as acknowledging the work of Gilleman and others in concluding that 'certain worldly human factors enter into the exercise of the various other virtues, but in exercising charity man gives himself in person'.[9]

On what he calls 'the governing principle of moral theology', Fuchs is quite clear in considering it

not man's reason but the faith through which are revealed Christ and the salvation he brings us. Moral theology explores and explains the implications of the practical side of this faith. It considers first the moral truths that have been directly revealed and then the truths that emerge from the revealed Christian mystery when the latter is examined by reason enlightened by faith. Moral theology must always be fully conscious, and must continuously emphasize that it, too, is theology in the same sense as is dogmatic theology, and that it relies on reason only in so far as reason contributes to understanding and explaining faith.[10]

This entails repairing the separation from dogmatic theology and from spiritual theology which left moral theology only custody of man's sins (and of canon law) and deprived it of 'a fundamental element of Christian morality'—'instruction regarding the perfection of consciences under the personal and individual guidance of the Holy Spirit'.[11]

At the same time Fuchs notes the Council's careful reference to the 'scientific exposition' of moral theology as a necessary guard on the one hand against mere sentiment or moralizing which is detached from reality, history, and the human sciences; and on the other, against an excessive preoccupation with a study of moral 'cases'—which can be equally remote from situations—'that absolutely unique, non-recurring personal combination of circumstances about which a moral judgement is formed in the conscience at the very moment that combination of circumstances takes

---

[9] Ibid., p. 25.   [10] Ibid., p. 31.   [11] Ibid., pp. 31–4.

place'.[12] Such scientific concern will take account of anthropology and psychology, as well as of dogmatic theology, ethics, and other Christian traditions.[13]

What Fuchs also brought out briefly at the conclusion of his article was that quite a number of these desired improvements in moral theology had already been under way, or at least under discussion, for some years, and notably in Germany, where one might say that writers like Tillman and Häring were reviving an earlier Christocentric tradition in moral theology and a type of systematic moral writing, as distinct from devotional literature, addressed directly to the laity in the Church.[14] It is useful to complement this observation of Fuchs in 1966 with the survey of the French theologian, Aubert, written in 1954 on the position of Catholic theology as a whole in the middle of the twentieth century. Aubert regarded the previous fifteen years as marked by a new vitality and as characterized mainly by a desire for closer contact with tradition, as well as for a better adaptation to contemporary society.[15] This, however, he observed, had not so far had much effect on the treatises of moral theology, which was in its presentation 'the most decrepit of the ecclesiastical sciences'.[16] Some stirrings were beginning to be observed, however, particularly under the influence of sociology and depth-psychology.[17] And the atmosphere of existentialism had directed attention to the topics of spontaneity and personality, in harmony with 'the preoccupations of those who had long been worried at seeing moral theology too often reduced to a collection of Byzantine discussions on the best way of evading the prescriptions of the Church while staying on the right side of the law, and who .... would rather see morality presented as the Christian's answer to the call of Christ, the generous response of a person to the ennobling call of another Person'.[18] The influential German theologian, Romano Guardini, whose study *The Lord* had been so seminal, does not tire of

[12] Ibid., pp. 41–2.
[13] Ibid., pp. 42–8.
[14] Ibid., pp. 51–4. Cf. bibliography listed there. Cf. also Jedin and Dolan, op. cit., vol. vi, pp. 528–31.
[15] R. Aubert, *La Théologie Catholique au milieu du XXᵉ siècle* (Paris, 1954), pp. 7–8.
[16] Ibid., p. 80.
[17] Ibid., pp. 73–4.
[18] Ibid., pp. 75–6.

repeating that Christianity is neither an ethics nor a system for interpreting the world, but a sharing in the existence of Christ.[19]

In this mid-fifties summation we are not, in fact, far from the central thrust of the message which Vatican II was to direct at moral theology, whether implicitly in many of its statements on the new awareness of Christian identity in the Church and on the roles of the Christian and the Church in society, or explicitly in its call for improvement. It is to be wondered, however, whether the Church's bishops quite appreciated the magnitude of the special challenge which they were delivering to moral theology, both in terms of the leeway which the discipline clearly had to make up, and in terms of the various directions in which it was being pointed by other conciliar statements, notably in the *Dogmatic Constitution on the Church* and in the *Pastoral Constitution on the Church in the Modern World*. It was not simply a matter of tuning the engine and tightening the steering of moral theology, but of a thorough systematic overhaul of the whole vehicle and of sending it off into quite new and (for it) uncharted areas of modern living. How was moral theology to respond to these challenges, and with what resources?

In some obvious respects, moral theology as envisaged by the Council is an applied science, or even a derivative science, which is dependent on other branches of theology, notably biblical studies and dogmatic theology. But the contribution to be sought from these other fields was not always so clear as might have been expected or hoped. The critical study of Scripture in the Church had long been frowned upon, and grudgingly approved only in 1943 by Pope Pius XII's encyclical *Divino afflante Spiritu*.[20] The result was that Catholic biblical scholarship, although making rapid strides, was still in many respects a preserve limited to comparatively few in the Church, which on the whole had derived much of its allegedly biblical teaching from a selective resource to 'proof texts' and in general was now in danger of transferring the extremes of the doctrine of *ex opere operato* from the area of the Sacraments to an almost magical belief in the efficacy of the Bible. Form criticism, redaction criticism, and the whole science of hermeneutics were not yet therefore, even if they ever would be, in a position to provide a firm base for a thorough biblical renewal in

---

[19] Ibid., p. 82.   [20] *AAS* 35 (1943), pp. 297–325.

moral theology except in very general terms. Moreover, the other major theological source for moral reflection and application, dogmatic theology, was now equally in a state of considerable flux in such areas as grace, original sin, the supernatural, Christology, ecclesiology, and ecumenism.[21] Added to this, moral theology, although willing, was somewhat hesitant and tentative in its approach to the human and social sciences, on whose relevance and value in any case the Church's papal *magisterium* was now more positive in theory, but still doubtful in practice, as evidenced by the Vatican's 1975 statement on sexual ethics and Pope John Paul II's more recent remarks on the human sciences and the 'loss of the sense of sin'.[22] When to all this is added the sheer novelty for the majority of the Church at large of the Council's teaching on so many topics, it is evident that the task facing moral theology in the post-conciliar age has been formidable indeed.

The various directions pursued by individual moral theologians since Vatican II, and since *Humanae Vitae*, could not in any sense be described as planned or co-ordinated, but they can be seen as falling under two main headings, that of methodology, and that of specific moral issues. For, of course, what had been set in train was not just a review of the traditional approaches and methods of the subject as it had developed, monumental as that was. There was also an attempt to meet in quite a new spirit the persistent moral issues connected with sexual and medical ethics, now seen in a wider context, and a whole range of increasingly urgent new issues on a global scale, such as modern warfare and the amassing of nuclear weaponry; world poverty and the imbalanced access to, and use of, the earth's resources; and many other aspects of the somewhat novel subject of social justice. And these two concerns with methodology and particular moral issues were to be found interacting with each other in ways which would, at least in theory, ensure that, on the one hand, the reviewed or new methods of approach to the moral life would maintain contact with reality, and on the other, that various moral issues would have the benefit of being considered in ways more likely to yield an appropriately Christian and up-to-date response.

[21] Cf. J. Mahoney, 'Ecumenical witness on moral issues', in *Seeking The Spirit*, pp. 27–33.

[22] *Declaration on ... sexual ethics*, no. 9; *AAS* 68 (1976), pp. 64–8; *Reconciliatio et Paenitentia*, CTS (1984), pp. 64–8; *AAS* 76 (1984), pp. 223–8.

In what have been the most active decades ever encountered in the Church's moral reflection, particularly as evidenced in the work of its moral theologians, it would not be possible to do justice in brief compass to the various new directions taken by moral theologians in loyal response to the commission given it by the Council. What we propose, rather, is to attempt an *Überblick*, or synoptic overview of the work of the past twenty years, as evidence of our conclusion that elements of a pattern of thinking may come to light in the great variety of attempts to improve the subject of moral theology, both in its method and in its address to specific issues. The dangers of such an attempt are, of course, obvious, whether in misreading the data or in distorting at least some of the data to fit into an alleged, or preconceived, pattern. Nevertheless, it does appear that elements of a pattern are discernible inductively in recent and current directions in the making of moral theology. And we propose to consider these elements under the three headings of totality, diversity, and mystery.

The Drive to Totality

What may be seen as a perhaps unconscious drive towards totality in much of recent moral theology is probably to be explained partly as a reaction to the excessively analytical approach of neo-scholasticism which had characterized moral theology since the end of the nineteenth century.[23] The systematic introduction of conceptual analysis and of the use of contrasting distinctions to reconcile opposing authoritative statements was a major contribution to theology by the Schoolmen of the twelfth and subsequent centuries.[24] And much of the intellectual satisfaction and success of the scholastic method derived from the way in which it thus perceived itself able to package and pigeonhole reality, whether created or uncreated. In moral reflection it was to be seen at its most potent in such areas as the analysis of the moral life of individuals into their final end and intermediate means chosen to that end; the analysis of the moral agent into body and soul, and the intellect, will, and other 'faculties'; the analysis of the moral act into object, circumstances, and goal; and, of course, the analysis of

[23] Cf. G. Fritz and A. Michel, 'Scolastique', *DTC*, xiv/2, coll. 1691–1728.
[24] On the application of 'dialectic' to theology, cf. Copleston, op. cit., vol. ii; Fritz and Michel, art. cit., coll. 1702, 1716–17.

morality itself into objective and subjective within an overall distinction between the natural and the supernatural.

Much of recent moral theology can be viewed as a bid to recover or to reclaim the living unity which links and subsumes all this into an intelligible whole which can easily be lost to view in the short-sighted peering at the parts, or which can slip through the cracks between the components. The drive to totality is thus not necessarily a move to abolish analysis, but a move to locating the parts (including analysis itself) in their context. In particular it is a refusal to ignore the relationships of the parts to each other and to the totality which is implied by their being 'parts' and within which alone their full significance can be recognized. This process is perhaps to be seen in its simplest manifestation in the move away from a previous sort of 'faculty' morality, which accords to various human capabilities such as speech or procreation an independence and a built-in purpose and morality of their own, towards viewing such human characteristics either within the bodily totality or, even more, within the totality of the human person. One traditional line of argument, for instance, considers lying a misuse and a 'frustration' of man's faculty of speech, whose inherent purpose is to communicate the truth. Another considers the reproductive system or faculty as possessing a built-in purpose of its own which must be absolutely safeguarded without much reference to the rest of the body, or, indeed, to the embodied person of which it is a feature, to the extent that a whole morality of human sexual behaviour can be, and has traditionally been, deduced from its connection with the male emission of semen.

It is true, of course, that the 'principle of totality' which has figured much in medico-moral theology (now bioethics) was propounded in 1930 by Pope Pius XI to justify surgical intervention on an unhealthy organ when this was considered necessary for the good of the whole body. To that limited extent some functional subordination of bodily parts to the whole was recognized.[25] But the utterance of this truism was required solely because surgery was conceived of as violence inflicted upon the body, or as 'mutilation' of its organs, without regard for the total context in which it was carried out. And the manner in which the principle of totality then became a tool for the moralist in a variety of human contexts other

[25] DS 3723. Cf. *supra*, p. 260.

than that of sterilization, in which it was first enunciated, serves only to highlight how detailed and systematic, as well as unreal, was the fragmentation of reality and of behaviour into such atomic elements. Moreover, subsequent attempts to expand the notion of the controlling 'totality' from the body to the whole human being and then, in a strongly social context, to community with one's fellow-humans met with strong papal resistance and disapproval.[26] The mind was concentrated simply on the act of bodily mutilation and the circumstances in which this might be argued to be morally justifiable. In other new areas of medical practice such as fertility testing, artifical insemination, and *in vitro* fertilization it is possible to see a similar exclusive concentration on the act of marital intercourse as the only proper exercise of man's reproductive faculty and a corresponding judgement of any other act as no more than a frustration of that faculty irrespective of the total context and purpose of such activity.[27] What is at issue in all such cases is an isolation of one element of the behaviour as doing violence to a particular part or natural function of the body with no consideration, for instance, of the insight of Aquinas that 'when anyone bends his limbs against a natural disposition, this may be in a sense considered violent so far as concerns the particular limb, but it is not violent so far as the man himself is concerned'.[28]

The most important and assiduous pursuit by moral theologians in recent years of the relation of component parts to a unifying totality, or of their significant integration into a single living unity, however, has been in the area of the analysis and moral evaluation of the human action in general. It is this drive towards totality which appears to underlie and link the two major themes of what we may call the breaching of absolutes and the incorporation of consequences. And we may begin by considering the debate about absolutes, or about the act and its circumstances, before proceeding to the debate about act and consequences. One of the most central

---

[26] Pius XII, *AAS* 44 (1952), pp. 782–6.

[27] Cf. J. Mahoney, *Bioethics and Belief* (London, 1984), pp. 12–18.

[28] 'Et similiter est dicendum cum aliquis inflectit membra contra naturalem dispositionem. Hoc enim est violentum secundum quid, scilicet quantum ad membrum particulare; non tamen simpliciter, quantum ad ipsum hominem', *STh* 1a 2ae, q. 6, a. 5 ad 3. In the following paragraphs we have attempted to maintain the distinction between single species or classes of behaviour considered in the abstract and particular concrete behaviour or individual pieces of behaviour by referring to the former as 'acts' and to the latter as 'actions'.

and now most controverted features of classical moral theology has been the maintaining that many types, or classes, of moral act are inherently evil and absolutely forbidden. It is not that to act in such a way is wrong simply because God forbids it, which would make such acts wrong 'from the outside', or extrinsically, as in traffic regulations which might easily take a different form. The classes of behaviour under consideration, which include, for example, lying, suicide, abortion, sterilization, masturbation, premarital and extra-marital intercourse, and divorce, are regarded as acts evil 'from the inside', or intrinsically, and it is for this reason that they are forbidden by God, whatever the circumstances in which they occur. Circumstances are mostly irrelevant. It is true that confessional practice, towards which, as we have seen, moral theology was mainly orientated, required special account to be taken of circumstances at times. But such times were either with an eye to what particular features would aggravate the sinful 'core' of the action, or with a view to identifying mitigating circumstances affecting subjective guilt rather than the objectively sinful nature of the act in question.[29] The point of moral absolutes was that, considered in abstraction from the circumstances surrounding them, their intrinsic malice was readily arrived at by the process of natural law reasoning elaborated by Aquinas, and that none of the other features of the situations in which they actually occurred could penetrate or alter this intrinsic malice.

What we have termed the assault on such moral absolutes has been a particularly noticeable feature of much recent writing in moral theology, both in regard to the general theory and with respect to particular instances, beginning with contraception, but quite rapidly spreading to other areas of behaviour such as those mentioned above. One line of general criticism has been to question the traditional distinction between act and circumstances as no more than a weak transference to pieces of human behaviour of the Aristotelian distinction to be found in objects between their substance and the accidental and transient properties which this bears and which can never affect it in its interior 'underlying' nature. There is this crucial difference, however, that a moral 'substance' such as 'suicide' or 'fornication' is not just an irreducible substance. It can itself be conceived of as a central core

---

[29] Cf. *supra*, p. 25.

of activity which is already 'accidentalized' or circumstanced. Thus, 'suicide', which is considered never justifiable whatever the circumstances, is itself capable of being described as 'taking life' in certain defined circumstances; and 'fornication' as more simply 'having sexual intercourse' in certain defined circumstances. The conclusion to this line of analysis is that there are some irreducible classes of human behaviour, such as taking life and engaging in intercourse, which are, considered in themselves, morally neutral but which can never as a matter of fact occur except in some circumstances or space–time co-ordinates; and that in certain circumstances they are morally justifiable and in others not. In this view circumstances are to be seen not simply as 'accidental' properties inhering in an already morally determined 'substance', like electrons around a moral nucleus. They are essential features of actual behaviour from which the moral quality of such actual behaviour derives. The act of taking life in some circumstances is morally justified, as is also the act of sexual intercourse, or the act of making use of some created objects, for example, whereas in other circumstances such acts would be wrong and would conventionally be described as murder, fornication, or stealing. The central questions then become: which of a particular cluster of circumstances, like electrons around a morally neutral nucleus, make a crucial moral difference; and what is the criterion for deriving morality from some, and not other, such circumstances as morally relevant. And below these considerations lies the more fundamental question of whether this conceptual analysis of behaviour in terms of an analogy with substances and accidents is a valid one.[30]

Another probe at a weak point in the theory of moral absolutes as it has derived from Aquinas originates partly from the authority of St Thomas himself and partly from the force of his argument. This approach makes much of his teaching that the primary precepts of natural law are completely unchangeable, but not the secondary precepts deriving from them. It appears to be the case that for Aquinas these secondary precepts would include the Judaeo-Christian Ten Commandments, and that he would consider these generally binding, but not invariably so in practice, and this

---

[30] Cf. J. Mahoney, 'The Classical Theory of the Moral Judgement', in *Seeking the Spirit*, pp. 54–5.

because of particular factors or circumstances in reality. Thus, in a much-quoted passage, he writes that the forbidding by God of unauthorized killing, of stealing, and of adultery is unchangeable, but what is changeable is whether this or that behaviour actually constitues murder, theft, or adultery. They may even appear to be such immoral actions, but in reality they may not be so. And if one further analyses Aquinas's thought in this direction one comes eventually to the recognition that in some cases particular circumstances can make a crucial moral difference.[31]

A more indirect attack on the citadel of moral absolutes, however, involves cutting off their supply line with human nature and arguing that if nature can and does change, either in general or in specific instances, then natural law conclusions claiming to originate in nature must themselves also change accordingly. One writer on objective morality could cite in this connection 'a seldom-quoted text of *De Malo*', in which Aquinas observes that 'the just and the good . . . are formally and everywhere the same, because the principles of right in natural reason do not change . . . . Taken in the material sense, they are not the same everywhere and for all men, and this is so by reason of the mutability of man's nature and the diverse conditions in which men and things find themselves in different environments and times.'[32]

It is possible to view these and other criticisms of moral absolutes as a new refusal to consider them in the abstract or in isolation from other factors, whether of the whole human nature with its variables as well as its constants from which they claim to be derived, or of the whole complex of circumstances in which such human nature finds itself immersed when it comes to act. And this move towards a larger totality of act and circumstances is also particularly evident in the lively debate which concentrates on what classical moral theology has considered simply one of many

[31] Cf. ibid., pp. 55–7. The attempt to meet this difficulty by retorting that in such cases the circumstances 'change the substance' of the act makes nonsense of the systematic application of the difference between substance and accidents.

[32] 'Iusta et bona possunt dupliciter considerari: Uno modo formaliter, et sic semper et ubique sunt eadem; quia principia iuris, quae sunt in naturali ratione, non mutantur. Alio modo materialiter, et sic non sunt eadem iusta et bona ubique et apud omnes, sed oportet ea lege determinari. Et hoc contingit propter mutabilitatem naturae humanae et diversas conditiones hominum et rerum, secundum diversitatem locorum et temporum; . . .', *De Malo*, q. 2, a. 4 ad 13, quoted in L. Dupré, 'Situation Ethics and Objective Morality', *Theological Studies* 28 (1967), p. 251. Cf. also *supra*, p. 260.

circumstances of a moral action—the effects which it produces, or the relationship between the morality of an act and its consequences. In an acute concern to incorporate the consequences of one's behaviour into the total moral appraisal of that behaviour, moral theologians are obviously reacting strongly against the traditional doctrine that certain acts are right or wrong quite irrespective of their effects in the concrete. Again one could see this strongly evident in the birth-control debate, with arguments adduced to favour contraception ranging from the global problems of world population to the heartbreak of strained families or broken marriages. And it is increasingly evident in the debates over abortion, the remarriage of divorced persons, and other areas of individual morality, not to mention global issues such as nuclear deterrence.

Underlying this question of consequences is the fundamental issue of the nature of morality and the extent to which this is viewed primarily as obedience to a moral law or primarily as the furtherance of certain values of human and social well-being, as expressed in the now hackneyed distinction between deontology and teleology. Even to express the question in these simple terms, however, is to raise a host of other equally fundamental questions, of which the most obvious include: what is meant by human well-being, and is to to be limited to this earthly life or must it take the longer view of including eternity and eventual happiness in return for present obedience? In what sense can virtue, or moral uprightness, or devotion to duty, be considered its own reward? And, of course, what is really meant, or entailed, by 'love of neighbour', or seeking the most loving behaviour? Is it that the Commandments, for instance, are authoritative and absolute indications of where genuine love is to be found and not found, as distinct from short-sighted sentimentality? Or is it, as Paul seems to have understood the matter, that if we really love another we shall find ourselves doing from the inside, as it were, what the Commandments enjoin from the outside—not unlike the experience of Molière's M. Jourdain, who discovered to his surprise that he had been speaking prose all his life? Or is it that loving is to be viewed as doing whatever furthers the well-being of others, and so the circle returns to what is it that constitutes human well-being?

It was almost as if, once moral theology had reacted against a tightly-woven morality expressed in terms of obedience to uncompromising natural law principles which took no account of consequences and had begun to attach much more weight to the effects of behaviour on the self, on others and on society, and to tug at the loose thread of consequences, that the whole moral act unravelled in the hands, and moralists were exposed to the danger of adopting an approach to moral evaluation which one sympathetic commentator described as buying heavily into a relatively uncritical utilitarianism.[33] In point of fact, much recent Roman Catholic moral theology is reminiscent of the history and fortunes of British utilitarianism in its concern to expand the totality of the moral action to include a serious consideration of consequences as much more than just another usually negligible circumstance of a conceptually distinct moral core.

One can see this pattern at work also in recent discussion of the traditional moral principle of double effect, for this is regarded by several writers as a major and significant instance where moral theology, at least since the seventeenth century, has systematically incorporated consequences into its considerations in a balancing of the foreseen good and bad effects of behaviour as one essential factor in evaluating the morality of that behaviour. Some writers argue that one cannot then stop short of pursuing to their radical conclusions the full implications of this approach to morality as assessing whether good consequences are to prevail over bad, or vice versa. Closely connected with this line of thought is another which may be partly influenced by the traditional statement of *Humanae Vitae* that contraception could not be morally justified as a choosing of what appeared the less serious evil, since we have it on the authority of St Paul that it is never permitted to do evil to bring about good.[34] Part of a rejoinder by some writers to this use of Paul is to explore just what is meant by the 'evil' which one is not permitted to do in order to achieve a good consequence, and to

---

[33] J. Gustafson, in *Theological Studies* 32 (1971), p. 524.

[34] 'Neque vero, ad eos coniugales actus comprobandos ex industria fecunditate privatos, haec argumenta ut valida afferre licet: nempe, id malum eligendum esse, quod minus grave videatur; insuper eosdem actus in unum quoddam coalescere cum actibus fecundis iam antea positis vel postea ponendis, atque adeo horum unam atque parem moralem bonitatem participare. Verum enimvero, si malum morale tolerare, quod minus grave est, interdum licet, ut aliquod maius vitetur malum vel aliquod praestantius bonum promoveatur [cf. Pius XII, *AAS* 45 (1953), pp. 798–9], numquam tamen licet, ne ob gravissimas quidem causas, facere mala ut eveniant bona [Cf. Rom. 3: 8]: videlicet . . .', *Humanae Vitae*, no. 14; *AAS* 60 (1968), pp. 490–1.

invoke the classical moral distinction between 'moral evil' or sin, and 'physical evil' such as hurt or harm to others. One might then consider that the inflicting of some harm or hurt upon others is often an unavoidable means to achieve a certain result, but that it is not therefore and *ipso facto* to be considered as morally evil. What counts, they argue, is whether the preponderance, in the total product of an action, is more helpful or more harmful; and it is only when this element of so-called 'pre-moral evil' has been evaluated that we are then in a position to adjudicate on whether or not it is also moral evil.

In such developments as these, then, there is evidence of a move towards viewing the morality of an individual concrete action within a wider context and totality than simply concentrating on what classical moralists termed the uncircumstanced 'object' of the act. It is being brought about either by incorporating circumstances within the description of the whole object of the particular action or by introducing a wide-angle lens to broaden consideration from the classical abstract object to a perusal and an evaluation which would also include the contrasting results of the concrete action. To any objections that such a way of proceeding is to elide an act with its consequences, and thus cloak its intrinsic immorality with a justification of the good which results, as if a good end justified a bad means, the counter-argument is evoked that, in abstraction from the results which are intended or are brought about, it is not possible to consider any particular piece of behaviour in strictly moral terms. Moreover, the distinction between act and consequences is not always an obvious and clear-cut one, and often to a large extent depends on how one chooses to describe what is being done or being contemplated, largely as a consequence of what independent moral significance one antecedently gives to various features of an action as distinct from the totality of the action.[35] Consideration of the ethics of surgical operations led to a realization that these could not be assessed simply by describing them as mutilation and then finding reasons to justify such mutilation. As a moral reality they had to be seen in a moral continuity with the effect of health intended and brought about; and only this totality, rather than incomplete stages or parts within

---

[35] Cf. E. D'arcy, *Human Acts: An Essay in their Moral Evaluation* (Oxford, 1963).

it, could be properly assessed in moral terms. Might not this approach apply in other medical areas, and, indeed, in other areas of morality?

A further instance in which there is evidence of a move away from atomic parts to an integrated whole is to be found in the regular bid on the part of some writers to consider the morality of individual actions not just in themselves but as they enter into a total continuity and pattern of the individual's moral history and life, or, in other words, in the light of a principle of moral totality. In this moral totality of individual actions the central referent is, of course, the person, and it is relevant to note here the recent shift of emphasis from human nature to the more comprehensive concept of person as the basis for objective moral criteria, as signalled by the Council. In October 1980 Pope John Paul II drew attention to the way in which scientific research and experimentation must be limited by 'respect for the person' and he called upon his medical audience to encourage 'a more unitary view of the patient'.[36] This holistic approach, or view of the individual person, can be seen operative not only as a controlling factor of all his moral behaviour, but also in his perception of what classical moral theology listed as a hierarchy of moral values, particularly in his approach to situations of moral conflict, whether of duties (either prima facie or otherwise) or of values. One can see tendencies against considering and comparing moral values in remote abstraction from the totality of life and experience. One can also see a growing awareness of the possible emergence of new values in society, whether in history or in the present, as in the case of identification with the poor and deprived and the consequent shift of emphasis on private property, or as in the case of the long-delayed emergence of women's rights, or the growing priority attached to world peace. Such consider- ations, both in society and for the individual at various stages of his life, can lead to the hierarchy of values which was elaborated by conceptual analysis of man's metaphysical nature into (in descending order) religious, spiritual, physical, and property values, giving way to what has been termed a 'hierarchy of urgencies',[37] even involving a policy of positive discrimination, in what is basically a continuous

---

[36] *AAS* 72 (1980), pp. 1126–29. On the new stress on person, cf. *supra*, pp. 113–14.
[37] J.-M. Aubert, 'Hiérarchie de valeurs et histoire', *Revue des Sciences Religieuses* 44 (1970), pp. 5–22.

attempt to strive for a balance, or equilibrium, of values in a more total perspective on life.

One such value which has emerged late in the Church's consciousness is that of human sexuality. And much recent and current work in moral theology centres on this most sensitive aspect of the human person. What has come increasingly into prominence is the relational aspect of sexuality and its fundamentally interpersonal character, such that, as one writer expresses it, married couples are to be considered as more than two individuals. They are two people who 'because of their sexual union change from two people into a single mysterious unit of one flesh', with moral consequences to be drawn from the appreciation that 'the need for frequent sexual union in marriage is the implementation, expressing, and strengthening of the oneness'.[38] Such a heightened appreciation of sexuality and marriage is one, and perhaps the most dramatic, instance of a shift of focus from personal isolationalism in moral theology to an awareness of a series of social totalities and of what this implies for moral evaluation of human behaviour. In such a climate of thought it is difficult to sustain the professedly personal opinion of Paul (1 Cor. 7: 32–5) as an argument for Christian (and not just priestly) celibacy that a spouse constitutes mainly a hindrance or a major distraction from the individual's service of God and not, rather, the first and most obvious focus of that love of neighbour which Jesus likened to love of God. It is, moreover, interesting to note how the Church has come to appreciate that moral decisions taken within a marriage must be seen as decisions shared by the partners in the marriage.[39] These and other developing insights into human sexuality stressing the nature and quality of human relationships are perhaps the most illuminating consequences of the growing appreciation that, as in God, so in his human creatures made in his image, reality is essentially relational, and that the fullness of personal identity is to be found only as interpersonal identity.

Such a move to a larger interpersonal totality is not an

---

[38] Elizabeth Price, 'Sexual Misunderstanding', *The Clergy Review* 65 (1980), p. 162.

[39] Cf. *Gaudium et Spes*, no. 87; *AAS* 58 (1966), p. 1110, 'deliberatio circa numerum prolis gignendae a recto iudicio parentum pendet'. Cf. also Pope John Paul II, *Familiaris Consortio*, no. 34; *AAS* 74 (1982), p. 124, 'Agnosci etiam debet in intima coniugum necessitudine voluntates duorum hominum implicari, vocatorum tamen ad mentium morumque convenientiam.'

absorption of the individuals but an acknowledgement of the inherently social nature of the human person which is being acknowledged not only in marriage but also in the larger variety of social groupings. It is, for instance, the resurrected social model of the Church as God's people, as the major contribution of Vatican II's *Dogmatic Constitution on the Church*, which has stimulated reflection on unity within the Church and at the same time acknowledgement of the unique dignity and fundamental equality of its individual members, so that it is no longer the case that 'theologians, who claimed to be speaking of the Church . . . were engaged in fact in describing its organs of government'.[40] And it is increasingly a matter not now, as we have seen, of the Roman Catholic Church being the single and absolutely indispensable ark of personal salvation. Focus has widened to encompass the whole Church of Christ for which he prayed and brings awareness on the part of at least some theologians of major problems to be confronted in ecumenical partnership, including the question of the degree to which other Churches and other Christians who share the one Spirit of Christ enjoy also authoritative Christian insights into the whole truth and moral reality. Nor does totality end there. For the new theological awareness of the Church as the sacrament of redeemed humanity and of its call to dialogue with the world in mutual respect and a quest for social justice indicates as a final cosmic drive to totality the function and role of the Church as symbolic agency of the totality of human history and of humankind.[41]

In the light of this overview of much that has been taking place in recent moral theology it is not unreasonable, and not a distorting of the evidence, to see it as so many manifestations of what may be considered a reaction against over-fragmentation of the human moral enterprise in the past and, more positively, a drive towards totality. It is an interesting phenomenon, which might be extended or extrapolated towards the ultimate unity of all created reality in Christ who alone gives ultimate meaning to morality. And one may speculate that if it is a valid inductive principle of moral theology it might also have some heuristic function as pointing towards a line

---

[40] R. Aubert, *La théologie* . . ., p. 87.

[41] Cf. the opening paragraph of Vatican II's *Dogmatic Constitution on the Church*, 'Cum autem Ecclesia sit in Christo veluti sacramentum seu signum et instrumentum intimae cum Deo unionis totiusque generis humani unitatis, . . .', *AAS* 57 (1965), p. 5.

of solution for new or outstanding moral issues. As such, it would tend to give favour, although not necessarily the last word, to solutions which gave a preference for the whole rather than the parts, and it would regard analysis as only a preliminary, if necessary, step towards synthesis, and require analysis always to include, and give due weight to, the relationships between the parts and the context and purpose of the whole.

It should be noted, of course, that what can be identified as an emerging cumulative totality is not one which annihilates the component elements, but fundamentally one which unites and integrates them. It is, in fact, one which concentrates on the pattern of the parts just as much as on the individual parts themselves, or, to be more precise, which constitutes them really as 'parts' and constituents of a whole rather than as a mere collection of unrelated entities. It is their being interrelated and patterned in a cosmic principle of totality which gives them their ultimate significance. And in identifying such an inherent interrelatedness we are, it may be suggested, acknowledging nothing other than the Augustinian and Thomist idea of divine *ordo* in all creation. It may be, indeed, that much of contemporary moral theology is unconsciously moving towards a recovery of that dynamic *ordo* which for Augustine and Aquinas was the very basis and context of all human morality.[42]

A Recognition of Diversity

In addition to the drive towards totality which appears to characterize much of modern moral theology it may be possible to identify another feature finding expression in the renewal of the subject requested by the Bishops of the Vatican Council—that of diversity. It may at first appear that totality and diversity cannot be compatible, since one appears to refer to unity and the other to differences. The point to be made, however, is that diversity in this context does not have to do with viewing the several parts of the whole, but refers to viewing the whole, or the totality, in a diversity of different ways.

It may be considered a feature of modern society, whether one considers history, or sociology, or anthropology, that we have

[42] Cf. *supra*, pp. 74–9.

acquired the ability to stand outside history and see it precisely as history, rather than being completely immersed in its stream. Man can stand on the bank of society as an at least partially detached observer and note something of the constants and the variables of human living. We are not, of course, capable of complete scientific, social, or historical objectivity, but we now at least are aware of it as something to be aimed at with varying measures of success. And perhaps the most dramatic instance and illustration of man's recently acquired ability to step back from the totality and view it objectively in the round was the morning when the world awoke to find spread across the front pages of its daily newspapers photographs of our earth taken by men on the moon.

This capacity for viewing things as a a whole from different standpoints, as it were, is one which appears to be finding expression in recent work in moral theology. Perhaps the most obvious sign of such diversity, or acknowledgement that the moral totality can be viewed and approached in differing ways, is the simple fact that moral theology is now conducted in many diverse languages, and no longer simply in the one medium of scholastic or ecclesiastical Latin. Aubert alludes to some of the 'fossilizing effects' on thought of neo-scholastic theologians, and refers to the feature of 'their penchant for repeating formulae instead of thinking them out afresh receiving added encouragement from the use of Latin'.[43] Not that English-language moral theology, at any rate, has totally succeeded yet in finding a native medium in which to reflect upon and to express the Christian moral experience in its own way, remaining too content to transliterate traditional terms and fresh barbarisms with references to 'unjust aggressors', 'probable opinions', 'ontic evil', 'fundamental option', 'intrinsically evil', and the like.

It is striking, for example, that the traditional Latin of moral theology is on the whole incapable of referring to 'right' and 'wrong' in moral behaviour, although it can speak of 'wrong' in terms of 'mistaken' or 'erroneous' conscience. Its basic terminological distinction in morality is between 'good' and 'bad', and this allows little scope for distinguishing between a 'good' thing to do and the 'right' thing to do, or between 'wrong' and 'bad'. Moreover, it cannot distinguish between 'bad' and 'evil', having

---

[43] R. Aubert (ed.), *The Christian Centuries (London,* 1978), vol. v, pp. 173–4.

only the Latin *malum* or *malitia* at its disposal. This has unfortunate and often misleading results when English-language moral texts exhibit an invariable preference and unconscious influence by referring to certain types of behaviour as 'evil'. In English usage of the normal kind to describe something or someone as 'evil' is to ascribe an element of emotional perversity or perversion, and the term tends to be reserved to instances of exceptional cruelty or of malicious behaviour. Yet in much moral theology in English reference continues happily to be made to such types of behaviour as contraception, euthanasia, and telling lies as being 'evil', or 'intrinsically evil', thus either devaluing the language or exaggerating the 'wrongness' or 'badness' of the behaviour. It also frequently induces deep confusion, and a subsequent need for clarification, between behaviour considered objectively and the subjective dispositions of the agent. In these and other ways of simply adopting Latin idiom unreflectively, both the incentive and the opportunity are lost to explore and to exploit more native English idioms and habits of thought and language which can give a welcome precision and richness to moral discourse and reflection.

Nor is this just a mere question of words. An illuminating parallel on the distinctive contributions to moral theology which can arise from its development in various languages is to be found in the case of the Church's liturgy, which has in recent years undergone similar diversification, at least in principle. Through vernacular liturgies the Roman Catholic Church's worship has undoubtedly become much more alive and effective for the vast majority of its members. This will be the more so as it is appreciated that liturgies appropriate to different regions of the universal Church are not simply, or should not be, so many faithful transliterations, in word and gesture, of the Roman liturgy, but are to be seen, as Pope Gregory wrote to Augustine of Canterbury, as equally valid expressions in local cultures and tongues of the central mysteries of the Churchs's cult.[44] It is not, then, in liturgy, or in moral theology, a matter of 'mere terminology', but of the underlying objective diversity of cultural and historical resources

---

[44] 'Sed mihi placet ut sive in Romana, sive in Galliarum, sive in qualibet Ecclesia aliquid invenisti quod plus omnipotenti Deo possit placere, sollicite eligas, et in Anglorum Ecclesia, quae adhuc in fide nova est, institutione praecipua quae de multis Ecclesiis colligere potuisti, infundas. Non enim pro locis res, sed pro rebus loca nobis amanda sunt', *PL* 77, col. 1187.

and heritages of which different languages are so many living repositories and expressions. From this point of view, then, the simple fact that moral theology is now beginning to be conducted in a diversity of languages is a feature whose cultural significances and full implications have not begun to be realized.

If language is the articulation and communication of experience and reflection then at a deeper level than diversity in language, and interacting with it, is to be found, as is slowly entering into the consciousness of moral theology, the diversity of human and moral experience. The common saying that Eskimos have many more terms to differentiate the phenomenon which those in warmer climes refer to simply as 'snow' can be seen as acknowledging how the subtleties and nuances of particular terms reflect and attempt to express the special significance and relevance to various individuals or groups of certain aspects of reality. In various cultures the relationships between things, the totality which is experienced, is not identical with the same totality as it is experienced by others. Identical things and identical terms can be perceived and comprehended differently within the context of a diversity of experiences. In Western culture over the centuries the frequent perception of particular relationships has resulted in a western vocabulary (with built-in moral overtones) which is on the whole at present (or has been until recently) commonly understood. Instances are such terms as war, marriage, ownership, communication, person, and parenthood.

The realities, however, and the relationships between them, which underlie these traditional western terms differ in other worlds of experience and of discourse. And even in the West they are changing today with increasing rapidity. War is becoming an inadequate concept, as are property and ownership. One of the most fundamental personal and social moral questions emerging today must be the question: what exactly is marriage? The development of *in vitro* fertilization and its various applications is urgently raising for society the question: what is parenthood? The long overdue emergence of women's rights is equally raising urgently the question: what is gender? And the technological possibilities opening up before society in the form of recombinant DNA and genetic engineering can only bring to a head as the most urgent and radical challenge facing our species the question: what is man?

Cultural and moral diversity is an increasingly recognized simultaneous phenomenon in the contemporary world. It appears also successively in history as the phenomenon of change, an unavoidable element of human existence on which the Church often appears to be at best ambivalent and at worst studiedly uncaring. Perhaps one, Platonist, extreme is aptly summed up in the popular hymn 'Change and decay in all around I see. O Thou who changest not, Abide with me', where change appears synonymous with dissolution, or with decline from the ideal. Yet it was Newman who observed, 'In a higher world it is otherwise; but here below to live is to change, and to be perfect is to have changed often'.[45] It appears to be one of the sources of the popularity of the Jesuit mystic, Teilhard de Chardin, that in his christological vision of the cosmos he provides a theology of change in terms of purpose and convergence. Moral theology, however, in its anthropology has never accepted human evolution and its implications, and the Church has great difficulty not only in handling the subject of change as such—all theories of 'development of doctrine' aiming to vindicate continuity and basic identity—but also in adjusting its teaching to 'changing circumstances'. One temptation is to deny that any change has occurred and to appeal in moral matters to the unchanging character of 'human nature' and thus the permanent force of natural law precepts.[46] Another is to describe such change as is reluctantly acknowledged as merely 'accidental', or not affecting the 'substantials' of life and morality.[47] And a third is to concur warmly that change has indeed occurred, and to deplore it as the inevitable consequences of ignoring God's immutable moral law. In all such reactions, permanency is at a premium, and impermanency viewed as regrettable and threatening.

There cannot be any doubt, however, that the Roman Catholic Church's teaching over the centuries and in recent decades has changed markedly in many respects—as in the field of biblical studies; in the possibility of salvation for unbelievers outside the Catholic Church; in ecumenism; in the matter and form of the Sacrament of Orders; in recognizing the moral possibility in marriage of birth-control through periodic abstinence from inter-

---

[45] *Essay on the Development of Christian Doctrine*, ch. 1, sec. 1.
[46] Cf. *supra*, p. 206.
[47] On some of the difficulties of this analogy, cf. *supra*, pp. 312–13.

course.[48] That in recent years such changes appear to have become recognized as legitimate in so short a period of time is not necessarily to be seen as simply reflecting the accelerating rate of change in society at large, but at least equally as indicating that many such changes were long overdue in the Church. It is possible to view the first half of this century as a quite uncharacteristic period of the Church's history in its apparent placidity and calm, and as the unnatural sequel to the blanket and indiscriminate condemnation and suspicion of anything savouring of—in the revealing term—'modernism'.[49] So much so, that the increasing remoteness of his Church from modern life and from modern society led Pope John XXIII to decide that nothing short of a General Council of the whole Roman Catholic Church would be required to bring about his much quoted *aggiornamento* of the Church, or quite simply to bring the Church up to date.

The first changes introduced by that Council which were really to strike home in the lives and practices of many Church members, those in the Church's liturgy, were much the more painful for many loyal members of the Church for their having been comfortably accustomed to permanency and unchange as a result of the calm induced by the Church's repulse of any attempt to incorporate change as a fact of human and Christian life and thought. When to the almost complete lack of preparation and education then for change in many parts of the Church there is now added the increasing rate of change in modern society and in the 'secular' lives of Church members the realization is unpalatable for many that Pope John's 'updating' is now over twenty years old. The activities and changes brought about, reluctantly in many instances, in the 1960s and 1970s were not an uncharacteristic or exceptional period during which the Church was leaving one comfortable plateau in order to scramble up to a higher plateau. At least in its official teaching, the Church is becoming aware that change is here to stay and that every age is an age of transition. That, after all, is what the 'pilgrim' Church means.

One conclusion for moral theology to be drawn from these considerations on change as an unavoidable element of human existence is well expressed by Rahner when he writes, 'the sum total

---

[48] Cf. on the subject, F. A. Sullivan, *Magisterium: Teaching Authority in the Catholic Church* (Dublin, 1983).

[49] Cf. *DS* 3475, proem.

of the norms of Christian living, together with a specific way of life felt to be binding on Christians, may once have been developed and held confidently and unquestionably in a particular age. Nevertheless they contained far more changeable elements than were ever conceived of as a matter of clear and conscious reflection by those belonging to that particular age itself'. And he goes on to see within the Church an unavoidable 'process of interaction between changeable and unchangeable factors which cannot fully be distinguished . . . . And this is something which must be sustained and endured in patience.'[50] Of course, the question of change, intimately linked as it is with questions of personal security and insecurity, is permeated with emotional elements, and when it takes the form of the need for corporate change, whether in doctrine or in behaviour, then such conclusions can easily be interpreted by authority as a criticizing of the past and of the past exercise of authority. The so-called 'minority' paper of the papal commission on birth control offers a case in point when it argues that for the Church to change now in its moral condemnation of contraception would be an admission that it had for centuries been mistaken.[51] And yet this conclusion does not necessarily follow so far as the past is concerned, whatever might be said about reluctance to change in the present. At any stage in history all that is available to the Church is its continual meditation on the Word of God in the light of contemporary experience and of the knowledge and insights into reality which it possesses at the time. To be faithful to that set of circumstances and not to some conjectural or possible future set of factors is the charge and the challenge which Christ has given to his Church. But if there is a historical shift, through improvement in scholarship or knowledge, or through an entry of society into a significantly different age, then what that same fidelity requires of the Church is that it respond to the historical shift, such that it might be not only mistaken but also unfaithful in declining to do so.[52]

Examination of historical change including changes in the Church and in its teaching illustrates, then, in dramatic form the

---

[50] 'Basic observations on the subject of changeable and unchangeable factors in the Church', *Theological Investigations*, vol. xiv (London, 1976), p. 14.

[51] Cf. L. Pyle (ed.), *Pope and Pill* (London, 1968), p. 291; *supra*, pp. 266–7.

[52] Cf. A. Dulles, *The Resilient Church* (Dublin, 1978), ch. 2, 'Church Reform through Creative Interaction'.

challenges and the problems thrown up by all diversity, whether successive or simultaneous. To this can be added, alongside diverse types of behaviour which correspond to whole societies differing in culture and experience, consideration of the diversity of individual persons and of the personal cosmos which each inhabits, as an instance in microcosm of various corporate diversities. For the most part moral theology has tended to concentrate on elaborating what God wants of all men. Any divergence or deviation from that by individuals has then tended to be treated at best understandingly and sympathetically, in a 'pastoral' manner, as a falling short of what is objectively required. And the degree of individual guilt in acting at variance with God's will for all men has been explored in terms of personal freedom, sin, and grace in the light of the Augustinian axiom that whatever God commands is possible of achievement.[53]

This traditional distinction, however, between the 'moral' and the 'pastoral' approach leads inevitably to an impoverished view of both moral theology and pastoral theology. It accentuates in moral theology an approach which is concerned exclusively with universals rather than particulars, and it lends itself too readily to the elaboration of morality in terms of the law as 'normal' and of anything else as requiring justification through the exploring of 'exceptions' to law.[54] It thus exposes itself to the dangers of an unhealthy form of casuistry which can easily incur charges of 'loophole' moral theology. To those who are not Roman Catholics and even to many Catholics unaware of the 'pastoral' tradition which has accompanied moral theology it presents a highly intransigent and remote moral teaching. While to those who have some acquaintance with this 'pastoral', or 'lenient', tradition and are also possessed of an Anglo-Saxon reverence for law such a dual approach can easily appear either cynical or hypocritical. And in those Church members who, for one reason or another, are unable to 'measure up' to the universal norms of moral theology, such pastoral concern, and sympathetic understanding, while often undoubtedly helpful, can also at the same time confirm or reinforce a personal sense of moral failure, delinquency, and hopelessness which is terrible to contemplate.[55]

[53] Cf. *supra*, pp. 54–7.
[54] Cf. *supra*, pp. 232–40.
[55] Cf. J. Mahoney, 'Moral Freedom, Grace, and Sin', *Seeking the Spirit*, p. 35.

It may be suggested that what is basically at issue here is the tension which exists between the challenge and the comfort of God's call, perhaps reflecting the tension between the divine transcendence and the divine immanence—the demanding call from a distance and the companying close at hand. Such tensions are not to be resolved, of course. Yet it appears that the elements of divine comfort, immanence, and companying call today for particular stress, partly in reaction to the past, but mainly because they appear more consonant with a religion which is essentially incarnational and particular. The reluctance of moral theology, as it has developed, to incorporate the particular, and the relinquishing of the individual to 'pastoral' theology and to 'pastoral solutions' to moral dilemmas (which has also until recently prevented any healthy development of pastoral theology), may arise partly from a desire to preserve the character of moral theology as a theological science, and from a care to maintain its self-esteem as a 'hard' rather than a 'soft' science in the face of moral philosophy or ethics.[56] And yet, as a branch of theology, the description of moral theology as a 'science' is but an analogy which is ill-used if its comparison with purely human counterparts is pushed too literally and univocally. It is interesting to note, however, how, alongside major new developments in pastoral theology, much recent work in moral theology has been at pains to explore avenues which integrate the particular into the renewal of the subject, largely stimulated by reflection on so-called 'conflict' situations. Theories of choosing the lesser of two evils, or more positively of choosing the best in the circumstances, of compromise, of proportionality, of situated or limited freedom, and others, appear to be so many acknowledgements that moral theology cannot today simply content itself with elaborating a list of moral universals without also carefully perusing their absolute or relative character, notably when they may, or may 'appear', to come into conflict in particular situations or for particular individuals. What such moves must betoken is a reappraisal of the traditional distinction between objective and subjective morality in terms of the diversity of individuals and of their distinct moral universes. The slow growth in the making of moral theology of respect for individual

[56] On the individual and moral and pastoral theology, cf. E. Doyle, 'Peaceful Reflections on the Renewal of Moral Theology', *Clergy Review* 62 (1977), 393–401.

conscience by way of the development of invincible ignorance and of the terrain of subjective morality could perhaps be seen in retrospect as an inchoate attempt to acknowledge objective diversity in the lives of individuals. And the rush of Christian commonsense to the head which resulted in the ecumenical revolution may be seen as a further stage in acknowledging that the Church is not armed with a complete survey map of God's ways for all men.[57] It may appear, then, that various current attempts to incorporate particulars into the science of moral theology, with all the mental and systematic adjustments which that implies, is a move to throw a bridge across the gap between 'objective' and 'subjective' morality and to judge that, far more frequently than has been suspected, what diverse individuals consider God requires of them is in actual fact what God does 'objectively' require of them, as legitimate personal diversities.

Moral Pluralism: Liberation Theology

The recognition of diversity between individuals and groups—not simply in their behaviour and not simply in some particular attitudes, but more generally in the way in which they perceive and interpret the whole of reality or large sectors of it—underlies the growing awareness of pluralism in society, which for the Christian often takes the form of exploring how to live and commend the Christian view of life in a pluralist society. As a simply descriptive term, pluralism acknowledges a plurality of coexisting philosophies or theologies of life, and a variety of value-clusters as espoused by different individuals or groups and operative simultaneously in society, without attempting to evaluate them or their correspondence to 'reality' or to the truth. As a term used increasingly in theology, however, pluralism considers not just the variety of ways of appropriating God's Word, or of contrasting and differing beliefs and their interpretations. It considers also the claim that several varying approaches may all contain some measure of truth, or may be considered as equally valid expressions of Revelation, and may together provide complementary aspects of the many facets of God and his activities. What theological pluralism claims as a matter of principle is that, not simply because of cultural and

---

[57] Cf. *supra*, pp. 218–23.

other differences in the perceiving subject, but also because of the inexhaustible nature of the divine 'object', it is impossible to comprehend God from only one viewpoint or to express that comprehension in only one manner.[58]

In earlier chapters of our study of the making of moral theology we have noted the enormously influential legacy bequeathed to the subject by Augustine's perception of reality in the light of his experience, both personal and polemical, and we have noted Gilson's remark that some people appear to be born Augustinian.[59] We have also seen something of the effortless influence of the imperturbable 'Common Doctor', Aquinas, on subsequent moral theology, and we have noted the movement of neo-scholasticism, and specifically neo-Thomism, strongly inculcated by Pope Leo XIII at the end of the last century and subsequently reinforced by his successors to culminate in Pope Pius XII's critical reaction after the Second World War to the developments of the 'nouvelle théologie'.[60] For most of the present century it would not be inappropriate to conflate Gilson with Shakespeare's Malvolio and conclude that some theologians are born Thomists, others acquire a love for Thomism, and some had Aquinas thrust upon them. One regrettable consequence for moral theology, however, was that the Aquinas so assiduously cultivated was not Thomas the moral theologian but Thomas the moral philosopher, and that in a very rigid portrayal of his natural law theory.[61]

Since the 1950s, however, with the growing influence of existentialist and personalist thought, as well as with the recovery of a historical sense in theology, it is a fact that pluralism, or a variety of approaches, has become an accepted feature of theology. It is increasingly recognized as a characteristic even of theology's normative sources, the Bible itself. Theological pluralism is, in fact, as the International Theological Commission noted in 1973, an inevitable consequence of 'the very mystery of Christ which, while being at the same time a mystery of universal fulfilment and reconciliation (Eph. 2: 11–22), goes beyond the possibilities of

[58] Cf. K. Rahner, 'Pluralism in theology and the unity of the Creed', *Theological Investigations*, vol. v, London, 1966, pp. 3–23.

[59] Cf. *supra*, p. 71.

[60] On Leo XIII, cf. Aubert, pp. 171–4. For Pius XII's encyclical *Humani Generis*, cf. *DS* 3875–99.

[61] Cf. J. Mahoney, *Seeking the Spirit*, p. 113.

expression of any given age and thus eludes exhaustive systematization (Eph. 3: 8–10)'.[62]

Within the discipline of moral theology it is possible to refer to
pluralism in more than one sense. Thus, the International Theological Commission, in its general treatment of the growing
phenomenon of pluralism, could describe as pluralism the diversity
of ways in which universal moral principles are applied to different
situations in the light of changing circumstances.[63] One can also
describe as moral pluralism the freedom of discussion and the
variety of possible moral attitudes in certain areas of morality
where there does not appear to be any clear teaching in Scripture or
from the Church's *magisterium*, much as Pius XII referred to 'open
questions' on which the Church had not, or not yet, pronounced.[64]
Such meanings given to moral pluralism, however, are comparatively superficial, and today the enquiry into pluralism is
undertaken at a much deeper level than that relating to variable
circumstances or officially debatable subjects. What is in question
increasingly includes moral cultural pluralism which is similar to,
but more thoroughly acknowledged than, the occasional difference
which circumstances will make to the application of principles. At
heart it concerns a pluralism in moral method which could result in
a pluralism in behaviour as the result of which of various diverse
methods is adopted and applied.

One major diversity which has in recent years occupied the
methodological stage focuses on a choice between a deductive and
an inductive approach to morality, not perhaps so much as offering
complete alternatives as in identifying how much attention is to be
accorded to the a priori over against the a posteriori, or to
intellectual considerations alone over against respect for the data of
experience and the significance of moral insight or intuition arising
from such experience.[65] The tension between these two broad lines
of methodological approach is perhaps most evident in fields of
individual morality, and within that on the particular subject of
sexual behaviour in the aftermath, and reaffirmation, of *Humanae
Vitae*. It may be more instructive, however, as well as refreshingly
different, to consider, however briefly, the major debate in

---

[62] *The Tablet*, 7 July, 1973, p. 646.
[63] *Pluralismo*, Commissione teologica internazionale (Bologna, 1974), p. 71.
[64] Ibid., Cf. *supra*, p. 159.
[65] Cf. *supra*, pp. 206–10, 287–8.

contemporary social morality which best exemplifies the tension of methodology and the growing phenomenon of moral pluralism in the Church—the whole powerful current of liberation theology.

The theology of liberation has its origins not in any abstract consideration of man but in the situation in which individuals find themselves in the social and political conditions of Latin America and other parts of the globe. Some critics of liberation theology would incline to view it as revolution in search of theological respectability, or at least, in the delicate French idiom, as 'soliciting' the text of Scripture for its own purposes. And this preliminary consideration is perhaps already evidence of a difference between analysis in remoteness, or from a distance, and analysis by way of immersion and involvement in the situation. Liberation theologians themselves view their subject from the latter vantage point. From their immediate experience and reflection upon that experience they are convinced that the point of the Gospel is not just orthodoxy, or 'getting things right', but orthopraxy, or 'making things right'. They believe strongly also, if the matter is capable of being expressed so simply, that the important feature of orthopraxy is to choose one's prejudices. Prejudices are the unconscious preferences operative in our actions, and the first need is to lay them bare and then to choose which ones to be influenced by, or to make a 'preferential option'. For the Christian in Latin America, they conclude, there can be only one such preferential option, and that is for the poor and the powerless. In such social circumstances not to choose deliberately for the poor is to conspire with the powerful. And that is a (if not the) central feature in the message of both the Old and the New Testaments.

The literature on liberation theology and its concentration on the socio-political implications of the Gospel today is vast and varying in quality, and much of it has attracted adverse comment outside Latin America, notably in Rome.[66] Its methodological approach is a two-way movement in which reflection upon the experience of widespread social and political oppression and prayerful meditation on Scripture throw a strong light on each other to deliver practical conclusions and justification for action appropriate to the situation of the participants. An illuminating and moving application of the method is to be seen in one major figure in the movement and in a

---

[66] Cf. Instruction of the Sacred Congregation for the Doctrine of Faith on Certain Aspects of 'Liberation Theology', *AAS* 76 (1984), pp. 876–909.

speech which he delivered in the academic world of the University of Louvain on the occasion of receiving its honorary doctorate in theology. The figure was Archbishop Oscar Romero, theologian and 'vicar of Christ'[67] in his own local Church. And the authority of his remarks and behaviour was further enhanced by his being publicly murdered for his beliefs one month later in the centre of San Salvador.

In the words of Archbishop Romero his Church had chosen to 'incarnate itself' with the Salvadorian poor, with a world which had 'no human face', and in so doing it was also led 'to rediscover the central truth of the Gospel'. This dual movement led to 'the discovery of the convergence of the desire for liberation of our continent and the offering of the Love of God to the poor'. But by extending that love and defending the poor the Church 'has entered into conflict with the powers of economic oligarchy, the political powers, and the military State', inevitably incurring persecution and thus 'a common destiny with the poor'. Such an evangelical identification of the Church with the poor, or preferential option for the poor, Romero reflected, avoids that 'false universality which ends always in a complicity with the powerful'. 'We see clearly that there is no possible neutrality: we place ourselves at the service of the life of Salvadorians, or we are accomplices in their death'. In a powerful and moving passage the Archbishop stated what Christians must learn from the poor:

The world of the poor teaches us how Christian love should be a love that seeks peace by unmasking false pacifism, resignation, and passivity; this love should be free but should search for a historical efficacy. The world of the poor teaches us that the sublimity of Christian love should first go through the imperative need of justice for the masses and it should not shun honest struggle. The world of the poor teaches us that liberation will happen not only when the poor will become the privileged subjects of government or Church attention, but more when they will be the actors and protagonists of their own struggles and of their liberation, revealing thereby the last roots of false paternalism, even that of the Church as well.[68]

[67] 'Episcopi Ecclesias particulares sibi commissas ut vicarii et legati Christi regunt', *Lumen gentium*, no. 27; *AAS* 57 (1965), p. 32.
[68] O. Romero, 'Political Dimension of Christian Faith from an Option for the poor', 2 February, 1980. English translation in *Convergence*, publication of Pax Romana, Switzerland–Belgium, no. 1–2, 1981, pp. 27–32.

In this eloquent witness by a martyr of the modern Church we can see dramatically illustrated a number of the considerations upon which we have already touched: the replacing of a static hierarchy of values by a hierarchy, or an urgency, of priorities which will give a particular, and possibly dominant, moral coloration to everything one does or does not do in the situation; a deliberate abandonment of moral impartiality as, in fact, untrue and humanly impossible; a choice of moral stance from which the totality of relationships is viewed in a particular light; the interaction of moral reflection and experience rather than the rational application of the practical syllogism; in a word, a particularly cogent and articulate choice of a moral method as an illustration of moral pluralism. It could be objected, however, that according to liberation theology itself moral pluralism is ruled out of order, since the theology of liberation is considered the only moral option open to the Christian. And this in turn raises the general question of the compatibility, or even the compossibility, of diverse theologies and methods and specifically of how extensive or how limited moral pluralism can legitimately be within the Christian community. In various of its magisterial decisions throughout history the Church has tried to control debate and controversy on certain topics. Sometimes it has done so by enjoining silence on disputing parties, as it did in the controversy over grace and freedom and in the Jansenist troubles, without much success. Or it has delivered judgements intended to close a subject, as in the crisis of Modernism; the development of situation ethics in post-war Europe; the papal encyclical on contraception; and perhaps in the critical judgements delivered in some quarters of the Church against liberation theology itself. In other instances, as we have noted in the Church's reactions to the excesses of laxism and of rigorism, formal condemnations have been delivered of what could probably not in moral matters be described as heresy, but which were undoubtedly regarded as instances of heterodoxy.[69]

With increasing attention, however, given to the possibility and indeed the inevitability of pluralism in theology, including moral theology, a comparable attention is likewise called for with regard to questions concerning heresy and orthodoxy. And a considerable body of writing illustrates and explores the difficulties today

[69] Cf. *supra*, pp. 90–1, 140–2, 158–9, 205, 271.

attendant upon attempts to identify what heresy and heterodoxy are with regard to individual statements or expressions of belief or behaviour when these are the product of theological or philosophical diversity or, additionally in moral matters at least, of cultural diversity in different parts of the world, or even in the world-views of different individuals.[70] Within the context of theological and moral pluralism such verdicts of heresy and heterodoxy as may be possible may have at root to take the form of adverse judgements on specific methods such as utilitarianism or 'situation ethics' or liberation theology. Or they may reject a particular 'projection' of reality as portrayed in a diversity of theological or moral maps. And yet such expressions of disapproval cannot themselves be exempted from the fundamental questions which the possibility of pluralism raises. In matters of morality, in the first place, there is scrutiny of the *Magisterium*'s own choice of method and the extent to which, for instance, natural law theory, and one version of it at that, is to be considered a moral method particularly privileged or even required by the Gospel to the exclusion of all others. Furthermore, there is increasing theological pluralism about the Church itself, on its *magisterium* in teaching on matters of faith and morals, and on the degree to which the comparatively recent distinction between the teaching and the learning Church can be maintained in all its starkness.[71]

To advance such considerations is not at all to conclude that heresy and heterodoxy are no longer possible to commit. They do, however, serve to illustrate that with the acknowledgement of pluralism heterodoxy is much more difficult to identify and, in some sense, may have to be judged either on its own principles, or within the projection of reality from which they emerge; that is, either as being at variance with those principles or as a logical extension of a projection which must as a whole be considered not just inadequate—for in theology all projections are strictly speaking inadequate—but positively erroneous. It may further be advanced that part, but perhaps only part, of an answer to the question of competing methods in morality, or to claims to possess a monopoly of method, whether on the part of the *Magisterium* or of liberation

---

[70] Cf., e.g., K. Rahner, 'What is heresy?', *Theological Investigations*, vol. v (London, 1966), pp. 468–512; 'Heresies in the Church today?', vol. xii (1974), pp. 117–41.

[71] Cf. *supra*, pp. 119–20, 296.

theology, may be that at any moment in history one can act only according to what knowledge and insight are available, but that some moments in history and some cultures may call for a particular method in preference to others or even for that time and place to the exclusion of others. If it be objected that such a view is tantamount to accommodating theology to the world as the handmaid of politics or sociology or cultural anthropology and constitutes a betrayal of its roots in Revelation or its scientific integrity and proper autonomy, then such objections in turn raise the deeper question of what theology is, and in particular what is the purpose and function of moral theology. In attempting to respond to this foundation question addressed to moral theology we also wish to propose a further consideration concerning contemporary moral theology which may serve to bring together and throw light upon the two characteristics which we have identified in post-Conciliar moral theology, that of a drive to totality and that of a recognition of diversity. It is the consideration that, as a branch of Christian theology, moral theology is concerned at heart with the mystery of God and 'the riches of the glory of this mystery' (Col. 1: 27); and that a renewed moral theology can find its theological identity only by a recovery of mystery.

The Recovery of Mystery

It is the mystery of God which earths all theology and at the same time makes theological pluralism unavoidable. So far as moral theology is concerned, there may appear to be a disinclination to accept this element of mystery in much of the writing devoted today to a central question—that of the specificity of Christian ethics, or, in other words, what features moral theology possesses which would not be accessible to moral philosophy. On the whole the move in contemporary moral theology is towards minimizing the difference by developing such themes as viewing Christian morality as human morality at its best and stretched to its fullest potential, in a manner similar to that by which the Incarnation itself did not annihilate or replace humanity but may be considered to raise it to the peak of its perfection. When attention is directed towards specific moral principles or conclusions concerning, for example, issues of birth and death, sexuality and marriage, and the structures of society, the debate on the specificity of Christian ethics often takes the form of asking whether, as in the view of Aquinas, the moral content of Scripture is identical with conclusions of natural law, and has nothing radically new to add to what can, at least in principle, be attained by unaided human reason. What would then be specific to Christian ethics, rendering it distinctive from human ethics, would be simply its confirming the content of human ethics and at the same time adding considerations to intensify both the motivation and the urgency of human ethical considerations. In this way, for instance, murder would be viewed as the unjustifiable killing not just of a fellow human being but, in theistic terms, of a fellow creature of God and, in explicitly Christian terms, of a 'brother for whom Christ died' (1 Cor. 8: 11).

Such an approach to Christian ethics, however, appears to labour under two difficulties. The first is that it appears to presuppose a clear and adequate distinction between reason and revelation, and underlying that, between nature and grace, whereas recent thinking in other areas of modern theology tends to regard all reality and historical experience as a source of divine revelation and as bathed in grace, whether consciously or not. The conclusion of this would be, with ancient writers such as Justin Martyr and moderns such as Karl Rahner, that all ethics is Christian ethics in some degree, whether in the fully explicit form to be found in Scripture and the Church, or as intimations to be found everywhere in human culture and history.[72] In other words, just as all men who try to live an upright moral life can be regarded, in responding to God's saving grace however implicitly or unknowingly, as anonymous Christians, or as saved by 'the blood of Christ, who through the eternal Spirit offered himself without blemish to God [to] purify your conscience from dead works to serve the living God' (Heb. 9: 14); in like manner all true human ethical insights are likewise anonymous Christian ethics, or to be considered as exemplifying the theological richness of the observation of Ambrosiaster, that 'every truth, no matter who utters it, has its origin in the Holy Spirit'.[73]

The second difficulty from which any attempt to separate out Christian from human ethics suffers may be illustrated by reflection

---

[72] Cf. *supra*, pp. 100–2, 114–15.

[73] 'Omne verum, a quocumque dicatur, a Spiritu sancto est', on which cf. Z. Alszeghy, *Nova creatura. La nozione della grazia nei commentari medievali di S. Paulo* (Rome, 1956), pp. 194–8.

on the terms 'Christian' or 'theological' ethics, and 'moral theology'. For many purposes the two terms are interchangeable, although moral theology can be also seen as emerging from, and expressive of, a Catholic background with its strong sense of Christian community and responsibility to *magisterium* in the Church, as has become evident in this historical study, while Christian ethics can be considered as more expressive of a Protestant background and ethos, with more direct reliance on the Bible and, perhaps, the individual. In addition, however, there may be a further difference between the two terms, or rather, a subtle differentiation of focus, arising from each being described as a specific form of quite different genera. On the one hand, Christian ethics implies a particular type of ethics, as contrasted, for instance, with rational, or philosophical, or secular, ethics, with the inevitable consequence that questions of identity must arise as to how this specific type of ethics differs from other types, as we have recently been considering. On the other hand, however, moral theology is a species, or branch, of theology, or the study of God and of his creative and saving actions. To that extent its primary focus is on how man, and not just explicitly Christian man, is to respond to God.

We may recall here the observation of Josef Fuchs, commenting on the type of moral theology appropriate to the Second Vatican Council's call for renewal, that it should not be 'that type of moral theology which evolved into "Christian ethics" in the age of rationalism and viewed Christ mainly as a moralist, albeit a truly sublime one. On the contrary, the primary task of moral theology, according to the letter and spirit of the Council, must be to explain that man is called personally in Christ by the personal God.'[74] In the light of such reflections on a possible difference of mental approach in Christian ethics and moral theology, influenced by their differing conceptual starting-points, it may be possible to conclude that much modern writing in moral theology, in its dialogue with philosophical humanist ethics on the one hand and with non-Catholic Christian ethics on the other hand, and in the desire to prove to the former that it is not irrational and to the latter that it is not simply authoritarian, is in danger of forgetting that it is a branch of Christian theology. As such it is concerned primarily

[74] J. Fuchs, op. cit., p. 8.

with mystery: the mystery of a loving God and of his dealings with, and destiny for, his creation. The artistic medium in which God is fashioning and crafting his human creatures is the medium of their personal freedom; and the stuff, or material, of moral theology is the sheer wonder of man's being as it responds in freedom to the design of God.

If theology is viewed with Anselm as 'faith seeking understanding', then moral theology is faith seeking expression in behaviour, or, as the Second Vatican Council expressed it, faith put into effect in morals.[75] Theology, as we have described it elsewhere, is both an attempt to make sense of human experience in the light of belief and an attempt to make sense of belief in the light of human experience, which is always a Christian experience.[76] Ultimately it is an attempt to make human sense of divine reality and activity. It is therefore always and inevitably imperfect, a peering through a dark glass of human limited intelligence and limited language, such that no one glimpse or expression can encompass or exhaust the divine reality, but that many such expressions can reflect in necessarily refracted manners aspects or facets of the totality in some measure, much as, in Shelley's *Adonais*,

The One remains, the many change and pass;
Heaven's light forever shines, Earth's shadows fly;
Life, like a dome of many-coloured glass,
Stains the white radiance of Eternity . . . .

In these terms, theology may be compared to a window of many lights in different colours, through which God's self-revelation filters to our human sight, or to a prism which discloses in a spectrum of colours the one undifferentiated source of light.

Such a bid to recover the mystery for moral theology, or to stress its strictly theological character, does not leave man in agnosticism or in impenetrable darkness about moral behaviour, any more than it condemns other branches of theology to stunned speechlessness and silence, even though they too can easily forget the analogy of being and the analogical nature of all theological discourse. What it does do, however, is to admonish man to a due humility in his conclusions and in his claims for himself or upon others, and to

---

[75] 'fidem . . . moribus applicandam', cf. *supra*, p. 174.
[76] *Bioethics and Belief*, p. 112.

inject a note of reverence for God and the work of His hands into all moral enterprise. It reminds him that in such matters, as the Second Vatican Council observed, man is ultimately 'alone with God' in the 'sanctuary' of his conscience, a sanctuary which may afford him protection from other men but which is also his meeting place with the living God.[77] Such a recovery of mystery for moral theology should also lead all in the Christian community to strive to attune themselves habitually to the Spirit of Christ who is still at work in his creation and redemption, and whose presence in our hearts and in the Church, as Augustine and Aquinas realised, is the primary and indispensable element of the New Law of the Gospel and the primordial source of all morality.[78]

The Morality of koinonia

In attempting to identify, then, a pattern in the renewal of moral theology we have suggested that post-conciliar work in the subject as a whole shows evidence of what we have termed a drive to totality and an attempt to recognize and respect diversity. We have also suggested that these two characteristics may be pointing to, and be satisfactorily united in, what we have further termed a recovery of mystery. Such a culminating feature for moral theology not only gives theological warrant for pluralism, whether of method or of a resulting diversity of behaviour. It also provides ample justification for a point which we have made more than once in this study, that moral theology has suffered in the past from treating analogical concepts as if they were univocal and could deliver detailed and unquestionable conclusions. The not infrequent consequence has been that moral theology, or the Church, has manoeuvred itself into remote corners from which it could only with difficulty emerge. And such unreflective pursuit of concepts is to be seen at its most momentous in the ways in which God himself has been perceived and portrayed. Whether he is seen as lawgiver or as lover, as liberator or as judge, as narrator or as artist, human perspectives of God may all with more or less inadequacy portray something of him, but none in isolation is at all capable of comprehending the height or depth or breadth or richness of divine reality. When Solomon laboured to build a temple for the Lord he

---

[77] Cf. *supra*, p. 292.   [78] Cf. *supra*, p. 255.

also recognized that if 'the highest heaven cannot contain thee; how much less this house which I have built!' And when the Lord in his glory did take up his abode, 'the house, the house of the Lord, was filled with a cloud' (2 Chr. 6: 18; 5: 13–14).

In more prosaic terms, the Christian God is a God who escapes systematization on the part of his human creatures. In any future 'systematic exposition' of moral theology, as desired by the Second Vatican Council, the hope may be expressed that deliberate care should be taken to incorporate a planning feature to which some architects refer as 'sloop', a term deriving from the initial letters of the phrase 'space left over on plan'. For architects the phenomenon appears to occur as an occasional oversight in the planning of a building. For theologians, particularly moral theologians, it should be a matter of design, since, in the light of our preceding observations, theological systems which account for everything and which leave no room for surprise are constricting to the Spirit of God, and are just too neat to be true to reality.

The consideration of the mystery of the Christian God and of his ways with men as a culminating feature of moral theology also appears to give further encouragement and clarification to what we have suggested is the other characteristic of more recent moral theology, the movement towards totality and integration as a context which must never be neglected if various elements of reality and of morality are to be accorded their full significance. As we suggested earlier in this chapter, the idea of progressive inter-relatedness which appears to fit a great deal of moral writing since the Council appears also to be leading to a cosmic principle of totality which gives ultimate moral significance to creation's, including man's, response to God. And we concluded that this may be seen as an unconscious move towards the recovery of the Augustinian and Thomist idea of divine *ordo* in creation, which for those founding fathers of moral theology constituted the very basis and context of all human morality.[79] It might be considered, however, that the idea of 'order', even when considered in a dynamic sense and not as a giant cosmic still life, and even when viewed in a purposive sense far surpassing the imaginings of Stoic and Aristotelian thought from which Augustine and Aquinas gladly accepted the idea, carries overtones of excessive rationalism and of

[79] *Supra* pp. 74–9, 321.

impersonality. It could be objected that these do scant justice to the Christian God who is pre-eminently love rather than the great designer and to his human creatures who are incomparably more than units in a planning programme or cogs in a cosmic machine. We have only recently observed and warned against the over-enthusiastic exploitation of human concepts in the theological enterprise, including that of moral theology. Nevertheless, when due note is taken of such cautionary qualification, the idea of divine purpose in a shared destiny for his human creatures, in response to which, or in deliberate disregard of which, man may be described as behaving within the moral order, appears to be emerging into prominence once again in moral theology. And it may be thought to find biblical confirmation and enlightenment, as well as the correction of any danger of excessive intellectualizing or of depersonalizing, in the great eighth chapter of Paul to the Romans which is at once the magna charta of the freedom of God's sons and daughters when 'led by the Spirit of God' and a sublime description of how creation, including man, is 'groaning in travail together' and 'waits with eager longing for the revealing of the sons of God' (Rom. 8: 14, 19–23).

That work of revealing God's sons and daughters is summed up in the equally Pauline idea of *koinonia*, or 'the fellowship of the Holy Spirit' (2 Cor. 13: 14), which has come into such prominence in recent years as almost a rediscovery made by the ecumenical movement about the nature of the Christian community. Entirely absent from the Old Testament as a description of men's relationship with God, or with each other in God's purpose, the concept contains layers of significance for the Christian community in its regular appearances in Acts and the Pauline and other Epistles. The term *koinonia* and its variants denote a passive and active sharing of God's gifts by individuals and among individuals, characteristic of the earliest disciples (Acts 2: 42) and of their material help collected for the Jerusalem church (Rom. 15: 26), as well as of spiritual blessings in which the gentiles 'have come to share' (Rom. 15: 27). It is expressive, further, of a corporate solidarity (Gal. 2: 9), and a solidarity in something received, whether the fellowship of Christ (1 Cor. 1: 9) or of his sufferings (Phil. 3: 10), or of his body and blood in the Eucharist (1 Cor. 10: 16). And not only is it also a fellowship imparted by the Spirit (2 (Cor. 13: 14; Phil. 2: 1) to all Christ's followers, but it is a gift of God which finds its climax in fellowship 'with the Father and his Son' (1 John 1: 3) to 'become partakers (*koinonoi*) of the divine nature' itself (2 Pet. 1: 4).

Given such a richness of meaning and implication in the theme of *koinonia* as characterizing Christians in community, it is no matter for surprise that the Anglican–Roman Catholic International Commission should consider it 'the term that most aptly expresses the mystery underlying the various New Testament images of the Church' and should utilize it as the key operative concept in its reflections on Eucharist, Ministry, and Authority in the Church.[80] And it is matter for further rejoicing that the Anglican–Lutheran dialogue, in endorsing the ARCIC focus upon this expression of the mystery of God's Church, could judge that 'Anglicans and Lutherans, together with other Christians, have rediscovered the communal character of the Church at a time of loneliness and estrangement. The Church lives in *koinonia* and is a community in which all members, lay or ordained, contribute their gifts to the life of the whole.'[81]

The New Testament and contemporary theology of fellowship, then, can be seen as expressing in much richer and more characteristically Christian terms the insight of Stoic philosophy into a cosmic order of the *logos*[82] which had already been considerably enhanced by Augustine and Aquinas in their systematic incorporation of *ordo* into Christian thinking as expressing a purposive principle of totality in God's dealings with his creatures. And it also provides a typically Pauline context of the Christian community for his reflections on the birth pangs of creation in responding to its destiny of 'the revealing of the sons of God' (Rom. 8: 19). To the extent, also, that Catholic moral theology has characteristically been the reflection upon Christian behaviour as developed, and, indeed, controlled, within the context of the Church, the theology of *koinonia* can be seen as providing an enriched awareness of the *locus* of moral theologizing. It also gives a fresh appreciation of its subject matter and of the conditions for its further development. In other words, it is within a refreshed

[80] Anglican–Roman Catholic International Commission, *The Final Report* (London, 1982), pp. 5–6.
[81] *Anglican–Lutheran Dialogue*, The Report of the European Commission (London, 1983), p. 21.
[82] Cf. *supra*, pp. 38, 102.

theology of the Church as *koinonia* that the matrix is to be found for a continually renewed moral theology, in which, as in every other branch of theology, to apply the remark of the Anglican–Lutheran dialogue quoted above, 'all members, lay or ordained, contribute their gifts to the life of the whole'.

The totality of the Church, then, is to be seen as the primary agent of moral theology, as it is also the primary recipient of the Spirit of Christ before such grace of the Spirit is diversified to the various individuals who are thus called to build up the fellowship of the Christian community. As a communion of all Christian believers, or 'the *koinonia* of the saints', it is a hospitable concept, embracing all who have gone before in the history of the Christian community and sensitive to that tradition without being fixed in it or being unaware of its historical limitations. It is coming to embrace in increasing awareness those who, despite tragic disunities within the fellowship, share 'the *koinonia* in the gospel' (Phil. 1: 5). And it also embraces all others who may know not the God of Jesus Christ but who have, nevertheless, been 'called into the fellowship of his Son' (1 Cor. 1: 9). In so perceiving itself as the place and the agent of moral theology, the Church at the same time receives as its charge the gift and the task of deepening not only its own, but also all men's fellowship with each other and with God, in whose own nature all are called to be sharers, or *koinonoi* (2 Pet. 1: 4). And such call to further the *koinonia* of all humanity constitutes also the first and overriding, or architectonic, task of moral theology.

Nor is this to be seen as an introspective or colonialist programme for the Church. For, it may further be suggested, the concept of *koinonia* is not simply a Christian addition to human destiny, but responds to the deepest aspirations of God's human creatures, who are made in his image. Throughout the Christian centuries theologians have variously interpreted the significance of the creation of man 'in the image of God', and have advanced explanations of what it is about man which constitutes that divine image. For the most part it has been considered to be man's powers of reason and of free choice, in so far as these differentiate him from the rest of creation. In recent years, however, more personalist thought and a deepened appreciation of human sexuality as a relationship of complementarity between the sexes have introduced the view that what singles mankind out from his evolutionary forebears is his capacity for personal relationship, and that it is this also which lies at the very heart of divine Being in the Trinity of Father, Son, and Holy Spirit. So much so, that the God who created man in his image is a God of interpersonal reality, or of substantive *koinonia*, and it is this quality of divine Being which is imprinted upon man. Nor is it an image to be found only in every human individual as such, as is his power of rationality, although it does found in each man a yearning for companionship and completion, and for living in the society of others and of God. It is also a divine resemblance impressed upon humanity as such, or in its totality, so that it is the completeness of human *koinonia*, or of human persons in community, which will most fully image forth the inter-personal riches of the Creator and be the culmination of his destining of his human creation to be together sharers in his own essentially interpersonal being.

Such a theology of the traditional Christian doctrine of man as made in God's image puts before all men and women, then, not only a common destiny but also a shared moral programme of a fellowship of persons as the creational and Christian task to be worked for at all levels of human society. And it is, to add the final detail to God's handiwork, a destiny and a programme which are presaged and already to some extent embodied in the Church, as a sacrament of divine and human *koinoinia*. For here again, recent theological reflection on sacramental theology and on the nature of the Church has resulted in a fresh appreciation of the function of the Church within God's unitary enterprise of creation and redemption. It is to give witness in human society to that fellowship of individuals to which every man is called and to give evidence of the degree to which he is already enabled, by the Spirit of Christ, to live in communion with God and his fellow men. To live its witness is the prime task laid upon the Church. But to preach that witness, in words as well as example, is also its charge. It is to be both a symbol and an agent of human community. And it is within this context of witness to society of the *koinonia* of God to be shared by men and among men as his creatures that moral theology finds its most challenging and enriching programme for the future as an ethics of *koinonia*. No less than such a programme will fulfil the characteristics of contemporary moral theology which, we have suggested, are in evidence in post-conciliar moral theology: a drive to totality and a recognition of diversity. And no less required for the future is the recovery of something of this mystery which, as we have suggested, both explains and combines these two charac-teristics. This sharing in the divine destiny and project for all his human creatures is what we also describe as moral theology, and it is perhaps most informatively and briefly summed up in the letter to the Ephesians (1: 9–10) as our having imparted to us 'in all wisdom and insight the mystery of his will, according to his purpose which he set forth in Christ as a plan for the fullness of time, to unite all things in him, things in heaven and things on earth'.

INDEX